Islam Evolving

ALSO BY TANER EDIS

Science and Nonbelief

An Illusion of Harmony: Science and Religion in Islam

The Ghost in the Universe: God in Light of Modern Science

Islam Evolving
Radicalism, Reformation, and the Uneasy Relationship with the Secular West

TANER EDIS

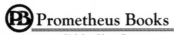

Prometheus Books

59 John Glenn Drive
Amherst, New York 14228

Cover image © Dudarev Mikhail / Shutterstock
Cover design by Jacqueline Nasso Cooke

Inquiries should be addressed to
Prometheus Books
59 John Glenn Drive
Amherst, New York 14228
VOICE: 716–691–0133
FAX: 716–691–0137
WWW.PROMETHEUSBOOKS.COM

20 19 18 17 16   5 4 3 2 1

Library of Congress Cataloging-in-Publication Data

Names: Edis, Taner, 1967- author.
Title: Islam evolving : radicalism, reformation, and the uneasy relationship with the secular West /
    Taner Edis.
Description: Amherst, NY : Prometheus Books, 2016. | Includes index.
Identifiers: LCCN 2016007383 (print) | LCCN 2016008783 (ebook) |
    ISBN 9781633881891 (hardback) | ISBN 9781633881907 (eBook)
Subjects: LCSH: Islam and science. | East and West. | BISAC: RELIGION / Islam / General. |
    SOCIAL SCIENCE / Sociology of Religion.
Classification: LCC BP190.5.S3 E354 2016 (print) | LCC BP190.5.S3 (ebook) |
    DDC 297.09/051--dc23
LC record available at http://lccn.loc.gov/2016007383

Printed in the United States of America

CONTENTS

1

VARIETIES OF ISLAMIC EXPERIENCE

HEADSCARVES AND BEARDS

If the piles of books that I worked through while writing this book are any indication, Islam should be symbolized not by a crescent but by a headscarf or a beard. Very often people on the covers of the books appear immediately recognizable as Muslims because they are women wearing headscarves or men with full beards. Whether the writer intends to emphasize conflicts between Muslims and non-Muslims or to defend Islamic contributions to social diversity, presenting an exotic picture seems to be a good way to advertise the presence of Islam.

In the midwestern university where I teach, there are only a few who are visibly Muslim, usually African Americans or international students. Still, I see a variety of Islamic displays. Very rarely, I see the full veil and body-hiding black dress, which can be a nuisance when administering exams. More often the headscarf or beard is less attention-grabbing, but it still stands out, especially compared to the far more common Christian students who prefer to display their faith on their T-shirts.

Those of us who are secular in the way we live and liberal in our politics, such as most of my colleagues, don't always know what to make of an Islamic presence. We are well-conditioned to allow for diversity, but the stronger forms of Islam raise questions: What does it mean when a woman in full veil thereby isolates herself from others? If a style of beard signals piety, does this accompany a Muslim form of religious Right politics, similar to that of Christians?

Indeed, the strongest challenges to secular liberalism today often seem to involve Islam. Among my fellow liberals, I take it for granted that we will treat religious faith as a personal matter and that we will reason about public issues in a secular fashion. Not all of us will take a liberal position on, say, wealth inequality or our healthcare system, but none of us will support our views by making theological claims. In contrast, devout Muslims often refuse to limit religion to a private realm. As philosopher Shabbir Akhtar describes it, Islam

> is a faith whose adherents are sounding a lone note of courageous defiance in the battle against secularism while other trumpets are blowing retreat. . . . In Islamic culture, all issues, moral and political included, are still effortlessly conceived of as religious. Muslims treat even secular and pragmatic issues as theological matters. Economic, foreign, and political policy is often a surrogate for a theological position.[1]

We secular liberals like to think of ourselves as the leading edge of modernity: we have figured out the best means of acquiring knowledge and institutionalized them in our sciences; we have learned how to reason about social arrangements and established liberal democracy. We have formed liberal varieties of Judaism and Christianity that serve as social clubs and refuges for attenuated supernatural convictions. But Islam seems to hold out. "Progressive Muslims" who try to reconcile their piety and their liberal views about gender equality and social pluralism[2] are very conscious that they stand against dominant conservative views. And conservative Muslims appear to have little use for our secular liberal political framework. We encounter a political culture where arguments constantly refer to sacred texts, and traditional gender roles and severe penalties for blasphemy are very often just the normal way of things.

Moreover, most secular liberals I encounter are not very familiar with Islam. Our political tradition was forged in criticism of the fact claims and the social ideals presented by Western Christianity. When we attempt to argue for a secular liberal public order, we usually bring up worries about theocracy, the violence that might be unleashed by sectarian conflict, or our inability to achieve consensus when political actors appeal to faith.[3]

Such arguments are not convincing in a Muslim context. The challenge presented by conservative Islam, then, is also an opportunity to revisit and revise arguments that form the core of secular liberal political convictions.

Therefore, secular liberals have some reason to explore the political landscape of Islam today. And we have to be careful about the details. Headscarves and beards come in many varieties, and they don't always have the same political significance.

The ways of advertising religiosity become especially complicated where Muslims are a majority. I grew up in Turkey, a dubiously secular country where the public environment has been considerably re-Islamized in the past few decades. When I return to wander the streets of Istanbul, my hometown, I see many different Islamic appearances. The most striking are the men in flowing robes, skullcaps, and full beards, and women in shapeless black with eyes barely visible. I rarely used to see them outside of ultraorthodox neighborhoods or as Arab tourists, but now they can appear everywhere. Even so, most Turks, though generally quite religious, do not try to look like someone out of an imagined version of Arabia fourteen hundred years ago. Two-thirds of women cover their head, but they typically use more color—from the distinctly modern trench-coat-and-scarf look of Islamic fashion houses to more traditional Anatolian headscarves. Only a minority of men wear beards, and only a few of them sport the sorts of beard that proclaim devoutness. Their conformity to customary norms of modesty becomes more obvious in the summer, when even in the heat few Turks wear shorts on the city streets.

There is, in fact, a complex code of religious self-presentation. The style of beard, headscarf, or dress can signal everything from how conservative one is about religion to the particular religious order one may belong to. The codes also involve speech and writing. Religious conservatives tend to use more Arabic loan-words, while I, secular semi-foreigner that I am, stick with a modernized, cleaned-up Turkish. I announce my own identity by wearing shorts. If someone addresses me with the common religious form of greeting, I don't make the proper reply, and then we all know where we stand.

If I'm curious about the varieties of Islamic experience being signaled

—at least to the level of amateur anthropology necessary to negotiate life in any culturally complex large city—it's not difficult to learn more about what the various forms of display mean. The more conservative Muslims, with their more obvious codes of modesty, are also more likely to segregate the sexes in everyday life. I would not offer to shake the hand of a woman who does not show any of her hair; it's possible her community does not believe contact with a male outside her family is permissible. If I want to meet a well-bearded man outside of work, an establishment that serves alcohol is perhaps not the best choice.

But my choices are not always clear-cut. What of an acquaintance who fasts during the month of Ramadan but who likes to grab a beer after work during the rest of the year? What of a young woman who covers her hair but dons her headscarf over blue jeans and a stylish blouse that avoids showing bare arms? Most Muslims I know—many of my friends and relatives—make compromises between the sort of Islam that goes by the book and the requirements and opportunities presented by modern life. Rigorous, orthodox Islam and its rules are an ubiquitous part of their cultural background, but that background is often remote. Only a small minority makes a concerted attempt to follow an ultraorthodox version of Islam. The rest may admit that they are imperfect Muslims, but they usually are not overly concerned about divine condemnation. Many think that the fully bearded men and the invisible women who walk around in black shapeless garb are fanatics who misunderstand the "middle path" of true Islam and needlessly impose a rigid lifestyles on themselves.

Still, it is tempting to start describing Islam and Muslim politics in terms of a spectrum of commitment. At the devout extreme, there are those who aim to follow what Muslims have traditionally acknowledged to be divinely ordained rules. Their piety may lead them along paths laid down by religious scholars, or they may devote themselves to the leader of a religious order. They may immerse themselves in texts or in praise of the subtle magic revealed by charismatic figures. But they are the religious overachievers of the Muslim world—the kind of people who may brush their teeth with a *miswak*, a twig from a certain tree, because tradition reports the Prophet Muhammad recommending such a twig.

At the other extreme of the spectrum I could put westernized, secular Muslims, who include my closer friends and most of the Turkish side of my family. They enter a mosque only for funerals and disregard the religious rules without a second thought. They associate the Quran with an aura of sacredness or spirituality but cannot be bothered to consult any scriptures for guidance in life. Such secular Muslims are also a minority, but there are many unobservant, cultural Muslims who vaguely believe that there is a God in charge of everything and that Muhammad was his messenger, treat the ultraorthodox as annoyances, and consider themselves as good a Muslim as anyone.

Most people, then, would fall in between the extremes. Ordinary Muslims are housewives and shopkeepers and students who try to be faithful to some notion of Islam in their daily lives. They often pick and choose from among religious observations. Plenty of Muslims like the idea of a divine order undergirding social and political life, but they also show little enthusiasm for religious figures getting mixed up with everyday politics. Occasionally they might worry about the influence of evil spirits, but they mostly complain about the cost of living.

There is perhaps a similar dynamic in all monotheistic religions. There are cafeteria Catholics and those who regularly attend Mass. Among Jews, there are those who belong to Orthodox and Conservative and Reform congregations, and maybe a handful of Humanistic Jews to highlight the secular extreme. In most cases, there are a few who strictly follow the rules, and there are larger numbers who in principle affirm the rules but are just as happy to let a minority of overachievers keep a vigorous faith. Most ordinary believers acknowledge that they fall short, but then concentrate on everyday life and trust to the mercy of their God.

THE RULES

Still, rules and doctrines are useful as a kind of ideal defining the faith. If I want an official version of Catholicism, I have a thick volume on my shelves providing the catechism. If I want a normative definition of Judaism, there are plenty of books describing central beliefs and observances. Personally, I am much more likely to find myself at a Reform service than in an Orthodox synagogue, but often even the Reform Jews in my wife's family define their religion by what they consider essential and what can be modernized from among historically Orthodox practices. Rules help to locate us on a religious landscape. I even have books on my shelves that describe Buddhism by providing lists of Noble Truths and explaining varieties of the doctrine of No Self. The priests and scholars who give shape to religious traditions evidently love to construct systems and draw boundaries.

And so, many of my books on Islam—those with beards or headscarves on their covers—present Islam in terms of common doctrines. Introductory texts list the Five Pillars of Islam. They make sure to emphasize the peerless, absolute Unity central to the Muslim conception of God. No less important are the glories of heaven and the tortures of hell, and what believers need to do to get to the afterlife they desire. Beliefs about angels and evil spirits also bear mentioning. If they are at all comprehensive, the books also discuss divine decrees about the division of inheritances or the spoils of war. They usually lay all this out with citations from the Quran and the prophetic traditions, which are the rulebooks of the faith. If I want, I can further find out in mind-melting detail about the precise procedures for ablutions before the daily prayers, or the rulings from acceptably orthodox legal schools about why it is impermissible for men to wear gold jewelry.

And it is not just books. I need to know for whom *not* to vote, so I often tune my radio to a local evangelical radio station while driving. The preachers emphasize their own religions' version of the rules, defining the pale of orthodoxy, defending the Christian faith as handed down to the saints once and for all. When I get a chance to hear the Muslim versions of televangelists and radio preachers, much of their talk is also concerned about the boundaries of proper belief and practice.

Maybe even more important, official versions of religions, whether backed by ancient churches or by governments, lay down rules. In Turkey, which the Western media somehow insists is a secular country, religious functionaries are government employees, and the constitution mandates religious instruction in public schools. Neither my Turkish father, who is unobservant and indifferent to Islam, nor my American mother, who is skeptical of Christianity, wanted their children to be indoctrinated in official Sunni Islam. But they could not always get me excluded from religion class, and so occasionally I too had to learn the official version of the rules, together with my classmates. How else could we possibly be instructed in "our religion"?

There are, however, problems with approaching a religion by investigating its orthodoxies. Emphasizing rules and doctrines implicitly turns less rigorous religious positions into compromises between sacred and profane. Catholics for Choice, who support abortion rights, become deviants. Muslims immersed in the worldly concerns of everyday life become justified objects of harangues by religious experts complaining about insufficient religious commitment. Conservative religious leaders naturally like to put forth their version of their faith as the standard. But from my perspective as a godless infidel, I don't always perceive religious believers who are careless with the rules as people close to my worldly extreme on a spectrum. If the signatures of religiosity are belief in supernatural agents, infusing life with significance through perceived connections with a transcendent realm, or social morality animated by a notion of the sacred, then most people I know are religious to some degree. And intensity of religiosity is not the same as purity or orthodoxy. Even very liberal religious believers are not necessarily de facto secular people with a lingering attachment to tradition. An easygoing style of faith, among the Muslims I know best, is often another way of being religious, with its own integrity, apart from the demands of religious experts.

The main difficulty with the rules or the official versions of a religious tradition is that they are not always representative. However useful it is to have an ideal form of a religion written down, few of the believers will conform adequately. Communities that attempt perfect orthodoxy often split into rival sects with emphases on different rules and interpretations. Furthermore, many of the faithful will disagree with the established rules, make up their own rules, or develop ideas about living spiritually that puts little emphasis on official versions. And from my secular standpoint, religion is what religious people do, or at least, it's what they do that they ascribe to their interaction with supernatural realities. Catholicism is about the laity at least as much as about the priestly hierarchy. Islam is the often-confused landscape of beliefs and practices usually centered on the Quran, Muhammad, and the will of God that I have to negotiate when I am among Muslims.

The limitations of a conservative-to-secular spectrum as a guide to the landscape of Islam become even more apparent with cases that are hard to classify. For example, a substantial minority in Turkey belong to the heterodox Alevi sect. And the majority Sunni Muslims, secular intellectuals, and even Alevis themselves have never quite figured out how to relate Alevi Islam to the dominant forms of the faith. Not following the mainstream Sunni rules is central to Alevi identity.

A good part of Alevi spirituality focuses on the tragic figure of Ali, the cousin and successor of the Prophet Muhammad. So at first glance, Alevism looks like a version of Shia Islam such as that dominant in Iran. But much in Alevi ritual and religious life bears little resemblance either to Sunni or Shia Islam. Alevi villages do not have mosques, and Alevis do not live by Islamic law as codified by the religious scholarly class among either the Sunni or Shia. Their religious authority structure is very different, and references to the Quran and other sacred texts are far less frequent in their devotions. Indeed, Alevis tend not to think of the Quran as the direct word of God, often ignore practices such as daily prayers or the Ramadan fast, and use Turkish rather than Arabic in their rituals. Alevi poetry and song contains plenty of effusive devotion to a monotheistic God and invocations of divine justice, but it also expresses criticism of the Sunni emphasis on rules, often asserting that it is not religious conformity but human justice that matters.[4] Revered figures such as Hacı Bektaş Veli in the thirteenth century made the arduous pilgrimage to Mecca and wrote commentaries on prophetic traditions, like many orthodox scholars. Alevis, however, remember him for verses such as

> The heat is in the fire, not in the iron
> Reason is in the head, not in the crown
> Whatever you seek, seek it in yourself
> It is not in Mecca, Jerusalem, or the pilgrimage[5]

Most scandalously, in the Middle East where the segregation of the sexes is routine, Alevi rituals involve both women and men participating together as couples. Among Sunnis, slander about Alevi rituals involving illicit sex is common. Naturally, Alevi women do not wear veils. In any case, Alevis are *different*. Some historians describe Turkish Alevi Islam as a product of syncretism involving elements of shamanistic beliefs nomadic Turks brought to Anatolia from Central Asia. Alevis wrapped their pre-Islamic traditions into the less orthodox varieties of "folk Islam," contrasted to the urban, official Islams of Sunni and Shia religious scholars.[6]

The isolated, impoverished villages where Alevis preserved their way of life have all but vanished. In the early twentieth century, Alevis supported the quasi-secular state established by the Turkish Revolution, hoping for an end to Sunni dominance. Later, migrating to the slums of metropolises such as Istanbul, Alevis established their own neighborhoods. They were a natural constituency for secular and leftist political parties, thereby becoming a political as well as a religious minority. Alevis did not wear headscarves or religious styles of beards. Many were attracted to socialism, and leftist intellectuals with Alevi roots recast their tradition as a prescient religious humanism that anticipated the European Enlightenment. Alevism, they said, was barely theistic, inherently secular, and had preserved the Turkish language and national culture from the Arabization imposed by Sunni Islam.[7]

In fact, however, Alevism is as fractured as the world of Islam that includes it. Many Sunnis consider Alevism to be an unacceptable religious deviation, and might even want public policy to draw Alevis to the mosque. Some conservative Alevis among the wealthier segments of Alevi society acquiesce, desiring to turn Alevism into an equivalent of a denomination within a broader tent of orthodox Islam. But others continue to rebel, even accepting the description of Alevism as non-Islamic. One Alevi citizen even demanded that "Alevi" be inscribed as his religion on his national identity card rather than the customary "Islam"; he won a favorable ruling from the European Court of Human Rights.[8] Some Alevis remain connected to a universalist political left, while some prefer a narrower focus on Alevi community interests. The difference between Alevi and Sunni Islam also has implications beyond Turkey. Many Alevi immigrants to Germany find that their traditional opposition to orthodox Islam and avoidance of headscarves and beards help them integrate into European society more easily than their Sunni neighbors.[9]

Now, perhaps examples such as Alevis are exceptions; after all, there are genuine questions about whether Alevis should be thought of as truly Muslim. Bearded or headscarved overachievers, in contrast, are obviously Muslims. So we might still place the majority orthodox Sunni beliefs and rules at the center of Islam, and surround it by deviant religiosities as well as weaker, secularized forms of devotion.

But everywhere we look among Muslim populations, there is an awful lot of deviation going on. The orthodox religious experts have never lacked reason to complain about religious laxity. Indeed, Muslims have historically been no less religiously creative than Christians have. Muslims also regularly reinterpret the stories that frame their faith tradition, and occasionally generate movements that break the rules.

As another example, consider the Ahmadis.[10] From an outsider's perspective, there is little distance between orthodox forms of Islam in South Asia and the multiple movements that originate with the teachings of Mirza Ghulam Ahmad in the late nineteenth century. The main point of divergence between the Ahmadis and the orthodox is the status of Ahmad. Most Ahmadis exalt Ahmad, considering him to be a renewer and revitalizer of Islam. Indeed, they think of Ahmad as a messiah or a messenger of God, but not as a full-blown prophet since he was not sent with a new scripture and a new law for the community. To strict Sunnis, this status ascribed to Ahmad violates the doctrine that the Islamic revelation was final and complete—that Muhammad was "the seal of the prophets."

Much of this looks like a dispute over doctrinal issues that only purists would care about, like the endless wrangling in the United States over whether Mormons are truly Christian. Ahmadis in India and in most of the world are treated as Muslims. But in Pakistan, which defines itself as an Islamic state, the question of who is a Muslim is more important. Pakistani Ahmadis are legally considered non-Muslims, which leaves them as second-class citizens.[11] And as with many persecuted minorities, Ahmadis are often a constituency favoring a looser, more pluralist relationship between states and religious communities.

Such examples can be multiplied, from Sufi movements that have been more or less absorbed into local majority forms of Islam, to the Bahais originating in Iran who eventually broke with Islam in self-conception and who continue to face severe persecution in Iran. Religiously, Islam is fragmented, even as the ideal of a single people of God united in a universal faith retains its appeal. The model of an orthodox center surrounded by deviant interpretations does not do justice to the variety in Islam. Indeed, such a model implicitly affirms the established, orthodox point of view, overlooking how orthodoxy is no less a product of human religious creativity than are minority sects.

Moreover, looking more closely within the circles of Sunni or Shia orthodoxy, we continue to find rival interpretations and attempts to reshape the rules. Religions typically respond to and co-opt other belief systems that claim the allegiance of believers, and Islam is no exception. The eclipse of twentieth-century Arab nationalism by Islamist politics may create the impression that Islam has faced nationalism as a rival and defeated it. But most Muslims are not Arab, and ethnic identity and nationalism have a strong grip on many Muslims. Post-revolutionary Iranian Shiism has acquired a stronger identification with Iranian nationalism and national interests. Popular Sunni figures in Turkey, such as the highly influential Fethullah Gülen, appeal to nationalism and speak of a "Turkish Islam" in contrast to harsher Saudi Arab and Iranian forms of the faith.[12] In Pakistan, Islamic loyalties are colored by an intense nationalist rivalry with India. In Bangladesh, memories of the bloody war of separation from Pakistan complicate any notions of Islamic unity.

Nationalism is not the only modern influence. As mostly illiterate tribal or agrarian societies have changed, so have the expressions of Islam, even as orthodox ideals have endured. As literacy surged and the traditional scholarly, rabbinical class lost much of its power, the past century or two has seen very important changes. Instead of trusting scholars or charismatic Sufi leaders to convey the dictates of religion, modern, urban Muslims are just as likely to try to consult the sacred sources individually or in lay study groups. In the process, they rewrite the rules. They often claim to return to an earlier, purer form of Islam, though it is their modern needs that drive them to seek religious guidance and that color their interpretations.

In this environment of reinvention and reinterpretation, many find resources to shift power away from would-be custodians of the rules. Muslim feminists such as Leila Ahmed, for example, look to the oral, folk traditions of Islam, picking and choosing to form a more congenial spirituality as opposed to the emphasis of traditional religious scholarship on rigid texts and laws.[13] Some groups decide that since only the Quran is supposed to be divine speech, they should disregard the traditions of the Prophet and look only to the Quran for guidance. In practice, they usually continue to interpret the Quran in a manner that is fixed by the traditions, but much to the annoyance of the orthodox religious experts, they also introduce a potential for innovation.

Official Islam with its rules and its enjoyment of state support remains strong, and the ideal of a pristine, God-given form of Islam retains a powerful attraction. But the result is not easy agreement. Muslims must, if they are to be religious rather than just cultural Muslims, believe that there is some divinely ordained True Islam. But in practice, even within the mainstream majority in Islam, there are rival claims to True Islam. Muslims constantly debate what it means to be a devout Muslim today.[14]

ISLAM FOR INFIDELS

Does this then mean that instead of a core set of rules and deviations from the ideal, we have a formless chaos? Can we say no more about Muslims than that they are monotheists who hold the Quran sacred and identify with communities rooted in an Islamic tradition?

One way to proceed would be to call social science to the rescue. We can make statistical generalizations about Muslims while acknowledging the variety. For example, the orthodox rules prohibit Muslims from enjoying alcohol. But Muslims who drink are not rarities. Indeed, even visitors to religiously strict countries like Saudi Arabia, where alcohol is banned, often tell stories about how the imported whiskey flows freely within the family compounds of the rich. So if the question is how Muslims behave—if Islam is defined by what Muslims do rather than by an orthodox ideal—we could also take a look at statistics on alcohol consumption. And indeed, the Muslim per capita consumption of alcohol is remarkably low, which is especially obvious when comparing European countries with those Muslim-majority countries where alcohol is freely available for sale.[15] Many Muslims indulge in alcohol, but statistically, Muslims are not drinkers.

In this age of the opinion poll, there is also information about Muslim attitudes concerning religion and politics, gender roles, and social tolerance. Instruments such as the World Values Survey provide snapshots from a wide range of Muslim populations. Such surveys are very coarse-grained—they have many limitations, and it is not always easy to interpret reported attitudes or to make causal connections to religious beliefs. But often surveys provide the best available description of Muslim views. Where appropriate, I will refer to such material, particularly the work of M. Steven Fish.[16]

I am, however, less interested in statistics than in addressing questions about Islam that are of special interest to secular liberals such as myself. Those of us who identify with the Enlightenment tradition favor disinterested analysis before wholehearted commitment. So the rich tapestry of supernatural beliefs associated with Islam—an interventionist creator-god, revealed scriptures, prophecy, angels and demons, an afterlife of rewards and punishments, miracles, and mystical practices[17]—will not appeal to us without a leap of faith. Nonetheless, such beliefs are politically potent. Secular liberals examining how Islam challenges our ideals have to start with what Muslims consider divine revelation. Looking at the origins and history of Muslim sacred texts will help us understand how Muslims interpret their religion today.

Secular liberals stand for progress and modernity. We celebrate science and hope to use advancing technologies to improve human prospects. So the uneasy relationship of Muslim populations with modern science, and the economic backwardness that appears to have characterized Muslim lands for the past few centuries, strongly affect how we think of Muslim political ideas. Our sense of superiority, however, is not as secure as we often think. We need to be more aware of Muslim efforts to achieve an alternative, pious form of modernity, which promises to infuse conservative Muslim social ideals with a feeling of success.

Monotheistic religion matters especially because of the way it imparts an aura of sacredness to social morality. And this is where disagreements take on a sharper political edge. Secular liberals want to know why traditional Islamic notions of divine law are so attractive to so many believers, and how deeply female subordination is inscribed into the social norms held sacred by many Muslims. We wonder if Islam can fit into a secular arrangement where government and religion stand separate from one another. And we want to know how varieties of Islam conceive of nonbelievers and dissenting minorities, and how freedom of speech rubs up against a common Muslim sensitivity to what believers consider to be blasphemous expression. In current events and in the media, Islam is often associated with violence, and outsiders have an urgent interest in better understanding various Muslim views beyond the "religion of the sword" and "religion of peace" stereotypes.

Addressing such questions means that I will not be giving a balanced or representative description of Islam or Muslims. After all, the questions I pursue come up in the context of disagreements between Muslims and nonbelievers—they do not always preoccupy Muslims themselves to the same degree. I am especially interested in occasions where Muslims present thoughtful alternatives to secular liberal views, and where I think secularists like me have to be more critical of our own positions.

Most important, I will take a fully secular view of religion. The observation that Islam is constantly being reinterpreted is common enough. Sociologist Asef Bayat, for example, points out that

> Islam is the subject of intense conflict between diverse segments of the faithful. Women, youths, the middle classes, the poor and the powerful, the "modern" and the "traditional," clerics and laymen are all engaged in redefining the truth of their creed through either ordinary daily practice or deliberate campaigns. In doing so, they render religion a plural reality with multiple meanings.[18]

I will go further. For devout believers, religion is often what gives meaning to their existence, structures their lives, and breathes fire into their moral convictions. My view is that this sort of religion is deeply meaningful precisely because it is almost meaningless. That is, there is very little that is determinate in the meaning of religious texts and practices. The *belief* in God-given meaning, in rules, is often a driving force for many varieties of Islam. But the obscure texts and traditions Muslims hold sacred often resist any clear-cut ascription of useful meaning, though the faithful constantly turn to them for guidance, often even for the problems of everyday life. This invites interpretation.[19] It invites *creativity*. Far from a residue of medieval or classical Islam, I see modern Islam as a dynamic, protean process. In all its conflicting varieties, it destroys and rewrites history as much as it attempts to recapture the glories of the sacred past.

This does not mean I set the rules aside. Official doctrines often reflect some degree of consensus. Moreover, modern mentalities and the pervasive tendency to try to establish clearly understood, rational bureaucratic procedures in complex societies can strengthen the desire for God-given rules. French political scientist Olivier Roy describes a globalized, "born-again Islam" stripped of local attachments that has gained strength among young Muslim immigrants in Europe.[20] A similar phenomenon exists in Muslim-majority countries. Migrants to the huge cities in Muslim lands are also often cut off from village structures like local scholars, holy men, and religiously-based informal negotiations of disputes. Varieties of fundamentalism that attack local forms of Islam as deviations and claim to return to a pristine set of rules have considerable appeal in the poorer suburbs of Cairo as well as in Paris. And intellectuals in Istanbul who craft an Islamic politics are as conversant with writers from Egypt, Pakistan, and Iran as with the conservative Turkish intellectual tradition.

So conservative interpretations of the faith enjoy a lot of influence and popular support. Very often, I will take them as my starting point because they capture what large numbers of Muslims believe. In any case, I want to concentrate on practices that challenge secular liberal positions. Conservative varieties of Islam, because they are often both modern and illiberal, provide occasions to rethink what we want from secular politics.

But in the shadow of influential varieties of religious conservatism, there are also new, sometimes supposedly deviant views. There are Islamic feminists who try to articulate a religiously faithful way of raising women's status. Urban professionals may be attracted to forms of neo-Sufism that ignore politics and construct a New Age style of Islam. Academics in the humanities try to steer their coreligionists in a more sophisticated direction. They might not enjoy as much influence as tradition-minded conservatives or thundering fundamentalists, but for secular liberals, the less conservative reformers are also worth attention. Dealing with the rough spots of relationships between Muslims and infidels will require adjustments on the part of everyone. Sometimes a resolution for the political questions secular liberals care about will turn on the prospects for reinterpretations of both Islam and secularism.

I should also make it clearer where I stand. I teach physics, and my past work on Islam has revolved around questions concerning the relationship of science and religion. I come from the culture of science, with its distaste for getting entangled with politics. But as the never-ending disputes about evolution and creationism show, questions of science and science education involving conservative monotheist populations are intensely and inescapably political. So some of the roots of my interest in Islam are in trying to understand the context of public disputes over science.

I also come from a secularist political background, and Turkey has had a long, not entirely positive experience with elites trying to impose their idea of a reformed, partially secularized Islam on a reluctant population. So I carry some baggage. Nevertheless, I no longer live in a Muslim environment, and I have long ago accepted that the Turkish version of secularism has been defeated.

Although I write as a nonbeliever, I also do not want just to engage in criticism of Islam. If my views have any influence, it will be with my fellow secular liberals. And I think that we secular liberals have grown too comfortable and perhaps become intellectually lazy in our approach to politics and religion. Examining Islam, with its reputation of being a more fire-breathing religion than more familiar, often secularized versions of Christianity or Judaism, might help us rethink some of our notions about secularity and secularism. My arguments are as much a criticism of my own Enlightenment rationalist tradition as of Muslim forms of religiosity.

2

THE SACRED SOURCES

THE MAGIC OF THE SCRIPTURES

As a child, when I visited relatives in the United States, I could enjoy about ten broadcast television channels—I was never disappointed when looking for morning cartoon shows. But in Turkey, until 1984, there was only one state-run channel. I was regularly annoyed when my favorite programs were preempted on occasions like the birthday of the Prophet. The screen would be given over to men chanting religious texts, usually the Quran. And we would never know quite when the event would end. Sometimes my parents would leave the performance on in the background, so we would know when a program we might be interested in would begin.

I have always been religiously unmusical, and where the Quran is concerned, quite literally so. But across the Muslim world, and especially in Arab countries such as Egypt, musical Quran recitation is a major art form, where the best professional reciters are national celebrities. This is not a secularized art, like the Renaissance masses I like to listen to even though I have no personal connection to Catholicism. Quran recitation is very rarely abstracted from worship; it is often one of the ways in which Muslims weave the scriptures into the fabric of their lives.

Indeed, especially for self-consciously devout Muslims, the Quran is a ubiquitous presence. As philosopher Ernest Gellner famously remarked, "Christianity has its Bible belt; Islam *is* a Qur'an belt."[1] But Muslims do not treat the Quran in the same way that evangelical Christians relate to the Bible. The conservative Protestant ideal is regular individual Bible readings and devotional study; most Muslims do not encounter the Quran so directly. The Quran is supposed to be a source of guidance, even for everyday problems, but few Muslims find this guidance through personal study of the text. The chanting on the radio, or a preacher's words on television, liberally laced with quotations from scripture, may be at the forefront of how many Muslims interact with the Quran.[2]

The Quran, after all, is in an ancient Arabic, and traditionally the Quran is supposed to be properly encountered only in the original. Muslims almost always take the Quran to be the direct, unaltered word of God; traditional doctrines declare that the Quran is eternal and uncreated. Translations, then, inevitably introduce a human element into the sacred.

So for most Muslims, who are not Arabs, the word of God is in a foreign tongue. Even most Arabs are removed from the language of the Quran—the Arabic of the Quran is not their everyday language any more than the Middle English of Chaucer is the language of soap operas. Like many liturgical languages—Latin, Old Church Slavonic, Hebrew in American synagogues—Quranic Arabic marks out a domain that is sacred. The Quran appears more elevated, not subject to the criticism or possibilities for doubt implicit where ordinary language is used. Often Muslims memorize parts of the Quran; the best reciters start at an early age. Memorizing the Quran is a religiously meritorious act, regardless of whether the reciter knows the meaning of the text or any Arabic at all.

As a sacred object, the Quran is not only a divine message; it has supernatural power. For example, in the Middle East and North Africa, a traditional magical device for warding off diseases and evil spirits is a talisman containing verses from the Quran or other sacred texts. Often holy men and Sufi masters will ritually blow on the talismans and say prayers to impart their supernatural influence. Even in everyday circumstances, Muslims usually set religious texts apart and treat them with ritual reverence. One of the casual acts of sacrilege I perform is the way I handle my copies of the Quran in the chaos of my office. Unlike a properly instructed believer, I do not take care never to have mundane books piled on top of a Quran.

Modern varieties of Islam have tended to focus more on the meaning of the sacred texts, cultivating a more Protestant attitude toward the Quran. There is, today, increased opportunity to consult translations, plus a degree of embarrassment with those magical elements of traditional religion that are not explicitly endorsed in the sacred sources. But even with more individualistic, born-again varieties of Islam, the Muslim encounter with sacred texts remains heavily mediated. Traditionally, interpreting the texts was the role of religious scholars, who gave shape to the rules by which divine revelation guided the lives of the devout. Together with the scholars, Muslims also relied on holy men and Sufi orders, who, through their supernatural connections, could draw out hidden meanings from the texts. The scholars and saints have lost much of their power, but they retain plenty of influence. Today, even online discussion groups may help the devout find guidance, but fundamental Muslim conceptions of the sacred sources have not changed much.

The Quran still stands at the center. And even if most Muslims do not always directly ponder its message, the basics are clear. The Quran proclaims itself to be from a creator god, indeed, from the God familiar to Jews and Christians. Muslims may disagree about the efficacy of talismans bearing Quranic verses, but they overwhelmingly affirm that

> God is the one who created
> the heavens and the earth
> and all that is between them
> in six days,
> then mounted the Throne.
> You have no other protector,
> and no intercessor.
> So will you not be mindful?
> God governs order from sky to earth;
> Then it will go up to God on a day
> that will last a thousand years by your count.
> That is the Almighty, the Merciful,
> knower of the hidden and the manifest,
> who did best by everything created,
> and began the creation of man from clay,
> and made his progeny
> from an extract of a lowly liquid,
> yet proportioned him and breathed

some divine spirit into him,
giving you hearing, seeing, and intelligence.
You are scarcely grateful. (32 Worship 4–9)[3]

The themes of the Quran are familiar to any monotheist—submission to the One God, hell and damnation, heaven and reward, angels and demons, the creation and the end times. There are anathemas on nonbelievers, commands concerning proper behavior, affirmations of gender roles, reassurances that injustice will be vanquished. The Quran tells stories about prophets sent to peoples of the past, and relates the punishments visited upon those who failed to heed divine warnings.

But the Quran is also a short book, especially compared to the Bible. It could not contain guidance for the full range of Muslim concerns, even if it were a clear text in an accessible language. Muslims may take the Quran to be the sacred word of God, but to make the Quran anchor a religion, they have to provide it with a context. Revelation needs a structure of interpretation—it needs mediating institutions.

Classical Islamic societies, which took shape a few centuries after the time of Muhammad, fashioned a religion centered on the Quran by surrounding revelation with lesser sacred sources. Muslims interpreted the revealed words in the context provided by traditions about the life of Muhammad and his close companions. After all, if anyone properly understood the word of God, it must have been those closest to the events of revelation. Moreover, it would only make sense for God to reveal moral principles and ritual details through the example of the Prophet and those beside him. Scholars collected thousands upon thousands of anecdotes that either cast light on revelation or related the behavior of the pious first generation in the faith. They also decided which of these reports were reliable.

For traditional Muslims, and indeed most Muslims today, the accepted prophetic traditions are only slightly less sacred and authoritative than the Quran itself. The approved tradition books even contain some "sacred traditions," which are divine revelations expressed in the words of Muhammad, in contrast with the Quran, which is the direct speech of the One True God. Moreover, the scholars who constructed classical Islam came to agree that in a select few legal situations, prophetic traditions could even overrule the Quran.[4]

Traditions about the Prophet and the early days of Islam can be very useful, including, for example, "occasions of revelation" that provide a meaning for many otherwise-obscure passages in the Quran. Still, compilations of reports are not enough for an interpretive context. They end up as a maddening pile of disconnected anecdotes, suitable for a lifetime of rabbinical study but of little use aside from being a supply of concrete examples. It is hard to generalize from anecdotes about ancient seminomadic Arabs to obtain guidance for life in urban centers, in early Islamic empires no less than in modern times.

Therefore another layer of sacred writing exists: the literature of salvation history, which tells the story of the rise of Islam. Traditions were woven together to give a narrative of Muhammad's childhood and pre-inspiration adulthood, his first revelations, the times in his hometown of Mecca where he found a few but growing number of followers, how the community of believers migrated to the oasis of Medina, the early raids and first wars, how Muhammad administered his community, his victory over the Meccans, his final pilgrimage and farewell address, the wars of apostasy immediately after his death, and the initial battles of the Arabs who formed an Islamic empire in the times of Muhammad's immediate successors. Revelation found its fullest context and proper interpretation in this sacred history.

To these various layers of sacred sources, the scholars who established classical Islam added volumes upon volumes of commentary, legal studies, and devotional literature. Almost everything in the Quran and the accepted traditions has long been explained, contextualized, and formulated into rulings, and yet Muslim orthodoxy has also remained flexible enough to apply its principles to changing circumstances.

The religious scholars are not as powerful today, but the ideal of following learned experts in religion remains. Even born-again Muslims who use translations to try to approach the sacred sources themselves almost always closely follow the classical legacy. They read the Quran, naturally, but they also consult the traditions and commentaries, because otherwise it is hard to make sense of the words of God. They take the sacred stories about the life of the Prophet and the exploits of the first generation of Muslims as given. They may feel free to disagree with official versions of Islam about how to apply the sacred sources to present concerns, but the texts remain the same.

How Muslims understand the demands of the supernatural on their lives varies. Directly and indirectly, how Muslims give meaning to what they hold sacred is mediated by tradition and by institutions. There is little that is as futile in trying to understand Islam as attempting to read the Quran as if it were a sequential narrative or a catechism. And yet, to anyone who considers herself a believing Muslim, the Quran is somehow sacred. And almost always, the Quran is surrounded by other layers of sacred texts that give shape to Muslim devotion.

THE QURAN FOR SKEPTICS

Those of us outside the faith may be tempted to treat forms of Muslim religiosity as exotic anthropological phenomena. But a secular liberal political engagement with Islam starts by recognizing how, for Muslims, the Quran has *authority*. A secular debate over homosexuality, for example, will have themes such as personal freedom and social harm. Muslims can explore such themes, but they will also want to consult the sacred texts. Moreover, conservative Muslims will resist liberal attempts to separate private moral judgments from the public political order. Even the minority of Muslims who find homosexuality permissible make arguments centered on interpretations of sacred texts.[5]

Therefore, secular liberals need a detailed secular view of the Quran. We have to explore the reasons we think that the Quran is religious literature, not a text with authority over our lives. Our politics are rooted in the European Enlightenment, which denied the churches and the Christian scriptures blanket authority over the public domain. Europeans came to understand the Bible as a cultural artifact, however valuable it may be within confessional communities. The process of explaining the Bible as a human document was intellectually fascinating, but it also had important political implications. The same is true about the Quran. Muslims who challenge a secular political framework insist on the authority of the Quran and the secondary layers of sacred texts.[6] A secular liberal response must at least present a plausible view that the sacred sources are artifacts, not revelations that bind all of us.

For an outsider, the Quran is an odd book. It has no coherent narrative, with tales of prophets and devotional poetry haphazardly distributed throughout a text that has no clear organization other than an arrangement in roughly descending order of chapter lengths. It jumps from one theme to another, changes voice in the middle of a discussion, and contains much that is incomprehensible without the interpretive structures of Muslim orthodoxy. Nonetheless, secular people should allow for the possibility that the Quran is a record of divine speech. Something about it might still impress us as beyond human capabilities. We cannot start by assuming the divinity of the text, but we can be persuaded.

Now, Muslims may wonder whether asking for reasons to believe is a wrong way to approach the Quran. After all, the Quran proclaims itself to be "a revelation from the Lord of all worlds" (27 The Ants 192), and the One God is the judge of all, not to be judged himself. We cannot approach the words of God without awe and deference. Standing back, putting distance between ourselves and the allegedly divine word, and presuming to evaluate the text might introduce a secular bias into how we read the Quran.

Maybe so. But for a reader not willing to rush into a religious commitment, the Quran's self-referential nature and its insistence that it is divine revelation is itself a curious literary quality. Furthermore, while referring to itself, the Quran also tries to convince an audience that might be skeptical. 10 Jonah 37 and 38 declares

> And this Qur'an is not something
> that could be manufactured without God;
> rather, it is a confirmation of what preceded it,
> and a fuller explanation of scripture,
> in which there is nothing dubious.
> That is from the Lord of all worlds.

> Do they perhaps say, "He forged it"?
> Say, "Then bring a chapter like it,
> and call upon anyone other than God you can,
> if you are being truthful."

A variant recorded in 11 Hud 13–14 demands critics to "produce ten invented chapters." Classical Islam developed the doctrine that the Quran was inimitable and beyond comparison to all human invention in its literary excellence. The Quran, in fact, was Muhammad's primary miracle, the answer to skeptics who demanded signs and wonders akin to those performed by prophets preceding Muhammad (29 The Spider 50–51).

Doctrine aside, however, the Quran is an argumentative text. 7 The Heights 50–52 threatens those who "refused Our signs," particularly the scripture sent by God, with the fires of hell. And just in case nonbelievers are not convinced, 17 The Night Journey 46 explains that God has prevented critics from understanding the Quran: "We put a cover over their hearts, lest they understand it, and deafness in their ears."

Much of the Quran echoes with such polemics. Both the believers and doubters the Quran addresses, however, already accept a monotheist cosmic outlook, even when they are rhetorically condemned as polytheists.[7] As Jews and Christians also believe, the God who speaks in the Quran has friends and enemies among humans, has created the world in six days, and will soon usher in the Day of Judgment. But the various beliefs about God or the acts of God that appear in the Quran are rarely developed to any full extent. The Quran *alludes* to the six days of creation and the making of Adam and Eve, assuming its audience already knows a common stock of relevant stories.

The stories about past prophets that fill the Quran show a similar pattern. Most of these are variations on biblical narratives. There are stories about Solomon, who could speak with birds, and his adventures involving the Queen of Sheba and spirits known as *jinn* (27 The Ants 15–44). There are tales featuring Jonah, Job, and one son of Adam murdering the other. Noah is there, as is the Flood.

In 2 The Cow 258–260, Abraham confounds a skeptic who says he also can grant life and cause death by demanding that since God brings the sun from the East, the skeptic should do so from the West. Then there is an allusion to a story of a man God caused to die, and then resurrected after a hundred years. And then Abraham gets a demonstration of how God gives life to the dead; God instructs him to "catch four birds and train them to come to you. Then place them one by one on the mountains all around and then call them and they will all rush to you." Since it is unclear what this has to do with resurrections, commentators usually add that Abraham cut up the birds before placing them. The passage remains obscure.

Most of the prophetic tales feature either Moses or Jesus, son of the Virgin Mary, who perform one fantastic supernatural feat after another. There is, to a secular eye, a fairy-tale quality to the Quran's compendium of stories followed by morals drawn about God's power and mercy. The edifying stories are not limited to those related to the Bible. An otherwise-unknown Arab prophet or two, such as Salih, put in brief appearances. There are noncanonical Jewish and Christian legends such as the Seven Sleepers who fell asleep in a cave and awakened hundreds of years later (18 The Cave 7–26).

The Quran, then, began in an environment of monotheistic controversy, where the audience knew many common stories, but there was dispute about the proper understanding of supernatural realities. But the Quran also strikes some odd notes. For example, there is a lot about Jesus in the Quran. While a prophet and precursor to Muhammad, Jesus is also the Messiah and will come again to battle the Antichrist at the end times. But Jesus is also supposed not to have died on the cross: although he appeared to have done so, in reality he was "raised to the divine presence" (4 Women 157–158). That the Quran endorses what had become a heretical position for Christians is perhaps understandable; there is no controversy without disagreement. But while strongly rejecting the Trinity, the Quran only describes it once, in 5 The Table 116, when God asks, "Jesus son of Mary, did you tell people, 'take me and my mother as deities rather than God'?" Taking Mary as one of the persons of the Trinity is reminiscent of fragments preserved from the *Gospel of the Hebrews*, in which the Holy Spirit descends into the world and becomes Mary.[8] Perhaps a remnant of Jewish Christianity remained alive where that part of the Quran was composed.

Controversy aside, however, the Quran agrees with the monotheists of its time about the palpable presence of the supernatural. The world as imagined in the Quran is full of magic and miracles, curses and evil spirits. But God created all, including the evil, and so 113 Dawn tells us to

> Say: "I seek refuge with the Lord of rising day,
> From the evil of what He has created,
> And the evil of evening darkness
> when it overspreads,
> From the evil of sorceresses
> who blow incantations on knots,
> From the evil of the envier
> when he envies."[9]

To a modern, secular reader, such an immediate presence of the supernatural marks the Quran out as religious literature of its times. Its conception of the universe is prescientific, containing fossilized remnants of ancient Near Eastern and Greek cosmologies. For example, the Quran often says God created seven heavens, as in 71 Noah 15–16: "Haven't you observed how God made the seven heavens in ascending order, and set the moon in their midst as a light, and made the sun a lamp?" This recalls the cosmology of antiquity with seven planetary spheres centered on the earth, including spheres for the sun and the moon as celestial lights.[10]

And yet, even for the nonbeliever, the Quran also contains poetry that resonates deeply, as well as pointed eviscerations of religious hypocrisy. 107 Assistance declares,

> Do you see the one who rejects religion?
> That is the one who rebuffs the orphan
> and does not encourage feeding the poor.
> So woe to those who pray
> yet are inattentive to their prayer:
> those who put on the appearance
> and yet are withholding assistance.

And many a believer in a God, though not always persuaded by Islam, has appreciated the uncompromising monotheism of the Quran. The "throne verse," 2 The Cow 255, is particularly impressive:

> There is no God but *the* God,
> the Living, the Self-Existent,
> whom neither slumber nor sleep can overtake.
> To God belongs what is in the heavens
> and what is on earth.
> Who intercedes with God,
> except by divine permission?
> God knows what is before them,
> and what is after them;
> but they do not encompass anything
> of that knowledge,
> except as God wills.
> The throne of God extends
> over the heavens and the earth,
> whose maintenance does not weary God,
> who is the Exalted, the Powerful.

For outsiders, the Quran can be fascinating, even inspiring—as centuries-old religious literature. The notion that the Quran is divine speech, that it is a miracle, is harder to accept. Where devout Muslims perceive divine perfection, nonbelievers are more likely to see a bit of a mess, full of dogmatically asserted supernatural beliefs that were not out of place in the eastern Mediterranean region fourteen hundred years ago. In other words, the Quran looks very much like a human cultural product.

DRAWING MEANING OUT OF OBSCURITY

The Quran says of itself that "this is the Book, without doubt, in it guidance for the conscientious, those who believe in the unseen, ... They follow guidance from their Lord; and they are the successful ones" (2 The

Cow 2–5). Muslims typically understand this guidance to include public behavior as well as individual rituals, political principles as well as moral injunctions. To achieve success, believers in the unseen must therefore figure out what exactly the Book says.

On their own, however, many passages in the Quran are difficult to understand. The Quran even anticipates such difficulties, saying it contains clear and unclear verses, and no one knows the explanation of the unclear parts but God (3 The Family of Imran 7). Some aspects of the Quran are completely obscure. Twenty-nine of the chapters start with combinations of up to five letters. What their significance was is now lost. Like the identity of Jack the Ripper, this mystery continues to attract the attention of experts and amateurs alike.[11] No compelling solution is known.

The difficulties in understanding parts of the Quran go beyond matters that are acknowledged as unclear. For example, chapter 111, Flame, is

> Ruined are the hands
> of the one who flares up,
> and ruined is he:
> His wealth is no avail to him,
> nor what he's acquired:
> He will roast in a flaming fire,
> his wife carrying the fuel,
> with a rope around her neck.

This imprecation is directed toward "the one who flares up," but the Quran does not say any more. Therefore tradition and sacred history come into play. "The one who flares up" is literally "Abu Lahab," or the father of flame. And traditions provide stories about Abu Lahab, explaining that it was the name by which an uncle of Muhammad was known. Apparently Abu Lahab, together with his wife, was an implacable early enemy of Islam. The histories are full of details about his life, genealogy, and death. Translations of chapter 111 usually leave "Abu Lahab" untranslated, assuming, from the traditional account, that it is a personal designation. Muslims typically think that the reference of chapter 111 is clear, but that is due to the traditions, not the Quran.

Sometimes the process by which tradition elaborates on the Quran is relatively obvious. Many of the shorter chapters are apocalyptic in character, warning listeners about an imminent Judgment Day. For example, 54 The Moon begins with "The end of time has drawn near, and the moon is split: But even if they see a sign, they turn away, calling it persisting illusion." The splitting of the moon might be a lunar eclipse, or perhaps a more serious episode among the end time events, as in "the sky will be split apart, for it will be fragile that day" (69 The Momentous Event 16). The Quran follows the monotheistic tradition where prophets are validated by their miracles. But the Quran also has "they say, 'Why weren't wonders from his Lord revealed to him?' Say, 'The wonders are in God's power alone; I am only an open warner'" (29 The Spider 50). Later interpreters were bothered by Muhammad's implicit lesser status compared to other prophets. So there is a tendency to make Muhammad into more than a warner, ascribing miracles to him, including a literal splitting of the moon as a demonstration of supernatural power.[12]

Another way to elevate Muhammad compared to other prophets—and thereby show the superiority of his religion—was through the story of his Night Journey and ascension to heaven. 17 The Night Journey begins with an obscure passage,

> Glory to the One
> who transported
> a devotee one night
> from the Sacred Mosque
> to the Furthest Mosque,
> whose precincts We blessed
> so We might show him
> some of Our signs.

It is unclear from the Quran whether "a devotee" means Muhammad, what the events are, or where they take place. The next verse jumps into an entirely different story about Moses and the Israelites.

The traditions and sacred histories vastly expand on this hint of a Night Journey. In them, Muhammad flies on a steed with wings. He travels to the site of the former Hebrew Temple in Jerusalem: the "furthest mosque."

From there he ascends through the seven layers of heaven, starting with the First Sky where he sees Adam. He then meets his predecessors, including Abraham, Moses, and Jesus. He finally speaks to God, who informs Muhammad that fifty daily ritual prayers will be obligatory for his community. Moses points out to Muhammad that this is too much of a burden, so Muhammad repeatedly returns to God and eventually bargains the obligation down to five prayers, each which will count for ten.[13]

Traditions also tell of those who found the Night Journey hard to believe and left Islam on that account. This, apparently, was the occasion for revelation of another otherwise-incomprehensible passage: "We have told you your Lord surrounds humanity, and We only granted the vision We showed you as a test for humankind, as also the cursed tree in the Recital. Though We alarm them, yet it only increases their tremendous excess" (17 The Night Journey 60).

Another problem the secondary sacred sources help resolve is those passages in the Quran that appear to give conflicting rulings. For example, 16 The Bee 67 appears to endorse the drinking of wine: "And from the fruits of the date palm and the grape you make wine and wholesome food; surely in that is a sign for people who understand." But 5 The Table 90 says "Believers—Wine and gambling and idolatry and divination are nothing but abomination from the work of Satan, so avoid them that you may thrive." Makers of religious rules have to favor one verse or the other; a common solution was to say that a later revelation would abrogate an earlier. What is early and late, and what the contexts of various verses are, are entirely dependent on the traditions concerning the life of Muhammad.

More serious matters of policy also turned on what verse abrogated what, or which verse could be deactivated by confining its occasion of revelation to a narrow context. The Quran famously declares that "there is no compulsion in religion: true direction is already distinct from error" (2 The Cow 256), but also includes the "sword verse," commanding

> But when the sacred months are past,
> then kill idolaters wherever you find them,
> and capture them, and blockade them,

and watch for them at every lookout.
But if they repent and practice prayer
and give alms,
then let them go their way;
for God is most forgiving, most merciful. (9 Repentance 5)

Today, the sword verse is more likely to be glossed over. But in the times of conquering Muslim empires, the sword verse was often held to abrogate more peaceful statements. Alternatively, "no compulsion in religion" was understood to narrowly refer to foster children choosing between Judaism and Islam, after a Jewish tribe was expelled from Medina.[14]

The practice of abrogation found support from the Quran, especially "We do not cancel any sign [message], or cause it to be forgotten, unless we bring one better, or its equivalent" (2 The Cow 106). The meaning of this verse is also ambiguous; it may more naturally mean that the Quranic dispensation overrules previous revealed texts such as that of the Jews and Christians. Nonetheless, scholars have at times liberally used the notion of abrogation to forge a consistent set of legal rulings out of the sacred sources. Some medieval scholars list hundreds of abrogated verses, but disagreement among scholars is also very common. The modern tendency is to downplay abrogation or even to eliminate it; as theologian Farid Esack points out, "When almost every passage or practice that is held as abrogated by one scholar is questioned by another, then there is little doubt that the question of scriptural authority itself is compromised."[15] And yet, the need to selectively deactivate parts of the text remains.

Since much of the meaning of the Quran turns on the traditions concerning the first generation of Islam, much depends on these originally oral traditions and their reliability. Consider, for example, a tradition recorded in the collection by Bukhari, over two centuries after the death of the Prophet, which is considered one of the canonical best.

Narrated by Abu Dhar

The Prophet asked me at sunset, "Do you know where the sun goes (at the time of sunset)?" I replied, "Allah and His Apostle know better." He said, "It goes (i.e., travels) till it prostrates itself underneath the Throne and takes the permission to rise again, and it is permitted and then (a time will come when) it will be about to prostrate itself but its prostration will not be accepted, and it will ask permission to go on its course but it will not be permitted, but it will be ordered to return whence it has come and so it will rise in the west. And that is the interpretation of the Statement of Allah: 'And the sun runs its fixed course for a term (decreed). That is the decree of (Allah) The Exalted in Might, The All-Knowing.'" (36 Yā Sīn 38)[16]

The anecdote begins with a chain of transmitters, which is very short in this case. Since forgeries were always a problem, the orthodox scholars developed a methodology—one of the "religious sciences"—for validating traditions. Much depends on the reputation of each link in the chain of transmitters for piety and memory, even today. As the religious scholar Fethullah Gülen puts it,

> The Companions strove to verify the meaning of every Tradition. None of them lied, for their fear of divine punishment was too great. . . .[17]
>
> Thanks to the tremendous efforts of such [orthodox] Traditionists, authentic Traditions were distinguished from fabricated ones. . . . Traditionists also wrote on the narrators' character so people would know who was reliable or unreliable, careful or careless, profound and meticulous or superficial, and God-fearing or heedless.[18]

There even developed secondary traditions about the greatest tradition collectors, including how they acted with the utmost piety, had infallible memories, recorded traditions only after attending to ritual purity, and even confirmed the authenticity of traditions via supernatural visions of the Prophet.[19]

Classical Muslim doctrine about the sacred sources becomes more ragged around the edges as we move away from the Quran at the center. Nonetheless, the scholars of classical Islam created an imposing system of beliefs. Even today, many find it compelling, especially if they accept supernatural claims and adopt a faith-based way of thinking.

A SECULAR HISTORY OF THE TEXTS

For a more secular observer, the sacred sources present an intriguing historical puzzle. Muslim scholars have preserved an immense amount of material to provide context for their revelation. But from a modern, critical historical point of view, it is striking how few primary sources survive from the earliest years of Islam. There is the Quran, but it is notoriously obscure and its textual history is not known. There are only a few relevant archaeological remains such as inscriptions, coins, a few early mosques, and the Dome of the Rock in Jerusalem. There are a handful of largely polemical non-Muslim sources dating to the Arab takeover of the Middle East. These do not add much to our knowledge of historical context.

The bulk of the Muslim material, though vast, is late and contradictory, and it is practically impossible to separate history from religious literature. The earliest extant versions of the sacred history accepted by Muslims were recorded more than a century after the events and survive today only within heavily edited texts from even later. Some material is no doubt authentic, such as the "Constitution of Medina" describing an agreement between Muhammad and tribes inhabiting the town of Medina. But both in outline and in details, the sacred history almost entirely depends on traditions collected during the two centuries after Muhammad.

Therefore much Western scholarship about the origins of Islam is permeated by skepticism about the reliability of Muslim historical traditions. Most traditions, including those in the canonical collections and the sacred histories, are situated in religious, political, and legal controversies in the two centuries after Muhammad. Providing a context for verses in the Quran through an occasion of revelation or ascribing a legal or ritual principle to the Prophet imbued a particular interpretation with authority.[20] This was naturally an open invitation to anything from fabrication of traditions to improving the pedigree of principles already accepted to be true.

So early Muslim scholars faced a flood of dubious traditions, and they developed a "religious science" of authentication. This was not, however, an early version of critical historical scholarship. For example, trust in the personal worth and piety of links in the chain of transmission was very important in establishing authenticity. But many Western historians today think that the chain of transmission was a late innovation. Traditions often appeared without historical context precisely because they were supposed to be timeless models for laws and religious beliefs; an elaborate chain of transmission can even be a reason to question the authenticity of a report.

So to many modern historians, authentication by orthodox Muslim scholars is a religious act that says little about the historical substance of a tradition. This leaves us with a literature that is motivated by religious polemics, full of anachronisms, with multiple contradictory versions of everything from early Arab battles to occasions of revelation for Quranic verses. The early Muslim scholars who imposed a degree of coherence on the traditions and the sacred history produced a plausible-enough narrative. At least in outline, the story of Muhammad, his first revelations in Mecca, his move to Medina, his eventual triumph, and the first Arab conquests in the name of Islam are reasonable. Nevertheless, the sacred history is religious literature, uncomfortably similar to religious fiction in its use of mythic elements and thematic conventions.[21]

In other words, the early environment of Islam very often erased history rather than preserved memory. Historians today regularly write biographies of Muhammad, but even the best efforts are mostly paraphrases of the orthodox story leavened with critical judgment.[22] If the traditions do not inspire trust, such biographies are also very uncertain. A more skeptical historian, Patricia Crone, describes the situation as follows:

> For over a century the landscape of the Muslim past was thus exposed to a weathering so violent that its shapes were reduced to dust and rubble and deposited in secondary patterns, mixed with foreign debris and shifting with the wind. . . . The religious tradition of Islam is thus a monument to the destruction rather than the preservation of the past.[23]

If such skepticism is even half-correct, the traditions need to be treated with caution. In that case, perhaps a detailed analysis of the Quran itself could help. We might at least construct a textual history, which could tell us more about the early environment of Islam. Devout Muslims, even when they allow plenty of latitude for scriptural interpretation, usually feel no

need for textual criticism. After all, the Quran is supposed to be an embodiment of divine perfection. For outsiders, however, the imperfections of the
text reveal the most about its history.

The Quran shows plenty of signs of its construction. Historian Andrew
Rippin points out that the Quran "displays all the tendencies of rushed
editing with only the most superficial concern for the content, the editors/
compilers apparently engaged only in establishing a fixed text of scripture."[24] Much of the difficulty of the Quran as a text comes from its being
a bit of a mess.

Some of the textual oddities of the Quran have long been noticed by
Muslim scholars. For example, there are noticeable stylistic differences
within the Quran, and shifts can occur haphazardly even within chapters.
Traditionally, scholars attribute such differences to Meccan and Medinan
periods of revelation, classifying each verse accordingly.

Other features of the Quran also suggest editorial interference. Western
scholars who have taken a critical look at the Quran in a manner analogous
to the Bible have noted many passages with arbitrary breaks of rhyme
or thematic deviations, often suggesting additions and interpolations.[25]
Discoveries of ancient manuscripts can also help establish variant readings, suggesting, for example, that the present Quran is based on an earlier
written text, or that parts of the Quran were once taken to be a record of
Muhammad's sayings.[26] Indeed, numerous passages in the Quran start with
"Say," converting what might have begun as liturgical material addressed
to God into divine speech.

Prophetic traditions, though perhaps unreliable, also include stories
about the collection of the Quran and the establishment of the text after
Muhammad. These include recollections that the official version of the
Quran omits material.[27] The most famous example is a verse that allegedly
prescribed stoning for adultery, while the existing text says "The adulterer
and the adulteress are each to be whipped a hundred strokes" (24 Light 2).

Although intriguing, all of these hints about the shaping of the Quran
do not amount to detailed knowledge. The textual history of the Quran
includes efforts to standardize the sacred text, which entailed some loss of
variants. As textual critic Keith Small points out:

Though Muslims may take pride in the fidelity of the preservation of this text, it does not reproduce precisely what was originally considered to be the Qur'ān in the early seventh century. Because of the standardizations of the text in 653–705/33–86 and 936/324, together with constant pressure throughout Islamic history to have one text match their dogma, many texts which had equally good claims to containing authentic readings were suppressed and destroyed. And, because of the emphasis on oral transmission and the vagaries of Arabic as it developed, the written text was constantly vocalized in new ways which did not preserve the original vocalization. The original vocalization must have been lost very early on if it did indeed exist.

While bearing testimony to the careful preservation of one particular consonantal text, the history of the transmission of the text of the Qur'ān is at least as much a testament to the destruction of Qur'ān material as it is to its preservation. It is also testimony to the fact that there never was one original text of the Qur'ān.[28]

Known alternative readings differ on minor matters; they testify to the fact that the text has a history rather than pointing to any major editorial alterations in the centuries after Muhammad. While there is only sparse early evidence of the form of the Quran immediately after the Arab conquests, it appears that the Quran, or the texts that form the basis for our version of the Quran, were considered sacred very early on and were preserved carefully.

While the words were preserved, however, the context in which the sacred scripture was to be understood was lost. About two centuries after Muhammad, after a revolution that resulted in a renewed Abbasid version of the Islamic empire, it was important to establish the new regime on a revised religious basis. Through commentaries, selection among competing traditions about the forgotten past, and the gradual hardening of orthodoxy, the Quran acquired a new context. But many of its original meanings are now lost to us. They were lost even to the scholars who created classical Islam.

This means that together with critical rewritings of the orthodox version of early Muslim history, there is also room for more radical approaches. Yehuda Nevo and Judith Koren, for example, set aside all late accounts and attempt to reconstruct early Islam based on evidence such as archaeological remains. They argue that Islam developed gradually after the Arab takeover of Syria, that the sacred history is a fabrication, and that Muhammad was not a historical figure.[29] After all, even in the Quran there are very few references to Muhammad, which may mean "the praised one" or "the chosen one"—possibly not a personal name but a title that may refer to Jesus.

Radical skepticism about the traditional history of Islam is often traceable to the influence of John Wansbrough, a polarizing figure in Islamic studies. Wansbrough insisted that the sacred texts of Islam should be read as literature generated in an environment of Jewish and Christian polemic, rather than as reflections on recent history. And in this literature, Wansbrough and his successors found, for example, a desire to establish the vicinity of Mecca in the Arabian Peninsula as the geographical context of Islam, while the Quran is more naturally read as alluding to places much farther to the north, closer to Palestine.[30] For example, 37 Those Who Stand Together 133–138 has

> Lot was an emissary too:
> We saved him and his people, all
> except an old woman among those who stayed behind;
> and We destroyed the rest.
> You pass by where they were, daily
> and nightly—so won't you understand?

In other words, the audience for these verses was located close to the Dead Sea—the "Sea of Lot" in Arabic—where the events of Sodom and Gomorrah were supposed to have taken place.

All of this is very interesting. And to a nonbeliever such as myself, there is some very appealing black humor in the suggestion that traditional Muslim claims about revelation are not just mistaken but spectacularly off the mark. Nevertheless, radical historians are far more successful in highlighting our lack of knowledge than in constructing compelling alternative scenarios. As a result, mainstream Western scholarship avoids the most radical views, especially since the balance of evidence indicates that the text of the Quran was fixed very early, even if much of its context may have been lost.[31] The most plausible accounts put more trust in the traditional historical outline, while recognizing uncertainties and acknowledging that at its origins, the movement that became Islam might have had significant differences from the faith that crystallized centuries after Muhammad. Historian Fred Donner, for example, postulates that an apocalyptically oriented "Believers' movement started by Muhammad, which grew into what we know as Islam, began as a monotheistic and pietistic revival movement that included at least some Christians and Jews."[32] It is hard to say more. Unless we discover a cache of early documents, historians have to work with sparse and often-questionable evidence. This evidence does not lend itself to any clear narrative of early Muslim history.

In that case, our knowledge about the origins of Islam is comparable to our knowledge about Christian origins. Modern scholarly analysis of the Bible and other early Christian literature demonstrates a high degree of uncertainty—we cannot fully understand the opaque and tendentious material available. So biographies of Jesus, notoriously, plausibly but contradictorily present the Christian founder-figure as an apocalyptic prophet, a Jewish Cynic, a magician or magical healer, a political rebel, a prototypical rabbi, and more.[33] At the fringes of respectability, there are even suggestions that Jesus never existed.[34]

Similarly, with Islam, we have different scenarios, including suggestions that Muhammad is a figure more of myth than of history. This seems as unlikely for Muhammad as for Jesus, but the fact that such possibilities have to be considered seriously highlights the uncertainty facing historians. The historical meaning of much of the Quran is lost to us. But then, infidels especially do not have to think of Islam as a faith handed down from on high. The meanings of Islam are often later constructions, the work of the orthodox scholars of the classical period but also of dissenters and the heterodox. Islam is a work of human creativity that is ongoing today.

CREATIVE MISREADINGS

A skeptical view of the sacred sources is, naturally, unacceptable to devout Muslims. Most ordinary Muslims are unaware of questions about their texts; more scholarly Muslims tend to reject criticism out of hand. In part, they suspect that allegedly disinterested historical criticism conceals an anti-Muslim agenda.

Indeed, modern criticism of Muslim texts has been an almost entirely Western enterprise, mostly carried out by Christians and Jews with a background in higher criticism of the Bible. And especially in its early forms, Christian scholarship about early Islam was driven by theology, with questions about Muhammad's sincerity or even mental health never far from the surface. Even today, efforts to show that Islam emerged from a non-Trinitarian Christian sect or that the Quran's source texts include Christian hymnody can be colored by liberal Christian theological ambitions.[35]

More secular approaches also do not impress Muslims. Farid Esack, for example, describes skeptical criticism of sacred texts as "a kind of voyeurism" that "has not been welcomed by those who openly acknowledge a relationship between the lover and/or the beloved."[36] Many Muslim academics argue that no standpoint is neutral, and therefore a secular historian treating Muslim sources as mere documentary evidence sees no more clearly than a committed Muslim who assumes the divine nature of the sources. Perhaps, as philosopher Seyyed Hossein Nasr declares, a Muslim who allows his mind to ascend to the higher levels of spiritual truth can do better than the so-called higher criticism, which results in "the closing of the gate to the spiritual world."[37]

This is not to say that Muslims always fail to acknowledge difficulties with their scriptures. Many academics want to leave room for human interpretation while preserving the sacred character of the texts. For example, scholars such as Nasr Hamid Abu Zayd and Mohammed Arkoun distinguish between the divine revelation of the Quran and the text as a historical artifact. According to Arkoun, "At the stage of the Qur'ānic fact, God presents Himself to man in a discourse articulated in the Arabic language." But separate from this is the "Islamic fact," which sanctifies the spiritual encounter and turns it into an ideology.[38] Such distinctions may seem dubious to secular critics, but they protect the divine nature of the Quran while also allowing some latitude to analyze the text as a book in history.

So Muslims who want a more sophisticated analysis than that of traditional religious scholarship can adopt views similar to liberal Protestant conceptions of the Bible. The inspiration of the Quran does not have to mean divine dictation. Its commands can be read as suggestions or as dictates specific to a time and a place rather than as permanent principles.

Indeed, such views fit well with postmodern attitudes within the humanities. Emphasizing interpretation above all destabilizes the sort of fundamentalism that privileges a particular authoritative reading. But a postmodern approach also resists Enlightenment-style critical approaches that risk undermining the sacred. So Muslim scholars who want to give priority to convictions of sacredness or moral inspiration can find a congenial environment in some corners of academia, although their versions of Islam tend to look more like a set of feminist or anticolonial postures than a supernatural belief system.[39]

For example, consider 4 Women 34, which gives men advice on how to deal with rebellious wives:

> The men are supporters of the women,
> by what God has given one more than the other,
> and by what they provide from their property.
> So women of integrity are humble,
> guardians in absentia by God's protection.
> As for those of whom you fear perversity,
> admonish them;
> then leave them alone in bed;
> then spank them.
> And if they obey you,
> then seek no means against them.
> For God is exalted, great.

Such instructions are not controversial in male-dominated environments, as Muslim societies always have been. They grate, however, against modern sensibilities. And so English translations of the Quran sometimes downplay the uncomfortable aspects of 4 Women 34. The word rendered "spank," for example, has usually been understood more straightforwardly, as "beat." A few translations insist that it is a metaphorical expression meaning "have intercourse with"; other alternatives include "go away from" or a generic "chastise."[40] Usually the reason for such translations is a conviction that the divine text cannot sanction wife-beating. The traditional reading of the text remains dominant, but even conservative scholars will often explain that the verse must only mean light beatings administered only if necessary.

Such inevitable disagreements about meaning are also opportunities to reinterpret the sacred text to conform with changing sensibilities. Today, it has become a commonplace that texts have multiple, contested interpretations. The secondary layers of sacred sources—the traditions, the biography of the Prophet, and the classical commentaries—fix the traditional meaning of the Quran, but the secondary layers are also more easily set aside as reflecting the society that produced them. A reformer can start by saying that the most sacred layer of texts has been misunderstood, that human social arrangements rather than the words of God have been sanctified.

Nonetheless, a devout scholar reads the Quran as a religious act. The text cannot easily remain indeterminate, since it is the divine message to the faithful. Furthermore, passages like 4 Women 34 are sprinkled throughout the Quran. At face value, the Quran endorses female subordination.

Muslims who want to improve the status of women have a way around this problem. Asma Barlas, who specializes in politics and gender studies, argues that the classical religious scholarship that formulated a severely patriarchal version of Islam was not true to the Quran. To develop legal rulings, the scholarly class took Quranic passages in isolation, without the context supplied by the overall vision of the Quran. Following influential theologians such as Fazlur Rahman,[41] Barlas states that the Quran is completely consistent and coherent when read in the light of its major themes such as a concern for justice. The Quran unequivocally condemns oppression and injustice; severe male domination is a manifest injustice; therefore patriarchy cannot be condoned by the Quran. Indeed, Barlas argues that opposition to patriarchy should be held as a basic interpretive principle.[42]

To someone outside the faith, such feminist readings of the Quran appear strained, even arbitrary. It is too obvious that prior moral and theological convictions are doing most of the work. Far from being coherent, the fact that the Quran is a bit of a jumble is exactly what allows latitude for nontraditional interpretations. The Quran does thunder against injustice toward widows and orphans, and in 4 Women 135, says

> Believers, be supporters of justice,
> as witnesses to God,
> even be it against yourselves,
> or your parents or relatives;
> whether one be rich or poor,
> God is closer and more worthy than either.
> And do not follow desire,
> lest you swerve from justice;
> and if you pervert or neglect it,
> God is aware of what you do.

But "justice" is a vague concept. Beyond basic notions of impartiality and giving people their due, it is hard work to give specific content to justice. The Quran only provides general statements and a few concrete examples. It is implausible that Quranic invocations of justice have much to do with modern notions of gender equality or social justice. Retributive justice, charity for the unfortunate, and giving women and men just rewards according to their proper roles and stations are much more at home in the Quran's historical context.

Similarly, wife-beating would have been common in the Middle East at the time the Quran was assembled, as it often is today. 4 Women 34 is more plausibly read as *regulating* an accepted social practice.[43] Much the same can be said, for example, about slavery. The sacred sources accept slavery as an institution but enjoin believers to be kind to slaves, and treat freeing slaves as a meritorious act. Reading the Quran in a manner that condemns wife-beating or slavery is theology, not history.

And yet, for a secular outsider, it is not enough to observe that modern readings of the Quran are often misreadings. Scriptural religions always attempt to draw profound meanings from ambiguous, barely coherent texts. We can be reasonably confident that historically, the Quran has been interpreted to accept a regulated form of wife-beating. But that does not mean that Muslims are forever constrained to read their texts in this manner. Islam is the product of a history of misreadings: the interpretations by orthodox scholars and their opponents in the classical period, but also the new misreadings that followed them and are continually invented to this day.[44] Devout scholars must continually try to get in touch with a revealed message. For a fully secular reader, however, any original meaning of the Quran is just one more interpretation among others.

A MARKETPLACE OF MEANINGS

The plausibility of the meanings ascribed to the Quran have a lot to do with the circumstances of the reader. Traditional religious scholarship still counts: the weight of institutionalized interpretation makes it the default position. But believers facing modern economies and changing gender roles still turn to the Quran for guidance. The sacred sources take on new meanings in the context of social movements and media fashions; interpretations succeed or fail depending on whether they find a market.

Indeed, the marketplace for meanings is particularly crowded today. Many observers note that Islam is undergoing a reformation. Muslim populations today are more literate, more able to communicate globally. Believing women and men are increasingly studying sacred texts translated into their own language, combining ancient authorities with modern needs to make new meanings.[45] As with the Protestant Reformation, this often means more intense, sometimes fundamentalist styles of piety. Increasing individualism combines with conservative moralizing. Contests over faith can even erupt into violence.

In such an environment, whether a feminist interpretation catches on depends on whether subtle shifts in meaning resonate with women in the workplace, or with women in Quran study groups, where conservative impulses to submission and piety compete with opportunities to claim the Quran for women.[46] The result is not a foregone conclusion. Ideas that might allow a scholar to conceive of the Quran as a historical document and also as the word of God, such as those of Abu Zayd or Arkoun, have not yet succeeded in the marketplace. Liberal but devout scholarly approaches are ignored by the public and treated as barely better than apostasy by the conservatives who dominate religious institutions. Liberal theologians in Muslim lands court trouble, even exile.

More moderate approaches, however, have better prospects. Conservative ideas need to be modernized to remain viable. Indeed, most reinterpretation today is a revitalization of social and theological conservatism.[47] For example, the devout middle class in Turkey has come to favor a version of political Islam that supports electoral democracy and neoliberal policies. Their version of Islam gives a conservative moral tone to a capitalist society instead of providing a comprehensive set of laws. Less traditional interpretations of the sacred sources are therefore finding a larger market in Turkey.[48]

Sometimes modernizing the faith requires another layer of almost-sacred texts. Again in Turkey, the Nur movement has been the most influential grassroots religious phenomenon since the early twentieth century. Nur followers study the *Epistles of Light*, interpretations of the sacred texts penned by Said Nursi, the founder of the movement.[49] Since the ancient traditions and classical commentaries are now distant to the modern Muslim experience, a revered explanation of the sacred sources such as the *Epistles of Light* almost functions as another layer of scripture. Since the Nur movement is impeccably orthodox in its fundamental doctrines, it receives very little opposition from more traditional believers.

New layers of commentary, however, do not work for everyone. A more individualist faith often accompanies a desire for unmediated, direct access to the sacred. Political scientist Olivier Roy finds that "born-again Muslims," especially in westernized populations, often take a decidedly anti-intellectual position. While remaining very conservative, they "reject culture, philosophy, and even theology in favor of a scriptural reading of the sacred texts and an immediate understanding of truth through individual faith, to the detriment of educational and religious institutions."[50]

Faith decoupled from institutions and fused with populism can have odd consequences. For example, classical religious scholarship, developing within Islamic empires, discouraged overly enthusiastic expressions of apocalypticism among believers. Many verses in the Quran suggest an imminent end of the world, but Muslims, with the exception of some among the Shia, have usually postponed the Last Day to an indefinite future. Even so, in Arab countries today, interest in the apocalypse has reawakened among Sunnis, particularly outside of established religious institutions. Very often, expectations of a catastrophic end of the world are woven together with anti-Semitic themes.[51]

The meaning of the sacred sources is, then, fluid. This is not to say, however, that Muslims will accept just any interpretation. The center of gravity of Islam remains close to the traditional interpretations of the texts. Constant debate over interpretations can itself prompt a reaction. Devout Muslims may accept all sorts of disagreement about details, but they also want agreement on the more fundamental commitments of the faith. For example, Ali Bulaç, a leading Muslim intellectual in Turkey, sounds a note of caution. He argues that the emphasis on reinterpreting and historicizing the sacred sources is a global project promoted by academics, but that this project cannot be fully accepted by believers. God's will does not change with the times, and Muslims do not have the latitude to disregard the clear commands of the Quran.[52] Putting too much emphasis on reinterpretation starts to make religion look like a human production.

So a few intellectuals will take radical positions, and perhaps they may even have a small number of followers. For example, "Quranists" or "People of the Quran" reject the authority of all prophetic traditions, taking only the Quran to be sacred.[53] But they stand too far beyond the bounds of orthodoxy to have much influence. Religious revival means interest in religious controversy, so even in highly religious environments such as Egypt today, the popular press will occasionally highlight questions about the authenticity of canonical traditions. Typically, such skepticism will attract a few supporters among intellectuals, draw condemnation from religious scholars, and help sell a few more newspapers. It is dangerous to cast doubt on the traditions, since the Quran is incomprehensible without them. In the end, debate occurs, but even the more liberal commentators will not dispense with the traditions, though they may suggest weeding out some of the more embarrassing examples.[54]

The Quran alone does not lend itself to a clear interpretation. But there is a religious need to find a coherent meaning. Muslims will disagree about what it is, but they will also try to persuade each other about *the* Quranic message. The classical heritage, in its modern conservative revisions, remains a compelling way to impose coherence onto the sacred texts. For the foreseeable future, Muslims will continue to argue about details. But the most viable options today do not challenge the fundamentals of orthodoxy. They only update the faith.

OUTSIDE THE FAITH

The Quran is not to my taste. Its supernatural claims—God, Satan, angels, jinn, miracles—seem wildly improbable. I have been too brainwashed into scientific and secular ways of thinking; the sacred sources, for me, have an aura of falsity about them. When the Quran moralizes, what I read seems archaic, or an obstacle to the ways I would like to change the world. And when the texts resort to threatening skeptics with hellfire, I lose respect for them.

And yet, I have to be impressed by how powerful a grip the Quran has on the imaginations of believers. For all the quarrels between Muslims about proper belief and practice, they sustain an overwhelming sense of sacredness about the Quran. Public expressions of doubt about religion remain rare among Muslims; most often, believers take the divine nature of the Quran to be just obvious. For many, it is as if the perfection of the sacred sources is clear prior to reasoning, perhaps framing rationality as they understand it. Asking whether the Quran is trustworthy is hardly conceivable. The authority of the sacred sources is so obvious, so fact-like, that questioning it is no more serious than doubt about the existence of the moon.

Nonetheless, few believers live in a sealed-off bubble of faith, and so there is an apologetic literature arguing that the Quran is the word of God. Some writers defend Islam against Christian polemics, others go so far as to allow doubt about the very idea of revelation. Sometimes the arguments are very old, for example, claiming an uncanny literary perfection and inimitability for the Quran. In deeply Muslim cultures the influence of the holy book is pervasive—it is constantly recited, chanted, quoted, alluded to. The Quran comes to define literary excellence. Sometimes the reasons for faith turn on fulfilled prophecies,[55] personal religious experiences, and miracle stories.

My favorite genre defending revelation are attempts to find modern science and technology prefigured in the Quran. Popular among Muslims across the globe, science-in-the-Quran apologists argue that everything from geophysics to cosmology to embryology is anticipated in the sacred book.[56] Even in modern times, the Quran remains the greatest miracle of Islam.

Not everyone is convinced the Quran is a divine revelation. There are always converts between Islam and Christianity. Some of those who become Christians, perhaps under missionary influence, come to believe that the Bible is the true word of God.[57] Much Muslim apologetics is intended to counter the Christian variety.

More interestingly, some lose faith in Abrahamic religion altogether. Historically, there have always been a few dissenters who favored the God of the philosophical tradition and rejected revelation, as well as poets who imitated the Quranic style or had a low opinion of the Quran's literary qualities. In the eleventh century, the Syrian philosopher and poet Abul Ala al-Maarri produced verses like

> So, too, the creeds of man: the one prevails
> Until the other comes; and this one fails
> When that one triumphs; ay, the lonesome world
> Will always want the latest fairy tales.[58]

We often have only fragments surviving from this doubting intellectual tradition. But today, it is even possible to find books by dissidents from Islam. This literature combs through the texts to produce long lists of contradictions, absurdities, and statements unacceptable to modern moral sensibilities or unworthy of a holy God.[59] Lately, the best place to run into such polemic is the Internet.[60]

By and large, however, the dissenters are a tiny minority. Few Muslims are religious overachievers; most pick and choose, or go through life acknowledging that they pay insufficient attention to the sacred texts. Nonetheless, most are immersed in the idea that the Quran is holy from early childhood. All that is noble and virtuous, Muslims come to believe, is connected to the sacred sources. Muslims are trained to perceive the divine nature of the Quran as obvious. And the Muslim sense of the sacred very successfully reproduces itself. Dissenters have always been suppressed or relegated to the margins of Muslim societies.

Islam, therefore, is much more culturally resilient than a secular examination of its texts may suggest. The very lack of coherence and clarity of the sacred sources prompts layers of interpretation and helps believers adapt to changing circumstances. States and religious institutions create structures to enforce agreement, but consensus always fractures into varying, mutating forms. For someone like me, a religion like Islam is steeped in the implausibility of supernaturalism and annoying demands to always approach scriptures with reverent belief. But I also have to remind myself not to think of faith as a pathology of rationality. The sacred sources are *religious* literature. The religious often demand more than that I adjust my perception of the facts. They also invite a change in the kind of person I am. When I reject the Quran, it is also because my values, my interests, my temperament lead me to take a critical distance rather than to become a person of faith.[61]

Standing outside the faiths, I see scriptures as devices for religious people to make meaning, to make their way in the world while remaining anchored in tradition. The dissenting literature, no less than the faithful, usually assumes that the Quran has a clear meaning—usually a conservative interpretation. The dissenters just happen to judge the claims of revelation to be false. This way of thinking comes naturally to me. I have a scientific background, and in science we put a lot of effort to achieve clear communication and definite evaluation. We try to reduce ambiguity and latitude for interpretation. We reach agreement.

Religious literature, apparently, resists being so constrained, though religious institutions continue to try. Today, when we need unambiguous procedures to negotiate the impersonal, complex institutions of modern life, even religion is under more pressure to present itself as a clear set of fact claims and behavioral rules. Fundamentalists particularly want to reduce the latitude for alternative meanings, and fundamentalism has been famously attractive to modern people trained in the applied sciences.

I also dissent from Islam, but I do not want to do so in a manner that inverts fundamentalism. As far as I can see, the Quran inspires plenty of falsehoods, and for those of us who care about an accurate description of the world, this sets us outside the faith. But the sacred sources do not fix Islam. Islam takes place in the meanings Muslims make. Conservative Muslims challenge secular liberal convictions not just because of their texts, but because of how their faith plays out in specific political circumstances. Any useful appraisal of Islam, therefore, has to focus on the complex ways in which Muslims put their convictions about the sacred to work. Lists of contradictions are interesting, but we cannot get lost in the texts.

A MUSLIM MODERNITY

PROGRESS

It has been more than a quarter century since I have lived in Turkey, but I still glance at Turkish news online. I usually skip the daily political speechmaking, and it has been a long time since I followed the football scores. The background story that has stretched over my lifetime, however, is the gradual re-Islamization of the country's public sphere. I find this fascinating.

As a result, lately I have been spending much of my time on a Marxist news site. This means I run into occasional stretches of Marxist cant, not to mention the odd delusional editorial. But though marginal, Marxists are also the bitterest opponents of the neoliberal Islamic politics that has come to dominate Turkey. So I can count on them to keep me informed about the latest in the culture wars, whether it is public officials denouncing religiously offensive art or a university hosting a seminar opposing evolution. I then visit religious media sites to see how they spin the events.

My left-wing site worries about religion because of the social and economic conservatism of politics colored by Islam, but also because it sees intense public religiosity as a regressive force. Its contributors uphold an Enlightenment ideal of universal social progress. And to have progress, they believe, we have to give science a free hand in describing the world, focus politics on worldly interests, and make religion a private affair. We have to secure a secular political framework to entertain hopes of improving the standing of the working class. Bringing Islam back to the forefront of public life is just going backward.

For secular people of all political stripes, it is hard not to associate Islam with backwardness. Whether in studies of levels of human development or in more straightforwardly economic comparisons, Muslim-majority countries usually do not fare well.[1] There are exceptions like the opulence of a Dubai or some oil-rich areas, but too often Islam goes together with poverty. The world is no longer sharply divided between technologically advanced and economically less developed regions. Parts of the world such as East Asia—South Korea, for example—have in the space of a few generations become developed countries. But heavily Muslim regions such as the Middle East, North Africa, and South Asia have not made as much progress. Indeed, even in countries with large Muslim minorities, such as India, the relative position of Muslims has declined, so that Indian Muslims have socioeconomically fallen behind low-caste Hindus.[2]

The backwardness associated with Islam is not just a matter of wealth. Muslims may look back to the glory days of Islamic civilization, but the Muslim presence in modern culture is much more muted. There certainly are world-class Muslim scientists, artists, and architects. But for a religion that claims well over a billion adherents, today's Muslim contribution to global high culture is much less impressive than it could be.

Since the Muslim world is so large, the reasons for relative backwardness differ from place to place. Indian Muslims face disadvantages in an environment increasingly shaped by Hindu nationalism. Across the border in Pakistan, the traditional tribal and kinship-based relationship networks that hold society together also undermine modern social and economic organization.[3] Oil-rich Arab countries suffer from a "resource curse," where an abundance of mineral resources, particularly oil, goes together with poor economic performance.[4] It is hard to see a common thread in such diverse obstacles to development. Secular liberals may be tempted to think that many Muslim populations exhibit a failed modernity. But in that case, it appears that modernity can fail in many different ways.

Nonetheless, many have suspected that religion, or rather the culture associated with premodern Muslim civilization, has had something to do with patterns of Muslim backwardness. Since the advent of modern science and the Industrial Revolution, technologically advanced Western countries have enjoyed a military and commercial advantage. Many Muslim lands were colonized or relegated to a subordinate role in the international political and economic order. This has been cause for sustained reflection among Muslim elites about the sources of the Western advantage and the reasons for Muslim backwardness.

In part, the problem has been clear. Western commercial and military power was due to advanced technology and institutions able to create and deploy this technology. Furthermore, the European powers' technological advantage was not a fluke—their capabilities were continually improving. Reorganizing Muslim states and adopting better weaponry was crucial, and in the late eighteenth and early nineteenth century military reforms swept through centers such as Istanbul and Cairo. But without more extensive modernization oriented toward technology and establishing an industrial economy, Muslim lands would remain subordinate, always having to play catch-up.

It has also been clear that Western technology derives from a new knowledge base. Modern science is a powerful way to probe and to understand nature, and scientific knowledge is closely tied to technological applications. Science, however, is more than a tool—it has more cultural depth than technology. In the late nineteenth century, European science already harbored plausibly comprehensive ambitions, and through developments such as Darwin's theory of evolution, had moved in a religiously uncomfortable direction. Materialist popularizations of science appeared and influenced European debates and were partially translated and read by intellectuals in the Ottoman Empire.[5]

Western science, then, posed a cultural challenge. As a result, while intellectual leaders in Muslim lands agreed on the urgent need to modernize, they did not reach a consensus on the extent of cultural change that was needed. Their object was to revitalize and advance *Muslim* societies—whatever the changes in the training regimens for soldiers or the costumes of government officials, after modernization the Quran had to outline the sacred and the call to prayer had to be heard from minarets. And yet the institutions and tools to be borrowed from Europe came wrapped together in a non-Muslim cultural package. Conservatives tended to be suspicious of all departures from what had become Islamic norms, while westernizers called for wholesale adoption of European ways. More often, the moderate view was to adopt Western technical knowledge and institutions but to reject ideas that challenged settled Muslim ways of thinking about nature and society.

For the past few centuries, Muslim populations under foreign influence have been driven toward modernization. States that retained some independence from Western powers, such as the shrinking Ottoman Empire and Iran, went through periods of state-imposed reforms and popular reactions. Where Muslims were under direct colonial rule, such as in British India, Muslim leaders aimed to both revive Islam and adopt modern technical knowledge and educational institutions. And yet, by the early twentieth century, even with all that had changed, little had improved in the position of Muslim societies relative to Europe. Modernizers blamed both the traditionalists who resisted reform and the colonial powers that prevented independent development.

One source of hope, however, was the Turkish experience. During the political chaos and collapse of empires in the aftermath of the First World War, the remnants of the Ottoman military and bureaucratic elite organized a war of independence against European occupiers and, after victory, got a chance to implement a comprehensive program of westernization.

The leaders of the new Republic of Turkey imposed a cultural revolution on the country. Ottoman efforts at westernization continued, but now under a nationalist ideology that proposed to confine religion to personal piety and ritual observances in the private sphere. The secularism of the Republic was always somewhat aspirational—the state remained closely involved with religion, criminalizing or undermining many popular forms of faith and attempting to channel popular Islam into a reformed variety of orthodoxy that would support modernization.[6] And yet, the revolutionaries abolished religious law, and a public sphere independent of religion emerged. Education was secularized and the natural and social sciences imported from Europe shaped how schoolchildren were taught about their world. Indeed, some Turkish revolutionaries wanted to completely westernize the public sphere, including attempts to transplant the aesthetic cultures of classical music, painting, and sculpture, though these were alien to the population at large.

Turkey is a special case: no other Muslim country experimented with westernization to the extent of the first two decades of the Republic of Turkey. Indeed, after the consolidation of the new regime, Turkey itself took a more conservative path. Nonetheless, the Turkish experience of victory over colonial powers followed by state-imposed westernization influenced Muslim elites worldwide. As colonialism fell apart after the Second World War, the most populous Muslim countries did not institute religious public orders but adopted religiously colored forms of nationalism. The Indonesian state recognized Islam, but only as a majority faith in a country with multiple official religions. Pakistan was formed by a partly secularized Muslim elite who thought of Islam in the Indian subcontinent as more akin to an ethnic identity than a comprehensive religious system. Arab nationalists honored the collective identity provided by Islam but confined the influence of the orthodox Islamic rules to personal and family law.

In all these cases, especially among elites, catching up in science, technology, and economic development remained national ambitions. There were many unresolved issues: establishing democracy when nationalist leaders had authoritarian tendencies, continuing economic dependence on Western powers, the contest between labor and capital. Nonetheless, observers of independent Muslim nations in the middle of the twentieth century expected gradual secularization to accompany economic development. Western countries, after all, had gone through a similar process. With the rationalization of economic life and rural communities giving way to urban individuals engaged in mass politics, religion would become a more private affair.[7]

Instead, religion became an instrument of political mobilization. Capital won its struggle against labor. And concerns for cultural authenticity distorted the public understanding of science. My Marxist news site does a great job telling me what the Islamic Right is up to, but otherwise it seems frozen in the past—it appeals to a conception of progress that does not make sense anymore. Muslims today, much like their predecessors two centuries ago, most often aspire to a specifically Muslim modernity rather than a secular notion of progress. The more powerful political movements, those who can plausibly claim to express the democratic consent of the majority, certainly want wealth and technology. But they want these without privatization of the sacred, and without the disenchantment of the world spearheaded by modern science.

A PURPOSE-DRIVEN UNIVERSE

In popular Islam, there certainly is plenty of enchantment. The traditionally devout often inhabit a world full of spirits, usually local variations on the Quranic jinn. Wherever modern medicine does not reach, or when it fails to deliver a cure, there are magical forms of medicine. Holy men still perform healings using their saliva and exorcize curses or the evil eye by following the example of Muhammad as related in the prophetic traditions.[8]

Indeed, for believers, nature is under divine control, infused with moral purpose. After a major earthquake or other disaster, whether in the Middle East or South Asia, preachers will explain the devastation as collective punishment for sin. Many among the believers appear to agree. Even in populations subjected to modern education, such as Turkey, a majority tends to attribute the cause of an earthquake to divine judgment.[9] The Quran (29 The Spider 40), after all, describes how God uses various disasters to punish sinful peoples.

This is not to say, however, that Muslims are exceptionally committed to supernatural notions or oblivious to modern science. Evil spirits, magical healing, or disasters as punishments are beliefs common to most world religions. American preachers also have a habit of blaming disasters such as hurricanes on collective sins, not to mention seeking healing through prayer. Popular charismatic forms of Christianity, particularly in the global South, emphasize supernatural feats such as exorcizing evil spirits. It is very difficult to compare the commitment to supernatural beliefs of different religious populations. But broadly speaking, the evidence from surveys does not portray Muslims as noticeably more intense than others in their religiosity.[10]

Furthermore, Muslims do not agree with one another about how super-natural power manifests in our world. The magical beliefs that appear most dramatically superstitious to secular people are typically connected to folk religion and rural piety. In Muslim lands, this usually means Sufi beliefs, where saints—called "friends of God" in Muslim tradition—mediate between the human and the divine realms. Saints, their descendants, and the shrines of saints are associated with miracles, and worshippers at the shrines will ask for intercession for everything from healing to finding a good husband. But if this form of piety looks similar to traditional Cathol-icism with its saints and miracles, Islam also harbors a Protestant-style alternative. Urban, middle-class Muslims often understand orthodoxy in terms of an uncompromising dedication to the sacred sources. More puritan Muslims treat popular devotion to saints as unnecessary supersti-tion at best and unacceptable worship of others besides God at worst.

So one sign of modernization—maybe even progress—might be a decline in the more flamboyant varieties of supernaturalism. Westernizers, such as the founders of the Turkish Republic, often inherited a Protestant-style disdain for popular enthusiasms and suppressed Sufi orders and devo-tion to saints. Puritan movements like the Saudi Wahhabis have done their best to destroy shrines and eliminate Sufism and heterodoxy in territories they have controlled. And however less developed, Muslim countries are still largely modern states integrated with a global economy. Proportion-ally more Muslims live in urban environments than ever before. This is not to say that varieties of Islam associated with impoverished peasants, feudal landlords, mountain tribes, and hereditary saints have vanished. The vast slums of megalopolises such as Karachi or Cairo mostly consist of recent migrants to the cities, who usually remain culturally rural. Sufi super-naturalism mutates and adapts, including New Age varieties that attract educated elites.[11] And yet, in the rapidly changing landscape of Islam, the more urban, Protestant-like, scripturally oriented forms of Islam are the more dynamic, increasingly dominant elements.

Perhaps, then, urban life and the demands of the marketplace may lead to some disenchantment. There should be less need for magic when we have reliable technology. But then again, even in premodern conditions, people ask the aid of supernatural forces not to bake bread but to make sure enough bread will be available. Complex technological societies do not always reduce our uncertainty about important matters—our economic prospects, personal relationships, and health are still full of risk and insecurity. Modern, urban circumstances need not reduce the demand for magic or determine whether the demand will be met by freelance fortune-tellers or those with stronger ties to formal religion. Modern conditions also need not diminish the role of the kind of larger-scale, more abstract supernaturalism that provides a cosmic moral template rather than help exorcize spirits. In other words, modernization in a conservative political context can favor an urban, scripture-oriented style of faith rather than disenchantment.

For example, during the Suharto era in the 1970s and 1980s, Indonesia went through important economic and religious changes. The nominal peasant Islam that characterized rural areas declined, and Indonesia as a whole came to present a more orthodox Muslim image. The loss of traditional rural ways of life accompanied economic growth and an increasing dominance of market-based social relationships, resulting in the stimulation of more Protestant styles of Islam. In a modernizing environment, it became more important to be seen to be observant, rather than to follow communal, possibly heterodox traditions. The ascendant middle-class, more individualist form of religiosity found political expression in a moderate Islamism that was instrumental in effecting a transition to a more democratic political system.[12]

Indonesia is not an isolated case. Malaysia has similarly Islamized while embracing economic modernity.[13] Turkish economic development and religious revival over the past few decades follow a roughly similar story. The Turkish example, however, also suggests that the linkage between economic development and strengthening orthodoxy is not simple. Modernization also includes opportunities for secularization and disenchantment. Conservative political choices, particularly in public education, have been instrumental in preventing disenchantment.

Westernizers in Muslim lands have emphasized education as the key to progress—when possible, they have removed education from clerical control, attempted to replace loyalty to the community of all believers with a nationalist ideology, and encouraged knowledge of science and engineering. Conservative modernizers retain this emphasis on education, including technical knowledge. But they also want to support perceptions of a universe infused with moral purpose. The centuries-old concern with the materialism lurking in Western science, and the desire to adapt Western knowledge selectively, remains very much alive.

Today, there are many areas of tension between the picture of the universe drawn by modern science and the commitments of supernatural religions. Quantum randomness and physical cosmology sit uneasily with beliefs about a world created and controlled by a cosmic mind. Cognitive neuroscience threatens to dispense with any notion of an immaterial soul. However, the main public flashpoint concerning science and religion is, as always, Darwinian evolution.

In Turkey, a major source of opposition to evolution is grassroots modernizing religious movements. In particular, since the mid-twentieth century the Nur movement has been very influential with its enthusiasm about capitalism and technology, nontraditional structure of religious authority, and insistence that modern science supports traditional Islamic beliefs.[14] Nur movement apologetics parallels the very popular belief among Muslims worldwide that some verses in the Quran miraculously anticipate modern science and technology, which would demonstrate that the Quran is the divine word. For example, verses mentioning the seven skies, which are a relic of ancient cosmology, are continually and implausibly reinterpreted to refer to the most current ideas in play in astrophysics.[15] Darwinian evolution, however, was difficult to assimilate into traditional beliefs. Conservative Muslims typically rejected human evolution outright. But Nur movement apologetics argued that science affirmed Islam. Therefore the movement needed a scientific-seeming alternative to modern biology.

Starting in the 1980s, conservative cultural policy in Turkey wove popular resistance to evolution together with desires to bolster national unity and to undercut leftist politics by strengthening religiosity. As a result, Turkish conservatives combined the creationist pseudoscience fashioned by Christians in the United States with Muslim and Nur-inspired sensibilities to produce an Islamic creationism. The Quran shows no interest in the age of the earth but insists on the special creation of Adam and Eve. The creationism fashioned in Turkey, therefore, ignored the flood geology of the Christians and was most rigid in denying human evolution. Almost immediately, this creationism began to influence Turkish education.[16]

Official creationism has waxed and waned with different governments in power, but Turkish politics today is dominated by a neoliberal Islamic conservatism with little sympathy to evolution. Textbooks contain small amounts of creationist material, but more important, Islamic creationism has also developed a popular and media presence far beyond its effects on formal science education. Indeed, Turkish creationism has acquired international influence, from Indonesia to the Muslim diaspora in Europe.[17]

Muslim populations worldwide often resist evolution, due largely to local religious conservatism rather than to Turkish imports. Though reliable data is hard to come by, it appears from surveys that deniers of human evolution outnumber those who accept it in populous countries such as Indonesia, Pakistan, and Turkey, while smaller countries in Southeastern Europe, Central Asia, and the Middle East show more ambiguous results.[18] This picture is incomplete, as the questions asked in the surveys do not distinguish between undirected Darwinian evolution and common descent under explicit divine guidance or intelligent design. Guided descent tends to be a popular way of preserving the enchantment of nature while superficially affirming science. Education policies vary widely, from the strict creationism of the Saudis to the forthright acceptance of common descent for nonhuman species in Iran.[19]

Where resistance to evolution blossoms into outright creationism, however, this is typically not a mere traditionalist reaction against secular education. The Turkish creationists present an impeccably modern image and are proud of their mastery of technology and success in a modern business environment. Like their Christian counterparts, they appeal to a modern constituency that depends on technology for a living, respects science, and requires an elaborate pseudoscience precisely because it promises harmony between science and faith.[20]

The strength of Islamic creationism, then, suggests that conservative modernization can successfully avoid disenchantment. Even when the magic of the saints and shrines recedes from public consciousness, Muslims can still perceive a supernatural, purpose-driven universe. As far as most of the faithful are concerned, there is a moral order inscribed into nature. In matters such as gender roles, our divinely created nature reflects the conservative moral order endorsed in the sacred texts.[21]

FAILING AT SCIENCE

In many ways, how conservative Muslim modernizers preserve an enchanted perception of nature is not unique to Islam. Christian conservatives in the United States reject science that threatens their religious and political ideals, whether evolutionary biology or global warming. Hindu nationalists in India consult astrologers and miracle workers and are partial to distortions of science that claim modern physics supports Hindu conceptions of spiritual realms.[22] Successful resistance to disenchantment is not unusual.

This resistance, however, need not undermine scientific performance. Though famously religious among technologically advanced countries, the United States is a world leader in basic science. India has some very good universities and research institutes, and it produces notable contributions to natural science. The Muslim presence in the natural sciences, in contrast, is disappointing—a continual concern for observant and secular Muslims alike.[23]

The reasons for why most Muslim-majority countries underperform in science are complex, and these reasons vary with each country, which makes it hard to generalize. Basic science is a public good that is primarily supported by public means. So very often, underdevelopment means a lack of resources for cutting-edge research in natural science. And yet, the modern scientific contributions of China and India suggest that even countries at a relative economic disadvantage can support respectable scientific enterprises. Secular liberals often expect some dampening of supernatural beliefs with social progress. But even if cultural conservatives successfully resist disenchantment, science is an elite, international enterprise. Science does not have to closely reflect the societies in which scientific institutions are embedded. That science-inspired skepticism about supernatural beliefs has not become widespread among Muslims is perhaps not surprising, since the Islamic world is hardly alone in this regard. But Muslim populations have also not adequately supported the institutions of basic science.

Consider, again, the United States. While Americans are a religious people, American science inhabits a different cultural world. Especially elite scientific circles are very secular.[24] This split occasionally leads to pressure on science, when some factions among political conservatives perceive academic scientists as cultural traitors. Nevertheless, American science has usually been both well-funded and independent from religion.

In part, this support for science depends on a public perception of benefits from technology, together with a common identification of science with technology. But religious liberals who are reconciled with some disenchantment also play an important role. For example, in the nineteenth century, the discovery of geological deep time, together with textual criticism, undermined confidence in the Bible as a historical narrative. Today, a notable minority of Americans—young-earth creationists—still reject deep time. Many more deny human evolution: over 40 percent in some polls.[25] But creationists of any sort have virtually no influence on American intellectual high culture and the educational establishment. This is partly because of the cultural and political strength of liberal Christian options. In the United States, public debates over creation and evolution are largely contests between different religious communities. And many Christians, especially among the well-educated managerial and professional classes, are comfortable with reinterpreting the Bible in a manner consistent with geology. As a result, intellectual high culture in the United States has little room for creationism and other gross distortions. Science and respectable religion largely occupy separate spheres, taking care not to interfere with one another.

In contrast, in Muslim lands, the intellectual high culture is often split between religious and westernized secular poles—and conservative religious intellectuals have a better claim to authenticity. For example, Turkish scientists in the better universities tend to be westernized and to participate in the international culture of science. They have not been able to effectively oppose the creationists in Turkey. Turkish scientists supporting evolution have had to argue that creationism violates the secular nature of the Turkish Republic, associating themselves with a failed secularism that does not enjoy popular support.[26]

Most important, Turkish defenders of evolution, while asserting that science is no threat to Islam, have not been able to draw on the support of a liberal religious establishment. Unlike liberal Christians and Jews who have at least partly adapted to deep time and biblical criticism, few Muslim intellectuals engage with historical criticisms of the Quran. Muslims are rarely bothered by fossilized bits of ancient cosmology in their sacred texts, and if they are, they too easily adopt apologetics that equate the seven skies in the Quran to peculiar interpretations of astrophysics.

Indeed, scientists and other academics often participate in what to outsiders look like strange attempts to appropriate science for Islam. Philosophers propose unproductive schemes for "Islamizing science" or deploy a postmodern rhetoric of suspicion to protect religion from science.[27] In regular conferences throughout the Muslim world, physicists announce that the speed of light can be calculated from the Quran, and geologists and clerics join forces to state that "modern science had at last provided evidence that Mecca was the true centre of the Earth"—and that therefore Mecca Time rather than Greenwich Mean Time should be adopted.[28] Anti-Darwinian views have a presence in academic departments, not just the popular media and educational administrations.

With both popular and high culture enamored with claims of science confirming Islam, many Muslims claim that Islam is a scientific religion. It has become commonplace to note that the Quran commands that believers should seek knowledge. However, philosopher Hasan Aydın points out that in historical context, "it is true that Islam defends science, but the science it defends is not the modern science that explains events through other events. It is a knowledge of intermediate causes, involving teleological and metaphysical causes; in other words, religious knowledge."[29] Indeed, for devout philosophers such as the Malaysian Osman Bakar, this is precisely what makes Islamic science superior to modern Western science. Looking to medieval philosophers as a model, Bakar states:

> Faith in the Quranic revelation unveils all the possibilities that lie before the human intellect. Submission to revelation at all levels enables the intellect to actualize these possibilities to the extent grace from revelation makes it possible. The cultivation of the Muslim intellect is based upon a complete awareness of this principle. Within this perspective, it is a meaningful thing for a scientist of the stature of Ibn Sīnā, certainly one of the best scientific minds in the whole history of mankind, to often resort to prayer to seek God's help in solving his philosophical and scientific problems. And it is also perfectly understandable why the purification of the soul is considered an integral part of the methodology of knowledge.[30]

Conservative Muslim thought about science is full of grandiose schemes to reinstate the medieval religious sciences at the top of a hierarchical scheme of knowledge where natural science occupies a peripheral role of gathering collections of facts about the material world.[31] Reason, many still think, should be subordinated to revelation. Such ideas have widespread currency. They are not helpful for advancing the state of science in Muslim lands.

ACCIDENTS OF HISTORY

Distortions of science are easy to find in Muslim intellectual culture today. None of these distortions aim to oppose science—at least, not what believers consider to be true science rather than materialist pretensions to knowledge. They try to show that science and traditional Islam are in perfect harmony, that revelation and knowledge of nature mutually reinforce one another.

If harmony reigns, however, it is curious that Muslims are constantly having to import modern knowledge rather than leading the world in science and technology. After all, before the scientific revolution in western

Europe, empires ruled by Muslim dynasties supported some of the most vibrant scholarly environments on the planet. Latin Christendom lost much of the intellectual heritage of antiquity, but areas of the Mediterranean and West Asia under Muslim rule experienced no Dark Ages. Muslims set the standard in astronomy, optics, medicine, and public health. Why, then, did Islamic civilization fall behind in science and technology?

Debates over the state of Muslim science invariably look back to a premodern golden age. Liberals often argue that the golden age came to an end due to an imposition of strict orthodoxy. Conservatives, however, more often think that Muslim decline is due to deviations from the true faith. The golden age shows what Muslims can achieve if they once again let their ideas of nature be guided by divine revelation.[32]

In any case, medieval Muslim science and technology has acquired mythic proportions. The myth is promoted, for example, in *1001 Inventions*, an impressively produced, award-winning exhibition that has appeared in London's Science Museum; Istanbul; the New York Hall of Science; Abu Dhabi; the California Science Center in Los Angeles; the National Geographic Museum in Washington, DC; and other places. Widely acclaimed, and endorsed by figures such as Charles, the prince of Wales, *1001 Inventions* presents a picture in which medieval Muslim scientists and inventors are ultimately responsible for many of the highlights of modern technology, from surgery to aircraft. Moreover, as *1001 Inventions* tells the story, these achievements expressed the personal religiosity of the inventors, within a civilization that integrated science and religion to the extent of teaching science in medieval mosques:

> There was little distinction between religion and knowledge as the mosque was both the place of prayer and the place of learning. Subjects included science, so science and religion sat side by side comfortably, which was not the case in other parts of the world.[33]

This, as with much of the history related in *1001 Inventions*, is so inaccurate as to be practically fictional. For example, *1001 Inventions* claims Muslim precursors of powered flight based on very poor historical documentation and claims of physically very implausible feats. Indeed, dubious stories about medieval technical achievements are well-established in the education and pop culture of many Muslim-majority countries.[34]

Moreover, the golden age myth misrepresents even the genuine accomplishments of medieval Muslim science and technology, stripping them of historical context. Whether Muslim, Christian, Hindu, or Chinese, premodern knowledge about nature existed in intellectual environments where astrology or various medical superstitions were as respectable as innovations in planetary models or medical practice. Today, we can pick out those ideas that fit with our current understanding of the world. But highlighting such examples means overlooking the important differences between premodern conceptions of knowledge and modern science.

The notion that medieval Muslim science declined is also something of a myth. Regardless of imposed orthodoxy or deviations from orthodoxy, Muslim efforts at building knowledge of nature continued to develop slowly.[35] What happened was that this medieval form of science was overtaken by the explosive growth in a new, significantly different way of investigating nature that took off in western Europe.

Europe was backward in terms of medieval knowledge. But with hindsight, historians can identify some reasons why the scientific revolution took place in what was once an intellectual backwater. For example, European law allowed corporate entities such as cities, which set the stage for intellectual enterprises independent of religious control. Islamic law did not recognize corporate bodies. Late medieval Christian theology began to emphasize natural causation, allowing nature a degree of autonomy. Muslim theology developed a suspicion of natural causation, preferring an omnipotent divine will in direct control of events. Other, similarly minor points of divergence added up to give Europe an advantage.[36]

None of this means that a religious civilization with the Bible as a sacred text was inherently friendlier to science than one where the Quran was central. Islamic law has no fundamental objection to corporate entities; it just happened not to develop ideas in that direction. A few Muslim theologians proposed ways to reconcile natural causation and divine omnipotence, but the whole debate was peripheral to premodern Muslim intellectual life, and such options just happened not to catch on. The scientific revolution began in Europe due to a number of historical accidents.[37] The most strongly held beliefs of either Christians or Muslims have little to do with either encouraging or suppressing the beginnings of modern science.

Perhaps, then, to do better at science today, Muslims could emphasize options overlooked by the religious mainstream. Conservative thinkers often want to revive the supernatural-centered conception of knowledge of the golden age, proposing a science that attempts to read "the book of nature" as a compendium of symbols and signs of divine purposes.[38] But since that appears to be a dead end, more liberal Muslims, often with a background in science, hope to combine reinterpretations of scripture with philosophical interpretations of science that leave room for divine action. The liberal Christian experience suggests that if such views were to gain more influence, science could enjoy a more secure cultural position in Muslim lands.

For example, physicist Nidhal Guessoum calls for a "multi-level," more metaphorical interpretation of the sacred sources, even suggesting that religious texts can be better understood after taking science into account:

> While the Qur'an cannot be turned into an encyclopedia of any sort, least of all of science, one must keep in mind the fact that if the Qur'an is to be taken seriously and respectfully, one must uphold the Rushdian (Averroes's) principles of no-possible-conflict (between the word of God and the work of God) and his hermeneutical prescription. In practice this principle can be turned into a no-objection or no-opposition approach, whereby one can convince the Muslim public of a given idea (say the theory of biological evolution), not by proving that it can be found in the Qur'an but rather by showing that at least one intelligent reading and interpretation of various passages of the Holy Book is fully consistent with that theory.[39]

Conservatives rightly worry that such liberal approaches risk putting human science ahead of divine revelation. But Guessoum does not ask religious conceptions of nature to give way to secular science. He proposes a "double programme" that makes demands on science as well:

(1) Some new theology must be proposed that would be consistent with modern science even if it does not adhere to the sacred beliefs and writings in a literal way; (2) a less materialistic cosmology must be produced, one that would allow for some meaning and spirit to be found in the universe and in the existence.[40]

A liberal but still religious approach, after all, cannot allow complete disenchantment. Distaste for materialism leads liberals such as Guessoum to favor ideas such as "theistic science" and non-Darwinian views of evolution that attempt to retain divine design in biology.

I do not mind materialism, and I do not find any liberal theology grafted onto science convincing. But while I doubt the intellectual merit of liberal reconciliations of science and the supernatural, I also think that scientific institutions in Muslim lands would do much better if liberal interpretations were to become more popular. Basic science needs public support, and its materialist tendencies cause difficulties in strongly religious societies. If science is to enjoy some independence, it needs the political protection provided by religious factions inclined to grant science a separate sphere.[41]

Religious conservatives have not been able to establish harmony between scientific and religious institutions. Believing that science can be found in the Quran—that seven skies refer to modern astrophysics—might ease religious discomfort, concealing the materialist aspects of modern science. But conservative views do not just clash with isolated facts established by science. More important, the need to perceive design and purpose in the universe conflicts with important conceptual frameworks of modern science. Materialism is pervasive in the blindness of Darwinian evolution, the randomness of quantum events, and the way the physical brain produces mentality. Religious discomfort with such materialism inhibits research and education within these conceptual frameworks. Science is large and specialized, and one can, for example, be an Orthodox Jewish world leader in electrochemistry who denies Darwinian evolution.[42] But widespread rejection of the theoretical frameworks established by science cannot lead to a healthy scientific enterprise.

Religious liberals also dislike materialism, but their attempts to preserve enchantment do not disrupt the conceptual frameworks of science to the same degree. Liberals will seek a divine hand disguised in quantum randomness, thereby annoying purists such as myself.[43] They will not, however, interfere with the ordinary practice of physics. Liberals may be dissatisfied with stark Darwinian evolution, but they will not impede the work of biology. While science-minded nonbelievers like me disagree with liberal versions of enchantment, this is closer to a friendly philosophical dispute that has little effect on the everyday practices of science.

There is a liberal Muslim option that can ease conflicts between science and Islam. The problem today is that liberals are in a politically weak position. The materialism and disenchantment associated with modern science will continue to cause intellectual tension with supernatural convictions. No variety of Islam can entirely escape this tension. But if liberal options were to gain strength, there would be one fewer obstacle to Muslim populations supporting flourishing scientific enterprises. After all, the present poor state of science in Muslim lands is due to historical accidents. Things may change.

APPLIED SCIENCE

Modern science and conservative Islam do not mix well—and theologically conservative versions of Islam are stronger today. If the flourishing of science and the disenchantment of public culture are important for progress, my Marxist news site is right to worry.

But then again, it is also worth asking if disenchantment is really progress. I teach physics, so I am professionally obligated to sputter and rant when I encounter misrepresentations of science. But secular liberals also attach a particular political significance to science. Why should devout Muslims care about science in the same way?

For secular liberals, science is often significant because of what we expect from a modern citizenry in a complex world. We cannot rely on faith-based conceptions of knowledge, often because our societies are religiously diverse. Instead, we want to pursue our common interests by acting on publicly available, secular reasons. This is best done by well-informed citizens equipped for free participation in public decision making.

It is impossible to acquire all relevant knowledge. So in practice, we often need to locate the appropriate experts and trustworthy institutions. This requires that we cultivate our critical abilities, including our judgments on proper expertise. Therefore liberal education becomes important. Citizens should have some understanding of history, philosophy, and science—not to solve highly technical problems in every field, but in order to be a reflective actor rather than a passive consumer of information.

That is the liberal ideal. The reality in technologically advanced countries can be very different. I used to be involved with research in atmospheric physics, which a few years ago led me to a lobbying trip to the United States Congress. The Union of Concerned Scientists hoped to advance legislation that might, however feebly, begin to address global warming. So they sent us out, in teams including scientists and economists, to try to impress the urgency of the situation onto congressional staffers. In the process, I started to learn that our political systems are incapable of responding to the climate crisis.[44] We are facing catastrophic climate change and we need to stop pumping greenhouse gases into the atmosphere. But that expert consensus was impotent in the face of the politicians' well-justified concern that if they passed any real legislation, they would be vulnerable to twenty-second attack ads funded by fossil fuel interests.

Perhaps improving education would help, since a better-educated citizenry should be less susceptible to political manipulation. But science education is expensive. And it is very difficult to get more than a small percentage of a population to properly grasp the conceptual frameworks, such as Darwinian evolution or quantum mechanics, that are so important for modern science. At best, mass science education can produce appreciation of science,[45] which might lead to more deference to scientific expertise.

Secular liberals, then, may ask too much from education—at least at present. In Western countries today, public education at all levels is more likely to face austerity than expanding resources. If American trends are any indication, education will be increasingly privatized, with high-quality science education available to few besides the wealthy.[46] And even in the recent past, when conceiving of public goods was not as difficult as it is today, scientific institutions have had an uneven record in influencing political decisions. For example, it took public health policy a long time to acknowledge the danger of smoking. Similarly, despite the concerns of worried physicists, nuclear warfare remains an ever-present possibility. Secular liberals envision science, along with the humanities, contributing to public debates about how to live our lives together. After all, science helps us predict the consequences of our actions, including harmful effects of our technologies. But wealthy countries support science because of the promise of technologies that lead to immediate commercial and military advantage. Science, in other words, primarily serves power and only secondarily informs public debate.

The need for commercial and military power is also the driving force behind Muslim modernization efforts. Selective importing and mastering of modern knowledge is supposed to help overcome the humiliations suffered by Muslim populations.

But countries lagging behind technologically advanced rivals will naturally invest more in applied science. They will train engineers, not physicists. Indeed, in Middle Eastern countries, engineering has higher prestige than does science. In Turkey, for example, entrance to universities depends on a national standardized test after high school. The highest demand is for degrees that promise status and earnings. Past decades have seen a surge of interest in business and management, but for generations, some of the best students have been attracted to engineering. I come from a family of engineers, and I did well in the national examination. So I started out as an engineering undergraduate; after all, physics held out few job prospects and did not require good scores. Curiously, Turkish universities may also offer a "physics engineering" degree, which is very similar to physics. The very name "engineering" attracts higher-ranking students than physics programs do.

Since Muslim countries have usually emphasized applied science in their efforts to modernize, we should ask how they have done in applied rather than basic science. And in this case, there are more success stories. Turkey is, again, a good example. Turkey has joined the ranks of "upper middle income" countries with a considerable concentration of manufacturing industries and internationally competitive engineering firms. Now, my friends who do engineering in Turkey often work on unglamorous tasks such as adapting advanced technologies to Turkish conditions, or maintenance. But this is a large part of what most engineers do, wherever they are located.[47] Turkey is still in an economically subordinate position, not at the cutting edge of high technology development. Nonetheless, it has a largely modern, technology-driven economy. Whatever its difficulties in basic science, Turkey no longer presents the image of utter backwardness of a century ago, when it was emerging from the collapse of the Ottoman Empire.

Many Muslim countries do reasonably well educating the engineers they need. They produce a sufficient number of applied science professionals for the marketplace. Two centuries ago, Ottomans or Iranians had to rely on European experts for the most basic transfers of technology. Today, there is still a sense that the best applied science is found abroad, so many Muslim engineering students will pursue graduate studies in the United States or Europe. Some of them stay. When I look at the faculty lists of American engineering departments, I run into many names from Arab countries, Iran, Turkey, Pakistan and so on—proportionally many more than in physics departments. Most, however, return home and contribute to their countries. Complete dependence on Western experts is long in the past.

In at least some Muslim countries, then, efforts to acquire modern technology without the disenchantment that accompanies natural science show signs of success. Indeed, the secular liberal concern about conflicts between science and religion can make us overlook how applied science and conservative modernization can work very well together.

When science leads to skepticism about theistic supernaturalism—not just small-scale magical claims—it does so because of its ambitious, naturalistic conceptual frameworks. Science receives support due to its promise of eventual military and commercial applications, but institutionally, natural science is on a long leash. To a physicist, high-temperature superconductivity is not primarily a means to achieving magnetically levitated trains, though the prospect of such applications may be an important reason superconductivity research is funded. Instead, superconductivity is a fascinating, difficult, and fundamental puzzle. There are reasons internal to physics to pursue such a problem, and our institutions allow a measure of freedom for physicists to respond to these reasons. The long leash also allows scientists to endorse comprehensively naturalistic explanations of the world, even if naturalistic views threaten to erode the myths that support conservative social orders.

Applied sciences, in contrast, are oriented toward pragmatic problem solving rather than toward theoretical understanding. Considerations of cost and purpose are much closer to the surface. Civil engineers have to respect physics, otherwise their bridges will collapse. But the process of designing an actual bridge cannot be abstracted from the social or economic utility a bridge is expected to deliver. Military or commercial imperatives keep applied science on a much shorter leash. The work of engineers and medical doctors is much closer to business and the marketplace, much easier to link with communities and their conservative social values as expressed in prevailing forms of religion.

As may be expected, social scientists find that the internal culture of applied science is much more religiously and politically conservative than the culture of basic science.[48] Proportionally, far more engineers than physicists are creationists; many more medical doctors than biologists deny Darwinian evolution. In Muslim lands, engineers have very often been leaders in Islamist politics. In Egypt, professional associations, including those of engineers and medical doctors, have been strongholds of the Muslim Brotherhood.

Education for purposes of conservative modernization is also easier to achieve than are ambitious secular liberal ideals. To conservative populists, liberal education often appears as a social engineering project aiming to instill trust in secular elites who claim special expertise. Instead, conservatives emphasize loyalty to communities with organically developed ways of understanding the world, in which moral and spiritual ideals are interwoven with descriptions of how the world works. They trust the visible achievements of technology but are more reserved about abstract theoretical descriptions of nature.[49] Leading conservative thinkers have often taken an anti-rationalist approach, emphasizing experience and "practical knowledge" over theoretical forms of knowledge that are, at best, an abridged summary of practical knowledge.[50] And education driven by conservative ideals can lead to success in commerce and technology.

Consider, for example, the followers of Fethullah Gülen, a powerful offshoot of the Nur movement in Turkey. Gülen's disciples emphasize education as a vehicle for piety and social mobility. The movement has operated many private secondary schools and a number of universities in Turkey and abroad. Sociologist Yıldız Atasoy emphasizes the secular appearance of the schools:

> The schools are locally run and follow a completely secular educational programme. They focus on the study of science and technology, and how to apply the resulting knowledge from such study to economic development. These schools are funded through the philanthropic support of business communities and are integral to the wealth creation strategy of the [Gülenists].[51]

Such education includes very little overt religion in the classroom, concentrating on instruction in technical knowledge. Students absorb religion indirectly, through social networks connected to the schools.[52] This emphasis on technical competence pays off—Gülenist and similar religious movements prepare students well for the minefield that education driven by standardized testing has become. This includes the national university entrance examinations in Turkey, where there are many questions on scientific facts and mathematical calculations. And once in university, students from conservative backgrounds can count on religious networks to provide housing and other support. As a result, many of the best engineers in Turkey have connections to religious orders. While educated elites in many Muslim countries, from Turkey to Pakistan, tended to be secularized a few generations ago, the pious middle class has a much stronger presence today in higher education and in the technical professions.

Technical competence, however, is not the same as science education in a secular liberal sense. Gülen's movement is cool toward Darwinian evolution and has been a significant source of support for creationism in Turkey. Conservative education that focuses on technical competence treats science as a collection of facts and a generator of technologies. It downplays important conceptual frameworks of modern science such as evolution, and therefore does not allow science the cultural depth to produce disenchantment. This outlook produces students who do well on standardized tests but also have a superficial conception of science. Such an education need not handicap students groomed for success in commerce and applied science. After all, there are many aspects of science that are crucial for understanding how the world works but do not lend themselves to immediate technological applications. Evolution is a good example. Notwithstanding claims made for "evolutionary medicine,"[53] Darwinian ideas remain peripheral to applied biomedical sciences.

Most strongly religious Muslims, like their conservative counterparts in other religions, have been ambivalent about secular liberal ideas of progress. Secular progress involves disenchantment, which threatens the moral integrity of religious societies. Advancing technology, however, has more appeal. Most people want the wealth and increased capabilities promised by modern technology. Competition with rivals such as the Western powers makes technological progress vital for survival as Muslim societies.

In that case, it seems appropriate to judge Muslim progress not by secular liberal ideals that seem increasingly irrelevant even in the West, but in terms of a more conservative approach. Muslim populations may lag in their support for basic science, but this lag is less consequential than where they stand on applied science. If even in advanced Western countries the primary social role of science is to support existing power structures, it is hard to criticize Muslim countries if their approaches to science and education reflect similar priorities.

TRADING UP TO MODERNITY

If lagging in science is as much a symptom as a cause of Muslim backwardness—if it is only part of the story—there still is the question of why Muslims fell behind. What prevented a modern economy from emerging in Muslim lands?

One reason might be Islamic doctrines. After all, when European colo-
nizers penetrated Muslim lands, they encountered relatively stagnant economies. We are still familiar with stereotypes of the static, otherworldly
East. In 4 Women 77, the Quran encourages those reluctant to fight and die
with "Say, 'Enjoyment of this world is little; the hereafter is better for the
conscientious, as they will not be wronged in in the slightest.'" Getting into
heaven, it might seem, should be the main concern for Muslims. Worldly
endeavors such as commercial enterprises would be distractions.

Muslims, however, remember Muhammad as a merchant. And together
with conquests and conversions of princes, Islam spread through trading
networks. Just as the best medieval science was practiced in Muslim lands,
the most sophisticated financial and commercial institutions used to be
associated with Muslim civilization. Islam could support otherworldly
inclinations, much like Christianity had its own varieties of otherworld-
liness such as monasticism. But Islamic civilization also looked back
toward the worldly success of its early days. Muslims engaged in trade,
and scholars of Islamic law directed much of their effort to rulings on commercial matters.

In that case, instead of religious doctrines, perhaps some broader characteristics of Muslim civilization promoted stagnation. For example, many
Muslim societies have been organized around cohesive tribes or clans,
without a strong central government. Urban specialists—including arti-
sans, merchants, and religious scholars—lacked cohesion and often have
been ruled by a warrior class deriving from seminomadic tribesmen. These
were not conditions conducive to accumulating capital or forging the connections between a strong state and commercial markets characteristic of
modern economies.

Even today, a social order derived from a tribal period can inhibit
economic performance. Modernizers in Muslim lands have tried hard to
break tribal social relationships, but in many regions—Kurdish territories,
many Arab countries, large parts of North Africa, South Asia—tribal and
kinship group solidarities remain strong. In what are superficially modern
states, political ties echo the older tribal relationships. As a result, philosopher Ernest Gellner observes that in a "Muslim state," there often is an

"extreme addiction to patronage politics: the weak can survive thanks to protection by the strong, and everything depends on networks. There is no trust without a special relationship, and not too much even then."[54] Modern institutions cannot function properly in such an environment.

Patronage politics has been a serious obstacle to development for many Muslim states. But the Muslim world also is, and has been, large and diverse. The idealized model of tribal societies is a rough fit, and it hardly applies to all.[55] Medieval and early modern European societies were also diverse and included many forms of organization and social solidarities that inhibited capitalist economies. Modernity just had to start somewhere and spread; a similar process could have taken place in Muslim regions. But it did not. Tribes and patronage politics, though important, do not explain the difference between the European and Muslim experiences of modernization.

A better explanation will be similar to the account of how Muslims fell behind in science. With hindsight, we can pick out features of medieval Muslim economic institutions that, while they worked well in their time and place, also set Muslims back when compared to European powers that developed a new way of organizing their economies. Economic historian Timur Kuran, for example, argues that

> the Middle East fell behind the West because it was late in adopting key institutions of the modern economy. These include laws, regulations, and organizational forms that enabled economic activities now taken for granted in all but the most impoverished parts of the globe: the mobilization of productive resources on a huge scale within long-lasting private enterprises and the provision of social services through durable entities capable of transformation. Well into the nineteenth century, the private sectors of the Middle East were composed of atomistic enterprises that did not outlive their founders. When individuals pooled resources in profit-making enterprises, their cooperation was meant to be temporary, often no more than a few months. By that time, most of the now-advanced countries had developed institutions essential to the mass mobilization of savings, the lengthening of individual planning horizons, and the exploitation of new technologies through structurally complex organizations.

Therein lies a key reason why the Middle East fell behind in living standards and why it succumbed to foreign domination.[56]

Religion had a role in this relative stagnation. Muslims regulated commerce, as with so much of daily life, through a body of sacred laws. Kuran points out that aside from the conservatism inherent in sacred institutions, Islamic law also had some specific features that inhibited large-scale, durable enterprises. For example, Quranic inheritance laws did not leave much to choice in the manner of splitting estates. This kept Muslim societies more equal, making it more difficult for wealthy aristocratic families to persist. But Islamic inheritance practices fragmented productive assets. Muslim polygyny also promoted fragmentation. After all, powerful and wealthy men could afford multiple wives and lots of children. On their deaths, their commercial enterprises would be divided and distributed over large numbers.[57]

More important, Islamic law, though influenced by Roman and Persian precursors, did not recognize corporate entities. There were short-term partnerships for business and pious endowments charged to perform a specific task in perpetuity. But there were no cities or colleges that could hold property or act as an organization. No religious corporate bodies existed either. Religious scholars enjoyed a largely decentralized, personal authority. Movements centered on Sufi saints were not institutionalized in legal form, other than endowments to care for shrines.

Without corporations, long-term business enterprises that could grow, adapt, and change their goals could not exist. Moreover, the Christian experience and the rise of modern science shows that corporate entities with some scope to determine their internal rules could lay the groundwork for institutions independent of religion. In Muslim lands, nonreligious domains of law were controversial at best.[58] As historian Bernard Lewis states, "In the Islamic context, the independence and initiative of the civil society may best be measured not in relation to the state but in relation to religion, of which, in the Muslim perception, the state itself is a manifestation and instrument."[59] Islamic law, then, happened not to provide for modern economic organization and did not endorse a separate sphere for economic activity any more than for science.

None of this, however, means that Islam was not adaptable. Kuran also observes:

> The Islamic heritage harbors elements that promote conservatism, and generations of Muslims have invoked scripture and perceived precedents to block institutional change. However, Islamic law is not inherently unchangeable, because reformers are able to draw legitimacy from the very same sources. Had a significant demand emerged before the nineteenth century for expanding the organizational options of merchants, religious sensibilities would not have posed an impregnable barrier. Judges could have altered the practice of Islamic law by tolerating deviations and relaxing interpretations. Muftis might have assisted merchants through commerce-friendly opinions (*fatwās*).[60]

For example, premodern Muslims were fully engaged in borrowing and lending with interest. The Quran denounces usury in 2 The Cow 275, saying that "Those who consume usurious interest are only in the sort of business in which one maddened by Satan's touch engages. That is because they say trade is like usury; but God has permitted trade and forbidden usury." But what usury consists of is open to interpretation, and Islamic law was flexible enough to allow a credit system while respecting the letter of a ban on usury. In practice, the taking of interest was fully present, public, and ubiquitous in premodern Muslim economies.[61]

The rise of modern economies, then, came about in a manner similar to the rise of modern science. Due to historical accidents rather than any core religious doctrines, the economic and legal institutions of some parts of Latin Christendom were more suitable for nurturing what became modern business enterprises. Western Europe took off, leaving Muslim regions behind. After that, modernizing Muslims had to adapt, starting by transplanting Western institutions.

Change started with foreigners, minority religious populations, and westernizers. Sometimes foreign ideas did not help—in the twentieth century, the communist example tempted the leadership of many newly independent Muslim countries to leap into modernity with massive state-led development projects. Patronage politics doomed many such efforts.

But by and large, Muslims adopted modern economic institutions. Furthermore, in commercial matters, borrowing from the West did not prompt the defensiveness that accompanied importing Western scientific knowledge. Kuran notes that

> By the early twentieth century the corporation had been transplanted to the legal systems of the Middle East. Nowhere did legal personhood or entity shielding generate reactions in the name of Islamic purity. Islamist movements of the twenty-first century do not want to limit legal standing to natural persons. They have no qualms about organizational longevity. They do not take issue with the Islamic world's rapidly expanding stock markets, in which millions of shares change hands daily. Certain institutions of early Islam kept the corporation from emerging indigenously. Once borrowed from abroad along with supporting institutions, it was absorbed into local legal systems without notable resistance.[62]

In contrast to their resistance to religiously sensitive aspects of science, even conservative Muslims easily allowed reinterpretations and adjustments to accommodate commerce. For example, interest-free Islamic banking has become a notable financial presence in the past few decades. As with its historical precursors, modern interest-free finance is somewhat fake—Islamic banks almost always provide returns identical to the secular banks with which they compete.[63] And as with many liberal reinterpretations of religion, Islamic banking is driven by worldly needs rather than reasons internal to religion itself. After all, many religious doctrines have little fixed meaning. They are sometimes most flexible in the hands of those who present themselves as upholding timeless traditional truths.

Economic need seems to have spurred more creative adaptation than with science. Improving commerce does not threaten disenchantment, which makes it more in tune with conservative modernization. If modern economic and financial institutions ensure growth, then many Muslim countries are well on their way to a more developed status.

NEOLIBERAL ISLAM

Today, most Muslims live within a neoliberal, enthusiastically capitalist system of economy and politics. In many countries, globalized investment and free trade means a small affluent business class organizing cheap labor resources. Those of us living in advanced Western countries hear little about the economy of Bangladesh, until a more than usual number of workers producing textiles for export die due to appalling safety conditions. Our media praises Indonesia as an "emerging market," occasionally airing stories about low-paid Indonesians sewing athletic shoes for leading global brands.

There is, as always, much variation in Muslim-majority economies. Businessmen are not always the dominant figures. Pakistan, for example, could be called a "neoliberal security state," where the military has enormous influence on the economy and politics.[64] Egypt's version of army-dominated crony capitalism might also fit this description. Some countries have lagged in liberalizing their economy and have been pushed into chaos and civil war, such as Libya and Syria.

Even though Muslim countries integrate with the global economy in different ways, there are commonalities. States tend to retreat to providing military and police functions, business concerns become more prominent, and a kind of plutocracy with elections takes over politics. But there is little that is specifically Islamic about this form of neoliberal development. Furthermore, if Muslim countries mainly contribute cheap labor and natural resources, they appear more comparable to Mexico than, for example, Germany. The Middle East and South Asia may boast of active stock markets and increasing numbers of billionaires, but it is hard not to see them as remaining backward when they are also the source of large numbers of economically motivated immigrants to richer countries.

To see how Islam affects economic development today, it helps to examine the Turkish example again. Turkey is relatively well-situated without suffering from a resource curse, and the strong Turkish state descends from the Ottoman Empire, heir to centuries of efforts to catch up to modernity. In recent decades, Turkey's economy has followed an orthodox neoliberal trajectory. At the same time, Turkey has significantly re-Islamized its public culture.

Grassroots movements, such as the ubiquitous Nur movement, had a significant role in mobilizing Turkish popular piety to support business dominance. They had plenty of political help. Neoliberalism took over Turkey in the aftermath of a military coup in 1980, which broke the labor movement and imposed a business-friendly public order.[65] The United States and the European Union, the major allies and trading partners of Turkey, also exerted pressure supporting free trade, privatization, and openness to foreign investment. Many manufacturing industries were leaving Europe for lands with cheaper labor and laxer environmental standards, and Turkey took advantage. The liberalization of the Turkish economy was not, however, just a secular project. The Turkish military and military-backed governments adopted conservative cultural policies, for example, introducing anti-evolutionary themes into science education. Moreover, economic liberalization strengthened the position of pious businessmen based in the provinces, compared to the established capitalist dynasties that had been closely intertwined with the secular elites in the modernizing state. The pious businessmen poured resources into Islamizing the public sphere.

Though religious influence grew stronger in the aftermath of the coup, Islamists in 1980s and 1990s Turkey often continued to sharply oppose the existing order. Even the cultural conservatism in place was, according to many Islamist intellectuals, a set of half measures, compromised by association with a secular state tradition. They explored radical ideas, including not just explicitly Islamic legal and governmental structures but also gestures toward a religious solidarity within the economy rather than pure market competition. The "just order" would take care of the pious poor as well as unleash free enterprise.

In the 1990s the Islamist opposition deepened its appeal, won elections, and claimed a leading role in government. The Turkish military then rediscovered its secularism and intervened to drive the Islamists from power. Political stability remained elusive, even as economic neoliberalism remained constant throughout changes of governments. Finally, in 2002, after a severe financial crisis, the newly formed Justice and Development Party (AKP) won its first election. The Turkish state had defeated the more radical forms of Islamism, but decades of Islamic cultural resurgence meant that political legitimacy had to come through a more explicitly religious politics. The AKP was a moderate Islamist, fully neoliberal party, and together with religious communities such as the Gülenists who controlled the police and judiciary, the AKP continued to advance the conservative modernization project.

The AKP period, then, represents a reconciliation between popular religiosity and state goals of succeeding at modernity. By embracing neoliberalism as the best path to development, conservative Muslim leaders abandoned ambitions to completely remake society. They joined the system.[66] In their quest for an alternative, Muslim modernity, Muslim leaders settled for governing Turkey according to the ambitions of pious businessmen and engineers, who were shaped by a global economy as much as by Islamic traditions.

Indeed, the ascendant versions of Islam today are a good fit with free market ideology. Influential religious orders conceive of religion as the moral backbone of a capitalist society. As Yıldız Atasoy observes, they demand that

> Muslims must emerge as morally inspired economic players and engage in a competitive market economy for wealth generation. The religious order is the moral architecture, providing the spiritual messages, ethical representations, and knowledge bound up with the values of market competition.[67]

Pious business organizations promote a concept of "Homo islamicus," adding a moral dimension to the "Homo economicus" of the Western capitalist imagination. They argue that the original economic model of the Prophet and his Companions was a free market order that also took care of the unfortunate by embodying charity in the religious rules. Instead of conflicts between labor and management, an Islamic moral framework emphasizes cooperation in a common cause, making unions unnecessary. Business publications include a "verse of the day," selecting among prophetic traditions according to their compatibility with a business environment. Meanwhile, Islamic networks promote trust between businessmen, assuring the smooth operation of production and distribution.[68]

Such versions of Islam also produce consent for the inequality generated by neoliberalism, by moralizing winning and losing in the marketplace. After all, traditional religious teachings enjoin patience in the face of worldly disadvantage—this world is a place of testing, and the true reward is in heaven. Striving for success is a duty, but God will choose to test some by poverty and some through the temptations that come with wealth.[69] And in the end, though pious workers and businessmen enjoy very different standings in the workplace, they all go to the mosque together.

Turkey, then, is a leading example of conservative modernization. Its evolution toward a market society has been driven both by elite interests and by popular religious mobilization. Religion has been central to Turkey's neoliberal transformation, through moderate Islamist governments and grassroots religious movements that celebrate business values.

How, then, has Turkey performed? Free markets are often claimed to deliver high growth rates. In these terms, Turkey has enjoyed a middling performance. The AKP's rule, for over a decade, corresponded to average growth rates of income per capita of 3 to 4 percent, matching the high growth of the decades preceding the 1980 military coup. Emphasizing Islamic affinities, Turkish industry took advantage of Central Asian markets and attracted investment from rich Persian Gulf States.[70] However, as economist Dani Rodrik points out, while Turkish growth was large compared to advanced countries,

> Turkish performance lagged significantly behind emerging and developing economies as a group. In the latter, real GDP rose by 95% compared to Turkey's 64%. Real GDP in large emerging markets such as China, India, Bangladesh, and Indonesia all grew more rapidly than Turkey, as it did in many smaller African and Latin American countries.[71]

The stability of neoliberal growth is also questionable. The heavily financialized global economy is vulnerable to periodic crises. Turkey has a large foreign debt load and a troublesome trade deficit, and has been overly dependent on flows of "hot money" from sources such as the Gulf States. As a middle-income country on the edge of Europe, Turkish leaders invite comparisons to advanced economies rather than, say, Bangladesh, even if Bangladesh has grown faster. But Turkey ranks last in overall quality of life among the 34 OECD countries.[72] The distribution of income is highly skewed, as it is with neoliberal regimes globally. Real wages have remained stagnant, even with productivity increases of about 80 percent per capita over more than a decade. Increasing industrial production has resulted in environmental problems, and growth has depended on the informal sector without generating much increase in formal employment. Insecure, precarious employment accompanied by persistent unemployment has become common.[73]

Turkey, therefore, is not an unqualified success story. Nonetheless, Turkey demonstrates that conservative modernization can deliver much of what its proponents desire. The Turkish example, together with other neoliberal experiments such as Malaysia and Indonesia, shows that some varieties of Islam can be instrumental in bringing Muslims into the global capitalist mainstream. It no longer makes sense to lump all Muslim countries together and ask whether their religion contributes to underdevelopment. The achievements of and difficulties faced by countries such as Turkey or Malaysia are similar to non-Muslim countries with comparable levels of income and in similar geographical circumstances. The advanced economies still enjoy a historical advantage. Statistically, less religious countries still have an edge in patents produced per capita.[74] But global neoliberalism has also meant relative economic stagnation in the advanced regions, particularly for those not in the very top income brackets. In any case, rich countries and emerging markets are no longer distinguished by new and distinct forms of economic organization.

The Turkish example also shows that it is difficult to generalize from a particular country's experience. Turkey under its moderate Islamist leadership has, until recently, been highly praised in the Western media, and the Turkish model has been offered as an example for other Middle Eastern countries to emulate. And indeed, conservative modernization—rejecting religiously challenging ideas while emphasizing modern economics and applied science—has considerable appeal to Muslim populations. In Turkey, however, modernization culminated in Islamic neoliberalism due to a complex history and specific political choices. Other countries need not follow the same course.

The Islamists of Turkey and Egypt, for example, have influenced one another—the Muslim Brotherhood and the Turkish AKP are political and intellectual allies. Indeed, the Muslim Brotherhood went through a similar evolution, losing its radical edge and becoming a populist conservative movement under the leadership of businessmen. The younger generation of Egyptian Muslim Brothers have adopted an ethos of commerce and networking and are less interested in the Brotherhood as a hierarchical organization regulated by an oppositional ideology. Instead, they express their Islamist convictions through consumption patterns and business activity. But unlike the AKP, the Muslim Brotherhood has not been able to sideline competitors and inherit the state's project of modernization. The Muslim Brotherhood faced obstruction from the established, military-allied kleptocracy and a strong fundamentalist competition, and it did not have the opportunity to organize a strong popular base for neoliberalism.[75] So while it is certain that Egyptian politics will retain a strongly Islamic character, it is much less clear whether Egypt can follow an economic trajectory similar to that of Turkey.

Economic backwardness, then, may continue to characterize many Muslim regions. It is not even clear whether neoliberalism is the best recipe for development. Economics, after all, is not physics. The basic assumptions of today's dominant forms of economic theory are far removed from even a first approximation to reality; the core of today's market worship appears to be conservative moral convictions about just deserts rather than a mutually supportive interaction of theory and experiment.[76] Nonetheless, politically, neoliberalism is triumphant. Muslims interested in economic development have to adapt to a neoliberal global environment. And Protestant-style varieties of Islam are capable of not just accommodating but celebrating a neoliberal, business-dominated social order.

A PIOUS MODERNITY

As a religion, Islam is a resounding success. Even in the last few centuries, as Muslim empires crumbled and Muslim civilization faltered, belief in the Quran and Muhammad as God's messenger continued to spread. Muslims have not always been able to defend their lands, but they have defended their faith. To arrest worldly decline, many Muslims embraced modern institutions, particularly a dynamic capitalist economy. They sought technology without disenchantment, wealth without moral upheaval. Today, even as Muslim lands too often appear to be facing political crises, the mosques are crowded, televangelists attract large audiences, and the conviction of divine design permeates Muslim perceptions of nature.

The effort to find a conservative path to modernity is not unique to Muslims. The Chinese, for example, when confronted by superior Western force, also hoped to master new technologies and new knowledge while remaining wary of ideas that might corrupt social harmony.[77] And after a disastrous experience under Mao, they appear to have settled on a Chinese form of capitalism. Muslims also want a culturally authentic modernity. Modern developments may have ripped apart and reassembled states and societies, but religion is a vital link with an often imaginary past.

Today, the presence of "reactionary modernity"[78]—perhaps better called pious modernity—is most obvious where resistance to materialist aspects of science flares up. For secular liberal heirs to the European Enlightenment, natural science is the clearest example of universal, progressively advancing knowledge. Whatever diversity there may be in our customs and morals, nature works the same way for all of us. And so it does. But attempts to universalize European disenchantment have not succeeded. Supernatural convictions are not separable from perceptions of nature, and when organized by religions, supernatural convictions do a lot of moral and social work. They inspire loyalty. Inevitably, responses to modern ideas are selective—technology and stock markets work, the godless bits of science and equality for women do not always work as well.

So in India, pious modernity comes together with a rising middle class and prowess in software and technology. Workers pray on the shop floor and their bosses consult astrologers.[79] Mainstream politics shifts back and forth between technocratic boredom and Hindu nationalism. Devout intellectuals protect their sense of the sacred, and their social hierarchies, by invoking the best postmodern suspicions about Western materialist science. Mainstream viewpoints include extravagant claims of how true science supports Hindu beliefs.[80] The colorful local details are different from those of predominantly Muslim nations, but much is similar.

Pious modernity is not just a side effect of late modernization. In the United States, which has long been the leading edge of modernity, conservative trust in science has been decreasing.[81] In some states, particularly in the South, there is a fusion of state and religious power, favoring business interests and suppressing evolution education.[82] I do not have to look abroad to see pious modernity; it is here in my backyard.

For secular liberals, this is all very frustrating. We tend to see strong religiosity as an atavism, a throwback to a premodern way of life. Religion, we think, should be Episcopalian in character, not charismatic or fundamentalist. We mutter about denying evolution *in this day and age.* If science is progressive, we think, our societies should keep up with the times. We take our ideals about liberal education and the political role of expertise for granted. And we expect to be able to persuade reasonable people because they will recognize their worldly advantage. We all can see who has the fastest cars, the most effective medicine, the smartest bombs. And so we do. Secular modernity delivers these goods, and so we have been tempted to think that material progress will win people over.

But then, conservative modernizers also claim to deliver the goods. And as with large segments of the Indian, American, Turkish, or Indonesian middle classes, pious modernity can inspire some of the most technologically sophisticated populations. Secular modernity, it seems, is not the only key to material success.

Secular liberals have been slow to accept that our version of modernity is not the inevitable direction of progress. We have long enjoyed disproportionate influence in education and among the armies of experts that serve modern states. But pious modernity undercuts our influence in those areas. On the one hand, our common emphasis on material advantage reduces education to increased earnings for graduates.[83] On the other hand, religious populists support, and divert state resources to, alternative educational institutions. In the United States these are private Christian academies and parochial schools, in Turkey, private schools run by religious movements and an extensive parallel religious school system maintained by the state. In either case, the flourishing of creationism is a symptom of pious modernity.

Academic observers of strong religion often suggest that there is a silver lining to this cloud. Religious politics represent, perhaps, a step toward secularization.[84] After all, moderate Islamist engineers and managers do not try to run factories or do urban planning according to the dictates of revelation. Pious businessmen have their enterprises conform to global standards, adding an Islamic flavor to an otherwise-generic business culture. Loyalty to scripture rather than to a tribe or a saint prepares believers for anonymous social roles in complex urban societies. Islamist political parties enforce ideological forms of discipline, and therefore often stand against traditional clientelist forms of corruption.[85] All of this seems to move in a secular direction.

I have my doubts. The notion that Muslims must subordinate everything to Islamic norms is an ideal of religious overachievers. It has never been a widespread historic reality. Running businesslike organizations is not necessarily partial secularization, nor is it all that new. It is more significant that pious modernizers resist disenchantment. They contract the secular public sphere and cover what remains with a moralized religious ambiance that evokes personal, organic, communal relationships. Religious politics is no more a step toward secular modernity than is Wahhabi destruction of Sufi shrines—not unless we assume the universality of secular progress. I think we should instead accept pious modernity at face value: not a compromise or halfway house but a reasonably successful alternative form of modernity.[86]

In fact, secular liberals are partly responsible for the success of their rivals. After all, neoliberalism, which has been so hospitable to pious modernity, is largely the work of secular liberals. We, not pious businessmen, remade our societies as loose aggregations of acquisitive individuals, where only religion could hope to provide a common vision. Our experts made states focus foremost on economic growth, leaving redistribution of resources or mitigation of environmental damage to technocratic regulation. We failed to foresee how wealth would buy political power, allying with religious conservatism to undermine technocratic expertise. And we did not anticipate a media environment that would completely subordinate informed debate to entertainment and selling soap.

My Turkish Marxist news site agrees. It scorns ineffectual attempts at social democracy and rails against the reactionaries with the confidence given by their belief in historical progress. I am not entirely moved. Marxism, for me, too often means yet more uncritical enamorment with technology and growth, and more utopian indifference to human and environmental costs, only with Soviet art celebrating heavy industry rather than advertisements hawking today's cool iWhatsits. But I also regret that the socialist tradition of imagining a secular alternative modernity has become so marginalized. Marxists may have promoted a quack cure, but they have been right about the disease.

Secular liberals are, today, confused about technology and uncertain about how science should fit in public culture beyond serving power. We are no longer at the cutting edge of modernity. And those varieties of religion that promote creationism are not, I think, backward. I fear they may be the gleaming new future.

4

DIVINE LAW

PERMITTED OR FORBIDDEN

Most Muslims perceive a universe of supernatural design. But their religion is rarely just about magical beings and miraculous events. It is about how to live right, and how to live together.

Traditionally, Muslims have consulted religious scholars, experts on the sacred sources and the Islamic legal tradition who make rulings about practical matters. Islam, therefore, has a reputation of being centered on divine law—of being a religion of rules that regulate almost every aspect of the life of a devout believer. Muslim piety, in this picture, revolves around what is permitted and what is forbidden. Being a good Muslim is supposed to be about correct ritual and moral practice, in the context of a divinely prescribed social order.

There is some truth to this perception. Especially for religious over-achievers and those in strictly orthodox communities, living according to divine law is very important. Saints may display supernatural power, but they need not always be morally straight. Anyone may lead the community in prayer and perform the rituals in order. But the real source of guidance is divine law, and the person who is most helpful is a scholar who can deal with questions about right conduct.

My favorite examples come from websites that showcase rulings by some very tradition-minded scholars. They answer questions from readers, carefully laying out their reasoning based on the sacred sources. Often the questions are about extending traditional legal reasoning to modern circumstances, asking, for example, whether artificial insemination could be regarded as taking back a wife who was revocably divorced. Or the issue might be the validity of a marriage contracted over the phone or online.[1] Sometimes the results are amusing. One query concerned a parrot, which uttered a formal Muslim greeting when the questioner walked by. Were they then obliged to return the greeting? The scholar answered in all seriousness:

> It seems that it is not prescribed to return the greeting of a parrot which has learnt how to say salaams, because saying salaam is an act of worship and a supplication which requires intention on the part of the one who said it, and there is no such intention on the part of this trained creature. So one should not return its greeting. The ruling is the same as that on a tape on which the greeting is recorded and can be heard. It is transmission of sound and does not come under the ruling on greeting when it is broadcast live, in which case returning the greeting is prescribed and is a communal obligation (fard kifaayah).[2]

Though the themes are modern, posing questions and seeking guidance is a very old religious activity. In my pre-Internet childhood, believers would have sought answers from local scholars and discussion sessions around mosques. Centuries ago as well, questions would have involved everything from trivialities such as the parrot to more serious family conflicts and even international relations. And the legal rulings that supply the answers do not just forbid actions but also outline what is reprehensible though permitted, such as divorce. Likewise, they describe what is obligatory, meritorious, or indifferent. In its classical form, then, Islamic law does not follow Western conceptions of law. Seamlessly joining the legal, the moral, and the religious, it aims to be a comprehensive practical description of the proper way to live.

Religious scholars, therefore, have historically been legal experts well-versed in the religious sciences such as scripture interpretation and tradition criticism. While they have been conservative, staying close to established rulings and chains of reasoning, they also have had to respond to changing circumstances. In this regard, Islamic law is similar to the common law tradition: it is law made by judges, manifested in a series of rulings and precedents modified through time.[3] The rulings of these judges are not necessarily acknowledged by all believers, nor always enforced by states. Their authority is often informal, personal. Nonetheless, the scholars have usually had very similar educations and have worked in similar institutional settings. Therefore Islamic law in its classical form enjoys a certain uniformity.

The religious scholars, however, have not just been judges. Often, their social position has been similar to Orthodox Jewish rabbis, who have been interpreters of sacred law in the context of the everyday problems of close-knit communities. Rabbis are expected to know their texts and to figure out what is forbidden and what is permitted according to the Jewish version of divine law. But they are also community leaders and religious guides who often draw on an intimate personal knowledge of the situations they are expected to rule upon. Traditionally, many Muslim scholars played a similar role in their communities. So looking over conclusions announced from a distance, through the Internet, emphasizing texts and rules, can be misleading.

Nonetheless, Islamic law has acquired a reputation for being dry and rigid. Christians, in particular, are apt to see traditional Islam as a legalistic religion, and they portray the Sufi mystical strain within Islam as a more spiritual alternative. Muslims, however, usually see law and spirituality as inseparable. There always has been tension between varieties of Islam that emphasize texts and rules and varieties that are enraptured by saints and mystics. But since Islamic law is supposed to be a set of signposts helping to direct believers to a devout way of life, the law and spiritual devotion usually go together. The most successful Sufi orders have been those that are impeccably orthodox, committed to an ideal of law as well as emotionally intense spiritual practices.[4]

So, though I do find the question about the parrot amusing, in it I can also see the naive but passionate intensity of a student trying to figure out what is important and what is trivial. The Islamic ideal of divine law as an essential guide to life is alive and well today, even in modern conditions when tight-knit communities are harder to sustain and the scholarly class has lost much of its status and cohesion. Even in religious study circles composed entirely of lay people, the questions inevitably turn to the law laid down by the sacred sources. Among Muslim immigrants to the West, there are many questions about what Islam demands in their circumstances. To be Muslim is, to a large degree, to acknowledge a need for divine guidance. Islamic law is all about divine guidance.

A DIVERSITY OF LAWS

The Quran does not contain much that explicitly looks like law. Still, scripture does show that interest in divine regulation of life came very early to the community of believers. The Quran lays down rules on an odd assortment of topics. Personal matters are at the forefront—divorce, marriage, adultery, inheritance, the prohibition of adoption. There are some famously harsh punishments such as lashes and amputations. Even a basis for commercial contract law makes an appearance, as in 2 The Cow 282:

> Believers, when you incur debt among yourselves for a certain period of time, write it down. Have a scribe write it down honestly; let a scribe not refuse to write; let him write as God has taught him. Let the liable one dictate, wary of God, his Lord, without withholding anything due. But if the liable one is incompetent or infirm, or cannot dictate, let his guardian dictate, honestly. And get the witness of two witnesses from your men; or if there are not two men, then a man and two women of your choice from among the witnesses, so that if one of them errs the other may remind her. Let the witnesses not refuse when called on, and do not disdain to write it down, small or large, including its term. That is more just in the sight of God, and more proper for testimony, and easier to forestall your doubting; excepted is the case of a spot transaction between you—there is no fault on you if you do not make a written contract. But have witnesses whenever you make deals with each other. And let no scribe or witness be hurt—if you do that, it is corruption in you. Be conscious of God; God teaches you. And God knows everything.

The early interest in divine law continued: practical guidance and resolution of legal questions was the main motivation for collecting the anecdotes that became the prophetic traditions. The growing community of believers had many questions about ritual, moral, and legal details, and collectors of traditions supplied them with sacred precedents.

The rabbinical type of religious scholars evidently emerged early as experts on traditions and divine laws. We know of many scholars, tradition collectors, and founders of legal schools from the early centuries of Islam. Even today, legal controversies regularly invoke famous names of early authorities. The role of human reason and "personal initiative" in extending Islamic law beyond what was explicitly in the sacred sources, for example, was a matter for vigorous debate,[5] often echoed in modern times. Nonetheless, the classical body of Islamic law and the role of the scholars were not directly inherited from the early days of Islam. We also have some evidence of competition with caliphal authority in defining the law, bitter sectarian disputes, and rival schools of law that were eventually acknowledged as accepted variants of orthodoxy.[6] Islam was still fluid in the early Arab empire, and different conceptions of divine law were in play.

Much of what came to appear as settled Islamic law and classical legal institutions, including state-supported training for scholars, is a legacy from after the Arab empire, especially from Iran after the Mongol invasions.[7] Sunni Islam, which claims the allegiance of about nine out of ten Muslims worldwide, has often served as an ideology of empires. And since Muslim scholars have had an ambition to provide rulings on nearly every aspect of life, including greetings by parrots, some critics have described Islamic law as totalitarian in nature.[8] But much of classical Islamic law and institutions crystallized in conditions of political instability. The consensus of the scholars and the popular authority enjoyed by the scholars were not imposed by empires.

Scholars of Sunni Islam constructed detailed opinions about the ideal ruler, but they also recognized reality and endorsed acquiescence to rulers who may have displayed very little allegiance to scholarly ideals of divine justice. The purpose of a state was to advance Islam, and so empires found their legitimacy in religion. But in practice, divine law often competed with imperial interests. Scholars treasured independence from the state, and in their role as jurists, often protected private life and wealth from imperial intrusions. The power of the scholars was itself typically limited, personal, and integrated with local communities.

Therefore, whatever the comprehensive ambitions of Islamic law, the existence of states has always made the complete fusion of law, political power, and religion an impossible ideal.[9] Empires have their own interests; therefore, rulers and their bureaucrats must issue decrees, especially concerning the many matters on which the sacred sources are silent. The scholarly guardians of divine law, then, have been adaptable. Sometimes, they absorbed imperial laws into Islamic law, approving the facts on the ground. Often they secured the realm of communities and families as their legal territory, and occasionally wandered off into describing ideals that were as relevant to the daily functioning of the state as rulings on parrots. Historian L. Carl Brown observes that in the classical Islamic political condition, though there is some tension, "neither state officialdom nor religious spokesmen have sufficient motivation to push matters to confrontation."[10] Religious scholars did not enjoy any organization similar to the medieval Catholic church, which was comparable to states in its power and reach. And the premodern state was too weak to micromanage religious affairs.

Before modern times, then, most believers would encounter divine law within tight-knit communities, where rulings by scholars provided the framework for a social order that was fleshed out more informally. Indeed, Muslim empires were multiethnic, multifaith states where different religious communities enjoyed considerable autonomy to regulate their internal affairs. The rulers were Muslim, sometimes very piously Muslim, and Islamic law endorsed and absorbed the laws needed to run empires. But it made little difference if peasants were Muslim, Greek Christian, Armenian Christian, Jewish, or Druze, as long as they did not belong to a sect liable to foster rebellion. In this environment of legal pluralism, the rules within each community stood for law and order, and almost everyone publicly respected the divine law.[11]

Following every rule, especially in private, was a different matter. Muslims, especially wealthier Muslims, have often lived in family compounds walling off the private sphere of the family from neighbors as well as tax collectors. And going to a judge has been but one of many ways to resolve disputes, most which were informal. Life in traditional Muslim environments can appear oppressive to secular liberals. But this is not because of any totalitarian sway of divine law, only the conservatism of close-knit communities. The lack of privacy in Muslim communities came from prying neighbors, not government agencies and giant corporations snooping through electronic communications. And communities enforced conformity through gossip, not through police equating dissent with terrorism. From a modern perspective, traditional Muslim communities suffer from a stunted public realm, not an overreaching theocratic state.

So even if divine law presented an ideal of timeless perfection, premodern Muslim communities typically enjoyed a flexible, adaptable legal regime. Consider, for example, the Ottoman Empire, which lasted until the early twentieth century. For centuries, the Ottomans, a Turkish dynasty, ruled a vast multiethnic empire, legitimating themselves by championing Sunni Islam through holy war and protecting the Muslim holy lands after they conquered the territories of rival Muslim dynasties. They claimed the caliphate—nominal leadership of Muslims worldwide—and persecuted non-Sunni Muslims during their long rivalry with Iran, where Shia Islam became the state religion. Orthodox Sunni law was supposed to be supreme in Ottoman lands, and especially during the decline of the empire, Ottoman sultans portrayed themselves as defenders of the true faith. Even so, Ottoman subjects faced a highly varied legal landscape. The Ottomans respected the legal pluralism of classical Islam and recognized the autonomy of various religious communities. Islamic law trumped other religious rules, so a dispute between a Greek Orthodox and a Muslim merchant would end up settled by a Muslim judge. But even then, multiple Sunni schools of law were considered orthodox. Litigants could even go shopping for courts that might, perhaps with the aid of some bribery, be expected to rule favorably.[12]

The Ottomans also recognized customary law. Indeed, they respected the Turkish and Mongolian tradition of law, and when reasons of state demanded, imposed some very secular laws legitimated by little more than imperial decree. For example, Turks today remember Süleyman the Magnificent, the sultan presiding over the peak of the Ottoman Empire, as Süleyman the Lawgiver, after his version of an imperial code of law.

Multiple coexisting systems of law might appear problematic. But the Ottomans went some distance toward integrating religious and imperial laws; historian Antony Black notes that "in some respects, they were fused into a single legal system: this was unique in Islamic history."[13] Religious scholars were partly brought into the state apparatus and were given formal ranks and offices. And jurists were trained and required to consider not just religious but also customary and codified imperial laws in rendering decisions. The state did not control matters of religious doctrine, and many of the community-based scholars still kept the state at arm's length. Yet by developing a hybrid, the Ottomans avoided the chaos that might have resulted from the presence of rival systems of law.

REVIVING THE IDEAL

Then the Muslim states encountered modern Western power. Where the colonial empires took over, they induced modernization; where Muslims could resist, elites felt a need to rapidly modernize. Armies and bureaucracies were reorganized, communication technologies advanced, and legal systems and law enforcement overhauled.

All of this upset the balance between the religious establishment and the rulers. Classical Islam had used the ideal of divine law to counteract the tendency of elites to prey on the population. More than European church hierarchies entwined with the ruling aristocracies, Muslim scholars could, to some extent, act as a countervailing power.[14] Divine law, beyond the control of dynasties and landowners, was supposed to ensure justice.

Modernization, however, strengthened the state. As traditional ways of life eroded, religious scholars lost much of their power and prestige. Modernizers, who intended to reform Islamic civilization in order to save it, often came to think of the traditional scholars as reactionaries who obstructed change. Indeed, many scholars dug in their heels and attempted to preserve the premodern social order. Others found niches for themselves in states that increasingly standardized Islamic education and turned scholars into functionaries. In the twentieth century, experts on Islamic law often became government employees. Their legal role tended to be restricted to areas such as personal and family law. They were often displaced by a professional class of lawyers, negotiating a legal system that, even in countries where laws were informed by Islam and granted religion a special status, was modern and Western in its character and administration.

The Turkish Republic, successor to the Ottoman Empire, neutered the scholars even further. Continuing Ottoman trends, the republic absorbed religious officials into the government, even making many independent forms of religious organization illegal. But the republic also secularized its legal system. Religious officials were reduced to issuing advisory opinions with no legal force. They were supposed to educate the population in what the republicans considered to be true Islam, which was scientific and rational, and which most certainly stayed out of government and let modernization proceed unimpeded.

To a secular person such as myself, reducing the role of religion in law represents progress. But then, I stand at a comfortable distance to the painful transition to modernity. The old order did not pass without resistance. Conservative reaction was often fueled by the authoritarian and predatory behavior of modernizing states attempting to centralize power[15] and therefore enjoyed a broad popular base.

The rallying cry of reaction was the restoration of Islamic law. In troubled times, trouble must be due to straying from the divine law. In the late Ottoman Empire, with military failure against Western powers, the presence of imperial law became controversial. Calls to implement a purified Islamic law arose, particularly from Arab regions of the empire.[16] For over a century, Ottoman modernizers faced the impossible task of restructuring their political and legal system while insisting that divine law reigned supreme. Their heirs, the Turkish republicans, abolished Islamic law, insisting that it was a medieval accretion that was not essential to true religion. But to consolidate power, they had to violently suppress repeated revolts demanding divine law.

Today, opposition movements with a culturally conservative constituency continue to press for Islamic law, while ruling, business-friendly conservatives follow the historical pattern of compromising and diluting the religious aspects of their legal system. For its advocates, however, the religious rationale for pure Islamic law is clear. As Shia scholar Sayyid Mujtaba Musavi Lari puts it,

> The establishment of laws is dependent not only on a complete knowledge of all the dimensions of human existence but also on a knowledge of all the other beings with which the human being has dealings. It also requires a knowledge of society and its complex relationships. Furthermore, the legislator must be completely removed from distorting and misguiding factors such as ambition, selfishness, personal inclination and desire, which militate against the acquisition of perfect knowledge.[17]

Human law is subject to change, and is easily corrupted by predatory interests. Laws made by humans therefore cannot substitute for Islamic justice rooted in divine omniscience.

Reviving Islamic law is not, however, very easy. A reinvigorated class of religious scholars might take control of the law. But the old institutions and the old community-based ways of life are no longer sustainable. Scholars have too often become officials. Furthermore, as literacy has spread and Protestant styles of Islam have become more popular, it has become more difficult to enforce any coherent Islamic law. Believers seeking answers can obtain rulings from either official scholars or dissidents, but they can also rely on televangelists and question-answering websites.

To bring order to this chaos, Islamist movements have often pinned their hopes on an Islamic state—a modern state with a judicial and police apparatus dedicated to enforcing divine law. An Islamic state would not, however, revive medieval compromises between scholars and imperial agents. Like Protestants who imagine a pure early church before Catholic corruptions, puritans among Islamists call for a return to the first generations of Islam. They imagine the time of the Prophet and the Companions to be an age of bliss under unadulterated divine law.

For some Islamists, submitting to the divine will has meant that no law but Islamic law should hold sway. Not just imperial lawmaking, but also democratically elected bodies that legislate based on human interests are unacceptable. These would elevate human authorities to the side of God.[18]

Today, however, the antidemocratic strain of politics centered on divine law has lost steam. Islamists are more likely to prefer divine sovereignty to be expressed through democratic means, via the popular will of a devout population. For example, Rachid al-Ghannouchi, intellectual leader of the Islamist party that came to power in Tunisia following the Arab Spring, advocates Islamic law in very standard apologetic terms. The mere human intellect is unable to discover our rights and duties, God is the first and highest lawgiver, and submission to One God is the basis for our fundamental rights and freedoms. Indeed, a Muslim state is legitimate only to the extent that it serves and protects religion. Islamic law comes first, above all state-imposed laws. But though al-Ghannouchi also invokes the imaginary historical precedent of the first generation of believers, he insists that the first Muslims were pioneers of democracy, transferring government power according to the free consent of the people.[19]

In that case, what is Muslim public opinion concerning Islamic law? A Gallup World Poll of many Muslim countries conducted between 2001 and 2007 suggests that a majority support Islamic law as *a* source of law. Fewer want Islamic law to be the *only* source of law, except majorities in Jordan, Egypt, Pakistan, and Afghanistan.[20] Surveys conducted by the Pew Research Center from 2008 to 2012 find that

> The percentage of Muslims who say they want sharia to be "the official law of the land" varies widely around the world, from fewer than one-in-ten in Azerbaijan (8%) to near unanimity in Afghanistan (99%). But solid majorities in most of the countries surveyed across the Middle East and North Africa, sub-Saharan Africa, South Asia and Southeast Asia favor the establishment of sharia, including 71% of Muslims in Nigeria, 72% in Indonesia, 74% in Egypt and 89% in the Palestinian territories.[21]

Favoring Islamic law does not mean support for Islamist political parties, although it does indicate a strong social conservatism. John L. Esposito and Dalia Mogahed point out that Muslim attitudes in polls are comparable to those of other religiously conservative populations, such as the United States:

Many regard religion as a primary marker of identity, a source of meaning and guidance, consolation and community, and essential to their progress. Majorities of both men and women in many predominantly Muslim countries want to see Islamic principles, *Sharia*, as a source of legislation. These respondents have much in common with the majority of Americans who wish to see the Bible as a source of legislation. Both groups emphasize the importance of family values and are deeply concerned about issues of social morality. In fact, what respondents in the Muslim world *and* a significant number of Americans say they admire least about Western civilization is an excessive libertinism in society.[22]

Indeed, conservative Catholics in the United States occasionally assert the primacy of divine moral law over secular laws.[23] Right-wing Protestant rhetoric can echo that of Islamists. Where advocates of Islamic law assert a duty to enforce the good and prohibit evil, the Christian legal advocacy organization National Legal Foundation has a mission of "pursuing legal and policy means of ensuring that all levels of government reward good and punish evil."[24]

Demands for divine law, then, are a normal part of the political landscape today. Like most secular liberals, I do not like the policies favored by religious political movements. But proponents of divine law, Christian or Muslim, usually want to enact such policies by winning democratic contests.

Moreover, Islamic law is an inherently vague demand. Muslims who favor divine law disagree on what it means in practice. For example, a 2012 Pew survey found that "an overwhelming majority of Iranians (83%) say they favor the use of sharia, or Islamic law. Yet only 37% of Iranian Muslims think their country's current laws follow sharia very closely."[25] Iran has had an Islamic state enforcing a Shia version of Islamic law for over three decades. The ideal of Islamic law has a strong appeal, but this does not mean Iranians always endorse how divine law is institutionalized. Iranians can express opposition as well as support for clerical rule while affirming Islamic law.

Muslims in South Asia, such as in Pakistan, usually support Islamic law. In part, this is because the formal justice systems in South Asia are notoriously corrupt and slow, in majority Hindu as well as Muslim areas. Islamic law is attractive not just because it is sacred, but because existing colonial-derived institutions of justice are chaotic, untrustworthy, and culturally alien. Women, for example, often prefer Islamic law even though traditional Islamic laws favor men over women. After all, secular law is corrupt and unreliable, while local ethnic customs even more savagely disadvantage women. Even so, public life remains dominated by patronage networks and tribal allegiances. The high level of approval for Islamic law rarely means electoral support for parties promising an Islamic state.[26]

In contrast, in Turkey, where neoliberal Islamic politics has been very successful, Pew found that only 12 percent supported making Islamic law the law of the land,[27] which is about the level of electoral support hardline Islamists used to receive when they were represented by more puritan opposition parties. In Turkey, the Ottoman tradition of a strong state has endured, and state-imposed law and judicial institutions enjoy considerable legitimacy. Turkish Muslims tend to think of Islamic law not as an idealized rule of law but as a strict, traditional form of religious law overseen by a clerical class. That appeals only to highly orthodox Sunni segments of the population.

BARBAROUS RELICS?

The rule of law is not a bad idea. Neither is respect for a culturally familiar set of rules that promises to curb abuses by the powerful. But for secular liberals, divine law does too much. Taking laws to be sacred goes beyond enforcing respect—it can freeze archaic laws in place. Liberals want to be able to criticize laws and figure out what is reasonable. We want to participate in shaping our legal environment, rather than just trust an alleged higher wisdom channeled by religious experts.

Consider some traditional Islamic laws that famously grate on liberal sensibilities: taking a woman's testimony to be worth half that of a man, severe punishments such as cutting the hand off a thief, and the death penalty for apostasy. Historically, Islamic laws have not granted women and non-Muslims status equal to Muslim men. And the punishments prescribed by divine law often seem barbaric from our more squeamish modern perspective.

It is hard to set aside the uncomfortable aspects of Islamic law as historical relics or aberrations. Status inequality and severe bodily punishments fit very well with the ethos of traditional, hierarchical Middle Eastern societies that both shaped and were shaped by Islamic law. Religious scholars, both ancient and modern, usually accept and defend the harsher aspects of divine law, even while softening them around the edges. After all, the textual basis for these laws appears strong. And in modern circumstances, with increased literacy and individualism, fundamentalist interpretations of law have become popular. Inequality and bodily mutilations are there in the sacred sources, in black and white.

In the Quran, 2 The Cow 282 makes two women the equivalent of one man as a witness for commercial debt, and only when a man is not available. This is not an isolated verse; the Quran takes for granted that in their public roles, women have lesser status. For example, the complex and barely coherent rules of inheritance in the Quran favor males; 4 Women 11 starts with "God directs you in regard to your children: the male gets the equivalent of the portion of two females." Islamic laws further elaborate the inequality between the sexes. For example, following longstanding Middle Eastern tradition, and the Quran endorsing "an eye for an eye" but also recommending compensation instead (5 The Table 45), traditional Islamic law institutionalizes the practice of blood money. As an alternative punishment, the family of a victim can accept financial restitution. Even today, Iran and Saudi Arabia set the blood money for women to half that for men.

Harsh punishments also come straight out of the Quran. For example, 5 The Table 38 treats the sexes equally, commanding: "As for the man who steals and the woman who steals, cut off the hands of both of them as a reward for what they have earned, as an example from God." The word for "cut off" has some ambiguity; though usually read as calling for amputation, it might also be interpreted as a less severe mutilation of the hand that visibly marks a thief. Also, 5 The Table 33 says "For those who wage war on God and the messenger of God, and work for corruption on earth, the reward is but execution, or crucifixion, or amputation of their hands and feet on opposite sides, or expulsion from the land." It is not clear whether these punishments are to be enforced by divine Providence or by the faithful, but scholars have traditionally interpreted such verses as divine endorsement of the justice of harsh bodily punishment for the worst of crimes.

The death penalty for apostasy is less securely based on scripture. The Quran is full of imprecations against disbelievers and apostates; for example, 16 The Bee 106 says "Those who repudiate God after having faith—except one who is compelled, while his heart rests securely in faith—that is whoever open their chest to atheism, wrath from God is upon them, and there is tremendous torment for them." The most natural interpretation is that this is a promise of hellfire, not a prescription for earthly law. Numerous canonical prophetic traditions, however, indicate that those who leave Islam should be killed. For example:

> Some Zanadiqa (atheists) were brought to 'Ali and he burnt them. The news of this event reached Ibn 'Abbas who said, "If I had been in his place, I would not have burnt them, as Allah's Apostle forbade it, saying, 'Do not punish anybody with Allah's punishment (fire).' I would have killed them according to the statement of Allah's Apostle, 'Whoever changed his Islamic religion, then kill him.'"[28]

Such texts only amplify secular liberal concerns about religious laws. We do not expect all laws to be identical; after all, countries have varying cultures, historical experiences, and political orientations. Belgium and the United States have different laws concerning private gun ownership; Japan and Bangladesh structure bankruptcies differently. We may prefer one example over another, and even have bitter political arguments about the better policy. But we also have a sense—awkwardly expressed in postcolonial times—that certain laws are simply uncivilized. When, for example, the Sultan of Brunei decides to implement Islamic law, including the traditional punishments, we do not just raise an eyebrow at bad policy in a distant land but also worry if medieval tortures will reappear.[29]

For secular liberals, then, acceptable cultural variation has limits. Some laws, whatever their other merits, oppress some of the people subjected to them. Under traditional Islamic law, women are handicapped when acting in the public sphere—their ability to form and pursue interests beyond the circles of family and community is restricted. Harsh bodily punishments make law into an instrument of vengeance rather than public order. And executing apostates denies individuals the freedoms of conscience and participation in peaceful public debate.

As a shorthand for all of this, we might say that some traditional Islamic laws violate human rights. If secular liberals take agreements such as the Universal Declaration of Human Rights to express minimal require-ments for a decent legal framework, conflicts with Islamic laws are readily apparent. Article 5 declares that "No one shall be subjected to torture or to cruel, inhuman or degrading treatment or punishment," which is hard to reconcile with chopping off hands. Article 7 emphasizes that "all are equal before the law" and calls for "equal protection of the law"; Article 2 extends the rights of the Declaration to everyone, without distinctions such as that of sex. And Article 18 includes a right to apostasy:

> Everyone has the right to freedom of thought, conscience and religion;
> this right includes freedom to change his religion or belief, and freedom,
> either alone or in community with others and in public or private, to man-
> ifest his religion or belief in teaching, practice, worship and observance.[30]

These are not abstract matters. I am happy to live in an environment that takes gender equality for granted, and it is to my advantage that legal obstacles to such equality are few and getting fewer. Harsh bodily punish-ments do not so much deter me from crime as inspire a visceral disgust at legal systems that allow them. And as for apostasy—I am not even sure if I qualify as an apostate. I have never thought of myself as a believer, even as a child. But once, in conversation, a conservative Muslim told me that I should be a Muslim. After all, my father was a Muslim, not because he was at all observant, but because he came from a Muslim family. Therefore I rightfully belonged to the community of Muslims. By openly admitting nonbelief, I was positioning myself as an apostate. Fortunately, even reli-gious conservatives in Turkey are unlikely to call for executing apostates, and the laws of the state remain relatively secular. But in some countries, such as Yemen or Saudi Arabia, I would worry. There, apostasy receives the death penalty, and those accused have their lives ruined even if the law is not enforced.[31]

Now, many religious traditionalists defend the laws I dislike. They are, after all, used to criticism. Both Westerners who thought of themselves as representing a superior civilization and modernizers among Muslims have long decried the traditional laws as barbarous relics. Both the critics and the apologetic defenders of traditional law fall into centuries-old patterns.

According to the apologists, the proper, divinely prescribed social order is based on a strong family. This family is structured hierarchically: the God-given nature of women suits them for a primary role in the home and in caring for the family, while men take on public roles to protect and provide for the family. Authority and public responsibility therefore rests with men, who are, unlike women, legally obliged to support their dependents. Proportioning resources to responsibilities, the Quran gives males a double share of inheritance. Recognizing the lesser competence of women in the public realm, divine law gives their testimony less weight than that of men.[32] Modern societies, with their libertine ways and easy temptations, continually threaten families with dissolution. Islamic law provides a framework that strengthens families by supporting clear-cut gender roles and responsibilities, which is now needed more than ever.

Punishments such as amputations are also, according to the apologists, entirely appropriate. Perpetrators must be confronted with the gravity of their crime, bearing a permanent mark as a reminder to society of their past and to themselves that they cannot stray from the straight path of God. Modern, libertine societies are also beset by high crime rates, to which strict Islamic law provides the answer. Indeed, social scientists do observe that, for reasons that are not entirely clear, murder rates are appreciably lower within Muslim populations.[33]

Since piety is the foundation of social order, religion must be protected by law. Apologists consider apostasy to be an active and public disavowal of Islam, not merely a quiet falling away from faith which will have consequences in the afterlife. It is a betrayal of the community, treason against a divinely ordained social order. Apostasy therefore should be punished as treason. If after repeated warnings, the apostate persists in trying to undermine Islam, the threat to the community should be removed.

But then, any complex social order comes with elaborate theological and worldly justifications. Liberals are no more likely to be impressed by rationales for traditional Islamic law than by arguments supporting slavery or a hereditary aristocracy. We do not like rigid status inequalities written into law. Today we are more likely to justify inequality, even severe inequality, through market competition rather than sacred laws.

More important, many modern Muslims are not impressed by apologetics for Islamic law. There is an air of futility about these arguments— they look back to a premodern social order that is already undermined by modern technology, state power, and economic organization. The strictest forms of Islamic law may survive in ultraorthodox enclaves or countries that are global backwaters, but even most religious conservatives have had to adapt. Scrapping divine law is not an option for most Muslims, but laws can be reformed, and their interpretations can change. A conservative sense of social order can be maintained by new institutions. Just as pious modernity can successfully meld high technology and modern economics with an enchanted perception of the world, Islamic law can also find a modern form.

The example of slavery, in fact, highlights the potential for change in the practice of divine law. The Quran accepts slavery as a matter of course, and as with many other premodern legal systems, traditional Islamic law regulates slavery as a legitimate practice. Modernization, however, has worked against slavery in Islam. This has occasionally provoked reactions. In the mid-nineteenth century, under European pressure, the Ottoman Empire instituted some reforms that included a ban on black slavery. This ban was among the leading causes of a revolt in the Arabian Peninsula, cited by rebel religious scholars as among the deviations from Islamic law proposed by the Ottomans. The Ottomans crushed the pro-slavery revolt, though they then refrained from extending the ban into Arabia.[34]

Eventually, the bans stuck. Today, old-fashioned slavery exists only in backwaters such as Mauritania or war-ravaged areas such as the ruins of Iraq and Syria. And while rich Persian Gulf State residents often treat their imported servants and workforces as near-slaves, this is as much a problem of the status of labor in modern economies as it is a legacy of slavery. Most of the body of Islamic law regulating slavery is an inactive historical curiosity. Bands of fanatics in Iraq and Syria hoping to usher in the end times embrace slavery to signal their religious purity. In contrast, serious Islamist movements with ambitions to govern modern states do not have reinstituting slavery on their lists of demands.

As with slavery, other aspects of Islamic law that offend modern sensibilities can change. It matters little if the laws are set in black and white in the sacred texts. No world religion that lasts for centuries achieves its success without resources to interpret black to mean white.

BRINGING THE LAW UP TO DATE

Modernizing Islamic law is not a new idea. Neither is it an idea that implies a more liberal law. For example, in eighteenth-century India, scholar and reformer Shah Wali Allah al-Dihlawi brought renewed emphasis to rational judgment in interpreting the law. The divine law could be interpreted according to changing circumstances, adapting to the times.[35] But Wali Allah is also remembered as a founding figure of the Deobandi current of Islam in South Asia, which is a more rigorous, scripture- and law-centered version of Islam. Wahhabi-style puritans argue against blindly following tradition, demanding a more direct engagement with the sacred sources. Those Islamists who imagine that they can recover the age of the Prophet and the Companions thereby bypass an important body of medieval rulings.

Change, however, also opens up space for more liberal interpretations. One common way to avoid archaic rulings is to state that many of the prescriptions in the sacred sources were only intended to apply to a limited time and place. Divine law accepts and regulates some practices as a concession to human imperfection and with an eye to their improvement or even abolition. For example, apologists say that divine law limited slavery, confining it to prisoners of war.[36] This response does not address female slavery. It also overlooks how the slave trade became a major component of the economy of some Muslim empires, or how slave-soldiers formed large parts of many medieval Muslim militaries. But even conservative Muslims are happy to ignore that history. Today, divine law need not recognize slavery.

Interpreters can also use features of traditional law to nudge it in a more liberal direction. Islamic law can bend its rules in the face of "necessity." The dire need of an individual or the common good of a community can require adjustments.[37] Since the extent of necessity is subject to interpretation, there can be substantial flexibility in applying the law.

To be religiously plausible, however, flexibility or reinterpretation cannot look like an excuse for human interests to override the divine law. So change usually proceeds under the guise of restoring a proper understanding of the law. Perhaps today's scholars can achieve a broader perspective than their medieval predecessors. They certainly can do better than an unsophisticated literalism. Khaled Abou El Fadl, a renowned expert on Islamic law, argues:

> The law helps Muslims in the *quest* for Godliness, but Godliness cannot be equated to the law. The ultimate objective of the law is to achieve goodness, which includes justice, mercy, and compassion, and the technicalities of the law cannot be allowed to subvert the objectives of the law. Therefore, if the application of the law produces injustice, suffering, and misery, this means that the law is not serving its purposes. . . . If the application of the law results in injustice, suffering, or misery, then the law must be reinterpreted, suspended, or reconstructed, depending on the law in question.[38]

Justice, in fact, is a favorite theme of reformers.[39] The Quran commands justice. Conservatives might take the Quran at face value, and read its "eye for an eye" and other instances of rough retribution as appropriate defining examples for justice, including the parts that make modern liberals feel squeamish. But then again, justice is a notoriously vague concept. After some recontextualizing in the light of what the interpreter wants justice to mean, black can now be shining white.

There are, for example, ways to reinterpret the laws in order to make the testimony of women worth the same as that of men. At the time of the Quran, women did not regularly participate in public and commercial life, hence their word could not be expected to carry the same weight as men. Just as liberal Christians understand 1 Corinthians 14:34—that women should keep silent in the churches, and remain submissive as divine law dictates— to apply only to the Corinthian church at one particular time, reforming Muslims assert that what the Quran says about women only applied to specific circumstances long ago. There is considerable debate about such matters,[40] but liberals can make some progress. The legal status of women has often been improved in many countries where traditional Islamic law has a strong influence on legislation. Bangladeshi lawyer Mohammad Ali Syed gives examples from Pakistani law, and concludes that

> female witnesses are in no way inferior to male witnesses according to Islamic law. Even in matters of financial contracts, in the changed circumstances of the modern world, female witnesses should be treated on an equal footing as male witnesses as the recommendations made in 2:282 on financial contracts is no longer obligatory on Muslims.[41]

If reform has political backing, it may succeed in the face of traditionalist opposition. For example, in 2004, with strong support from the monarchy, Morocco changed its personal laws to improve the standing of women. The changes went well beyond traditional Islamic law, while stopping short of equality.[42] Legal change is a constant in Muslim countries, and whether the law moves in a more liberal direction is dictated by politics.

Similarly, advocates of Islamic law can be flexible about the more violent punishments in traditional Islamic law, such as chopping off hands for thievery. After all, with modern penal systems and policing, scholars can reconsider if the rationale for severe punishments is better served today without bodily mutilations. Whether this happens is a matter of politics. I have never encountered Turkish Islamists emphasizing lashing, stoning, or mutilating. In other times and places, imposing the traditional punishments has a symbolic role, showing that the government is serious about Islamic law. Harsh punishments appeal to a law-and-order constituency, similar to how American conservatives celebrate the death penalty.

The traditional death penalty for apostasy also inspires similar adjustments, especially because liberal reformers themselves can be accused of leaving Islam. Tunisian historian Mohamed Talbi argues that the discussions of apostasy in the sacred sources always takes place in the context of rebellion and highway robbery, and that apostasy in the early period of Islam invariably involved a violent threat to the community. Moreover, he suggests that the most famous traditions calling for the death penalty might have been forged.[43] Often the debate between reformers and traditionalists turns on technical matters such as whether the famous "there is no compulsion in religion" verse (2 The Cow 256) has been abrogated. If not, the death penalty for apostasy could then contradict at least part of the Quran.

Accordingly, how leaving the faith should be discouraged is again a matter for local politics. And change can work against liberalization as well as for it. Iran, for example, did not used to have the death penalty for apostasy in its penal code, leaving much to a judge's discretion. In 2012, the Guardian Council approved an amended penal code that more explicitly affirms non-codified Islamic laws, including the death penalty for apostasy.[44]

Islamic law is supposed to proceed from the sacred sources. But it is hard to hold sacred texts to any fixed meaning—for the faithful, they have a way of becoming what they ought to be. So the politics of the day shapes the law as much as does the weight of tradition. Even interpretations that are so liberal as to scrap nearly the entire tradition of Islamic law are available. For example, to conform to modern human rights, law professor Abdullahi Ahmed An-Na'im proposes to disregard even parts of the Quran as precedents for law:

> Unless the basis of modern Islamic law is shifted away from those texts of the Qur'an and *sunna* of the Medina stage, which constituted the foundations of the construction of *shari'a*, there is no way of avoiding drastic and serious violation of universal standards of human rights. There is no way to abolish slavery as a legal institution and no way to eliminate all forms and shades of discrimination against women and non-Muslims as long as we remain bound by the framework of *shari'a*.[45]

But An-Na'im's calls for setting aside the supposedly "Medinan" commands of the Quran follow the teachings of the Sudanese religious leader Mahmoud Mohammed Taha, who was executed by the Sudanese government in 1985—for apostasy. An-Na'im teaches law in the United States, not Sudan. For now at least, the most liberal interpretations of Islamic law are marginal.

Much more common are vague pronouncements on the extensive rights and liberties granted by Islam, which can easily go together with a deep social conservatism. Reform efforts find it hard to directly challenge this conservatism. Swiss scholar Tariq Ramadan, for example, has become well-known for his views on adapting Islamic law to help Muslim immigrant populations become more at home in Europe. But Ramadan's views on religion, from how human reason is circumscribed by the sacred sources to the unimaginative, conventional list of qualifications he provides for an interpreter of the sacred texts, do not depart from the conservative mainstream. The credibility of reformers often depends on their claim to orthodoxy.[46]

And so, for secular liberals, even moderate, modernized versions of Islamic law can provoke suspicion. After all, removing severe legal handicaps from women is not the same as establishing equality. Refraining from killing apostates is not the same as creating a legal environment supporting free religious choice. And while liberal interpretations of the sacred sources and the classical legal heritage are possible, there is always the question of whether they have real prospects for success or if they are academic curiosities. Reformed, reinterpreted Islamic law is more usually part of an effort to preserve a conservative ethos.

UNIVERSAL RIGHTS?

It is hard to imagine that Islamic law, even in a reformed guise, would endorse exactly the individual rights affirmed by modern Western legal systems. Therefore secular liberals will continue to criticize Islamic law, especially when Muslim states violate human rights in the name of religion.

But for many Muslims—especially those Muslims who think that conservative modernization works, that Islam can no longer be associated with backwardness—such criticism has lost much of its sting. Secular liberals may speak of universal rights, but God's true religion also demands allegiance from everyone. Self-confident Muslims need not follow the Western example. They will, naturally, continue to reform and reinterpret their traditional laws. But they will do it for their own reasons connected to their own faith, not to match a secular liberal conception of rights.

Indeed, liberal notions of individual rights remain controversial with Muslim populations. At the official level, many Muslim countries have been cool toward international human-rights agreements, especially concerning those items that implicitly criticize patriarchal families or affirm a right to change religions. When Muslim countries ratify human-rights treaties, they often do so with detailed reservations intended to protect the application of traditional Islamic laws.[47] Conservative Muslims have even produced alternatives, such as the Cairo Declaration on Human Rights in Islam, which to secular critics read like a list of religious justifications for human-rights violations.[48]

Muslim reservations about liberal conceptions of human rights also play out in popular politics. This is partly due to opposition to the libertine tendencies of secular modernity and a desire for cultural authenticity, but also because of a political taint that human-rights advocacy has acquired. Western colonial powers have long used concerns for the rights of minorities and women as excuses for interference; today's disastrous "humanitarian interventions" in Muslim countries suggest, to many Muslims, that Western objections to Muslim practices continue to be more about power than about concern for human welfare.

This is not to say that conservative Muslims are against rights or insensitive to oppression. Islamists often have occasion to condemn the imprisonment and torture of dissidents, as they have been regular targets of persecution by authoritarian governments. Not only is religious conservatism compatible with electoral democracy, in countries such as Indonesia and Turkey, increasing public religiosity has gone together with political systems becoming more receptive to broader popular influence.

Moreover, demands for rights are now part of a common modern political language. There are many nongovernmental organizations advancing Muslim versions of human rights, particularly defending the religious liberties of Muslims. When such organizations promote the civil rights of Muslims, they act much like any organization focused on the interests of a group.

However, advancing Muslim interests to act in the public sphere without compromising traditional faith also gives rise to difficult conflicts. For example, Muslim organizations often demand a right for public employees to wear headscarves or clothes of extreme modesty. This can clash with a secular interest in keeping the public sphere free of religious entanglements. Achieving a compromise between such interests can be difficult, since rights are not supposed to be subject to political negotiation. In practice, any solution is political. In 1993 and 2005, for example, the European Court of Human Rights decided that Turkish laws against headscarves for public employees were acceptable.[49] Today, as religious conservatism has consolidated power in Turkey, such bans have become irrelevant. Barriers to headscarves are now considered the human-rights violations.

Muslim rights organizations draw on the prominent place religious liberty has in human-rights declarations. Each person, the declarations announce, is entitled to their conception of life, and governments may not interfere in anyone's personal exercise of conscience. But religiously oriented rights organizations also have a distinct understanding of universal human rights. For example, the mission statement of the Turkish organization Mazlum-Der has this:

> Ma[z]lum-Der believes that human rights are universal, and that the source of human rights is the fact that individuals were created as human beings. Thus, natural law—divine law—constitutes the foundation of human rights. . . . Human rights are rights bestowed by God, without any exception, to every individual with full equality in line with human dignity.[50]

Mazlum-Der's reference to divine law is not incidental: its understanding of both the basis and the content of human rights differs from the secular liberal version enshrined in the Universal Declaration of Human

Rights. Secular liberals tend to see human rights as practical instruments, justified by their use in preventing commonly acknowledged forms of oppression. Among Muslims, however, the legitimacy of rights requires a religious foundation, which is most easily found through concepts of natural rights underwritten by a divine moral order.[51] Therefore Muslim conceptions of human rights are often similar to conservative Catholic notions of human dignity and concomitant God-granted rights.

Secular liberals might be tempted to think that this is not a rival conception but a subversion of human rights. Nonetheless, much current academic thinking about human rights and democracy is more sympathetic to the efforts of grassroots religious groups than to elite Western cultural artifacts such as the Universal Declaration.[52] Human-rights declarations piously affirm religious liberty but also leave it vague. But with the exceptions of some ultraliberal forms of Christianity or Judaism, or disorganized New Age–style individualist spiritualities, most religion for most believers is practiced within communities. Any universal concept of religious liberty must be sensitive to how most people develop their identity and their deepest aspirations in such communities. These communities are not voluntary associations like golf clubs; they make significant, even coercive demands on those who belong. Believers need to live according to their religion in a sense more profound than a golfer needs to swing her clubs. Accordingly, a postmodern conception of democratic rights, recognizing how most people are embedded in religious communities, is more in tune with today's religious conservatism.

A postmodern perspective also clarifies Muslim reservations about human rights. When Muslim thinkers object to liberal versions of rights, it is usually because of excessive individualism. While a more individualist, Protestant-style Islam has spread together with capitalism, modern Muslims do not seek to replicate the Western experience. Even the most neoliberal Muslim political movements insist on preserving the integrity of a religious community, even if, in today's circumstances, this may become an ideological or a virtual community.[53] As sociologist Mark Juergensmeyer observes,

The Islamic versions of human rights are seldom, however, the same as the humanistic secular versions. From the point of view of traditional religious cultures, stark individualism and a laissez-faire attitude toward personal expression run fundamentally counter to the collective loyalty and disciplined demeanor typically found in the religious life. It is unlikely, therefore, that religious nationalists will ever fully support a libertarian version of individual rights, even though in many other ways they may look and talk like human-rights advocates anywhere in the world.[54]

For secular liberals such as myself, individual rights are not stand-alone commitments—they make sense in the context of other intellectual positions and social ideals. There is, obviously, individualism. I resent authority that does not come with what *I* judge to be good reasons. Acting collectively for common interests is perfectly fine, and when I participate in a cooperative enterprise such as science, I thoroughly enjoy doing so. But I need to be able to make the reasons for collective action *mine*. Traditions and allegiances can influence but cannot dictate my decision. I do not do submission to gods. But for traditional varieties of Islam as for many other religions, overcoming that self-centered impulse is the beginning of wisdom.

The liberal tradition also reflects a particular historical experience. We propose to avoid conflicts rooted in religion by separating religion from politics. Intellectually, we draw a line between the natural and the supernatural, between the secular and sacred, and between what is accessible to a public process of reasoning and what appears true only through private faith. And we declare that the state does not have any competence in resolving theological disputes, and that therefore the state should be confined to administering worldly affairs.[55] We need not fully agree with such a position—as far as I can tell, supernatural claims are very likely false, not unknowable in a way that needs to be resolved by a leap of faith. But in any case, for secular liberals, our views about social order are not tightly packaged together with what we think about our gods. Politically, there is little that distinguishes a godless infidel like me from liberal religious people.

Muslim political traditions, however, do not treat otherworldly knowledge claims as private affairs. Islam represents a public truth, indeed, it is a framework that encompasses all genuine truths. We are finite creatures, and so human knowledge of the divine is always imperfect. The scholars do not have ready answers for all questions; perhaps we must also make rules through imperial decrees or parliamentary proceedings. And yet, God has not left us without guidance. Not acknowledging the divine law that we do know would be willful blindness.

Secular liberals ignore God, and, for religious conservatives, that can only invite trouble. For many Muslims who have suffered under authoritarian, modernizing states, trouble comes in the form of an overbearing state that tends toward totalitarian rule. Secular liberals demote the intermediate institutions of premodern societies, such as religious organizations, to private associations comparable to golf clubs. We prefer to interact with the state as individual citizens. This, many Muslims think, leaves modern individuals vulnerable to the state.

Now, liberals also face the danger of arbitrary power, and we also need to limit how states can interfere with our lives. So we link citizenship to participation. Political legitimacy comes through democratic consent, through our taking responsibility for our collective decisions. And as citizens we bear rights. Indeed, we invoke human rights just so we can resist arbitrary exercises of power, creating what political philosopher Stephen Eric Bronner calls "a form of solidarity that is more than legal and extends beyond the limits of class, race, and nation."[56] When liberals suggest that enforcing human rights would improve Muslim lives, they point to the need to curb the arbitrary power of postcolonial states.[57]

For most Muslims, however, divine law is the instrument for restraining a rapacious state. By emasculating intermediate institutions and eroding the basis for community, liberalism sheds itself of the moral resources to oppose worldly power. In that case, Egyptian Islamist Abdulwahab al Masseri argues, "To talk of human rights (in the abstract) is, therefore, to continue the original assault on the intermediate institutions that began in the Renaissance and left humanity completely naked before the state and its institutions."[58]

Accusations that secular liberals deify the state and prepare the ground for totalitarianism are overwrought. Nonetheless, conservative and postmodern critics do have a point. Starting with denying political force to otherworldly convictions, liberal political and legal philosophy has tended to disallow legal recognition of any comprehensive conception of the good. But in that case, secular liberalism appears to cripple our ability to collectively decide on and institutionalize moral convictions about a good life. Especially in its neoliberal versions, secular law becomes a matter of working out technicalities, divorced from political negotiations about public goods. According to the "law and economics" approach that is very influential in the United States, the law becomes a device to make markets run smoothly, and where considerations of economic efficiency are decisive.[59]

There is, then, plenty to criticize in liberal conceptions of secular law and individual rights. There are also practical problems. In highly religious Muslim societies, achieving respect for the law without continuity with the divine-law tradition is difficult. For those Muslims who care most about cultural authenticity, many of the individual rights cherished by secular liberals are too closely embedded in an alien historical experience to be broadly accepted. While modernizing, Muslims will seek a different social equilibrium expressed by a different regime of laws and rights.

For secular liberals, however, there is still something wrong with such critiques of individual rights. They sound like a diversion. Unrestrained individualism raises many questions. But that should not obscure how Islamic law is often an instrument to oppress women and non-Muslims.

Secular liberals want a neutral, universal standpoint from which to criticize Islamic law. While allowing for cultural variation, we do not want to depend on any particular tradition. After all, we want to see if existing institutions measure up. Perhaps a society need not be liberal in all respects—it may promote more hierarchical, more traditional moral ideals. Nonetheless, a decent society is based on cooperation to achieve common interests rather than pervasive force and raw authority. Some respect for human rights should be a minimum requirement for a decent society.[60]

But in that case, it is not so clear that a full set of human rights constitutes a minimum baseline. Traditional Islamic law endorses social hierarchies that favor Muslim men over women and non-Muslims, but it has flourished due to the cooperation and consent of believers, not raw coercion. And Islamic law, especially in its more modernized forms, does condemn the less subtle forms of oppression and torture.

We do have widespread agreement about the more violent sort of human-rights violations. Muslims do not typically accept such acts perpetrated by their governments, even in the name of Islam. Moreover, at this minimal level, human rights are not just an instrument to criticize Muslims. The United States practices torture of alleged terrorists, indiscriminate killing of civilians, and surveillance and entrapment directed toward communities that might harbor dissidents. These human-rights violations have primarily targeted Muslims. International human-rights organizations have protested such actions, and their protests have somewhat improved their credibility among Muslims.

Beyond such a minimal framework, however, disagreement abounds. For example, some activists have criticized the human-rights community for focusing on states and downplaying human-rights violations—particularly of women's rights—by violent Islamist groups.[61] There are longstanding debates over extending human rights into economic rights. Many conservatives reject such extensions, preferring a focus on property rights. Cultural rights, which would be enjoyed by ethnic and religious groups, are also thoroughly controversial. Recently, the United States has consistently either failed to ratify more extended human-rights covenants or has done so with reservations.[62]

Indeed, beyond a minimum, I think talk of rights tries to do too much. I am, for example, all for socialized medicine, but the slogan "healthcare is a human right" does not entirely work with me. Demanding rights promises gains that will not be subject to the vicissitudes of political negotiations. But how we might collectively arrange healthcare is, I think, a political matter, and so is the standing of Islamic law. Traditional Islamic laws express deeply held social ideals, and changing these ideals requires a lot more than rewriting a few rules. If change happens, it will be due to extensive political work.

I do not, then, think that Islamic law fails a test that is universal and neutral. Those of us who find divine law unattractive do not enjoy a deeper insight into human nature and all our countless conflicting needs. Indeed, when we assert human rights, we do so not because of any abstract foundation for rights but because of convictions forged in politics and messy, particular historical experiences. We may pretend otherwise—secular philosophers often justify liberal views by invoking "human dignity"—but dignity is a vague notion that is more at home in Christian moral theology and that is easily adapted to conservative Islamic use.[63]

We oppose traditional Islamic law as secular liberals, because of our identity, our interests, and our stable considered judgments that make us secular liberals. Some Muslims may come to think that Islamic law is not salvageable with patchworks of implausible reinterpretations. Our overlapping interests will help us work together. Secular liberals have some perhaps excessively individualist tendencies, which tempt some of us to disengage so as not to interfere with the choices of others. But we also have tendencies toward equality and solidarity. We fumble our way toward some kind of balance between our inclinations. With any luck, appreciating the complexity of Muslim attachments to divine law may help us strike a better balance. We might even come to see, with some sympathy, how for many believers divine law is inseparably entwined with justice and order. We oppose them nonetheless.

RESPONDING TO ISLAMIC LAW

Islamic law is a permanent feature of Muslim life. When Muslim populations have an opportunity to express their preferences, such as in Egypt after the Arab Spring, they usually affirm Islamic law. Fluidity in interpreting Islamic law is also permanent. In recent opinion polls, over 80 percent of Egyptians rejected the most literal form of Islamic law, responding that "they prefer applying the spirit of Sharia but with adaptation to modern times."[64] Most modern Muslims have little enthusiasm for the suffocating presence of religion in countries such as Saudi Arabia and Iran. An updated interpretation of traditional law sounds attractive, and debates about what that means in practice will continue.

For religious overachievers, divine law is supposed to be a comprehensive guide to life. Beyond the scale of small communities, however, living according to the rules has always been an impossible ideal. Muslim states have always had hybrid legal systems, combining imperial decrees or parliamentary legislation with rulings by religious scholars. This also will continue to be the case. Even fundamentalist states need to make some laws by secular processes, such as Saudi Arabia, which calls its codes "regulations" to avoid offending against the conviction that only God can legislate.[65]

Those of us who are uncomfortable with Islamic law in Muslim countries have to be resigned to political defeat. Some measure of Islamic law is, evidently, what most Muslims want. In that case, our interests in mitigating the harms associated with traditional Islamic law will be best served by liberal reinterpretation. We once might have thought that divine law could be swept away, like the revolutionaries who discarded Islamic law when they formed the Turkish Republic. But that experiment has produced ambiguous results, and in any case, revolutions nowadays veer toward conservative populism. So reinterpreting divine law is the only viable option. I think that the art of torturing ancient texts to make them say whatever we want is intellectually corrupting. But it might serve liberal interests.

For secular liberals, the more immediate challenge comes from Muslim minority communities. Devout believers want to live their faith, and for many Muslims, this means being able to live according to Islamic law. Religious liberty demands that they should be accommodated as much as possible.

We are used to modern nation-states, where within geographically defined administrative units, everyone is subject to the same laws. Typically the nation has a dominant cultural group, which has the strongest influence on the legal system. The laws of the United States, for example, have generally had a Christian character, from the informal Protestant establishment of the nineteenth century to the more secular legal landscape of today. But the United States has also accommodated groups that fall outside its dominant cultural norms. The local authorities know not to enforce all ordinances in Chinatown. The courts make exceptions to allow the Amish to keep their youth out of school, or to serve Orthodox

Jewish neighborhoods. But most religious groups find it easier to adapt to an American pattern. In order to enjoy religious liberty as understood in the United States, many varieties of Judaism became more like Protestant denominations. They became more overtly religious, more defined by creed and ritual rather than by a pervasive common culture.[66] Islam in the United States has evolved similarly. Congregations have replaced communities, and their leaders function like ministers rather than like judges.

Religious liberty is not a clear-cut principle but a messy, constantly renegotiated political affair. But accommodation can stretch only so far. It is not hard to imagine, in today's pluralistic, multicultural societies, that some tight-knit Muslim communities will refuse to fit the individualist, congregational pattern. They may demand the freedom to live in fuller accord with divine law.

Secular liberals are individualists—we demote religions to private associations, and we apply one law to all. Those Muslims who want to make space for divine law offer not just a religious communitarian rejection of liberal individualism but an alternative and historically rooted way of living together. In the multireligious Muslim empires of the past, different communities conducted their internal affairs according to their traditional laws. Perhaps, then, legal pluralism should be resurrected for multicultural societies. Islamist intellectual Ali Bulaç, for example, suggests that in a pluralistic legal framework, even secular liberals, including atheists, would have their own legal system.[67] Why, after all, should accidents of geography rather than community determine the laws we live under? Why not let communities run their affairs according to what they hold sacred, and concentrate on negotiating a loose overall framework for a multicultural society?

There are also current examples of legal pluralism. In India, Muslims and Hindus are subject to different personal laws. This is a colonial legacy, and the Indian constitution mandates a uniform personal law—eventually. In practice, separate personal laws is a compromise that has been hard to disturb. Keeping the peace in India may require that religious communities be able to protect their integrity by applying their traditional laws. In Malaysia, Muslims are a majority, but Islamic law applies only to Muslim

Malays. Israel has a personal status system that recognizes a multitude of ethnically and religiously defined groups. Again, coexistence depends on separate personal laws for distinct religious communities.

Liberal Western countries, which have become multicultural societies due to immigration, have so far not accepted legal pluralism. European Muslim leaders such as Tariq Ramadan encourage Muslims to live according to Islamic law, but only insofar as this does not conflict with the laws in their host countries.[68] Often, Islamic laws operate unofficially or as an instrument of arbitration. In Britain, Muslims can seek advice from local sharia councils, but the rulings they receive do not have the force of law. Islamic law in Britain is, instead, an institution of nonbinding mediation. Sharia councils very often serve women seeking religiously valid divorces, so that their marital status is also recognized in Muslim countries with which they maintain close ties. However, these councils do not treat women equally, seeking to reinforce traditional family structures. Therefore they attract criticism for being incompatible with human rights standards.[69]

Though Western legal systems have tended toward accommodating Muslim concerns,[70] none of the ways in which Islamic law is present in Western countries approach explicit legal pluralism. Neither are they new—they are similar to how Jewish law has been accommodated. But I do wonder whether the scope of Islamic law in liberal societies will expand. Usually, in speculations about such a possibility, the leading characters of the story are multiculturalists, who protect community integrity at the expense of individual rights. There is something to this. The desire not to interfere with others, to enable difference, and to acknowledge how central community is for many individual aspirations, are all important *liberal* tendencies. It is worth asking if these tendencies can undermine a secular liberal social order.

My worries are somewhat different. I suspect that our tendency toward acquisitive individualism, to reducing all human relationships to market exchanges, provides a more serious opening for religious law. Under neoliberalism, we have become accustomed to governments serving markets. The state retreats to its coercive functions: enforcing contracts, watching for and punishing criminals and dissidents. But privatization and the entanglement of state and corporate institutions do not stop there. We now have massive private security firms, privately operated prisons, and military functions farmed out to private contractors. Our national security and surveillance states are closely intertwined with the corporations that provide those services. And we are not, in practice, all equal before the law. Our extraordinary inequalities of wealth and power too often mean that our elites are not accountable.[71]

In these circumstances, I can easily imagine that legal systems could be further privatized. Binding arbitration clauses in the fine print of many contracts we sign are already a step toward a parallel private system of justice. Religious groups, such as some American evangelicals and Scientologists, are already taking advantage of binding arbitration to enforce religious rules.[72] We can extrapolate from such developments to envision a larger role for Islamic law. Neoliberal varieties of Islam have very effectively intertwined business and religious associations, so they could well provide an instrument for subcontracting localized legal regimes. Religious leaders and their lobbyists would advertise their services as cost-effective, relieving the taxpayers of another burden. They would represent decentralization, the realization of local efficiencies, and the expression of norms organic to their communities. Neoliberalism, in other words, creates opportunities to strengthen intermediate institutions.

All of this—Islamic law via multiculturalism or neoliberalism—is speculation. But if the prospect of revived religious laws bothers secular liberals, we should also give some thought to how we are bringing it onto ourselves. Whether in our preoccupations with diversity and difference, or in our obsession with buying and selling, we have lost much of our sense of solidarity with others. We have reason to be ambivalent about solidarity, since it conflicts with noninterference. Solidarity always implies some erasure of difference. But if the secular liberal tradition does not revive its sense of solidarity, if it abandons the field to religious loyalties, it will not have much of a future. And I, for one, will not mourn its passing.

5

WOMEN AND MEN

COVERED UP, CONFINED, AND OPPRESSED

Afew years ago I ran into an opinion piece in the tabloid the *Daily Mail*, in which journalist Yasmin Alibhai-Brown voiced her worry about the "Talibanization" of Muslim children in Britain. The photographs accompanying the article included one with a group of about eight women and children, all wrapped up in conservative Islamic dress, wading in the sea. The caption said "Joyless: A Muslim family stay covered up as they bathe on a British beach."[1]

Coming from a secular subculture in Turkey, my image of conservative Islam has been similar to the photograph. For over two centuries modernizers in Muslim lands have looked to the example of the West, working for new laws, importing science and technology, and sometimes even trying to keep religion out of government. But for the most committed westernizers, the need for cultural transformation extended into the most intimate domain: the family. Muslim women—especially higher-class, respectable Muslim women—were segregated from men, often confined to the home, and covered up on the occasions when they had to venture outside. Such exclusion of women, many westernizers came to believe, was one of the reasons Muslims had fallen behind. Moreover, they became convinced that modern civilization was universal, and that civilized people did not remove women from the public realm.

For the westernizers of my father's generation, born a decade or two after the Turkish Revolution of the 1920s, women's entry into the public sphere was a work in progress. In my family's circle of academics and professionals, women and men had started to work together; they certainly mixed in dinner parties and on the beach. They also worried that most Turks continued to keep women and men apart. The beaches of the secular middle class inspired apoplectic sermons warning of the fornication that mixing of the sexes would inevitably produce. In turn, when westernized women saw their more traditional sisters wading in all covered up, they probably thought that the religious rules imposed joyless lives on too many women.

By that time, the laws of the land did not contribute as much to the subordination of women. The Turkish revolutionaries had abolished Islamic laws, and even granted women full political rights by the 1930s, ahead of many European countries. Overhauling laws, however, goes only part of the way toward social change. Muslim-majority countries have continually reformed their laws over the past centuries. Though many retain laws inspired by religious rulings that favor men, legal changes have usually improved the standing of women. On paper, Turkish laws mostly treat the sexes equally.[2] But tradition still dictates that women must live under the authority of men. Professional and managerial elites of my generation who grew up in Turkey's secular subculture are much like those of our class across the globe: many of us almost take gender equality for granted. And yet, after many decades of secular law and pressure from a modernizing state, after urbanization, industrialization, and mass education, two-thirds of Turkish women wear headscarves or similarly cover up. In the common cultural imagination, if not always in practice, women's place remains in the home and under male guardianship.

Traditional religion endorses a subordinate status for women. Authorities, from scholars to Islamist opinion makers, immediately point to the sacred sources, starting with the Quran. They note that 4 Women 34 says that men provide for women, and it appears to imply that men have authority over women even to the extent of being allowed to beat women who misbehave. Likewise, 2 The Cow 282 makes a woman's witness worth half that of a man in commercial transactions; and 4 Women 11 starts by assigning women a half share of inheritance compared to that of men.

There is more. The Quran regulates marriage and divorce to the advantage of men. It gives male desires priority: 2 The Cow 223 says that "Your wives are a field of yours; so come to your field as you wish, but do something for the good of your souls beforehand." The Quran then discusses some matters such as oaths and divorce, and in verse 228 adds "And the rights of the females are as their responsibilities, while the men have a rank above them." Men are allowed to take multiple wives, since 4 Women 3 has "And if you fear that you cannot do justice by the orphans, then marry women who please you, two, three, or four; but if you fear you won't be equitable, then one, or a legitimate bondmaid of yours."

Indeed, it is notable how the Quran often speaks to men alone. This is not always the case; 33 The Confederates 35 includes men and women equally when describing the characteristics of a pious person. It starts with "For the men who acquiesce to the will of God, and the women who acquiesce, the men who believe, and the women who believe"; goes on to list men and women who are devout, are truthful, are constant, are humble, give charity, fast, are chaste, and remember God a lot; and concludes with "God has arranged forgiveness for them, and a magnificent reward." Tradition suggests that the occasion of revelation for this verse was that one of the wives of the Prophet complained that the Quran addresses only men.

The Quran assumes a patriarchal, extended-family structure normal for its time, and it goes into some detail instructing men about marriage, resolving marital disputes, and divorce. Nonetheless, as usual, the Quran is also a bit of a disorganized mess, providing little context to clarify its prescriptions. Most mainstream Muslims have looked toward the secondary scriptures of the prophetic traditions and further scholarly elaborations to understand the divine template for gender roles. Historically, the results have often intensified male authority. For example, under traditional Islamic law, men can unilaterally divorce their wives, even by verbal repudiation. While women can also initiate divorce, this is a difficult process that requires a judge's approval. Indeed, strict Islamic law has required women to always live under the guardianship of a man—usually a father, a husband, or even a son. Public acts of a woman, including appearing in public, have been subject to the consent of her guardian.

Tradition also supplies reasons for the lesser status of women: by nature, women are inferior to men in their capacity for public action. One famous prophetic tradition states that women are deficient in intelligence and religion:

Once Allah's Apostle went out to the Musalla (to offer the prayer) of 'Id-al-Adha or Al-Fitr prayer. Then he passed by the women and said, "O women! Give alms, as I have seen that the majority of the dwellers of Hell-fire were you (women)." They asked, "Why is it so, O Allah's Apostle?" He replied, "You curse frequently and are ungrateful to your husbands. I have not seen anyone more deficient in intelligence and religion than you. A cautious sensible man could be led astray by some of you." The women asked, "O Allah's Apostle! What is deficient in our intelligence and religion?" He said, "Is not the evidence of two women equal to the witness of one man?" They replied in the affirmative. He said, "This is the deficiency in her intelligence. Isn't it true that a woman can neither pray nor fast during her menses?" The women replied in the affirmative. He said, "This is the deficiency in her religion."[3]

Traditional religion, then, has endorsed and helped maintain male dominance. In heavily Muslim regions such as the Middle East, North Africa, and South Asia, religion blends in with deep cultural beliefs about the need to control female sexuality. One infamous example is various forms of female genital mutilation, common especially among Africans. Usually cutting much more extensively than male circumcision, female mutilation is often celebrated because it reduces female pleasure and dampens female sexual agency.

Moreover, in many Muslim populations, the family honor is associated with the sexual purity of its female members. Even the suggestion of a woman engaging in unauthorized sex—eloping, being left alone with a man, being raped—exposes the men of the family as unable to control their women. Violations of honor mean that the standing of the whole family suffers dramatically. The family is seen to lack power and to be unable to supply unblemished women for marriage. All of this means enormous pressure to confine and guard women. Even rumors about violations of honor can create an intolerable situation for the extended family. Sometimes injury to honor can lead to drastic measures, including honor killings, where murdering the woman involved serves as a public signal that the family will guarantee the purity of its women.

An orthodox Islamic order, then, can sanction violent control of women. Indeed, those countries that claim to most strictly enforce Islamic law, such as Saudi Arabia or Afghanistan today, are usually the most restrictive for women, to the extent of perpetuating a system of gender apartheid. Where Islamists attain power, in places such as Egypt and Tunisia after the Arab Spring, it is often accompanied by intimidation intended to prevent the mixing of the sexes and to make women cover up in public.[4]

So for the westernized women I grew up with, the prospect of the strict, rules-following versions of Islam gaining power was frightening. Almost all considered themselves Muslim; they just thought they followed a more enlightened Islam than the faith of ignorant preachers. In practice, they picked and chose among ritual observances, cared little about sacred texts, and were convinced that westernization represented progress—even, perhaps, a purification of religion.

Much has changed. In Turkey, conservative Islam has come roaring back into the public sphere, though in a mutated, modernized form. Today, Muslim women worldwide are often covering themselves up, even as they become more educated and increasingly take up paid employment. And everyone is talking about the sacred texts, whether to reinterpret them in the favor of women in public, or to proclaim that God's will is that men should wield authority in the family.

WOMEN UNDER ISLAM

Secular liberals would not want to live according to the Islam of the classical jurists, or in Saudi Arabia today. But especially where women's rights are concerned, it is worth asking whether it makes sense to single out Islam. After all, we also would not want to live in intensely Christian Uganda, which criminalizes homosexuality and passes laws that regulate skirt lengths.[5] Varieties of religion that seek to control women and impose conservative rules of sexuality are present globally.

It is hard to say whether, historically, Muslim environments have been exceptionally difficult for women. In the Western imagination, Muslim women have been associated both with extreme restrictions and with fantasies of erotic freedom, coming together in dreams about harems. But the vast majority of Muslim women have been peasants or working class. If, for example, Middle Eastern peasant women have been oppressed, this has most often taken the form of having to labor in the fields with a child tied to their backs while their husbands sat idle. Confinement to the family compound and having to completely cover up when emerging outside has been a luxury affordable by few. And in this regard, Muslim upper classes have not been very different from their predecessors and neighbors. Female seclusion and covering up were Middle Eastern customs before Islam, and they have occurred in Christian and Hindu environments as well. In the matter of marriage, as feminist scholar Leila Ahmed observes,

> The type of marriage that Islam legitimized was, like its monotheism, deeply consonant with the sociocultural systems already in place throughout the Middle East. Within Arabia patriarchal, patrilineal, polygynous marriage was by no means starkly innovative. Rather, Islam selectively sanctioned customs already found among some Arabian tribal societies while prohibiting others. Of central importance to the institution it established were the preeminence given to paternity and the vesting in the male of proprietary rights to female sexuality and its issue.[6]

Family honor requiring strict control of female sexuality is also not exclusive to Islam. In Turkish newspapers, I regularly see gruesome reports of honor killings, together with calls for action to stamp out this barbaric custom. A few years ago I read about the murder of a newly wed couple. Apparently the bride's family strongly objected to the relationship, trying to dissuade her. Finally the older brother of the bride said that he was provoked and had no choice but to kill the couple, who had been married for only ten days. News items like this are depressingly common. Ordinarily I would not read the details. But it turned out that a major reason the wedding was contentious was that the bride and the groom belonged to different religions: Islam and Christianity. The bride's family could not countenance the mixed marriage. Furthermore, the bride's family were Assyrian Christians, now a very small minority in Turkey. They had insisted that the groom should convert to Christianity and that the wedding had to take place in a church. But even then they were reluctant. The couple had already tried to elope once, and the woman had returned home after threats. But then, they got away again and got married in secret.[7]

Throughout the Middle East, traditional families jealously guard their honor—Christians as well as Muslims. In South Asia, Hindus also perpetrate honor killings. Very often, their sense of the sacred is inseparable from their perceptions of honor. For conservative Muslims, traditional interpretations of religion endorse close control of female sexuality. And yet, there is no explicit statement in the sacred sources that sanctions honor killings. There are many local customs that are consonant with traditional Islam but are not part of any official body of doctrine or law. Female genital mutilation is another example. It is common in many African localities, and it is practiced by people of many religions. But in Turkey genital mutilation is unknown except in some Kurdish populations. Most Turks would react with incomprehension and disgust if anyone suggested it was part of Islam.

So Muslim ideals of family and womanhood vary regionally and are close to the ideals of their neighbors. Little about women under Islam stands out as unique to Islam as a religion. In that case, historical differences between Muslim lands and western Europe might tell us more. As historian Bernard Lewis describes it,

> The difference in the position of women was indeed one of the most striking contrasts between Christian and Muslim practice, and is mentioned by almost all travelers in both directions. Christianity, of all churches and denominations, prohibits polygamy and concubinage. Islam, like most other non-Christian communities, permits both. European visitors to the Islamic lands were intrigued by what they knew or, more accurately, what they heard concerning the harem system, and some of them speak with ill-concealed and ill-informed envy of what they imagine to be the rights and privileges of a Muslim husband and master of the house. Muslim visitors to Europe speak with astonishment, often with horror, of the immodesty and forwardness of Western women, of the incredible freedom and absurd deference accorded to them, and the lack of manly jealousy of European males confronted with the immorality and promiscuity in which their womenfolk indulge.[8]

The travelers' reports Lewis mentions emphasize the practices of wealthier classes. Nonetheless, they do reveal some broad differences. Christianity preserved the Roman prohibition of polygyny, and polygyny does tend to reduce the status and well-being of women.[9] A more significant historical difference is the mixing of the sexes in European societies. It is plausible enough to think that the lack of segregation prepared the ground for a more equal relationship.

Even so, it is hard to make a blanket statement about whether premodern European societies accorded women more power. European women mixed with men, but it was also Westerners who, until recently, often erased married women as independent public actors. Islamic law never barred women from holding property and participating in commerce, even though they often had to act through male agents.

By modern secular liberal standards, traditional Islamic gender roles look very restrictive. But then, none of the premodern cultures associated with world religions look attractive in this regard. On our side of modernity, we have a political outlook where we hope to take charge of our own fates. We are not bound by texts and traditions proclaiming sacred social orders. We are suspicious of predetermined hierarchies. And we have used our technological prowess to create opportunities for women to more fully participate in public affairs. Armed with birth control, breast pumps, nannies, female suffrage, and a feminist political consciousness, educated elites today enjoy an environment where women and men are close to equal in their families and workplaces, even as the gap between rich and poor has widened.[10]

In that case, perhaps further modernization will mean that Muslim women will achieve a more equal status. After all, Muslim women are becoming better educated, although in most Muslim majority countries they still lag behind men. Even in a theocratic country such as Iran, women in higher education have caught up to and surpassed men in many fields.[11] Industrialization and diversifying economies generally lead to more formal employment, and the rate of participation in the labor force has been increasing for Muslim women. At the same time, fertility rates of Muslim women have been decreasing.[12] Reduced fertility usually goes together with less patriarchal family structures.

While economic development has tended to work against traditional gender roles, however, Muslim populations are still very much male-dominated. When comparing Muslim countries to other countries with similar levels of development, female labor-force participation tends to be lower and fertility higher. The strong religiosity of Muslim women promotes more traditional roles, though it is not the only contributing factor.[13] More broadly, comparative studies usually show a deficit in female welfare among Muslims that is not fully accounted for by levels of economic development. Political scientist M. Steven Fish observes that "Whether we focus on status in public life, popular attitudes, or structural inequities in well-being, females tend to fare relatively poorly in places where Muslims predominate."[14] Muslim women receive inferior healthcare and education, so that "Muslims have an especially acute problem with gender-based inequality."[15]

In other words, while modernization has changed gender roles, Muslim societies also remain conservative about gender in a manner that cannot be explained simply as a developmental lag. Politics and particular histories also matter. After all, the story of modern Western countries is not one of straightforward feminist progress. The European Enlightenment helped make it possible to break with tradition and imagine more equal gender roles. But it was never obvious that liberty, equality, and fraternity had to be extended beyond free, property-owning men, the natural actors in the public sphere. The present near-equality of well-educated Western women and men is a very recent achievement, which is by no means complete. With so much depending on historical contingencies, there is no guarantee that Muslim societies will evolve toward a similar form of gender equality.

Indeed, the common Muslim desire for a pious, culturally authentic modernity, and the popularity of conservative modernization, suggests that Muslims may explore different options. Muslim regions have long had secular women's movements rooted in westernized, educated elites. For a while, an unveiled, even sunbathing image looked like it might be the modern Muslim woman's future. But religious politics and the cultural conservatism of the rising middle classes has eclipsed secular feminism.

Currently, the modern conservative image of a Muslim woman includes both a veil and a public presence. Secularists in countries such as Egypt and Turkey first worried about re-veiled women among university students in the 1970s. These were women claiming an education and aspiring to employment outside the home, but doing so while affirming their religious background and displaying their adherence to traditional norms of modesty. Their peasant foremothers could not afford to conform to upper-class forms of respectability, but now, socially advancing women could take the veil. In Algeria, where colonial violence had been at its bloodiest, veiling was also resistance to the West. More recently, urban conservative families in Turkey value education for their girls and expect fewer children. Few women wear the traditional fully concealing black dress—they adopt less confining, more modern ways of covering up. Among the better off, headscarves and modern modest clothing support an important part of the fashion industry.[16]

That more Muslim women will assert themselves in public appears to be a foregone conclusion. But this is happening in a context of pious modernity. Just as many Muslims seek technology without disenchantment, and continually debate reforming Islamic law around its edges, Muslim women are likely to try to advance their interests without adopting Western feminist sensibilities.

EVERYONE IN THEIR RIGHT PLACE

For many devout, orthodox Muslims, conforming to God's template for gender and the family is not just to be accepted as a sacred obligation. Especially today, when the faithful are more aware of other ways to live, religious rules require rationales. Headscarves or traditional rules for divorce are supposed to be not just Muslim customs but universally valid prescriptions. There is a right and proper way for women and men to relate to one another. Apologists say that revelation guides us, but they also offer reasons for why traditional Muslim ways are best.

Some scholars still straightforwardly state that "the male gender is superior to the female gender in general," citing sacred texts.[17] In modern circumstances, however, apologists are more persuasive when they acknowledge that they do not propose to treat women and men identically, but claim that justice and equity is served by the religious rules. Islamist journalist Abdurrahman Dilipak explains that a half share of inheritance should be understood in context:

> Even if it seems at first glance that a Muslim woman is given less than her brother at the first division of property, this woman has the right to ask for the difference and perhaps more as dowry from the man she marries. Meanwhile, the brother will end up giving the surplus money he received to the girl he marries.
>
> According to this understanding, money and land won't be split into many ineffective pieces, change hands, and be taken out of circulation altogether. The quantitative growth of the money is also prevented, so the woman will be desired for her own character, not for her wealth.[18]

The prominent Islamist intellectual Rachid al-Ghannouchi states that Islam institutes a relationship of equality between the sexes, with some exceptions due to the different natures of women and men. For example, Islamic law prohibits a Muslim woman from marrying a non-Muslim, while men are allowed to marry Christians and Jews. Al-Gannouchi explains the difference as being due to a need to protect the religion of the woman and her children to be born. After all, the woman will come under the guardianship of the man and become part of the man's social circle and religious influences. This is acceptable if the man is the Muslim party in the marriage, but not if he is non-Muslim.[19]

The notion of separate God-given "created natures" that sets the sexes apart is prominent in the apologetic literature, which often includes interesting distortions of biology.[20] Some writers elaborate that women are by nature more delicate, more emotional, and more in need of protection due to their spiritual purity. This allows women to respond to a child's shifting moods, but it is a handicap in public.[21] Modern Muslims usually interpret the different natures of the sexes as a basis for differing gender roles in the family and society at large. Male and female roles are supposed to be complementary, separate but equal. Suzanne Haneef, a convert to Islam, explains that

Islam recognizes that men and women have different natures, strengths and weaknesses, and hence it assigns different but complementary roles within the society to each, dividing the total work which must be done for the process of living between them in a way which best suits their innate capacities and natures. Within the family group, Islam assigns the leadership role to men, together with financial responsibility for its members; the support and maintenance of the women and children are their concern. Women in turn are responsible for looking after their husbands' comfort and well-being, guarding their honor and administering their properties, providing for the physical and emotional well-being of their children, and, with their husbands' help rearing them in the best possible way as sound Muslims. Although as a matter of convenience most women do the work of their households, this is not required by Islam, and a woman is perfectly free to turn over all or part of the domestic work to others, as circumstances permit, and to pursue her own work or interests, provided the family—particularly in the area of the training of children—is not neglected.[22]

For conservative Muslims, respecting created nature—the boundaries imposed by God—is important because to cross the lines puts social order at risk. The secular liberal conception of women's liberation confuses liberty with license, encouraging women to rebel against their sacred duties as wife and mother.

Historically, male preachers and writers have often held women responsible for sexuality that breaks the rules. Indeed, to many Muslims, women have appeared to have an irresistible seductive power that threatens social chaos. Therefore they must be confined or covered up. But conservative Muslim women can also endorse the religious rules, reading them in a way that emphasizes female interests. Human nature includes created weaknesses, such as unbridled male desire. The Islamic family, however, provides a context in which such weaknesses can be turned into strengths. God's social order disciplines *men*, harnessing their otherwise-destructive desires and competitiveness in the service of women and children.

A more modern apologetic theme, then, emphasizes how separation of the sexes, women covering up, and other rules allow women to enter the public without making a sexual display. Haneef says that "due to this modest dress and the propriety of her manner and behavior, men can regard and treat her as a person, not a sex object: that is, her value to the society has no relationship to her physical attractions but solely to her worth as a human being."[23] As she ages, a Muslim woman remains valuable for her wisdom and experience. And Muslim men have to behave with the same restraint and purity, as "a conscious Muslim man avoids just as scrupulously as his Muslim sister anything which would lead him toward what is forbidden or would lower him in his own eyes or before his Lord: likewise his dress and manner demonstrate that he possesses self-respect and is free of indecent intentions and desires."[24]

Women need not passively acquiesce in an orthodox Islamic social order. In Turkey, for example, Islamic politics in the last few decades has actively engaged women. Indeed, moderate Islamist parties are well-known for organizing devout women who can enter homes in conservative neighborhoods and mobilize religious people in support of a highly moralizing political agenda.[25] Religious conservatives regularly propose to introduce public spaces reserved for women, such as pink women-only buses, women-only beaches, even a hospital with women personnel only. In doing so, they appeal to women's interests, even suggesting that this is affirmative action in support of women. Iran has women-only parks.[26]

Women express a need for separate facilities because Muslim men do not always act with restraint and purity. Devout, covered-up women also face unrelenting sexual predation in public. But such problems only intensify the need to discipline men, especially since conservative Muslims often blame modern influences for unsavory behavior. Ali Bulaç complains that liberal capitalism forces women to work outside the home, emasculates men, and breaks down family bonds. Indeed, "men losing their role due to their created nature leads them to merciless violence against women and savage murders."[27]

Conservative women face the strains modern economies place on traditional families, and endure male violence. But they also face pressures to marry and to submit to men, and are well aware that actual Muslim communities are less than perfect in according women the respect that idealized descriptions of Islam promise. Educated, professional women often find that conservative Muslim men in the business world are conflicted and confused when relating to women amongst them, even when the women cover up and act according to conservative norms.[28] Conservative, devout women respond, however, by trying to get closer to a religious ideal. Indeed, they may begin to suspect that traditional Islam, as interpreted by men in the past, should be seen anew through the eyes of women.

ISLAMIC FEMINISM

Until recently, women have been excluded from shaping official, orthodox versions of Islam—the texts and rules. Still, women have always participated in religious life. Segregating the sexes has meant that Muslim women have developed distinct styles of religiosity, which often have been informal, oral, infused with popular supernaturalism and everyday concerns rather than with an emphasis on doctrines and rules. As Muslim women have found more opportunities to assert themselves, feminists have sought resources for women within Islamic traditions. Feminist Leila Ahmed, for example, argues that the informal Islam associated with women has as much claim to authenticity as the Islam of the texts and the male jurists, and celebrates the ethical orientation of women's Islam.[29]

Indeed, Islam as lived is often not as it might seem through the texts. Male dominance of the public realm does not reduce women to abject powerlessness. In extended Middle Eastern families, women have often not just controlled their family relationships but also indirectly influenced public matters, particularly through their sons. Men present themselves as superior, but they also worry about being manipulated by women. Furthermore, in the past decades, academic feminists have sought to recover women's voices and agency even when following rules made by men. It has, for example, become a commonplace to describe women covering up as a form of empowerment, since many women actively adopt the veil to affirm their religiosity.[30]

And yet, acting indirectly and covering up are still signs of female subordination, even if done lovingly to express piety. Oral and folk forms of religiosity are less institutionalized, more ephemeral. They can exist in the background without challenging male dominance in the public realm. Furthermore, such informal alternative traditions are under considerable strain today. Under urban, modernized conditions, the typical Muslim family is changing, becoming more nuclear. The age at marriage is rising. How spouses meet and marry is no longer as much under the control of parents. Dating and plenty of sexual behavior against the rules takes place, even under the cover of the veil.[31] At the same time, religious politics has come to dominate the public imagination among many Muslims. This has meant that increasingly, all politics, including the politics of gender and the family, has to lay claim to Islamic authenticity. Today, efforts to advance the interests of Muslim women cannot sidestep the rules and texts.

Most Islamic feminism answers to such needs. Older generations among westernized women in the Middle East were often attracted to a more secular style of feminism tied to nationalism. The more recent forms of feminism are more explicitly religious, centered on reinterpreting the sacred sources.[32]

Feminist reinterpretation often begins by describing the classical structure of Islam, with its blatant subordination of women, as a medieval development imposed on an earlier, purer time closer to revelation. A Protestant-like desire to go back to the sacred sources and recover an Age of Felicity before corruption set in is common to many Islamic movements today. But feminists such as Asma Afsaruddin look back to "the early Islamic period" and imagine it as a time "when Muslim women were more visible in the public sphere, took part in humanitarian, social, and political activities with men, and were prominent in religious education."[33] We know little about the early period of Islam, though it is not implausible that early Islamic society might have been more fluid, and that there was a hardening of male control over time.[34] Speaking of "the gender egalitarianism of the early period," however, is not an accurate historical description but an attempt to claim Islamist myths for women.

Islamic feminists also make use of ambiguities and lack of clarity in the Quran. The sacred texts are not as univocal as orthodoxy has presumed, and they harbor possibilities for alternative interpretations. Some-times, as with men marrying up to four wives, this is a matter of claiming that a verse was intended only for the circumstances at the time and place of revelation, and that the Quran improved the condition of women by restricting the number men could marry. Sometimes, the scope of a verse can be limited. For example, religious scholars have usually interpreted the statement in 2 The Cow 228, that "men have a rank above" women, to mean that men are superior to women in general. Amina Wadud-Muhsin, an American scholar of Islam, points out that this verse occurs in a discus-sion of marriage and divorce, and argues that it should be understood to give men the advantage only in the narrow context of divorce.[35]

The scriptural warrant of even the most widespread customs can be less than solid. Traditionally, religious authorities have required women to cover up due to 24 Light 31, which starts with "And tell the believing women to lower their eyes and guard their privates, and not show their ornaments except the obvious ones, and to draw their coverings over their breasts and not show their graces except to their husbands, or their fathers, or their husbands' fathers, or their sons" and on to a long list of people who are allowed to see "the nakedness of women." This commands modesty in public, but there is nothing here about covering the head, or the detailed regulations about covering all but the hands and the face that appears in the legal tradition. Also, 33 The Confederates 53 asks believers to interact with the wives of the Prophet "from behind a screen"; 59 says "O Prophet, tell your wives, your daughters, and the believing women to put on their outer garments; that is most convenient so they will be recognized and not molested." The details of these "outer garments" are supplied by later tradition. Usually interpreters have extended the Quran's commands con-cerning the Prophet's wives to all Muslim women, but this is also open to challenge.

Some verses are more difficult, as with 4 Women 34, where the Quran appears to endorse wife-beating. Asma Barlas, an American academic exiled from Pakistan, questions whether the Arabic necessarily means hitting a wife, concluding that "the fact that there are so many different readings of this [verse] means that it is ambiguous and, to that extent, we should be willing to rethink our commitment to its centrality in our own understanding of the Qur'ān's teachings, as well as an exegesis that reads sexual inequality and husband privilege into the Qur'ān."[36]

Even so, why should Muslims prefer these new readings of the Quran? Islamic feminists often follow reforming theologians such as Fazlur Rahman and argue that the Quran's themes include justice and equality. Or, as Leila Ahmed puts it, we can recover the "ethical egalitarianism" found in early Islam that has traces in the Quran.[37] This overall context—drawn, Islamic feminists claim, from the Quran itself, not the prejudices of medieval men—means that verses that appear to affirm male dominance should be reread in a gender-egalitarian fashion.

This argument heavily relies on those verses in the Quran that treat women and men primarily as believers, even if they happen to have different social roles. A favorite is 33 The Confederates 35, since it lists the same characteristics of a pious believer for both men and women. And 4 Women 124 proclaims that "if any do good deeds, whether they are male or female, and they are believers, then they will enter the Garden, and will not be mistreated at all." The Quran also famously goes into some detail about the pleasures of the Garden from a male perspective, but Islamic feminists think that such verses must be metaphorical, or that they address the patriarchal Arab men who first received the revelation, or that in any case the Quran does not say that women will not receive similar rewards.

Then there are verses such as 4 Women 1:

> Oh humankind,
> be conscious of your Lord,
> who created you from one soul,
> and created its mate from it,
> and propagated from the two
> many men and women.
> And be conscious of God,
> by whom you ask of each other;
> and of relationships;
> for God is watching you.

Barlas and Wadud-Muhsin take them to mean that whatever the biological and functional differences between women and men, they are created as metaphysical equals. Neither is ultimately inferior or superior, and piety is, in the end, what matters.[38]

Now, all of this is as plausible a reading of the Quran as any. Feminist interpretations of the sacred texts involve some contortions. They impose prior convictions on the texts in the guise of overall themes. But then, religious engagement with obscure, sometimes almost-incomprehensible texts like the Quran is always an act of creating meaning. Pious people can get sacred texts to say what they want—from my infidel point of view, I am more interested in the results. Metaphysical equality, for example, does not mean much. Christian scriptures also contain affirmations of equality, as with Galatians 3:28, "There is neither Jew nor Greek, there is neither slave nor free, there is no male and female, for you are all one in Christ Jesus." But it also has 1 Corinthians 11:3, "the head of a wife is her husband," and 1 Corinthians 14:34, "the women should keep silent in the churches. For they are not permitted to speak, but should be in submission, as the Law also says." Ultimate equality in heaven together with hierarchy on Earth is a common-enough monotheistic conceit. Religions are made by people, not by texts, and practices vary widely. What would Islamic feminism mean in practice?

Islamic feminism has important conservative aspects, especially when it remains close to the texts. Metaphysical equality is all very well, but it is hard to set aside the concrete prescriptions of the Quran, where it differentiates between male and female roles and assumes that authority belongs to the male. Wadud-Muhsin, for example, has to resort to the common apologetic for the half share women get in inheritance: "there is a reciprocity between privileges and responsibilities. Men have the responsibility of paying out of their wealth for the support of women, and they are consequently granted a double share of inheritance."[39] Indeed, Islamic feminists tend to present an ideal of separate but equal roles working in line with female interests. Wadud-Muhsin accepts that women have a primary responsibility in childbearing, stating that "ideally, *everything* she needs to fulfill her primary responsibility comfortably should be supplied in society, by the male: this means physical protection as well as material sustenance."[40] Men are not to be lords and masters, but properly disciplined caretakers and providers. And since ideals are difficult to realize, there has to be some flexibility and balance in applying the rules. There is little here that challenges modern conservative views of gender roles and religion.

Another option might be to follow Leila Ahmed, downplaying texts and emphasizing a selectively defined "ethical voice" of Islam favorable to women. This has a more radical potential, if only because a vague cosmic benevolence can be more easily shaped according to feminist purposes. Just as liberal Christians ignore the Bible's commands that women should submit, liberal Muslims would use the sacred texts as a repository of traditions that can be freely reinterpreted or discarded. Older generations of westernized feminists often, in effect, did exactly this—though today's feminists, including Ahmed, often distance themselves from the "colonized consciousness" and cultural inauthenticity of early Muslim feminists.[41]

The prospects for such a liberal Islam, however, are not certain. Liberal Christians and Reform Jews were able to institutionalize their liberal outlook. Independent denominations that trained their own clergy and were responsive to their congregations helped ease their break with conservatives. If Islamic feminism is to be more than an academic preoccupation, it needs to be institutionalized. And Islam does not have a denomination or church-like structure.

One possibility is to have women more closely involved with the established institutions of Islam. Religious-studies scholar Pieternella Van Doorn-Harder observes that Indonesia provides a unique example: "Indonesia has thousands of institutions where women can become specialists in Islam. . . . Not only can these women debate with extremist Muslim groups who propose a different interpretation of the holy texts concerning gender issues, they participate equally in the interpretation and reinterpretation of these texts."[42] Judges in Islamic courts include a significant number of women, and women can get degrees certifying their expertise from Islamic state universities. Indeed, women in Islamic education have begun to outnumber men.[43] Indonesian women in religious institutions tend to emphasize the complementary, separate roles of women. Nonetheless, they are an important barrier to more oppressive views of male control.

Another avenue for Islamic feminism is through nongovernmental organizations. For example, in an interview, Zakia Nizami Soman of the Bharatiya Muslim Mahila Andolan, an Indian Muslim women's rights group, says that

> Islam speaks of a God who is just. The Quran has given women equal rights and equal dignity. We are as much God's followers as men are. The problem arises not from the Quran but from distorted, patriarchal inter-pretations of the Quran and other texts by some sections of the ulema. This is something that we have to fight against. Islam is a religion of justice. So, how, if it is interpreted properly, can it discriminate against women? For us, religion is something between the individual and God, a belief grounded in the faith that God cannot be unjust towards women. So, even if a thousand maulvis stand up and demand that women are inferior and that we should remain shut in their homes we will refuse to listen to them.[44]

Such organizations can attract local suspicion, particularly when they depend on Western funding. But in many cases, they can effect change at the grassroots by affirming complementary gender roles but restricting male authority. Especially rural women often think they need to submit even to abusive husbands, and Islamic feminism can provide religious reasons for them to believe otherwise.

Islamic feminism need not lead in a secular liberal direction—it is not likely to change scenes of groups of women shrouded in black, wading on a beach. Community and family, rather than a secular liberal conception of individual autonomy, remain at its center. But Islamic feminism can help support tangible improvements in the lives of women. This is no small thing.

WHAT DO WOMEN WANT?

Islamic feminism may help some women. But from a secular liberal point of view, its conservative aspects raise eyebrows. Retaining the overall framework of divine laws and trying to make separate-but-equal work falls short of the fuller equality envisioned by liberals. Finding more room to breathe within a male-dominated religious tradition is not liberation. Tinkering with the rules of a community is not the same as developing an expansive sense of individual autonomy.

The difficulties presented by Islamic feminism become especially clear when it takes on an apologetic role. Arguing that Muslim women's interests are best recognized within a mildly reinterpreted set of religious rules can get in the way of establishing and enforcing a universally applicable framework for women's rights. British human-rights activist Pragna Patel encounters Islamic feminism as an ally of religious Right movements seeking state recognition for minority Muslim identities, and argues:

> The critical point that is ignored is that female agency is constrained and framed through religious forces and that what we are witness to is the unfolding of a bigger power struggle for the control of female sexuality and women's freedoms and rights more generally—a central goal of all religious-right projects. This is the danger that religious feminists do not recognise but ordinary women engaged in struggles for greater freedom in the private sphere so readily recognise.[45]

Conservative Islamic communities deny women freedom—not just in the sense of overt restrictions, but also by constricting women's opportunities to develop as autonomous individuals. Still, autonomy is a somewhat abstract concern. Freedom starts with women's capabilities to get what they want. And very often, what women want comes wrapped up in religion.

Women are, statistically speaking, more religious than men. As philosopher Robert N. McCauley observes, "Regardless of the stage of life in question and, in nearly all cases, regardless of the kind of religious system and accordant beliefs at stake, women express interest in religion, affirm personal religious commitment, attend religious services, read religious materials, and pray more frequently than men."[46] Surveys of Muslims fit the same pattern. Being female corresponds to slightly greater religiosity, with slightly less enthusiasm for the traditional patriarchal rules.[47] Worldwide, most people are religious, and women especially so. Their ideals and aspirations are inseparable from their religiosity.

The reasons for women's higher religiosity are unknown. Evolutionary psychology may offer some explanations, but these are highly speculative. It is, however, clear that subordinated groups are usually more religious, and that improved material security, autonomy, and education are correlated with weaker religiosity.[48] More individual power means less reliance on traditional, religiously defined forms of community. Furthermore, traditional gender roles assign women heavy responsibilities in providing care and in maintaining social ties. So women are often more religious, and many are attracted to those varieties of conservatism that promise to discipline men and make both women and men useful to the community.

Women's religious conservatism is not just a Muslim phenomenon. Feminists in English-speaking countries have faced plenty of opposition from religious women, from the struggle to win the vote to the failure of the Equal Rights Amendment in the United States. Nineteenth-century liberals and secularists worried whether, since women were more religious, giving women the vote would strengthen religious conservatism.[49] In Catholic countries in Europe, such as Spain, Portugal, and France, secular leftists long opposed the enfranchisement of women, as most women were solidly supportive of the Church. Indeed, women often supported the Catholic Right once they were able to vote. In theocratic Iran, the all-male religious establishment has not felt a threat from women being allowed to vote.

Liberal feminism aspires for women to enjoy individual autonomy, but it does not speak for women in general. Devout Muslim women do not want the sort of liberation promoted by Western feminism. Anthropologist Lila Abu Lughod says that

> I have done fieldwork in Egypt over more than 20 years and I cannot think of a single woman I know, from the poorest rural to the most educated cosmopolitan, who has ever expressed envy of US women, women they tend to perceive as bereft of community, vulnerable to sexual violence and social anomie, driven by individual success rather than morality, or strangely disrespectful of God.[50]

Still, there is more to the story. Looking only at the preferences women express can make us underestimate how, until recently, male dominance was nearly total. The means of self-definition available to women have all affirmed their subordination.[51] What women say they want is limited by their constricted set of options in life. A feminist politics, then, may need to be oriented toward expanding women's horizons, toward letting women develop a fuller autonomy.

Consider, for example, honor-based societies, where families are compelled to kill women who transgress sexually. From the outside, these appear to be unequivocally oppressive toward women. Some on the inside agree; after many an honor killing a mother will rage and call for God's wrath upon her husband who killed his own daughter. But by and large, both women and men in such societies internalize the overwhelming value of honor. Women fully participate in endorsing and enforcing the policing of honor; even victims often think of themselves as deserving to die. I react to this with bewilderment as well as horror—such codes of honor seem doubly oppressive, not just due to the savagery of their punishments, but also by how their victims appear to have their judge and executioner installed in their own heads.

Criticizing an honor-based society is difficult when the value of female honor is internalized and affirmed by its participants, even though we do have some resources that can help.[52] Nonetheless, from the outside, it is reasonably clear that any movement looking to improve the lives of women will oppose the most violent honor-based practices. Secular feminists will support more autonomy for women, expecting that women who affirm and enforce an ethic of honor will then change their views. Islamic feminists will seek resources in their religion to mobilize against a tyranny of honor.

But then, what about women's experiences of Islam, even an Islam where women are subordinate, where no overt oppression is involved? Women have often participated in religion through informal networks of female kin and friends, in events with women preachers, poetry, Quran recitals, and rituals from which men are excluded. Even in more modern, urban settings, women often find an echo of these networks through female study groups. Such enactments of piety do not challenge male authority, since these groups usually emphasize purity and the women's domain of family, remaining within the rules. And the sacred texts, though not always in the foreground, are always present. Quranic stories and stories from the traditions about female role models, such as the wives of the Prophet and his daughter, are still central to how women today imagine themselves as pious Muslims.

Anthropologist Saba Mahmood describes her research involving such a study group, which was part of the women's mosque movement in Cairo. The women involved engage with the texts beyond what women would have traditionally done, and penetrate male-dominated religious institutions, but they also uphold submission as a goal. In particular, the women "seek to cultivate virtues that are associated with female passivity and submissiveness," including "shyness, modesty, perseverance, and humility."[53] Muslim tradition encourages patience and endurance in the face of adversity for men as well: a believer must submit to the divine will, accepting that it expresses a wisdom that cannot be fully understood by human reasoning. However, the shyness and submissiveness involved makes the virtue of patience different for women.

What women in such study groups do is not mere acquiescence, and neither is it an uncomplicated subversion of male-dominated religion. Their reason for engagement is to deepen their piety—they want to develop their selves in a manner that better reflects the virtues appropriate for pious women. Acts like wearing the veil, even if one does not want it at first, are parts of this training. Obeying divine commands, such as veiling, eventually comes willingly. Following the rules does not just train souls but partly constitutes piety.

For such women, submission is part of a religious process of disciplining and shaping the self. They display agency, free choice, and active endorsement of their religious discipline, and even make themselves present in historically male public religious institutions. But they do not cultivate personal autonomy as secular liberals understand it. The freedom they seek is the freedom to submit. Their experience casts doubt on how secular liberal feminists assume that autonomy is a universal goal.[54]

Anthropologist Sylva Frisk observes that Malay women who take the veil express the reasons for their decision in similar terms:

The practice of veiling was an important part of women's efforts to become pious persons in the sense of drawing closer to God. Women who covered emphasized the veil as something that was required of them by God. To cover was seen as an important everyday act of obedience to God's will. Through veiling they manifested their submission to God, but veiling was also a means whereby an awareness of God was created and upheld. Women explained that when they were covered they were "closing" their persons to some things in the world, but as they "closed" to those things, they also experienced that they opened themselves to God.[55]

Turning to the Islam of European minorities that challenges human-rights activists, we can find similar themes of a construction of pious selves. When young Muslims take up the veil and call for Islamic law in Europe, they do not follow tradition. Instead, they usually adopt a globalized, scripture-centered Islam stripped of local idiosyncrasies and interpretive complexities. They emphasize individual study and prayer, and they try to return to the sacred sources. As with the world of youth culture and consumer choice that they inhabit, their style of faith and assertion of identity owes much to liberal individualism.[56] Nonetheless, historian Joan Wallach Scott observes that with this form of religiosity, distinctions between private and public and the liberal orientation toward autonomy tend to break down: "the self is not constituted by its own authority but by religious norms."[57] All analysis aside, according to many Muslims, living according to the religious rules is the will of God. Making free choices is an important part of the story of how such Muslims construct religious selves, but they do not choose to become autonomous in a secular liberal sense.

Whatever we might think of the choices made by Muslims who want to train themselves into increasing piety, unlike the honor killing example, they hardly seem oppressed. If their choices are constrained, that is true for everyone, including secular liberals. Often maturity involves making the best of what is not chosen, even if it is just accepting the responsibilities that accompany giving care or belonging to a community. We still might want to achieve a world in which more of us embrace the kind of individual autonomy secular liberals care about. But today, a more pious life is attractive to many, sometimes precisely because it involves subordinating the self to a goal that transcends worldly purposes.

TRUTH AND FAITH

Women covered up and veiled, like those in the "joyless" photo in the *Daily Mail*, make me uncomfortable. Those of us who grew up secular in a Muslim country often define ourselves against the religious rules. Veiled women or bearded men in skullcaps and robes remind us of a social order we want to escape. We develop an aesthetic aversion.

Veils also, however, elicit confusion. On the one hand, it seems women are deprived of freedom, which invites some solidarity against oppression. On the beach, being all covered up restricts movement; such clothes hardly seem appropriate for frolicking. Veiled women are denied the pleasures of running and swimming unencumbered. On the other hand, particularly if the women cover up as an act of piety, it may be none of my business. Moreover, in the "joyless" photo, the women appear to be having fun. They are not dispersed but standing close to one another, even though there is room to spread out. Devout Muslims may well say that this is exactly the point: a day at the beach is a happy occasion for an extended family. They might look at a beach full of half-naked Westerners and point out the rarity of large family groups—it is a sad scene of individual isolation.

They would add that the restrictive clothing is not an arbitrary imposition. In the family compound, free from the public gaze, the bulky clothes would come off. But in a public environment full of temptations and dangers, protective measures are necessary. The family is the proper setting for a fully human, emotionally satisfying life. A traditional Muslim might see liberal Westerners as acquisitive automatons, pursuing individual ambitions, oppressed by their lack of strong human connections but not even aware of the fact.

Defending the traditional family is, after all, a common conservative theme. Monotheists of all faiths accuse secular liberals of undermining families. Liberals evidently attempt to redefine the family, inviting state intervention in institutions formed through tradition, within civil society. We turn what is supposed to be a sacred union for the purpose of producing and raising children into an arrangement to serve personal interests— yet another contract between autonomous individuals. "But to reduce familial existence to a series of contractual arrangements," philosopher David Novak writes, "is to belittle it and to detract from the richness of an existence many people very much desire."[58] Furthermore, privileging autonomy, liberals downplay the needs of the vulnerable: the young, the old, the infirm. Therefore we also do not value giving care, which has traditionally been women's work, done within families.

Normally, I would try to come up with a carefully reasoned response to such charges. After all, conservative criticism does have a point. Much of the success a secular liberal outlook has enjoyed has come within increasingly market-based societies. Gender equality is most obvious among educated professionals who can afford to buy care such as nannies, visits to the doctor, and cleaning services. We *do* have a tendency to overlook caregiving in how we imagine autonomy. And yet, many secular liberals also care about richly textured personal relationships and do not want them engulfed by contracts. We might even try to turn the table on conservatives. If putting a price on everything we value is a problem, the conservative tendency to celebrate market-derived power but also attempt to set aside families as protected zones is hardly a solution. We liberals have our own ideas—many conflicting, rival ideas—about how to tame markets so that they may be our tools rather than our masters. Autonomy might require a measure of freedom from commercial and contractual imperatives as well as from tradition and predetermined hierarchies.

Nonetheless, there is something here that cuts deeper than a political argument. Conservatives and liberals do not, I think, agree on what we want or what we need. Instead, we care about some very different things, and much of our personal identities are invested in what we care about. We are not entirely settled in our ways—conservative Muslims can see the temptations of secular liberal ways of life, and liberals can appreciate the satisfactions of close-knit communities. We desire many possible goods, but as with family and professional success, they often overlap and conflict, and none come without demands on our time and resources. We cannot be both the matriarch of a large extended family and a globe-trotting journalist. As we negotiate a balance between different and incommensurable values, arguments have some power to move us. But sometimes we ask for too much from a reasoning process. We cannot make a completely reasoned choice about who we are and what we care about.

Strong religiosity demonstrates these limits of reason. Consider someone training herself in the traditional religious virtues. We can recognize the self-discipline demanded by such an effort. Less obvious, perhaps, are the pleasures of religious ways of life: how piety is often entwined with fierce loyalty, a conviction of divine love, and flashes of joy in the midst of hardship. For an infidel such as myself, that sort of loyalty compromises autonomy, the love does not have a genuine object, and the joy is misplaced. I stand on the outside, adopting a critical stance, always somewhat disengaged, never entirely submerging myself in faith.[59] But for a committed religious person, that may be exactly the wrong attitude toward a personal God. Love—divine love no less than human love—demands us to surrender, to let go of the self, to fully commit. Indeed, human love is an analogue, a shadow of divine love, helping us to get closer to the infinite. And in turn, the love and fear of God is not a free-floating emotion but an anchor for our worldly loves and loyalties toward family and community.

Perhaps, then, while the rules give Islam structure, the heart of faith is expressed by the mystical poetry so beloved in Muslim lands. A pious woman trains herself in submissiveness and feels that she has opened up to God. A theologian treats the sacred sources as communication from "the beloved"; the texts are there not to be analyzed as historical artifacts but to be encountered with awe and in reverence. The supernatural is revealed through a life of prayer and devotion, which makes doubting God as artificial as questioning the reality of the moon. Hints of the unseen realities shine through into our mundane world when we admire the selflessness of a saint, lose ourselves in a Quran recitation, or quell our rebellious spirits to live as God intended. To strike out in search of autonomy is to needlessly distance oneself from divine love.[60]

Now, I am an infidel—I am not convinced. From a critical distance, setting theological claims in the context of love and loyalty is an impressive trick, but it is a trick nonetheless.[61] I see no reason why a critical approach, which is so fruitful in seeking truth, should be abandoned with religion. Nonetheless, such tricks highlight how arguments about religion are not just about alternative explanations or theoretical truth. They are also about who we are, what we care about. Even caring about truth, demanding that religious claims should be evaluated through criticism that calls on our best scientific and philosophical skills, has important costs and conflicts with other goods we often desire.[62] And how we weigh these costs is not independent of what we happen to care about.

Again, this does not mean that trying to reason about our differences is futile. We all constantly make readjustments and compromises, seeking to balance conflicting values. Traditional religiosity is full of reinterpretation, and liberal religious people abound. But local adjustments have limits. My point of reflective equilibrium is close to a godless secular stereotype. A religious way of life has no attraction to me. If I were to come to faith, I would have to undergo a radical conversion. And I expect that many, perhaps most devout Muslims are well-satisfied with their way of life and would be unsettled very little by any criticism I can offer.

All of this makes the universal claims of liberal politics difficult to sustain. The secular liberal political tradition gives a central role to the public exercise of reason. We assume that autonomy is a universal good desired by all, and the more the better. We also accept that autonomous individuals will make widely varying choices, and we are reluctant to interfere with such choices. Usually we handle the tension between reason and choice by separating public from private. In public, reasons available to all must rule. In private, arbitrary commitments may prevail. But such a social order has to be populated by a particular sort of autonomous selves. And a liberal order is stable only to the extent that it reproduces and even deepens most individuals' capabilities for autonomous choice. Our religious traditions usually encourage us to construct rather different selves. It is difficult to say that strongly religious selves manifest wrong, rather than just different, also coherent and reflectively stable ways of life.

In that case, how do we live together? We could, possibly, accept that people will cluster around different, often overlapping ways of life, and recognize that modern societies will harbor many cohesive groups as well as autonomous individuals. A reasonable extension of liberalism might demand that we not just tolerate one another, but also affirm diversity and extend our fullest respect to those different ways of life that join in peaceful coexistence.[63]

Respect, however, may be too much to demand. Secular liberals and religious conservatives also have deep conflicts of interest, particularly about how we arrange our public spheres. For devout Muslims, including Islamic feminists, piety comes first: nonbelievers such as me are bound for hell. They cannot warmly affirm my sinful state without harm to the integrity of their way of life. And in my turn I cannot, even with all the sympathy to strongly held faith that I can muster, celebrate women wading on a beach all covered up.

Those of us with a secular liberal perspective can still oppose those varieties of Islam that subordinate women. But if we do so, this is not because devout women are unambiguously oppressed or because autonomy has to be an overriding value for all ways of life. We resist conservative Islamic ideals because in the political rivalry between pious modernities and secular liberal modernity, we happen to belong to the secular liberal side. Historically, our kind of identity was forged in contest with strong religion. Acting according to our interests and aspirations means striving to maintain and expand social spaces that support individual autonomy.

ACCOMMODATING ISLAM

What, then, about Muslim demands on public space? When conservative Muslims are a minority, or if they cannot command a political consensus, they often ask to be accommodated. In public education, for example, Muslim families might ask for their children to be allowed to wear headscarves, to be excused from gym class, or not to be required to learn about evolution. A patient may insist on a doctor of the same sex at a public hospital. Or a Muslim community may request a public pool to set aside times where only women or only men are allowed to use the facility. On the one hand, accommodating religious concerns seems reasonable. After all, people of faith also pay taxes, so public institutions have to serve their needs. On the other hand, acceding to many of these requests would sacrifice the *common* nature of public spaces.

The Anglo-American political tradition favors accommodating religion. Conservatives usually support religious communities and are suspicious of the state. If all schools, hospitals, and pools were private, the communities running these institutions could decide on their own rules. But if we have to have public spaces, religious freedom demands that faith should not be an obstacle to access. Our liberals emphasize free choice but often end up in a similar position. Provided that they are not forced and do not harm anyone else, religious choices should be accommodated.

And so, when approaching the question of headscarves or segregating the sexes, American liberals start by asking whether the choice is genuinely free or coerced. Does a student cover herself to express a sincere faith, or is she acting under family and community pressure? When the French ban full veiling in public spaces, we see coercion at work. Acting against headscarves is state interference in personal decisions, which is not what we want in a liberal environment. Indeed, Muslim advocacy groups often use liberal rhetoric, portraying religious obligations as private choices.

Our emphasis on choice, however, makes American liberals treat religious observances like options available to a consumer. While this might work for a New Age pastiche of spirituality, it hardly makes sense of the community and coherence involved in more traditional religions. Nor do we recognize how close family and community ties inevitably have coercive aspects. Community pressure will be worrisome for some women, but for others, pressure will be a reassuring sign of collective commitment to a moral ideal. When we treat religion like a choice of toothpaste, we overlook how autonomy is not an impossible absence of constraint but a condition that needs nurturing and support. Indeed, we assume faith is an individual choice when what is at stake may be whether one should be a liberal individualist at all. What sense does choice of dress style make if the point is to immerse oneself in a communal sense of the sacred so that obedience, not choice, becomes a central virtue?

In contrast, secular liberals in the French tradition usually defend the secularity of public space and the mixing of the sexes as important goods. French secularism harbors a suspicion of traditional communities and associated intermediate institutions as possible obstacles to individual autonomy. With the right policies, the state can help develop autonomy. As anthropologist John R. Bowen observes,

> If the American insistence on freedom of choice assumes the possibility of choosing, and thus sees the matter as a private one, the French emphasis on autonomy and dignity sees it as the state's obligation to take steps to create the conditions for meaningful choice. From an autonomy perspective, "choice" appears as a naively thin concept.[64]

Veiling is not just a personal choice but an enactment of gender segregation in public spaces. It is not politically neutral—there are important public interests at stake.

In fact, the politics of the veil is full of complexities that are not often appreciated by commentators who favor a morality tale about state coercion and personal choice. In France, veiling is often associated with conservative Muslim communities maintaining separation from the wider society and trying to control their women. Hence bans on veiling have drawn considerable support as well as criticism from secular feminists and liberal Muslims.[65] In Turkey, headscarf bans in public spaces have often been criticized by postmodern conservatives, who see the struggle to allow veiling as a democratic contesting of an autocratic state. And so it was—devout women engaged in activism to win rights for themselves. But demands for freedom for headscarves were also part of a process of constructing neoliberal, religiously legitimated forms of public authority.[66]

Today, some secular Turkish women have begun to keep a headscarf in their cars, just in case they run into a traffic checkpoint. The police are often religiously conservative, so when a woman drives by with a headscarf on, she may be less likely to be stopped.[67] Again, asking about whether covering up is a free choice does not help in such situations. Both wearing and not wearing a headscarf are complicated options that are never as simple as an expression of faith or a fashion choice.

With all these complexities, it is difficult to guess the future of veiling. Conservative views of gender are strong among Muslim populations worldwide. Muslims remain resistant to reproductive rights, homosexuality, and sex outside of marriage.[68] Even as modern economies have eroded extended family ties, a hierarchical family structure that disciplines both women and men remains a strong ideal institutionalized by custom and law. Conservative Muslim gender politics are part of a global religious Right, where headscarves are only a particularly visible symbol of traditional roles.

But then, the religious Right does not represent all Muslims. Conservatism is wide and deep, but it has cracks. Muslim women are becoming more educated. Even conservatives can support education, saying that an educated woman will be a better mother to her children and a better helpmate to her husband.[69] Women are active in Islamist politics. I find it hard to imagine that so many educated women will remain content with more sophisticated motherhood and support roles in political movements.

The increasing public presence of Muslim women does not mean that Muslim majorities will inevitably move beyond separate-but-equal toward views that go as far as gay marriage. The continual praise I see among Western liberals for Islamic feminism is also an admission of defeat for a liberal politics that used to aspire to break free of the sacred. Still, the history of Western feminism suggests that things can change. American suffragists rejected their more radical colleagues who criticized Christianity, but they also used notions of women's piety and domestic purity to claim a public voice. And until just a generation or two ago, it would have been absurd to claim gender equality and sexual freedom as "Western values."

The prospects for more liberal attitudes toward gender depend on the viability of liberal versions of Islam. After all, in Western countries, if liberal attitudes have put down roots, it is not because of a tiny minority of secular extremists like me but because of liberal Christians and Jews, the indifferent, those with mixed loyalties. Educated elites in some countries such as Turkey have often sustained such a liberal Islam. Indeed, I admit that I prefer this older style of liberal Islam that ignores the texts and picks and chooses among the rules, pretending that religion is all sweetness and light.

It has not vanished. Academic observers of Islam are too often enraptured by veiling as empowerment and authenticity, but there are no few intellectuals among Muslim women who continue to think of the veil and such customs as restrictions above all—and consider unveiling an act of liberation.[70]

I don't know whether banning the veil helps to encourage liberal attitudes. I expect not; legal intervention is a blunt instrument at best. How to accommodate strong religion in a liberal social order is a difficult question, which is usually resolved by compromises sensitive to local conditions rather than by overarching principles. But the French approach is more attractive to me than American choice-of-toothpaste liberalism.

In any case, however clumsy, bans on veiling highlight how, if we are to advance secular liberal interests, we cannot honestly claim neutrality toward strong religion. Nor can we entirely avoid coercion. Gay marriage, no less than veiling, is a public political act. It does weaken the traditional family, if only by removing its aura of being the obligatory, God-given way of things. For social conservatives deeply committed to their conception of a proper family, changes like gay marriage represent genuine losses. They rationally oppose such changes, even though their expectations of social Armageddon are overblown. And when postmodern conservatives portray French-style secularism as working against women's present interests in the name of emancipating them from the particularisms of ethnicity, religion, and family, they are not entirely wrong.

So we have reasons to be careful. I am not interested in ripping the veil from women's faces in the name of progress, as modernizers in Iran once did. And any reasons I can offer for more subtly discouraging veils are not likely to move anyone who does not already have secular liberal sympathies. Those reasons, however, will have to be enough.

ISLAM VERSUS SECULARISM

THE AFFAIRS OF THIS WORLD

For secular liberals, including many liberal Muslims, there is a solution to the difficulties posed by conservative varieties of Islam: secularism. Muslims need, we think, a greater distance between mosque and state. It would also help if more liberal forms of Islam enjoyed a stronger social position.

In that case, believers would continue to take the Quran to be sacred, but the states Muslims live in would not favor any particular interpretation of the faith. Science and religion would attend to their separate spheres, neither trespassing on the other, and Muslims would make full use of modern knowledge. Muslim states would become just Muslim-majority countries governed by laws that address exclusively worldly concerns. Religious experts would propound rules only for those who freely choose to be members of their congregations. The meanings of gender would be socially negotiated, dictated neither by state nor by religious officials.

There is an air of nostalgia about such hopes. The Turkish secularists among whom I grew up thought they were making progress toward such a future. Secularists were few in number, but we thought we were the vanguard of a modernizing nation. Most of the population was more traditional in its religiosity, which meant that most people needed to be educated to accept a reformed faith. So in school, our teachers carefully explained secularism for us. In the shortest, most effective formulation, secularism was about separating the affairs of this world from the affairs of religion. In the public sphere, what united us was Turkish nationalism, and our leading worldly interest was to overcome the collapse of the Ottoman

Empire and fully join modern civilization. We were also supposed to be good Muslims, but that was a matter of sound morals and correct ritual acts in private life.

In practice, Turkish secularism had many oddities. Officially, everyone enjoyed freedom of worship, but it was also clear that more traditional religiosity had a second-class feel to it. Advancement in the military and civil service required a Muslim background, but it also helped if one indulged in some alcohol once in a while and had a wife who was uncovered. Furthermore, religion and state remained closely entangled. The Republic of Turkey employed an army of religious functionaries, many of whom had the awkward job of preaching orthodox doctrine while affirming a secular state. Secularists, however, saw all these as special cases and temporary measures. Western European states were closer to the universal secularist ideal. But Turkey had to catch up; meanwhile, the population had to be educated into a modernized form of religion so that they were less susceptible to the influence of ignorant preachers.

According to the secular liberal ideal we aspired to, we have to rely on reason to sort out our worldly affairs. Revelation or sanctified tradition have their place, particularly in personal morality, but these are private matters. The institutions of the state and our public affairs belong to all of us, regardless of religion. Organized religions are private associations.

Public or civic reason, in the liberal tradition, is a skill and a process available to everyone. Faith goes beyond reason and is a matter of individual conscience. Government, therefore, has no competence to decide theological disputes. And in turn, we cannot count on religious agreement when conducting the affairs of this world. After all, if a policy proposal emerges from the demands of faith alone, it cannot persuade those who do not share that faith. Without persuasion, we are left with coercion—we invite violence, even chaos. In modern societies, where religious uniformity is not possible, we have to offer nonreligious reasons if we hope to persuade others when discussing our worldly affairs. As the Sudanese liberal Abdullahi Ahmed An-Na'im puts it, we need "reasons that can be publicly debated and contested by any citizen, individually or in community with others, in accordance with norms of civility and mutual respect."[1]

A secular liberal state will show equal respect for its citizens, because its legitimacy depends on consent. Therefore the state cannot endorse any of the competing visions of a good life on offer. It has to be neutral toward religion; its basic structure cannot favor any comprehensive vision. In the political domain, the public exercise of reason can lead to a consensus on common values such as impartiality or human rights. Citizens of different faiths should be able to accommodate such political values without seriously altering their notions of the sacred.[2]

Such a secular arrangement provides for a large measure of personal and political freedom. Nonbelievers appreciate this freedom, but there can also be religious reasons to endorse a secular order. A freely chosen faith is a more authentic commitment. In places where there are religious police— Saudi Arabia, Iran, Aceh—conformity need not mean genuine commitment. A woman's headscarf reliably signals piety only when she is free to do otherwise.

This is not to say that neutrality, equal respect, and individual freedom work seamlessly together. Secular liberalism stands in tension with tight-knit communities and religions that make comprehensive demands on their adherents. For example, engaging in public reason is not a trivial skill. Citizens have to acquire the intellectual habits and basic knowledge required to join public debates. Therefore we all need a liberal education in order to exercise political freedom. This education should help citizens become independent, creative thinkers; because of this, such an education may promote skepticism about inherited faiths. But then, if the strongly religious are not to be coerced into living by a liberal order, their needs also have to be accommodated. A state may have good worldly reasons to promote a scientific understanding of health against beliefs in spiritual healing, or to have evolution rather than special creation taught in the biology classroom. But to the strongly religious, these occasions will appear like the state is interfering with their ability to live according to their faith.

In such cases, secular liberals need to balance competing interests and find some political accommodation. We hope that a public reasoning process will help sort out exactly such cases. Simply imposing the will of the majority will not do. Indeed, directly confronting religious beliefs in the classroom can be as questionable as a conservative Muslim majority deciding to ban alcohol.

Now, it may appear that nonbelievers and the liberally religious would be more comfortable with a secular political order than religious conservatives would be. Muslim supporters of secularism have usually come from among the heterodox, the less observant, and those who wear their piety lightly. However, secular liberals can still claim that separating state and religion is the best way to manage social diversity. After all, as secularists have always insisted, secularism is not state-sponsored atheism. Secular liberalism also harbors tensions with a full-blown Enlightenment rationalism. Public reason is a limited, politically circumscribed practice—it is not an attempt to push human reason as far it can go. Scientific critiques of supernatural claims or philosophical skepticism about the gods have an uncertain place in public environments sustained by a secular state.

A secular liberal order, then, is supposed to be a regime of compromise. It helps us keep the peace and allows us to attend to our common worldly affairs. And since keeping the peace depends on compromise and accommodation, secularism will play out differently in different countries and different religious environments. Indeed, Turkish secularism was once praised as an adaptation of the universal ideals of the Enlightenment to Islamic circumstances. In making the boldest attempt at separating the affairs of this world from the affairs of Islam, Turkey was to be a model for the rest of the Muslim world. Lately, however, I am more likely to read praise for how Turkey integrated religious politics with a modern economy.

VARIETIES OF SECULARISM

I would love to recommend secularism. But for Muslims, secularism has become a term of condemnation. The secular political tradition among Muslims is, by and large, a failure. Recovering anything from this tradition depends on asking why it failed and examining the kinds of compromises made in more successful varieties of secularism.

The United States, for example, is famous for its constitutional disestablishment of religion. We are supposed to have no religious tests for public office. Furthermore, in the twentieth century, constitutional interpretation shifted toward a stricter separation of church and state, where governmental institutions were prohibited from directly promoting religious beliefs or favoring religious organizations. Today, creationism cannot be taught in public science classrooms, as special creation is supposed to be an essentially religious idea. When a local government or school board endorses prayer or displays religious symbols, it risks lawsuits from civil liberties groups that demand neutrality about religious matters. Religious conservatives in the United States consider our current regime overly secular, decrying the "naked public square" left by the removal of faith.

Even so, government and religion have always been entangled in the United States. Church membership is voluntary, and it has long been understood that the federal government cannot favor one sect over another. But for much of the first two centuries of its existence, the United States supported an "informal establishment" of Protestant Christianity.[3] Most of this establishment has eroded, especially religiously motivated laws concerning personal morality, Sunday closings, alcohol restrictions, and school prayer. But religious organizations are still not burdened by taxes, even though they make significant demands on public resources.[4] Governments at all levels often provide services indirectly, through grants to private contractors. Faith-based organizations play a large role in social services and include religious activities in their operations. State support for faith-based charitable organizations is therefore another way to channel public money to religion.[5] In highly conservative areas of the country, such as the South, state governments can be so shot through with religion that philosopher Barbara Forrest describes their condition as a "de facto 'general theocracy.'"[6] Moreover, recently, the dominant interpretation of the constitution has moved away from strict separation toward a broader accommodation of religious institutions, where government may provide aid to religions but cannot treat any religion more favorably than another.[7]

Like its British cousin, American secularism has significant conservative aspects. The Anglo-American political tradition values religion as a source of community cohesion and as a check on state power. The British maintain lightweight established churches and fund "faith schools" of diverse sects, while Americans prefer more indirect means. But in either case, Anglo-American secularism allows state support for religion in general. Furthermore, this is a secularism that tends to conceive of religious freedom not just as an individual liberty, but also as the freedom of religious institutions from state interference. For example, the desire of religious organizations to enforce conservative reproductive morality has presented an obstacle to even feeble reforms of the health insurance system in the United States.

Religious conservatives still harbor suspicions about Anglo-American secularism, but this is because even a weak political secularism might provide an environment favorable to secularization—a decline in religiosity and the social role of religion. Otherwise, American conservatives are happy with an institutional distance between church and state, as long as governments can still support a generic religiosity cast in a Protestant mold. Indeed, in the United States, Jews, Buddhists, and Muslims all have found it best to organize themselves in church and denomination-like bodies.[8] Anglo-American secularism promotes voluntary membership in a wide variety of sects but has difficulty recognizing a *lack* of religion.[9] Nonbelievers may elect to remain outside churches, but they also forego the indirect state support enjoyed by the religious.

French secularism, in contrast, emphasizes liberty of conscience rather than freedom of church membership, extending to freedom from religion. In French history, the defining example of religion has been a dominant Catholic church rather than multiple quarreling Protestant sects. Accordingly, French secularism includes the freedom not to belong, to publicly criticize religious faith, and to be free of religious indoctrination. Anglo-American secularism can appear as a halfhearted concession to prevent sectarian strife. French secularism actively affirms a public sphere free from religious control, and therefore can seem aggressively anticlerical.

In the French republican ideal, citizens are individuals—they set aside their collective identities such as religion and ethnicity in their interactions with the state. A common public space for political debate, then, requires a degree of conformity from citizens. As anthropologist John R. Bowen describes it,

To willingly conform, citizens must interact with each other or must participate in institutions that teach shared habits and values. Social "mixing" (*mixité*) leads people to see each other as fellow citizens rather than as tokens of particular ethnic, racial, or gendered types of person. Social mixing effaces particularistic identities and gives individuals a Republican sameness, a social anonymity in the public sphere.[10]

According to the French version of secularism, religious identity is a private matter. Citizens act politically as individuals who have different interests but who share a common civic culture, rather than acting through intermediate institutions. Indeed, the state ensures that there is space for citizens to escape from the claims of religions and other communal associations.

Creating a common civic culture falls to French republican education. Citizens are *made*—the state has to ensure that students receive an education that prepares them for public participation. This education includes the skills to challenge and debate social norms and political proposals, which cuts against the nonnegotiable rules and beliefs that often define religious and similar strong ideological identities. Close-knit community associations that exercise a strong influence over their members are therefore somewhat suspect.[11]

Such is the ideal. But religions are not golf clubs, and they cannot be reshaped into private associations freely entered into and left as a matter of convenience. Therefore the French state recognizes the power of religious organizations and regulates their influence on the public domain. Some religious movements, such as Scientology, have been prosecuted and penalized for being a "dangerous cult" and for defrauding people.[12]

Regulation requires the French state to recognize particular religions as corporate bodies. So in negotiating the public presence of Islam in France, the government has devoted much effort to form a representative body for Muslims similar to those for various Christian and Jewish sects.[13] The state maintains most Catholic churches in France, funds many religious functionaries, and subsidizes faith-based private education.

In many ways, French secularism has been remarkably successful. Anglo-American conservatives dislike the French central government's responsibility for a secular public sphere, seeing it as a manifestation of an all-powerful state, or "civic totalism."[14] American academics who study Islam, such as Jocelyne Cesari, regularly denounce French secularism as "a kind of anti-Church with ambitions to monopoly, the creed of science serving for dogma."[15] But it appears to work in France. French conservative politics usually has a culturally Catholic coloring, but today, center-right politicians rarely question the basic laws separating church and state. Moreover, secularist ideals aside, the French republic can enjoy only partial success in creating secular spaces and educating its citizens to participate in secular political deliberations. In practice, intermediate institutions and their representative bodies exist, and the French government is often entangled with religion.

Among Western varieties of secularism, Anglo-American and French secularisms have made the strongest universal claims and have often been defining examples in debates among Muslims. Other European countries have different arrangements, reflecting their historical negotiations distributing power between church and state. Germany is somewhat secular, but German public schools teach religion, public universities train theologians, and the state collects a "church tax" supporting ecclesiastical institutions. Churches enjoy tax breaks, and some social service funding is funneled through religious organizations.[16] The Netherlands and Belgium used to "pillarize" their populations into relatively isolated groups such as Protestants, Catholics, socialists—and now Muslims—determining national policy through negotiations between groups with their own social organizations, media, political parties, and sports clubs. But such varieties of managing religious diversity have been too locally specific to inspire secularists among Muslims.

Secularism is not just a Western peculiarity. India has been a secular democracy for decades, and there is a vast literature on Indian secularism. India's very large population is divided between Hindu religions and a large Muslim minority, along with smaller minorities of Christians, Zoroastrians, and many others. Indian secularism emphasizes equal respect for the religions of different communities. Mani Shankar Aiyar, a "secular fundamentalist" politician, explains that because Indians are highly religious,

Indian secularism cannot be based on the denial of religion. It has to be based on the affirmation of dharma while recognizing that dharma appears in the form of different religions (or *panth*) to different groups of Indians. Hence, *sarva dharma sambhaava* (all religions are worthy of equal respect) as the first principle of Indian secularism.[17]

Equal respect also entails separate religious laws for each community concerning personal status and family matters. Secular liberals such as Aiyar also hope that Indian religions will eventually become more liberal, eliminating gender inequalities and allowing the state to realize the constitutional goal of a uniform civil code. But in any case, equal respect means significant state support for religion, including building and maintaining pilgrimage facilities for Hindus and Muslims and sponsoring religious festivals. Indeed, equal respect can be interpreted to mean that various religious communities should have all necessary resources for cultural reproduction.[18]

The rise of Hindu nationalism, however, has thrown Indian secularism into question. Meera Nanda, a philosopher and historian of science, describes how the Indian middle class has become even more invested in public demonstrations of supernaturalism than the poor have, and how Hindu ritual observations have become a way for politicians to spend public money on religion. Secularists in postindependence India sought to promote a scientific temper, as well as hoping to achieve more gender equality and a uniform civil code. And yet, "equal respect" secularism has begotten an intensifying religiosity. Nanda observes that "the Indian brand of secularism has allowed the state to maintain an intimate and nurturing relationship with the majority religion. As the neo-liberal state has entered into a partnership with the private sector, a cosy triangular relationship has emerged between the state, the corporate sector, and the Hindu establishment."[19]

In the twentieth century, as Muslim-majority states gained independence, westernizers in power often instituted a modest degree of separation between Islam and the state. They promoted nationalism and attempted to bring religious institutions under state control. Throughout the Middle East, and especially in Syria, Tunisia, Turkey, and Iran, many secularists were inspired by the French example. But later in the twentieth century, the middle classes and elites, as well as the impoverished, turned toward increasingly religious ideologies of social order. The trajectory of Muslim secularism has come to resemble that of India.

SECULARISM WITH A MUSLIM FACE

Secularism arose in Christendom and has found its most stable expressions in Western countries where the influence of Christianity has declined. It is a solution to political problems that arose in negotiating the balance between church and state, not mosque and state. The ideas of secularism developed in a Christian context. Perhaps secularism is, in a backhanded way, an expression of Christian culture.[20]

There is some truth here. As with natural science, capitalist economies, or representative democracy, there are many features of secular modernity that bear the marks of their western European development. They are, nonetheless, open to appropriation. Bernard Lewis links secularism to Christian doctrine about giving God and Caesar their separate dues, while Islam does not distinguish between the domains of religion and state.[21] Yet for most of the history of Christendom, the lines between church and state have not been clear. And Muslim dynasties have had plenty of occasions to overlook religious principles for reasons of state. Doctrine is not destiny, and how the past is imagined is politically very important. Present interpretations are often rationalizations after the fact. For example, Muslims often cite 42 Consultation 38, "and those who hearken to their Lord, and practice regular prayer, and conduct their business by mutual consultation, and give of what we have provided them," as a divine endorsement of elections and representative government. Such an interpretation is strained, and yet it is widely accepted.

Still, history matters. Secularism among Muslims arose in different circumstances and faces different prospects today.

Secularists usually start their story in Western Christendom, with contests between pope and emperor, and power struggles between local princes and the Catholic Church. They focus on the Protestant Reformation and the following wars of religion. As a result of that bitter experience, Western thinkers began to contemplate separating politics from political theology. They sought to achieve a worldly order independent of divine commands.[22]

Emphasizing how a secular political imagination emerged, however, can be misleading. The wars that convulsed Europe in the sixteenth century involved religion, but mainly because religion was central to questions of loyalty. The wars of religion took place as increasingly centralized states consolidated power against rivals such as the nobility and the Catholic Church. Catholic and Protestant rulers fought one another, but they also entered alliances. For secularists, this period of western European history inspired secular political thought. But for many conservatives and Catholic historians, the main theme of this history is the rise of an absolutist state that took control of religion in its territory and prevented checks on its power. Secularists, in this view, propagate a myth of sectarian violence arising from the uncompromising demands of faith, thereby legitimating central state control. Instead, the strife of the early modern period was due to emerging modern states establishing local monopolies on violence.[23]

In any case, the European states that emerged from the wars of religion were not overly secular by today's standards. Instead of separating religion from government, early modern states tended to control religious institutions and support religiosity as a foundation of social order. Increasing institutional complexity and a clearer conceptual separation between worldly and religious affairs made changes toward political secularism possible. But religion remained important for political legitimacy, central to education, and deeply entangled with government. Modern states could, occasionally, still be considered instruments of religion. Imperial expansion was, as always, mainly due to the prospects of worldly gain. But imperial power was also supposed to spread the Gospel or propagate Christian civilization in its modern form.

Anglo-American secularists often look back to political philosophers such as John Locke and Thomas Hobbes, emphasizing their themes of toleration, the exclusive legitimacy of worldly reasons in politics, and the need for a powerful state to prevent internal violence. But even in the nineteenth century, some distance between religious and governmental institutions in the British Empire and the United States existed together with immense Protestant influence on laws, education, and the political imagination. The French reestablished Catholicism soon after their revolution, under tighter state control. The relationship between religion and state in France continued to be contentious well into the twentieth century. Secular political thought may have arrived, but conservative political theology also flourished.

Secular Europe was born out of political struggles. Ruling elites had to confront demands about the status of minorities such as Jews,[24] religiously motivated restraints on economic activity, or the freedom of speech desired by political and social radicals. Since the Catholic Church supported established power structures, French left-wing politics had an anticlerical bent, seeking restrictions on church influence and aiming to secularize education. British liberals and radicals struggled against laws punishing blasphemy and obscenity, and protested restrictions on nonreligious representation in Parliament. Above all, as modern nationalism inspired popular loyalty and became the basis for state legitimacy, the idea of secular government took shape in the context of attempts to define the nation.

Secularism was made not just by political philosophers in the Enlightenment tradition but also by politicians such as Jean Jaurès and Charles Bradlaugh and the usually left-wing social movements that demanded a more secular public sphere. States achieved control over churches, but the story of European secularism is also a story of forcing states to become more liberal. With more religiously diverse populations engaged in national politics, making religious convictions a matter for private choice and individual freedom became more attractive. Many grew disillusioned with organized religion and adopted political ideals that did not claim supernatural sanction. Different countries patched together varieties of secularism, as a way of managing religious diversity but also in response to the diminishing political influence of religion within their populations. Secularism flourished with growing secularity.

The Muslim experience has been different. The histories of early Islam tell of wars against apostasizing tribes, battles with sects that separated from the mainstream community of Islam, and the enduring split between the Sunni majority and Shia minority over the legitimate leadership of the faithful. Later, both sectarian conflict and coexistence continued, weaving through complex political configurations such as the Shia dynasties that occasionally ruled large territories with Sunni populations. In the Ottoman Empire, popular heterodox movements tinged with Sufism and Shia beliefs regularly rebelled against the Ottoman dynasty.

But while there has been a link between heterodoxy and political disloyalty in the lands of Islam, wars of religion have not loomed large in the Muslim political imagination. Conflicts between the Shia and Sunni have usually resulted in local dominance by a sect, or in the rulers and sectarian religious scholars accommodating one another. Sufi movements have mobilized large numbers, but they have typically been absorbed into orthodoxy. And wars, such as those between the Sunni Ottomans and Shia Safavids, have predominantly been imperial conflicts rather than religious disputes, even as ideals of religious purity have played a role. Stalemates resulted in rival orthodoxies, with Ottomans controlling most of the Middle East and the Safavids establishing a Shia faith in Iran. Muslim political theology usually handled religious diversity by recognizing autonomous religious communities. As long as the ruling dynasty preserved order, and as long as the communities paid their taxes, peace could prevail.[25]

As in Europe, political secularism arrived in Muslim lands together with the centralizing modern state. As Muslim states sought to resist colonial powers and modernize, their structural reforms introduced elements of secularism. As the major Middle Eastern country and the leading independent Muslim state, the Ottoman Empire led the way. Nineteenth-century reforms brought Islamic laws and institutions under more direct state control and even moved toward equal citizenship regardless of religious affiliation. Muslim political thinkers were not concerned with wars of religion, but Ottoman attempts to strengthen the state and bring local religious forms of loyalty under control had secularist consequences, much as in Europe.

Ottoman efforts to modernize floundered as the multiethnic, multireligious empire was undermined by local nationalisms. The Turkish Republic that emerged after the First World War, however, continued the

Ottoman project. A strong, centralized, modern state would bring religion under control, but unlike the lost empire, it would legitimate itself through Turkish nationalism. In this Turkish, Muslim context, secularism was similar to the European examples Turks closely followed.

Indeed, most Muslim elites struggling against colonial powers became convinced that a strong state was necessary. And as Muslim countries achieved independence, particularly after the Second World War, they typically followed the Turkish pattern. As in Turkey, nationalism came to the fore, even as nationality was often defined partly through religion. Indeed, religious minorities such as Christian Arabs were especially attracted to secular nationalisms. Militaries, as the leading national institutions, often set themselves up as guardians of secular modernization projects. Turkey remained an extreme example of removing traditional Islam from the public sphere, but Iran and Tunisia also instituted vigorous programs of secularization. Arab nationalist regimes in Iraq and Syria adopted secularism, partly as a way of containing sectarian divisions; under the mid-twentieth-century dictatorship of Gamal Abdel Nasser, Arab nationalism also dominated Egyptian politics. Even a relatively isolated country such as Afghanistan had secularizing governments. Most independent Muslim countries officially recognized Islam to some degree, while committing to some elements of political secularism as an integral part of achieving a strong, modern state.

Muslim secularism has a reputation of superficiality—it is supposed to be an ideology of military and bureaucratic elites closely associated with the state, which did not find a larger constituency and did not acquire any cultural depth. But while explicit secularism has had weak support beyond elites, nationalism has put down deeper roots, eroding traditional forms of religiosity in the process. Turkish religious conservatives still denounce the damage late Ottoman nationalists such as the Young Turks did to established Islam. Theologian Hasan Gümüşoğlu describes the Young Turks as adopting a policy of creating a Turkish nation similar to Western examples, and pursuing systematic distortions of revealed religion by trying to shape a more Turkish Islam:

The Young Turks created deep instabilities in the fundamental beliefs of Muslim society, and the Committee of Union and Progress [successors to the Young Turks] dealt a major blow to values that were already severely damaged. In the later period, on top of this wreckage, there was a policy of creating a new state and society based on Turkish nationalism. The dynamics of this state and society were fundamentally Western while different from Western models in many respects, and it was given direction by modernist, and even more, positivist and materialist thought. This policy . . . allowed a partial role for religion on the basis of "ritual and morals," and isolated religion from social life by withdrawing it to within the boundaries of individual consciences.[26]

After all, state control of religious institutions and broad-based secular education cannot help but affect expressions of religiosity. Nationalists did not have to overtly displace religion. Instead, they promised a modern, improved interpretation of faith suitable for a nation destined to recover former glories. And just as Turkish nationalism affected popular religiosity, Islam transformed nationalism. Nationalism had first attracted modernizing elites, and had opposed traditional religion as a bulwark of the old order. This opposition was soon compromised as religion became integral to the definition of the nation.[27]

Turkish nationalists went farthest in their secularism, but Turkey was not an exception. Arab nationalism was similar, in many respects, to Turkish nationalism, and it also promoted a secularization of states and societies. Arab nationalism also penetrated beyond elite circles, transforming popular mentalities and even enlisting religious figures in its cause.[28] Postcolonial Pakistan and Indonesia were led by elites who emphasized nationalism as the ideological basis of the state, relating to Islam not as an organized religion but as a shared cultural background that could define a Muslim nation.

And yet secular nationalism failed. Modernization in postcolonial Muslim-majority states was associated with massive social changes, such as migration from rural areas to the slums and industrializing areas of increasingly unmanageable cities. Secular nationalism came with growing expectations from governments, and unsteady and faltering economic development produced unmet demands. Moreover, secular policies often undermined secularist prospects. The first generation of nationalist leaders heavily invested in education, which later produced large numbers of graduates who had difficulty finding employment outside of bloated bureaucracies. With secular nationalism losing its sparkle, underemployed graduates and urban populations aspiring to social mobility became attracted to Islamist politics. As elsewhere on the globe, propertied classes allied with the emerging class of managerial technocrats, embracing neoliberalism and encouraging tamer forms of religion.[29]

The political fortunes of secularism, therefore, declined steeply. The traditional guardian of Turkish secularism, the military, was also instrumental in hollowing it out during and after a period of military rule starting in 1980. After then, Turkish politics—both status-quo conservatism and opposition varieties of Islamism—would increasingly be colored by religion. Arab nationalism never recovered from the failures of Nasser in Egypt. By the end of the twentieth century, what remained of secularism in Arab states was indelibly marked by kleptocratic dictatorships, which conceded almost all the public sphere to religious influence while acting to suppress Islamist popular movements. Acting against secular leftist political currents, Pakistan's military regime led by Muhammad Zia-ul-Haq instituted an Islamization program in the 1980s, which has had lasting effects. Indonesians massacred hundreds of thousands of leftists and communists in the mid-1960s and experienced a gradual Islamization of public life and politics in the following decades.

Muslim secularism has, indeed, been weaker than its European counterpart. Secularism has not enjoyed as much support from broad-based movements—it has been an inverted secularism, based among elites associated with a modernizing state, excluding social classes who might oppose established power structures. Moreover, secularism has been linked to authoritarian regimes rather than being associated with the liberalization of postcolonial states. Secular nationalists have often not fully tried to move religion to the private sphere, instead hoping that a suitably reformed Islam would help their nation rapidly achieve the power and wealth associated with modernity. Muslim versions of secularism have usually been political frameworks put in place without substantial secularization of societies.

So today, the lands of Islam have become the leading examples of resistance to secularism, of fervid religion in politics. Muslim versions of secularism lost in political struggles, country by country. Secularism was often undermined by the very states and militaries that at other times had nurtured it. Still, though political secularism is weak among Muslims, this is not a simple reflection of deep social realities, nor is it an inevitable manifestation of a religiosity that pervades all aspects of life. Muslim secularism had to be defeated—it did not wither away on its own.

RELIGIOUS NATIONALISM

Secular liberals worry about theocracy. In the absence of secularism, we imagine priests overseeing governments and holy texts serving as constitutions. We envision a state devoted to the sacred, which imposes a religious morality on everyone and interferes with secular lifestyles. And Islam, to us, often seems to have theocratic tendencies. After all, there are no few religious figures who announce that Islam is a complete, all-encompassing way of life that does not separate politics and piety. Everything, from bathroom habits to guidelines for taxation, comes under the religious rules that may be enforced by an Islamic state.

Moreover, as Catholic authoritarianism and state-enforced Protestant moralism have faded, Islam has appeared to move in an opposite direction. The most obvious recent examples of theocratic government come from Saudi Arabia and Iran, and the experiments with Islamic states in Sudan and Afghanistan. Since the worldwide Islamic resurgence starting in the 1970s, even countries like Malaysia, where Islam had historically been at the margins of politics, have abandoned the idea of a secular state and Islamized their public spheres.[30] After popular uprisings topple corrupt regimes, as in the Arab Spring, Islamists and fundamentalists often find an opportunity to inject more religion into politics.

Nonetheless, even a political environment saturated with Islam rarely means a clear-cut demand for theocracy. Saudi Arabia, for example, is not an inspiration for many Muslims. The Saudis have influenced the more fundamentalist orientation of many current forms of Islam, due to their funding of movements close to their puritan interpretation of religion. But fundamentalists can withdraw into their community as well as engage in national politics; most often, fundamentalists emphasize piety and Islamizing daily life rather than taking control of states. In any case, most Muslims do not live in oil-rich absolute monarchies, and few Islamists point to Saudi Arabia as a political model.

Iran, after its revolution in 1979, caused more excitement, even among Sunni Islamists who were inclined to be suspicious of Shia heretics. The clerics who took control eliminated Iranian leftists and secularists, imposed a strict version of Islamic law, and sought to cleanse Iranian public life of godless Western influences. Most significant, the clergy claimed direct oversight of the affairs of state. This required new institutions. For example, a Guardian Council of religious jurists took on a role similar to a Western constitutional court, but it went further. Not only does the Guardian Council make sure that laws conform to Islam as understood by the Shia clerical hierarchy, but also it screens candidates to national offices such as the parliament and the presidency. Leading politicians and officeholders in the Islamic Republic of Iran have very often been clerics.

In fact, clerical rule in Iran has required significant religious innovation. Historically, both Shia and Sunni religious scholars have typically been political quietists, setting themselves apart from governing tasks that inevitably involved a degree of corruption. Shia scholars developed a more formal clerical hierarchy than did their Sunni counterparts, but their authority also depended on a reputation of independence from an often-predatory state. Indeed, the relative independence of Iranian clerics allowed them to become a focal point of organized opposition to the dictatorial, oppressive secularizing monarchy ruling Iran before the Islamic revolution. Taking power and running the state, however, was unprecedented. The clerical leadership, particularly the Ayatollah Khomeini, developed a doctrine of the guardianship of the jurists, even though this was an innovation that enjoyed only weak textual warrant and lacked support in traditional practices. Moreover, Khomeini put the interests of the Islamic state above all. Even traditional religious laws could be violated in the interests of the state.[31] The Islamic Republic combined its version of Shia Islam with Iranian nationalism.

Iran, therefore, was never able to export its revolution. Its ideology depended too closely on Shia beliefs, and its strongest influence remained limited to Shia movements outside its borders. And as revolutionary fervor faded, the Islamic Republic became normalized. Clerical rule became the ordinary, everyday order, but as a consequence, the ruling clergy also became identified with a sputtering economy and the usual corruptions and disappointments of daily politics. Few, especially in the much larger Sunni world, consider Iran a political model.

Indeed, grandiose ambitions associated with an Islamic state are no longer very attractive. Sunni experiments with Islamic states, such as Sudan and Afghanistan, are widely perceived as failures. Hard-core theocratic factions in countries such as Egypt and Algeria have been crushed. Throughout most of the Muslim world, the revolutionary varieties of Islamists have been suppressed, coopted, or assimilated into a status-quo conservatism. Politics among Muslims today is deeply infused with religion, but that is not because of dreams of an Islamic state. Instead, elites— especially business elites—have lost interest in secularism, and popular movements to promote personal piety and re-Islamize the public sphere have succeeded. Muslims have, by and large, become convinced that they can achieve a pious form of modernity.

In fact, focusing on theocratic ambitions and the waning fortunes of secularism can obscure the underlying continuities within Muslim countries. Nationalism, for example, has hardly disappeared. Islamists have often proclaimed the unity of all believers, denouncing nationalism as a deviation from true religion. But Islam failed to hold even the Muslim peoples of the Ottoman Empire together, and it failed to prevent the bloody split of Pakistan when Bangladesh came into being. Today, even as both Turks and Kurds insist on their Sunni Islamic identities, they also support separate nationalisms. While some religious conservatives have hoped that emphasizing religious commonality will keep Turkey intact, Kurdish nationalism has succeeded to a degree that makes it difficult to imagine Kurds not gaining independence.[32] Muslim states often harbor separatist movements—Kurds, Baloch, Acehnese—even while originally artificial colonial borders remain remarkably resilient. Islamist politics today are largely confined within Tunisia or Libya, Malaysia or Indonesia. The unity of believers is a politically impotent idea.

Nationalism, then, appears inescapable. Muslims today typically live in modern states, with a modern apparatus of government, from parliaments to secret police. The state has substantial control over religion. Muslims have, however, largely rejected nonreligious ways to legitimate government, and they have refused to confine Islam to a realm of private conscience. Religion works through the state. Secular nationalism has become religious nationalism.

Religious nationalism, however, is not theocracy. Today's most plausible models for Islamic politics are not attempts at puritan Islamic states but countries, such as Malaysia, Indonesia, or Turkey, that have enjoyed some success joining neoliberal economic development with grassroots religious revival. Prominent Islamist movements, such as the Muslim Brotherhood in the Middle East, have been increasingly linking business and technocratic conservatism with religious conservatism. The pious modernity aspired to by today's moderate Islamists fuses a culturally conservative identity politics with a businesslike approach to governance. The governments they run receive international praise for their neoliberal structural adjustments and their conservative populist embrace of electoral democracy.[33]

Moderate Islamists today mobilize mass political engagement. They rely on modern forms of collective association and hope to bring their societies up to date rather than return to a peasant or tribal ideal. They are not religious protest movements with a charismatic leadership—they usually separate their spiritual leadership from their political organizations, which are run by lay leaders who derive their authority from success in secular enterprises such as business or engineering. Indeed, it has become commonplace for social scientists to describe Islamist politics as inadvertently promoting secularization. After all, they represent modern mass politics, and their policies often appeal to pragmatic, religion-independent conceptions of what works for a modern state and economy.[34] Iraqi politician Ali

A. Allawi describes the "Muslim democracy" in place in Malaysia and Turkey in secular terms:

> The political dimension of Islam is irrelevant to the governing pro-gramme of these parties, and Islamic values become subsumed under a general conservatism and a right-of-centre politics. In essence, Muslim democracy is a pathway to a secular and ultimately western definition of the political rather than a re-expression of the political in Islam. It may prevail in the face of the nihilistic and destructive alternative of radical Islamism and in the face of more openly secular and westernising political currents in the Muslim world. As a phenomenon, it has garnered the support of western governments—even though the Turkish model of Muslim democracy owes its success to the particular conditions in Turkey and to the rise of the religiously observant and socially conser-vative Anatolian middle classes. But Muslim democracy is unlikely to resolve the conundrum which Muslims face when they are dealing with the political: the need to evolve a privileged place for the sacred in the structuring of the Islamic political order.[35]

Such claims are overblown. Modern, national politics that appeals to urban constituencies inevitably must downplay some aspects of Islam as traditionally understood. Economies or urban-planning policies can only be notionally Islamic. But such partial secularization goes hand in hand with very unsecular lives and politics. Religious nationalism demands an overall Islamic legitimation of the state, which in turn provides an Islamic ambience for public life. Many different Islamic lifestyles can compete under such a wide umbrella, from various religious orders to more individualist, even social-media-driven forms of faith. But there is no mistaking Malaysia or Turkey for a fully secular state. Fundamentalist political parties may nudge Pakistan or Bangladesh toward a more modern, less tribal form of politics. But while pious modernity is modern, it is not secular.

Theocracy makes us think of nondemocratic regimes. Religious nationalism, however, encourages conservative populism, validating a reli-giously colored public domain as the will of the people expressed in elec-tions. The compatibility of Islam and democracy has long been debated, but in terms of popular attitudes expressed in surveys, Muslims support electoral democracy, so that, as political scientist M. Steven Fish observes, "living in a country with a large Muslim population does not have any discernible statistically significant effect on one's support for democracy."[36] Moreover, Muslims worldwide do not require any deep piety in the politicians they vote for. They do not want religious leaders to be involved in politics. While many Muslims favor a religious public sphere, they do not appear to be too different from Christians in this regard, and they "share in a global consensus in favor of dividing political and religious power."[37]

In this environment, religious politics can be considerably more democratic and pluralist than fears of theocracy allow. In Turkey, the public sphere today is full of religion. Even opposition, historically secular parties in parliament contest policy proposals by invoking prophetic traditions. Moderate Islamist governments in power have supported a generally Islamic ambience covering the public sphere. For example, they have promoted creationism in education, engaging in symbolic cultural politics. But the Islamists have not imposed any comprehensive way of life, instead presenting Islamization as expanding freedom for the devout majority. Plenty of academics support moderate Islamists as a democratizing influence acting against a historically authoritarian state, and they praise the pervasive political influence of religious orders as an expression of civil society.[38]

Islamist movements in Arab countries, such as branches of the Muslim Brotherhood, have also followed a trajectory of moderation on matters such as tolerance of alternative interpretations of Islam, democratic pluralism, and a limited expansion of rights for women and non-Muslims. The Muslim Brotherhood accepted becoming a player in democratic contests to further its interests. But it has also undergone a real change of values due to its experience with repression and the responsibilities of power.[39]

This is not to say that democracy among Muslims always conforms to liberal norms. The Muslim Brotherhood still tends to hold a very narrow conception of democratic legitimacy, and its brief experience with power in Egypt does not inspire confidence. In many Muslim countries, democratization is often window dressing, entailing regular elections interspersed with sporadic repression. For example, Pakistani democracy has trouble finding breathing space in the shadow of the military. Indonesian democracy is rife with corruption and vote-buying. Malaysian democracy suffers from extensive corruption, a lack of accountability, and institutionalized discrimination against non-Muslims. Islamic politics does not preclude infighting: the Malaysian government has also attracted attention for jailing Islamist opposition leader Anwar Ibrahim on trumped-up charges.[40]

Turkey has been much praised for its improved democracy, but its ruling Islamists have continued in a conservative tradition of illiberal majoritarianism. Turkish religious conservatism has a paranoid streak exacerbated by the historical association between secularism and authoritarian rule. Islamists often perceive secular opposition as enmity. Having taken control of the judiciary and police forces, the ruling religious conservatives jailed many reporters and prosecuted a diverse group of secular opposition figures for planning a coup, using evidence that was very likely fabricated.[41] Afterward, the Gülen movement and the ruling Islamist party, which had collaborated against the secularists, publicly fell out with each other, revealing much corruption in the process. Lately Western observers have been unable to ignore the illiberal aspects of Islamist rule. Turkey has now become known for jailing journalists and persecuting critics through a flood of lawsuits for allegedly insulting the president.[42]

Nonetheless, religious nationalism brings devout, often lower-class and historically underrepresented populations into national politics. Religious populism has had a democratizing effect, even if it will still take time for the Muslim democracies to achieve maturity. Many Muslims aspire to a fuller democracy that goes beyond mere elections, and the prospects of liberalizing the existing tendency toward democracy will depend on politics, particularly social movements.[43]

I do not like religious nationalism. I am not religious, so I have little option but to hope for some version of a secular state. But it makes no sense to defend secularism by suggesting that theocracies such as Iran or Saudi Arabia are the alternative. Muslims tend to oppose secularism, rejecting an amoral public sphere devoid of religious direction. But a state that encourages a religious public environment need not descend into clerical despotism or sectarian strife. In the past, secular elites controlling the state often claimed a tutelary role in bringing their nations into modernity. Today, secularists have to persuade religious populations in a more democratic environment. But if that is to be possible, the familiar arguments for secularism will not be enough.[44]

THE EVILS OF SECULARISM

Religious nationalism is not peculiar to Islam. In the Christian parts of Africa, Hindu India, or Buddhist Sri Lanka, religious politics can be broadly similar. Right-wing Jews in Israel and the Christian Right in the United States also have religious nationalist aspirations. When I lived in the American South for a few years, the religious landscape was strange to me. I was fascinated by the many congregations and by the new forms of religious life I encountered. On the other hand, the Christian public ambiance, the pervasive Christian influence on politics and education, and the fusion of business and religious conservatism seemed much more familiar.

Even with all the cultural differences, there is perhaps a generic conservatism that applies across borders. After all, Turkish conservatives have long admired the United States. And the moderate political Islam that has shaped Turkey in the last few decades has adopted a noticeably American style of politics. Conservative political theorists partly claim inspiration from the European Christian Democratic tradition, but their animating thought derives largely from Anglo-American conservatism.[45] Indeed, some recent Turkish conservative literature presents a political outlook that is very similar to that of the Republican Party in the United States.[46] Greek political scientist Christos Teazis observes that "the Islamist movement in Turkey was only able to strengthen and express itself as part of a process of democratization (Americanization). Therefore, in this process American institutions have been adopted and applied in every respect."[47] And among American religious conservatives, a few will occasionally drop their reflexive distrust of Islam and highlight common social goals and a shared opposition to secularism.[48]

American-style conservatism encourages a suspicion of secularism, but that does not mean that conservatives demand that theology should dictate policy. Successful opposition to secularism includes significant compromises with worldly interests. Just as varieties of secularism always include compromise and accommodation, so do viable forms of religious politics. Many Muslims praise the American conservative ideal of separate state and religious institutions coupled with considerable state support for religion.[49] In the Muslim version of the American model, religious freedom would be a central concern, with emphasis on the freedom of members of religious communities to live according to their faith commitments. The state would recognize the sacred, but it would not be the custodian of faith. It would encourage but not coerce religious virtue—the state would, in fact, largely attend to worldly affairs.

Such an ideal draws on theology about the sovereignty of God, but also on a conservative criticism of secular liberal practices. For example, the influential Islamist intellectual Rachid al-Ghannouchi objects to the secular liberal ambition of a public order based on reason. We forget, he says, that God is the owner of all and we are but vicegerents of his rule. Human reason is not capable of discovering our true rights. On its own, reason cannot order our social life and keep freedom from degenerating into slavery to our passions.[50] Other monotheists express similar doubts. We might want to establish human rights based on our historical experience and a liberal exercise of public reason. But such reasons are merely contingent: they lack a transcendent anchor, a supernatural authority. Secular, implicitly naturalistic understandings of the world cannot capture the full conceptual depth of ideas such as human dignity or what people truly deserve.[51] Our religions often claim to reveal a moral order beyond mere worldly interests. If we take such claims seriously, it is hard to set them aside in politics.

Secularists usually think that our worldly interests are robust enough for us to productively reason about our common political questions. But liberal public reason cannot just coincide with godless moral philosophy. Public reason is supposed to be a narrower exercise that does not require religious people to abandon their convictions. And if secularism means that the state cannot decide whether otherworldly claims are correct, and hence cannot take them into consideration, legitimate political demands have to be translated into secular language. As philosopher Russell Blackford puts it, "the adherents of a religion that forbids alcohol might trust that their god disallowed it for essentially secular reasons, perhaps to prevent harms caused by intoxication. Nothing stops them from identifying those harms and putting evidence forward in political debates."[52] Protestants in the United States and Muslims in Turkey have often opposed alcohol in just this fashion. They have also promoted supposedly secular notions of medical harm due to abortion and pseudoscientific arguments that evolution is false. Translating religious morality into secular reasons results in fakery that is true neither to secular reasoning nor to religious motivations.

The effort of translation puts religious people at a disadvantage. After all, worldly interests—and no more—are exactly what a godless infidel such as myself recognize. I do not think the transcendent moral anchors invoked by religions are real, so I do not burden myself by referring to them in public debate. It seems odd that the common ground for all should be the same as what the nonreligious do.

Moreover, being religious is not just a matter of accepting secular notions of worldly interests and adding some extra supernatural sauce on top. For example, strongly religious people disagree with secular concepts of harm.[53] For a secular liberal, teaching creationism causes harm: it deprives students of the best that human knowledge has to offer. But for many conservative monotheists, teaching evolution is harmful, as it casts doubt on a conception of humanity that is integral to a person understanding their position in a moral community.

Secular liberals want to appeal to a universal, abstract conception of reason to resolve such conflicts. Almost all of us want to avoid certain things, such as being tortured for political dissidence. So we establish human rights. Almost all of us can come to accept evolution, if we follow the evidence. So we teach proper science. But if we want public reason to be narrowly applied, without privileging the godless, we will most often embrace a superficial pragmatism. We will rely on the instrumental reason of market transactions or well-defined engineering projects. In that case, we might avoid gulags, but it is much less clear that insufficient appreciation of evolution is bad for business. Pious modernity is a viable alternative to the secular version. Moreover, a public sphere permeated by piety gives moral depth to an otherwise-dismal pragmatism.

Still, secular liberals prefer a more neutral stance toward religion. This is not to say that complete neutrality between rival conceptions of a good life is possible. Liberalism inevitably takes individual autonomy as an important good. As political scientist Peter Berkowitz says, "Individuals whose fundamental beliefs give less primacy to individual choice, to say nothing of those who see celebration of individual choice as a revolt against God or betrayal of the nation and those who long for theocracy or despotism, will certainly be at a disadvantage in a free society."[54] Nonetheless, liberals do not require that anyone adopt a *comprehensive* view of the good life. Favoring individual autonomy is compatible with many different ways of life, including liberal religious ways of life. We can achieve an overlapping consensus about individual freedom without the state favoring any particular religion or lack of religion. This might not satisfy purists—perhaps not fundamentalists or militant atheists—but it is a practical form of neutrality.

There remain, however, many reasons for discontentment with liberalism without endorsing theocracy or despotic rule. An emphasis on individual autonomy works well enough for someone like me: I don't have deep community ties. I belong to plenty of organizations, from being an academic to serving on the board of my homeowners' association. Each of these social roles involves responsibilities that I take seriously. None, however, make deep moral demands that go beyond the narrow purposes of the institutions involved. They are not entangled with family and community, birth and death—they do not generate fierce loyalties. I am comfortable with social fragmentation and individually trying to reason my way to a more encompassing stance on life. But I am, perhaps, something of an extreme. For many people, and especially devoutly religious people who belong to tight-knit communities and congregations, liberal individualism is not as attractive. For many of us, a cohesive moral community gives substance and context to our individual aspirations. Moreover, few of us choose the communities that define our identities. A liberal neutrality that assumes we are all loosely tied, autonomous individuals who freely choose our affiliations is hardly neutral toward religious associations.

There are further problems. Secular liberalism has taken life within the modern nation-state, where the practices of a dominant ethnic or religious group sets the national defaults. From official languages to the days we are off work—Sunday for Christians or Friday for Muslims?—there are many decisions where it does not make sense to pretend to neutrality. Instead, to be fair, a state has to recognize the groups to which its citizens belong, and make appropriate accommodations. Liberal political theorists have, in fact, increasingly described neutrality as incoherent or unfair with regard to ethnic and linguistic minorities. But in that case, sociologist Tariq Modood asks, "If neutrality is incoherent, how can we apply it to religious groups? If it is unfair to ethnocultural groups, then is it not unfair to ethno-religious groups?"[55] If majorities determine dominant languages or official holidays, it is not a far stretch for Muslim-majority states to acknowledge the moral and political centrality of Islam for most of their citizens. And if minorities deserve protection, countries with Muslim minorities may have to acknowledge how religion often defines minority communities.

Recognizing communities limits individual freedoms. But then, religious conservatives have usually been suspicious of freedom without discipline. According to Rachid al-Ghannouchi, the Western, liberal notion of freedom lacks moral foundations. It is liberty as license, based on mere interests, without the responsibility and self-discipline urged by religion. True freedom emerges from the desire to follow the path of God. It is a product of the moral maturity to freely and wholeheartedly do what God commands and refrain from what God forbids.[56] Alternatively, some Muslim academics such as Anouar Majid criticize the liberal notion of freedom by romanticizing how a tribesman is free from the state, or assert an "Islamic definition of freedom as being in total harmony with the environment."[57]

Such conservative concepts of freedom downplay freedom from conformity to tribe or religious community. But freedom is an expansive concept, with rich conflicts within itself. A postmodern, pluralist political framework might have to strike a balance between individual freedoms and the freedom to live according to the demands of tight-knit communities. Freedom of religion, therefore, includes freedom for religious institutions—institutions that make deep moral demands, that entangle adherents in bonds of fierce loyalties and all the intimate matters of family ties and birth and death.

From a secular liberal point of view, such an interpretation of freedom of religion establishes special privileges for religion. This conflict is familiar from the United States, where right-wing Catholics and evangelicals continually feel that their religious freedom is under threat,[58] and liberals perceive conservative concerns about healthcare laws or public education as a desire to impose a religious morality on everyone. But purely secular laws and exclusively secular reasons in the public sphere inevitably burden strong religion. For example, there are good secular reasons for providing public education and for teaching evolution. But evolution also inspires deep religious resistance. If a conservative religious family sends its children to public school, they confront state endorsement of views they oppose. If they choose a private school, they still pay taxes to support public education.

Conservatives naturally see such a situation as an imposition on religious freedom. Moreover, changing this will require either a less secular state, or removing goods like education from the public realm—an opportunity for an alliance with business conservatives interested in privatizing public goods. In either case, the secular state appears as a source of interference in forms of social order that emerge spontaneously: religion, markets, and their attendant hierarchies of power.

Indeed, state-enforced secularity does not appear democratic, particularly within a Muslim political tradition that does not sharply distinguish between worldly and otherworldly needs and perceives religion to be the source of social order. A religious population will exert democratic pressure for its spiritual needs to be met. As conservative journalist Abdurrahman Dilipak puts it,

> When devout people have citizenship rights, they will make demands of the state to bring about and maintain a social structure that does not conflict with their religious needs, and they will quite naturally do all they

can to protect and promote the religious values that render their lives meaningful, and for whose sake they would even be prepared to sacrifice their lives.[59]

Such demands have political consequences. For example, in 2012, Fatma Şahin, the Turkish Minister of Family and Social Policies, defended elective courses on the Quran and the life of the Holy Prophet in public schools, since "humans don't just have material and physical needs; they are material and spiritual wholes."[60] Apparently "a welfare state has the duty to meet human needs in order that they live happily and in peace," and this includes spiritual needs as understood by a dominant majority of the population.

Secular liberals often respond to popular religious demands by trying to rule them out of bounds. American liberals have relied on the courts to block creationism and prayer in schools; Turkish secularists used to get their Constitutional Court to dissolve Islamist political parties. Arab autocrats have often presented their rule as progress toward secular democracy, since they supposedly prevent popular Islamist movements from establishing a theocracy. Secularism appears, then, as a precondition of a proper political order. In that case, just as conservative Muslims take cognizance of divine law to be a prior requirement for public order, secular liberals may see secularism as an "unalterable, built-in, pre-existing feature of democracy."[61] Hence when courts intervene to disallow religiously motivated policies, they act not to override democracy but to preserve it from majoritarian abuse.

Conservatives are not impressed. Such arguments expose the statism of secular liberals, and their tendency to take refuge in technocratic elitism. Liberal political philosophy has often included a suspicion of populism, even popular democracy. The state—guided by educated elites institutionalized in the judiciary—determines the requirements for social justice, leaving only details of policy to be ironed out by the political process.[62] When liberalism reigns, it might protect some minorities, but it also undermines the ability of communities to collectively decide and institutionalize moral convictions about how best to live together. Indeed, secular liberalism only protects minorities by pressuring everyone to become liberal individualists only loosely tied to any moral community.

Conservative opposition to secular liberalism often draws on particular religious traditions. After all, there are specific conceptions of transcendent order at stake; Catholic, Protestant, Hindu, or Muslim social ideals are not the same. But many conservative themes are also universal, appearing in arguments made by moderate Islamists as well as Western social conservatives. The secular liberal idea of public reason cannot supply the moral depth found in supernatural convictions. Liberals are not neutral toward religion; they displace organic religious communities with a civil religion that serves the state. Secular ideals of individual freedom easily degenerate into a libertinism that threatens social cohesion. Enforcing secularism interferes with the freedom of religious institutions. And in a democratic political environment, secularism reveals itself as an elitist view that avoids subjecting itself to political contests.

Many of these criticisms ring true. More to the point, they seem persuasive to many. Secularism has been discredited among most Muslims, but not just Muslims. Few politicians vying for national office in India or the United States would emphasize secularism. Islam, to some observers, has seemed uniquely resistant to secular modernity. But today, Muslims do not seem unusual. Liberals hoped for an overlapping consensus converging on a secular political order. It appears that conservatives from different religious traditions have reached their own consensus, favoring family, property, piety, and community over rootless liberal individualism.

CONSERVATIVE PLURALISM

Still, after all the criticism, perhaps secularism remains necessary to manage diversity. Modern societies harbor many ways of life and many individuals who complicate matters with their multiple, overlapping loyalties. Even where most people are religious, there are various interpretations that contest dominant forms of faith. Social conservatives celebrate the close-knit communities in which their sense of morality takes life, but we cannot scale up a neighborhood sense of community to order large, complex societies. So religious conservatives have to acknowledge irresolvable moral differences, even if they consider it a problem that invites a supernatural resolution.[63] Modern people face a moral landscape of incommensurable values that contain conflicts within themselves as well as with other values. Social diversity and value pluralism are facts of life. And if we are to affirm diversity rather than grudgingly accept it, we may be led to a liberal political order.[64]

But then, secular liberalism also comes in for severe criticism from postmodern thinkers who defend cultural diversity, minorities, and those disadvantaged by secular modernity. Secularism, they say, is nothing without the modern state shaping or even controlling religion, politically dominating those who do not fit its ethnocentric framing of politics masquerading as liberal universalism. Nationalism, the typical context of secular politics, imposes uniformity to define the nation, excluding those who do not conform in faith or ethnicity.[65] Non-Western peoples, who do not sharply distinguish public and private, worldly and otherworldly as in the secular West, find themselves marginalized by liberal politics, either when resisting the colonial legacy forced upon them or as immigrant groups in the West. Secularism fails to respect their difference. It interferes with the way they live, attempting to remake them in a secular image.[66] Worse, secularism is very often part of the discourse of empire, a tool of American strategy.[67]

Many socially conservative political philosophers converge on a similar point of view. While they give community primacy and value religious institutions as a bulwark against an overbearing state, they understand that the communities they belong to are but one among many such communities. Therefore they acknowledge political and cultural pluralism.[68] The liberal emphasis on individual autonomy appears to clash with an affirmation of a diversity of ways of life, especially those that include self-abnegating religious commitments. A better political order embodies respect for our various communities.[69]

If we are to favor a diversity of communities rather than the rootless individual choices of secular liberals, we will be led to multiculturalism.

Complex societies are made of multiple ethnic and religious communities, and people take on identities and flourish or not as part of their communities. Therefore states must not adopt the secular pretense of abstract individuals interacting with government without the benefit of intermediate institutions. Liberals care about the equal standing of citizens, but equality also has to be applied to groups, not just individuals.[70] Crucially, political multiculturalists demand equal respect for groups. They envision, as Tariq Modood describes it, "neither separatism nor assimilation but an accommodative form of integration which would allow group-based racialized, ethnic, cultural and religious identities and practices to be recognized and supported in the public space, rather than require them to be privatized."[71]

Public support for group identities means recognizing that communities are not like private associations. We become part of identity groups due to events such as birth, marriage, or conversion. We cannot, therefore, treat them like associations we choose to join or leave as autonomous individuals weighing costs and benefits. Recognizing groups means acknowledging the real power religious and ethnic institutions must exert over their members. We cannot treat this power as deriving from a contract, the way a golf club may use a secular legal system to demand unpaid dues. A multicultural state, therefore, must devolve some of its coercive powers to identity groups. At least, multiculturalism brings up the prospect of group rights or cultural rights.

Most liberal democracies already recognize groups to some extent. The Supreme Court of the United States, for example, has exempted the Amish from laws that make high school education compulsory. Its reasoning explicitly recognizes the cultural needs of a religiously defined group. The Amish, a sect that partly isolates itself from its surrounding society, want their children to have an elementary education, enough to be able to read the Bible. But further education would reshape Amish youth, hindering their transition to becoming mature community members. Amish cultural integrity demands an exemption from secular laws that otherwise apply to all. The United States does not, however, extend such rights to all groups. So far, unlike most countries, the United States only provides indirect public assistance to religious education, even though Catholics have long demanded aid to their parochial schools. It would be no surprise if, in the future, the United States extended recognition to Catholics as well as the Amish, acting to undo the financial penalty Catholics presently pay for sending their children to a faith-based school.[72]

In other countries, group recognition can go much deeper. Social scientists Paul M. Sniderman and Louk Hagendoorn point out that in the Netherlands,

> the state funds a Muslim school system in which children are taught in the language of their country of origin and, in an independently designed curriculum, about their own culture. The state also builds separate Muslim housing; provides mass media (including radio and television) dedicated to Muslim interests and concerns; imports imams; supports separate social and welfare arrangements for immigrant minorities and has established a separate consultation system with community "leaders."[73]

The Netherlands is still, perhaps, a secular state, since it attempts not to favor any particular religion at a national level. Nonetheless, religious identities enjoy public support, and within their communities and in a substantial part of their lives, conservative Muslims occupy a nonsecular space. Multiculturalism requires a public institutional presence for religion, which can often be satisfied by intensifying the religious accommodations already in place in liberal democracies. Where Muslims are sizeable minorities, as in many European countries, they often support multicultural accommodation rather than strict secularism.[74]

Such multiculturalism attempts to avoid conflicts by fragmenting and shrinking the public sphere and negotiating how to distribute the remaining public resources between communities to ensure equal respect. In a secular school system such as that in France, conservative Muslims regularly protest evolution in science, nudes in art, the Holocaust in history, and swimming and female participation in sports. A more multicultural country will defuse such conflicts by supporting faith schools where communities can decide on the education they prefer, perhaps within constraints of national curriculum requirements that can be politically negotiated.

Muslim minorities are also often caught between the demands of divine law and the laws of the country in which they reside. Often Muslims will try to follow divine law except where it conflicts with national laws. But multiculturalism introduces the possibility of fragmented legal systems, particularly for personal laws, as in the Indian example.

Countries with a Muslim majority are not subject to pressures to adopt a European style of multiculturalism. Nonetheless, they still have religious and ethnic minorities, including sects within Islam. But then, many Muslim political thinkers argue that pluralism is inherent to the Islamic political tradition. A variety of religious communities is God's revealed will, and an ideal Islamic political order would be the best guarantee of cultural pluralism.[75] The historical practice of recognizing autonomous communities within Muslim empires is a promising way to manage diversity. It might even be a better way than Western secular nationalism.

Nostalgia for autonomous communities is not confined to Muslims. The social critic Noam Chomsky thinks it would help the Middle East today:

> The best solution would have some of the elements of the old Ottoman Empire. . . . Now of course no one wants to reconstruct the Ottoman Empire—it was brutal, corrupt, and everything else. But they had the right idea about how to treat the region: People were left alone. In the Ottoman Empire, to go from Cairo to Istanbul to Baghdad, you didn't have to pass any borders. The Greeks in the town ran the Greek areas, the Armenians ran the Armenian areas. . . . It's the right kind of solution for a complex mosaic of populations. In fact, I think the same is true in Europe; to impose the nation-state in Europe required centuries of extreme violence. It's a very unnatural system—where do you draw the borders?[76]

None of these ways of institutionalizing pluralism are free of problems. The non-Muslim subject peoples' historical memory of Ottoman times emphasizes centuries of oppression and the spectacular atrocities and ethnic cleansing that accompanied the collapse of the empire.[77] We do not yet have a model of how a modernized system of autonomous communities might work—only vague hopes that it might be done without imperial oppression and with equality of respect. European varieties of multiculturalism are not unambiguously successful in keeping the peace either.

The way multiculturalism accentuates cultural identities can increase competition and hostility between groups.[78] Even French-style secularism is not out of the running, with defenders arguing that France has less specifically religious friction with its large Muslim minority when compared to more multicultural European countries.[79]

The political debate over managing diversity is complex. Instead of a universally applicable solution, we will probably continue to see many local accommodations patched together to fit particular circumstances. Secularism is, now, one option at best. Proponents of secularism continue to highlight the opportunities for oppressive theocracies or sectarian violence if religion and state are too closely entangled. This is no longer convincing. Secularism increasingly seems like an old-fashioned option, out of place in a world of resurgent religion, where too many of us have become disillusioned with myths of progress. These are conservative times. Strict secularism has not just been defeated among Muslims, it has often been weakened and qualified in the Western democracies that are supposed to be its home. To many, Muslim resistance to secularism appears to be a virtue rather than a liability.

WHY SECULARISM?

I am not a secularist because I think secularism is neutral with regard to religion, or because I think it is the best way to keep the peace between sects. I am a secularist because I am a secular person.

Indeed, I am a godless infidel. I don't think there are any realities transcending nature. I argue that we live in a world of chance and necessity, that all we know and have any prospect to encounter can be accounted for by physical explanations.[80] As far as I can tell, our societies harbor complex moral ecologies with multiple stable, successfully reproducing ways of life and attendant value perceptions. Moral behavior and politics are rooted in our interests and our prospects for conflict or agreement.[81] Claims about ideal social orders, varieties of secular liberalism as well as Islam, are neither dictates of reason nor revealed truths. They are competing aspirations of different coalitions of people.

Naturally, my political views also emerge from my psychological predispositions,[82] personal history, and understanding of the world. These make me suspicious of tight-knit communities and conservative moral convictions.

So I start with an everyday, visceral sort of secularism: I do not want group loyalties to have too much power over me. I do not need to know about my plumber's religion, and neither do I want my skeptical views to affect the service I receive. I want the same from my relationships with the institutions I encounter, including the state.

I might be able to avoid strong religion if our societies were divided up into isolated enclaves and I inhabited a small but irreverent social bubble. Alternatively, if most of my interactions with others were commercial exchanges such as that with a plumber, religion could fade into the background. There is, however, more to my secularism than insulation from the pushier forms of religion. Many of my interests derive from my commitments to long-term projects, some of which extend far beyond my lifetime. These projects call for collective efforts and depend critically on the existence of a vigorous secular public sphere.[83]

I teach physics at a public university, and science and education are both good examples. I see the sort of knowledge produced by basic science as a public good, produced by a public enterprise, that I want to make available to all. Science, indeed, is the most unambiguous example of success for Enlightenment hopes. It is universal, without fragmenting into a pluralism of incommensurable points of view. It makes progress. At its best, it works by being open to informed public criticism from all, without deferring to sacred tradition, market forces, or sheer power.

I don't want to claim too much. After all, I have plenty of occasion to complain about science shading into ideology, and education becoming corrupted by indoctrination or credential-seeking. A serious secular liberalism has to respond to conservative critiques, and it has to learn from catastrophic secular failures such as communism. Nonetheless, I think there still is life in the Enlightenment tradition. For people like me, who have been shaped by this tradition suspicious of traditions, this community wary of communities, Enlightenment aspirations still frame our purposes in life.

Indeed, a broadly secular public sphere is an end in itself. Not only does it enable secular liberal conceptions of a good life, participating in making public space is partly constitutive of a good life. I consider the secular institutions we have managed to construct so far as important achievements. Therefore I am reluctant to sacrifice them to the cultural integrity of groups, sacred texts, or the commercialization of everything.

Not everyone has to agree. Modern religious conservatism also appears to represent a stable, coherent set of interests. It emerges from a way of life that has been very successful in reproducing itself. Traditional supernaturalism does not accurately describe the world. But achieving the best description is costly—and costs, like harms and benefits in general, cannot be evaluated independently of our interests. Even when supernatural faith appears most vulnerable to criticism, it comes with impressive defense mechanisms. The faithful can always take refuge in vagueness or associate doubt with hellfire. Even after considerable reflection, a believer will usually end up concluding there is still life in Islam.

Compared to me, a religious conservative will have different political ideals, different long-term projects. A godly society is not compatible with my hopes for an expansive secular public sphere. I see little to do other than acknowledge that our views conflict and our politics compete. Our interactions will sometimes present opportunities for compromise and common actions, but often there will be winners and losers. In a godly society, I will be disadvantaged, maybe even a second-class citizen. And if a secular public sphere expands, it will trivialize traditionally devout ways of life and interfere with their cultural reproduction.

I cannot, then, propose my version of secularism as a form of neutrality, or as a universally applicable compromise. I do not know if there can be any political settlement where nobody's oxen are gored, everybody feels treated fairly, and the state stands equidistant to all. I suspect not, but in any case, secularism does not fit this description. I prefer, therefore, to defend secularism in terms of a broad conception of a good life shared by secular people, including liberal religious people. A state that treats religions as private associations provides the best context for individual autonomy and a healthy public sphere.

With my background, I am especially concerned with how science fits in a secular public sphere. Our judgments about public goods and harms depend on getting an accurate picture of how the world works. Our sciences—not just natural science but also social science and the humanities—are the institutions best suited for producing a picture that can withstand public critical scrutiny.

This is not compatible with neutrality or respect for the beliefs of all groups. Deeply mistaken fact claims are inseparably woven into our traditional cultures, especially our religions. Public policy would, if I had my way, recognize the falsity of many theological beliefs. If someone wants to try to heal herself by prayer, that is her business. But I want the ways we publicly deal with health to appreciate that the claims of prayer—and psychic healing, and homeopathy—are very likely false. In many cases, I am reluctant to even let believers opt out unless they are already largely disconnected from the secular public sphere. If, for example, a sect refuses immunizations for religious reasons, their false beliefs can lead to serious public health problems.

I do not agree, then, that public institutions such as the state are incapable of adjudicating theological claims. Without explicitly stating so, liberal democracies already implement a large array of policies that imply specific religious beliefs are false.[84] This is an unavoidable consequence of making good use of our sciences to identify and serve our collective worldly interests. But for many secular liberals such as me, the cognitive privilege we extend science is not just due to pragmatic reasons. We want evolution taught in schools, not because of the questionable benefits it may confer on students in the job market, but because we hope such knowledge helps citizens contribute to the making of a secular public sphere.[85]

This is not a call for a blanket hegemony of science. Scientist-kings would be even worse than philosopher-kings. Caring for individual autonomy means allowing a wide berth for people to get things wrong. Moreover, science, where we get used to demanding correct answers on exam questions, is not a good model for politics, with its inevitably shifting and diverging coalitions of interests. I cannot lightly brush away demands to respect diversity.

But then, diversity is not, to me, an overriding value. I'd like to strike a balance. After all, diversity often works against an expansive public sphere. Ethnic, racial, and religious diversity in a polity often reduces willingness to invest in public goods.[86] A degree of similarity helps us enter the public sphere on common terms—at the very least, there is a considerable information savings associated with a default cultural background. In our work, for example, we usually have to adapt to a shared business or academic culture. Constructing a public sphere is also a task of forging a common public culture.

Some demands for diversity are calls for inclusion, for widening the public sphere, to let others in. For example, our sciences have a history of taking wealthy white men to be the human norm. Secular liberals should be able to support diversifying our public-knowledge-producing enterprises: we can make the institutions of physics more open to women, and write more history from minority perspectives. But other demands for diversity would fragment the public sphere. Islamizing science, for example, would increase diversity by creating parallel institutions devoted to a sectarian perspective. Secular liberals should not be enthusiastic about such an enterprise.

My version of secular liberalism depends on a commitment to a common public sphere, and this commitment can override the values of particular communities. Liberal education aims to dampen allegiances to tight-knit communities and unquestioned authorities.[87] Indeed, secular liberal politics will most often appeal to those already participating in a secular way of life. Secularism is instituted by politics, acting to bring religion under state control, forcing education to support national projects rather than community interests. Such policies help create more secular people. And in turn, a secularizing population produces a demand for secular politics.

Secularism is the framework in which secular people shape a common public sphere. Its constituency is people who wear religion lightly, people who mostly attend to worldly concerns. Secular people treat their religions as social clubs that include transcendent inspiration. We may break from tradition and explore individualist spiritualities, or go entirely without supernatural beliefs. We enjoy enough material security, social equality, and political agency to meaningfully participate in shaping public life. Secularism is not atheism. But it does encourage laxity, heterodoxy, low-intensity religiosity, and even substantial nonbelief.

Therefore, secularism goes together with secularity. The most secular liberal region of the planet is western Europe, even with its vestigial monarchies and established churches. Not only is European politics secular, but each recent generation has been less attached to organized religion than its predecessors.[88] When secularism had purchase in Arab politics, observers also thought Muslim societies were secularizing. There was a time when pop culture icons in Egypt could be sexy, uncovered women singers and dancers, but today, many actors and actresses get religion, cover up, and push the entertainment industry in a more religious direction.[89] And where we see secularism in an ambiguous position, such as in the United States and India, it is because intensely pious populations sustain religious nationalist politics.

I therefore prefer a French style of secularism, which more explicitly affirms secularity as a social condition. Secularism cannot be sustained by judicial rulings or by military decrees. It needs a strong political constituency. And secular people cannot rely on modernization to nudge everyone in a secular liberal direction. There is no right or wrong side of history, no inevitable progress. If we care about secularism, we have to value secularity. And if our lives are wrapped up in secularity as a long-term project, we have to attend to the cultural reproduction of secularity. No one else will do it.

A POST-SECULAR WORLD

I teach at a historical relic. In the 1980s, my university transformed itself into a public liberal arts school intended to attract talented midwestern students who could not afford a private liberal arts education. Back then, this was relatively uncontroversial. High-quality education was not just a device to reproduce elites. It was a public good.

Today, our state legislature is enraptured by right-wing populism. Periodic bills to clear the way for creationism are the least of my worries—they die in committee. Hostility to liberal institutions is more easily channeled to defund public education, especially higher education. Learning is now a private good: a means of acquiring human capital. My generation of university faculty went into graduate school in the late 1980s, and many of us thought of our teaching and research as a way of contributing to a secular liberal public enterprise. We were behind the times.

There is always plenty of funding for research that ties in to corporate interests, and for the sort of teaching that produces credentials valued in the marketplace. But liberal education, which has been a major instrument for the cultural reproduction of secular liberalism in the United States, faces permanent austerity. The history of secularism demonstrates that education has always been hotly contested territory. And so politically, it appears that secular liberals have lost an important battle. But we lost not to religious conservatives alone, but to a more protean right-wing alliance that has delegitimized liberal notions of public goods. The state has become a force to serve the powerful and discipline the rest.

Since I started paying attention to public affairs, a constant theme has been a gradual hollowing out of public institutions, except those with police functions. Our banks and oil companies do wonderfully, but our educational or healthcare institutions do well only to the extent that they adapt to serve private gain. And politics—if there is anything Americans agree on, it is that our politics has become appallingly corrupt, if not a sham. Critics describe our process as "low-intensity democracy" or even an "inverted totalitarianism" where corporate lobbyists write the legislation and economic interests dominate politics.[90] Public participation means little more than voting. And elections are personality-driven public-relations exercises, where policy options that might inconvenience the powerful are excluded from consideration.[91]

In these decades, I also kept my eye on Turkey and the Middle East, where something similar was in the air. I saw the local cultures of business opening up to the world. But together with that, already-wobbly public institutions were hollowed out or simply plundered. Corruption flourished, inequality exploded, and a curious blend of money and piety washed over the mass media. Secular vehicles of solidarity, such as independent labor unions, which were never very strong, virtually collapsed. For a while, politics seemed different from the United States, when Islamists used to at least express a genuine opposition. But then, they figured out that they could worship both markets and the Quran, and that was the path to power. Turkey became more democratic. It stages regular personality-driven public-relations exercises, where policies that might inconvenience the powerful are not on the table.

So these are neoliberal times. Even after financial crisis and the prospects of environmental catastrophe, globally we remain committed to neoliberal economics and politics.[92] The secular political tradition among Muslims had already lurched into these last few decades in a state of defeat, indelibly stained by authoritarian practices. Now it is even more irrelevant, as most countries continue to dismantle what remains of a public sphere. The plunder proceeds, led by an alliance of business and religious conservatives—an alliance where religious conservatives have usually been the junior partner.

But then, it is less clear what all of this means for Islam. After all, plutocratic rule and a market society is hardly anyone's idea of a godly social order. Neoliberal ideology seems full of transcendent fantasies,[93] but it is not supernaturalistic in any conventional sense. I may dislike the course of events because of my nostalgic attachment to secular liberalism, but is neoliberal ascendancy not another form of secularization?

Not quite. The currently successful varieties of religion do very well in the marketplace. Conservative American Christianity and born-again Islam are both in many ways creatures of the market: populist, entrepreneurial, saturated with advertising. The religion of parish priests or local religious scholars has suffered much. But mutated varieties of their supernatural beliefs have come to flourish, often under the pretense that they are even more strictly faithful to the original revelations. In a market society, religion delivers therapy. It emphasizes personal encounters with scripture and the individual experience of faith. All of this undermines the intellectual, high-culture traditions sustained within world religions. But it also cuts against secularization.

Moreover, religion is also a refuge from the marketplace. In the United States, churches are often the only institutions that break social isolation, that can organize caregiving. From pastoral visits to the sick to church members pitching together to help a recently unemployed member, especially for those who are relatively poor or in reduced circumstances, churches are often the only source of help available. Congregations are our social safety net. Christian volunteerism is our exception to possessive individualism. We may not believe we owe anything to each other as fellow citizens, but we help others within our flocks. Even more middle-class versions of caregiving or social solidarity, such as a support system for college students, often work through religion. The largest student organizations on our campuses are religious.

Among Muslims, charity work and Islamist organization are often closely intertwined. The Muslim Brotherhood or Hezbollah are notoriously better providers of social services than the corrupt neoliberal states in which they operate. People can still count on ethnic, regional, and religious solidarity. For the poor, religious involvement is critical for getting support beyond an extended-family network. After all, few unions or other secular organizations can promote mutual aid. Religious groups also support middle-class and upwardly-mobile needs. For example, Turkish college students, if involved with religious orders, can receive decent housing, tutoring, and a supportive social environment. Indeed, there are religious groups that pay special attention to recruiting needy students. Secular public alternatives, when they exist, are usually starkly inferior. People are on their own as citizens, but as believers, they have access to care.

Historically, when secularism found political support, it also had broad appeal. Keeping religion out of government went together with agitating for free and universal public education, social insurance, an eight-hour workday—an expansive sense of social equality and access to the public sphere. Left-wing political movements in Muslim countries rarely confronted religious belief, but they were firmly secular. They used to attract some support. Even today, in countries such as Egypt, there remains a working-class constituency for more redistributive, less neoliberal policies. The religious care and solidarity organizations of the Islamists, however, allow them to more easily convince voters that they are on the side of the disadvantaged.[94]

Now, I do not expect the fortunes of secularism among Muslims would much improve, even if secularists learned to care better. But it would help more than the suggestions of many Western secular liberals. I sometimes run into commentary that argues, for example, that the military coup deposing the Muslim Brotherhood in Egypt was good for secularism. Evidently we never learn from experience with military regimes that continue the neoliberal dismantling of the public sphere and work closely with the official clergy. Western media celebrates liberal factions in Iran, but their liberalism usually means more electoral democracy plus free marketeering. According to polls and other indicators, the notion of an Islamic republic enjoys the consent of a strong majority. Iranians disagree about what an Islamic republic should mean, in light of their experience with rule by clergy. Some want greater cultural pluralism and social liberalization, particularly among wealthier social strata. But not secularity. The Green Movement protesting the 2009 elections was portrayed by some Western observers as an anticlerical, more secular movement; but as the Greens became associated with secular views, their constituency dwindled.[95] Some of the more rigid Muslim countries may see some slackening of theocracy. But secularism is not a mere lack of theocracy.

Secular liberalism among Muslims is largely dead. It was killed off. And it is not looking very healthy in India or in the United States either. Those of us who remain secular liberals have to acknowledge defeat. And if we care about secularism as a real-life political option, rather than an abstract legal deliverance of liberal political philosophy, we have to think about how to care for each other without depending on intimate, suffocating religious communities. We have much to rethink, and many obstacles. And neoliberalism is, at present, a more important obstacle than Islam.

7

BLASPHEMERS AND INFIDELS

TAKING OFFENSE

Questions on science and religion, and the relationship of science and Islam in particular, have occupied me for many years. I have occasionally had opportunities to speak about my work to a general audience. The questions afterward are always fascinating. Since conservative Muslims have a reputation of being easily offended, I have repeatedly been asked if I had run into any trouble because of my views. On a couple of occasions, I got a question about whether I was concerned about my safety.

I have never had reason to worry. In my talks I make it clear that I am not a believer, and that I think that some traditional doctrines make it difficult for many devout Muslims to fully appreciate modern science. Sometimes this draws a strong reaction; perhaps a few take offense. But though I have had some in my audience tell me I was grievously wrong, I have never run into anything more than firm but polite disagreement.

The most memorable response I received was at a Canadian university, where after my talk, a woman in a conservative Muslim dress including a full head covering announced that she was a chemistry professor, and that I was completely mistaken. She stated her views at length, did not appear impressed by my reply, and stormed out of the auditorium. She later wrote to the campus newspaper, expressing disappointment that the student groups that sponsored my talk, including the campus Freethought Alliance, "invited a speaker who didn't only give a distorted and incomplete description of the current status of science in the Muslim world, but also propagated a wrong definition of the scientific method."[1] All of this is completely normal. I have seen worse flare-ups at physics conferences.

Things might have been different outside of North America. After all, the group that invited me to Canada appealed to atheists and agnostics. Anybody who consults a search engine can easily find out that I am a godless infidel. Outspoken nonbelief does not go over well among Muslims.

In Britain, for example, it appears that secularist student organizations have been experiencing difficulties. Students have been prevented from wearing a T-shirt with images from a cartoon series, *Jesus and Mo*, which satirizes monotheistic religions; universities have been equating criticism of religion with racism and sexism, disallowing speakers who might give offense to religious sentiments. At the same time, Muslim organizations have hosted events where the audience had to be segregated by sex, because to do otherwise would interfere with their ability to express their views.[2] My talks on science and Islam are mild affairs, but I have to wonder if they would be welcome.

I certainly have not given a public talk about Islam in Turkey, which has a law criminalizing insults to religious sentiments. Recently, internationally renowned musician Fazıl Say was given a suspended sentence for blasphemy on Twitter, including retweeting a set of skeptical verses by Omar Khayyam. After three years, much hassle, and considerable international embarrassment, a higher court invalidated the ruling. Since Turkey still harbors fading ambitions to join the European Union, laws restricting speech now come with the latest rationales. The head of the Human Rights Investigation Committee of the Turkish Parliament announced that Say had received a just punishment for "hate speech." CNN Türk, a television news channel, received a fine for hosting Pınar Kür, a well-known Turkish author and secular feminist, who criticized the Islamic head covering. Evidently this "promoted discrimination based on race, color, language, religion, or sex."[3]

In most other places in the Islamic world, blasphemy and infidelity would be punished more forthrightly, as a crime against God or a danger to social order. After all, publicly expressed criticism of the faith is a disturbance of the peace. Religious scholars are happy to cite justifications from the sacred sources, with elaborations in Islamic law.

The Quran sets the stage, with its litany of threats of hellfire against those who do not accept the divine message. Nonbelief is a moral failing, since "We have revealed clear signs to you, and no one rejects them but the immoral" (2 The Cow 99). Therefore, "Believers are not to take scoffers for friends instead of believers" (3 The Family of Imran 28). In case believers ever have to encounter negative comments about revelation, 4 Women 140 counsels them to avoid such occasions: "When you hear the signs of God being scoffed at or ridiculed, do not sit with them until they enter into a different topic, for then you would be like them. God will gather the hypocrites and the atheists in hell, all of them." For the Quran, faith and righteous conduct are inseparable,[4] which reinforces the monotheistic tendency to associate nonbelief with evil and pollution.

Still, the Quran says little about what the faithful should do about blasphemers and infidels, other than avoid their presence. The prophetic traditions and sacred histories provide more direction. For example, Muhammad is said to have ordered the assassination of a few poets who propagandized against the faith, mocked Muhammad, and insulted Muslim women.[5] Such insults and criticisms had a political context: they threatened to undermine the community, or later, the embryonic Islamic state.

It is not always clear from the Quran if the nonbelievers include rival monotheists. Verses such as 2 The Cow 62 include all monotheists among those acceptable in the sight of God:

> The Muslims, the Jews,
> The Christians, and the Sabians,
> any who believe in God
> and the last day
> and do good
> have their reward with their Lord.
> There is nothing for them to fear;
> they will not sorrow.

But then, 5 The Table 51 says "Believers, do not take the Jews and Christians for patrons; they are patrons of each other." Surrounding verses suggest an environment where the Muslim claim to revelation has been rejected by other monotheists.

The prophetic traditions heighten the sense that Muslims constitute a separate community of true believers. Even prescribed details of social interaction come to reflect a more exclusive sectarian sense of identity. For example, one tradition commands "do not greet the Jews and the Christians before they greet you and when you meet any one of them on the roads force him to go to the narrowest part of it."[6]

There is a long way from the denunciations in the Quran to the severe penalties for blasphemy and apostasy prescribed by Islamic law in its developed forms. There is an even longer path to British universities being protective of religious sentiments, or the laws on religious offenses in modern Muslim countries. Muslim environments have not been very hospitable to an expansive understanding of free speech. But the current Muslim sensitivity to religious insult does not directly arise from the hostility to nonbelief expressed in the scriptures. If most Muslims want to discourage and even punish blasphemy, and if many are motivated to political action through a sense of insult, the reasons are more complicated than the commands of sacred texts.

CHRISTIANS AND JEWS

Islam took shape while Muslims were a minority. Most inhabitants of the Arabs' new empire followed their ancestral faiths, usually varieties of Christianity. It was possible to convert, and many did, starting with those among the conquered peoples who became clients of various Arab tribes. Nonetheless, the conversion to Islam proceeded slowly. Middle Eastern peasantries remained majority non-Muslim for centuries.

Muslim elites had incentive not to encourage mass conversions. In 9 Repentance 29, the Quran endorses the practice of collecting tribute from subjected tribes in exchange for protection, and extends it to those "to whom scripture has been given." Christians and Jews under Muslim sovereignty would pay an extra tribute tax, whose details were fixed by later traditions and legal rulings.

In classical Islam, then, non-Muslim monotheists had a recognized status. If independent, their territories were fair game for further expansion of the True Faith, although in the meantime there could be occasions to cooperate. If ruled by a Muslim dynasty, Christians and Jews would live in autonomous communities. In most daily affairs, the practices upheld by the local priests and rabbis would hold sway. Islamic law, however, had the final word when necessary. Moreover, Muslims were supposed to be superior to those belonging to the protected communities. Protected peoples were to dress such that they could not be confused with Muslims, to behave in public in a manner indicating submission, and to perform their religious rituals in an inconspicuous fashion. They could not build or repair houses of worship without permission. According to some common medieval interpretations of Islamic law, non-Muslims could not testify against Muslims in court; their testimony was considered less valuable in general.[7] Rulers did not always enforce the more onerous restrictions on the protected peoples. But the religious scholars, who were the guardians of the divinely appointed social order, often interpreted lenience toward non-Muslims as a sign of a more general laxity in following the will of God. In bad times, non-Muslims made a convenient scapegoat, and restrictions would tighten.

Popular writers such as Reza Aslan like to say that "Islam has had a long commitment to religious pluralism,"[8] evoking images of Jews, Christians, and Muslims in harmonious coexistence in the medieval Middle East or in Muslim Spain. This picture, however, is based on little historical evidence, as are recent Jewish and Christian polemics portraying protected communities as existing in a state of unrelenting oppression.[9] Autonomous Jewish and Christian communities have persisted for many centuries under Muslim rule over a large geographical range. There has been wide variation in the quality of relationships between communities. But Muslims have been in a decidedly superior position, and Muslim rule has usually impeded the cultural reproduction of rival monotheisms.

Eastern forms of Christianity certainly did not benefit from Muslim control. Western Asia used to be home to widespread varieties of Christianity that were usually considered heretical by the Byzantine and Latin authorities. Under Muslim rule, most Eastern churches were destroyed or reduced to small remnants.[10] Their flocks were absorbed into Islam.

Orthodox Christianity survived the Muslim conquest of the Byzantine Empire and flourished in Balkan and Middle Eastern communities, where it maintained local majorities and close links with ethnic identities. As a result, in the nineteenth century, Orthodox Christian churches often became tied to nationalist opposition to Ottoman control. Under European influence, Ottoman modernization included gestures toward equal citizenship, but this satisfied few. Muslims resisted the erosion of the privileges extended to the True Faith. Many resented the sudden presence of church bells which had once been forbidden in many cities, and the lack of submissiveness displayed by the newly emancipated Christians.[11] Indeed, Ottoman Muslims started to perceive Christians, who tended to ally with Western powers and move toward independence, as a fifth column in Muslim lands.

Bloodbaths attended the breakup of the old order of Muslim superiority and protected communities. Christians slaughtered Muslims, and the Ottomans perpetrated atrocities, even genocide, against Christians. And as the Ottoman Empire fell apart, Muslim minorities were ethnically cleansed out of much of the Balkans. This history is personal for me: members of the Muslim side of my family were removed from what became cities in northern Greece, Kavala and Salonika, in the 1920s. They settled in houses vacated by the even larger numbers of the Greek Orthodox expelled from Turkish territory. The Greeks did not think of their subjection as a protected people as an exercise in religious pluralism. When I visited Salonika some years ago, I saw very few traces of the many centuries of Muslim rule, either in the architecture or the local history museum. Greek nationalist fury had attempted to erase the very memory of Ottoman times.

Jewish communities usually had a better experience. Even large communities—Jews were, for example, once the largest religious group in Salonika—remained regional minorities, not threatening Muslim dominance. And many Jews in Muslim lands had roots in communities driven out after the Christian reconquest of Spain. In comparison with the treatment of Jews in Christendom, relatively autonomous second-class subjecthood under Muslim protection did not look so bad.

This is not to say that Jews always enjoyed an easy coexistence within Muslim empires. Occasionally, relationships got weird. For example, in the seventeenth century, many Jews were swept up in the Sabbatean messianic fervor that originated in Ottoman lands. Sabbatai Zevi, the would-be messiah, was prophesied to take the Ottoman sultan's position. The Ottomans considered the messianic movement a nuisance, imprisoned Sabbatai, and gave him a choice of conversion to Islam or death. He converted, causing much upheaval throughout the Jewish world. A few of his followers remained loyal, coming to believe that conversion was part of the messianic plan. They formed a crypto-Jewish Muslim sect that remained a significant community in Salonika until the twentieth century.[12] The wider Jewish presence in northern Greece survived the expulsion of the Muslims, but not the Nazi invasion.

Long before the upheavals in Europe, however, the Jewish position in the Middle East was affected by modernization and nationalism. Even in majority-Muslim areas, non-Muslim minorities were at the forefront of change and dominated trade relations with European powers. As a result, a wealthy Christian and Jewish business elite arose—much to the resentment of Muslim latecomers trying to gain entry to modern economic sectors. Ottoman and then Turkish nationalists tried to create a Muslim capitalist class through state support. In the early Turkish Republic, non-Muslim citizens had some hope for equal citizenship. In practice, they faced low-level discrimination or pressure for assimilation under an ostensibly secular nationalism.[13] Many Muslims, remembering the last years of the Ottoman Empire when Christians had threatened to expel Muslims even from Istanbul, thought it just as well that few Greeks and Armenians remained in the country, and continued to resent wealthy minorities such as Jews.

The Arab countries did not experience the same religious cleansing. Large and influential Christian minority populations remained, along with smaller groups of Jews and variant monotheists such as the Mandaeans, the Yazidis, and the Druze. But traditions of Muslim superiority were not forgotten, and they found renewed strength after secular Arab nationalism collapsed. Demographic factors, including higher emigration rates from non-Muslim communities, have continued to make the Middle East more Muslim. But there is still an echo of the premodern, maddeningly complex mosaic of sects.

The Arab versions of Islamist politics that replaced nationalist dicta-torships, however, have not been good for non-Muslim minorities. Coptic Christians in Egypt face constant conflict with Muslims. Iraqi Christians were better off with Saddam Hussein; Syrian Christians were safer under the Assads. Some Islamist factions today harbor a desire for a religiously pure population more reminiscent of right-wing nationalism in European history than of classical Islam and the premodern Muslim empires.

Most of the Jews who lived among Arabs have already left. Jewish migration to Palestine, the formation of Israel, and the ethnic cleansing of Palestinian Arabs from Israeli-controlled territories poisoned Jewish-Muslim relations. Following the logic of communal conflict, Arab govern-ments drove away most local Jews to Israel, even though they were from Sephardic communities who had little to do with European Zionism. Some of the most vicious anti-Semitism today flourishes within Arab popula-tions. Much of this enmity is dressed up in religious language, laced with Quranic verses and prophetic traditions urging distrust of Jews. Sometimes such anti-Semitism takes on an apocalyptic tone, even though classical Islamic apocalyptic literature pays little attention to the Jews. There is, for example, a tradition that quotes Muhammad as saying

> The last hour would not come unless the Muslims will fight against the Jews and the Muslims would kill them until the Jews would hide them-selves behind a stone or a tree and a stone or a tree would say: Muslim, or the servant of Allaah, there is a Jew behind me; come and kill him; but the tree Gharqad would not say, for it is the tree of the Jews.[14]

This anti-Semitism is shaped as much by modern religious nationalism as the historic rivalries between monotheisms. Even apocalyptic fervor today is woven into a broader conspiratorial imagination that perceives Jewish plots everywhere.[15]

The Arab-Israeli conflict has affected Muslim perceptions of Jews worldwide. The modern, conspiratorial form of anti-Semitism has spread far beyond the Middle East. Still, Islam's main rival is Christianity. Africa is now becoming increasingly monotheistic, and Islamization competes with Christian expansion. Tensions can run high where the rival proselytizing faiths meet, as in Nigeria or the fragments of Sudan. In Asia, Pakistan is infamous for mistreating its small Christian minority, and Christian-Muslim conflicts regularly flare up in Indonesia and the Philippines. In all such cases, there are preachers on hand who activate sacred texts that urge distrust of non-Muslims. But strife is rarely the result of naked aggression or arbitrary religious incitement—there are always perceived injustices and communal conflicts of interest. Christian missionary activity, for example, regularly triggers hostile reactions among Muslims, who see enticements away from their faith as an assault on their community.[16]

It is easy to get an impression of unrelenting distrust and conflict between Muslims, Jews, and Christians. But Muslim community leaders also have reasons to cultivate coexistence rather than strife. They can emphasize the more pluralist aspects of Muslim tradition. Indeed, a standard approach highlights how Islam broadly accepts the revelations that gave rise to Judaism and Christianity. Muslims honor Jesus and the Jewish prophets as divinely inspired predecessors of Muhammad. The Islamic revelation is more complete and uncorrupted, but that is a detail compared to the statement in 2 The Cow 62 that Jews and Christians believe in the true God and will be welcomed into heaven.

There are, to be sure, texts that promote distrust or conflict. But that is a matter of interpretation. For example, according to Abu Amina Elias, a popular online religious teacher, the apocalyptic gharqad tree tradition does not refer to faithful Jews but "a group of unbelieving Jews who are followers of the False Messiah" in the end times. The story "of the gharqad tree is a narration whose implications must be understood in the full light of Islamic tradition. Violent extremists and anti-Muslim activists alike will cite this narration out of context in order to spread discord and hatred among Jews and Muslims. We seek refuge in Allah from their corruption and we pray that Allah will frustrate them by bestowing peace upon Jews and Muslims."[17]

Even among theologically conservative Muslims, there is considerable fluidity in discerning the divine will about relations with rival monotheisms. To many Palestinians who daily face Israeli oppression, demonizing Jews may come naturally. But in other circumstances, the possibilities are more

open. For example, for decades I have paid close attention to Turkish creationist movements. The Harun Yahya enterprise, a major actor in Islamic
creationism, flirted with Holocaust denial in its early years. But the Yahya
enterprise soon adopted a conciliatory position, urging unity between the
"three heavenly religions" against the godless aspects of modernity. Their
Holocaust-denying writings disappeared, and not even a memory remains
within the present Harun Yahya material. The Gülen movement, which has
regularly supported pseudoscientific harmonizations of science and faith,
is better known for its efforts on behalf of religious tolerance and interfaith dialogue. Gülenists strive for warm relationships with Christian and
Jewish institutions, including the state of Israel. They have criticized the
actions the ruling Turkish Islamists have taken to irritate Israel; disagreements about foreign policy involving Israel contributed to the eventual
falling out between the Gülen movement and the Turkish government.[18]
The Iranian government, in contrast, is not warm toward Israel, but has
had little difficulty incorporating Iran's Jewish community into its Islamic
political order.

There is no clear, overwhelmingly agreed-upon Muslim position concerning Jews and Christians. The sacred sources are open to interpretation,
including modern interpretations that move toward accepting Judaism and
Christianity as valid expressions of monotheism.[19] Depending on the state
of community relations, preachers can amplify distrust, or they can insist
on the essential brotherhood of the three divine religions.

BEYOND THE MONOTHEISTS

What, then, about those of us who do not belong to a monotheist tradition? The sacred sources are much more clearly negative about polytheists,
apostates, and atheists. Discussions on Islam and pluralism tend to focus
on how Islamic social orders have accommodated Christians and Jews,
who have an established status as protected peoples. What about others?

One possibility is to approach other religions as if they were varieties of monotheism. In India, even as a substantial population converted

under Muslim rule, Islam remained a minority religion within a Hindu culture. Muslim rulers had to rely on alliances with Hindu princes, and Islam in South Asia took on local characteristics. The predominant school of Islamic law in India considered non-Arab polytheists to be eligible for protected status, and so many Indian Muslims came to treat polytheistic Hindus as protected peoples. As usual, this was not always a happy pluralism; Hindu nationalists today find plenty in the history of the Indian subcontinent to portray Islam as a violent incursion that attempted to eradicate Indian faiths. Nonetheless, Islam adapted to India, blending Sufi sainthood with local ideas about holy men, even reproducing echoes of a caste system in social relationships between Muslims.

There are also opportunities today to extend Muslim inclusivity beyond the three divine religions. Muslims can emphasize what they perceive to be the elements of divine inspiration in different traditions. For example, American Muslim leader Feisal Abdul Rauf writes that "the real divide is therefore not between Muslims, Jews, Christians, and Buddhists, but between godly believers and ungodly people—which includes religious hypocrites." He endorses how some Muslims have envisioned revered Hindu and Buddhist figures as monotheistic prophets.[20]

Nonetheless, popular Muslim attitudes are less hospitable to such a degree of religious pluralism. Surveys by the Pew Research Center indicate that, with regional variations, a strong majority of Muslims worldwide believe that Islam is the only way to heaven. Most think that they have a duty to convert others. Indeed, faith groups are often socially isolated. Muslims tend to have few friends among other religious communities, and few are comfortable with a Muslim marrying outside the faith. The more observant Muslims are more likely to consider Islam to be the exclusive path to salvation and are less likely to consider intermarriage acceptable.[21]

Such attitudes, however, need not result in hostility. Religious communities can coexist even when their members think the theologically correct view is that the others are going to hell. It is more difficult to accept those who threaten the community from within—the heretics, the apostates, the atheists. Abdul Rauf remains cold toward the ungodly. And Muslims, though not less tolerant of other religions than comparable Christian populations, stand out for their strong rejection of atheists, especially in positions of power. There are also far fewer people in Muslim countries who say that they are nonreligious.[22] Anthropologist Samuli Schielke observes that openly expressed religious nonbelief often produces severe social rejection. Therefore,

> the public invisibility and/or ambiguity of atheists and non-believers makes it very difficult to estimate their numbers. In any case, they are a small minority. . . . Data from the World Values Survey on religiosity in Muslim-majority societies show the following figures on "not a religious person" and "convinced atheist," respectively: Turkey 16.9 per cent and 0.5 per cent; Indonesia 15.2 per cent and 0.3 per cent; Iran 16.2 per cent and 0.1 per cent; Morocco 8.2 per cent and nil; Jordan 7.7 per cent and 0.1 per cent; Egypt 7.5 per cent and nil. Such data are to be treated with caution. . . . However, they do show that explicit atheism is a marginal choice, and that also being not a religious person is a clear minority position, albeit a significantly more popular one in Iran, Turkey and Indonesia than in the Arab world.[23]

Historically, Islamic social orders have not allowed open atheism, equating failure to acknowledge God with apostasy and blasphemy. All traditional schools of Islamic law have held apostasy to be punishable by death. It is lawful to plunder apostates' property and shed their blood.[24] This is not a Muslim peculiarity—there is, for example, a parallel in Judaism. An apostate Jew may be killed as a traitor. In Israel, religious right-wingers have used accusations of apostasy to incite the murder of Prime Minister Yitzhak Rabin and to denounce dissident Israelis as enemies of the Jews whom it is legal to kill.[25]

Since dire consequences attend on apostasy, Muslims have traditionally avoided accusing others of unbelief. Even minimal observance has been sufficient to be counted as Muslim. As historian Bernard Lewis describes it,

> Outward performance is sufficient, according to a tradition of the Prophet, since God alone can judge a man's sincerity. Thinkers as diverse

as the tolerant and mystical al-Ghazali and the fanatical and puritanical Ibn Taymiyya agree in stretching the limits of Islam to the utmost. . . . In a trial for apostasy, any legal rule or precedent, even a weak one, which would give an acquittal must be followed. . . . The Shāfiʿī law insists that the sectarian, even in revolt, is entitled to be treated as a Muslim; that is to say, that his family and property are respected and that he cannot be summarily despatched or sold into slavery once he becomes a prisoner.[26]

Some of this restraint about apostasy carried over into intellectual life. Muslim empires kept the Hellenistic legacy of the Eastern Mediterranean region alive, and a few philosophers expressed doubts about prophecy. They preferred a metaphysical God revealed through philosophical contemplation rather than the God spoken of by preachers and scriptures. Such doubters were far from mainstream—we tend to know about them secondhand, through the denunciations of the orthodox. But even today, the memory of their dissent is cultivated by some Muslims who hope for a less rigid form of faith.[27]

Muslim intellectual tradition, however, has never generated a serious form of atheism. Philosopher Shabbir Akhtar attributes this in part to theology. He observes that Christian thinkers have been preoccupied with the problem of evil, which generates doubt and remains a main theme of philosophically motivated atheism in historically Christian countries. In contrast,

Islamic thought does not concede as fundamental the problem of evil (and the associated problem of the overwhelming amount of suffering it causes) in a universe created and ruled by an omnipotent God. No Muslim thinker or educated layman has identified theodicy as a project worthy of elaborate consideration. And yet, among western philosophers of religion, the problem of evil takes a place at least as prominent as the problem of proving God's very existence.[28]

Even if few worried about the compatibility of divinity with evil, Muslims could still have been tempted toward doubt with the rise of modern science. A handful of westernizing intellectuals in the nineteenth century toyed with a scientifically inspired materialism. But neither their imported skepticism nor antimaterialist denunciations by religious scholars had much intellectual depth.[29] Departures from orthodoxy among westernizers affected secularist politics, and in the twentieth century Marxist skepticism about religion influenced some among educated people. Nonetheless, such forms of doubt remained foreign to most Muslims. Even sophisticated theologians tend to perceive nature as an obvious intelligent design and often do not feel a need to provide more than a superficial argument that a divine power is responsible for the universe.[30] There is a vast apologetic literature that argues that other religions fall short of Islam, but there is comparatively little that addresses atheism. Those works that do, including recent creationist writings, almost always echo themes developed by Christian apologists in the West.

While nonbelief finds very little purchase in a Muslim intellectual culture, popular culture demonizes atheism. This makes it very difficult for nonbelievers. Indeed, even religious liberals often have to ward off suspicions of apostasy. Sociologist Mark Juergensmeyer finds only a faint hope that completely secular people can be accepted in an environment of religious nationalism:

> Could the accommodation approach work with secular minorities? Even in traditional religious cultures there are people who were raised in religious households but who, through travel, education, or association with modern urban culture, have lost interest in religion. Should there not be a safe cultural haven for such people in a religious society, just as the cultures of Copts and other minorities are maintained as islands in seas of religiosity? From most religious nationalists to whom I posed the question, the answer was a resounding no. They could accept the idea that other religious traditions provide valid alternatives to their own religious law but not secular culture: it has, in their eyes, no links with a higher truth. From their point of view, it is simply antireligion. Some religious nationalists found it difficult to accept secularism even in Europe and the United States, where, they felt, Christianity failed to keep its backsliders in line.[31]

Heresy is also problematic. How varieties of Islam that appear heterodox to the local majority fare depends on political circumstances. They may flourish as separate communities, or they may face conflict. Today, as Pakistan persecutes its Ahmadi minority or as fundamentalist preachers and Sunni factions spoiling for holy war brand the Shia as heretics to be exterminated, conflict is very visible. Much of this is something new—it sets aside the traditional reticence to denounce those who belong to different sects as non-Muslims. Violent sectarian conflict, as in the ruins of Syria and Iraq today, signals a collapse of historical patterns of accommodating religious diversity.

Atheists are even harder to accommodate. Though few, those without religion are no longer virtually absent from among Muslims, especially in modern urban environments. Since they do not form a community, atheists are not easy to treat as a well-defined island within a religious society. The severe stigma attached to atheism drives nonbelief underground, but the Internet has helped atheists find and discuss criticisms of religion in an anonymous fashion. Open criticism of Islam is another matter.[32] Public expressions of nonbelief will inevitably be perceived as insult or blasphemy, especially if they appear on the mass media. As a further complication, many Muslim states legitimate themselves through religious nationalism. Atheism, then, retains its aura of a threat to public order even where the tight-knit premodern societies that generated mistrust of apostasy have disappeared.

So the Iranian Shia theocracy prohibits expressions of religious doubt, not just because of tradition but also because it is a modern authoritarian state that limits press freedom. In Egypt, Al-Azhar, the leading Sunni Muslim institution of religious learning and law, is also involved in official censorship.[33] And so the practices of Muslim states regularly challenge secular liberal ideals. After all, we want coexistence, but on individualist terms that include liberties such as freedom of expression. But in Muslim environments, this often means an unacceptable freedom for blasphemy.

PREVENTING BLASPHEMY

In their 2015 World Press Freedom Index, Reporters Without Borders classified the state of freedom of the press in almost all Muslim countries as a "difficult situation" or "very difficult situation." This has not changed for many years. In 2013, they also issued a report on how some Christian and almost all Muslim countries stifle freedom of expression through laws against blasphemy or insulting religions.[34] Secular interest groups assemble reports detailing worldwide discrimination against nonreligious people; Muslim persecution of religious dissent is particularly notable.[35]

Examples come from all over the Muslim world. Just in the last couple of years I read about a journalist in Mauritania who was handed a death sentence for apostasy and criticizing the Prophet, where moderates wanted the judicial system to handle the offense and hotheads demanded a lynching. A Nigerian atheist was forced into a psychiatric ward and received death threats, and an Islamic court sentenced nine people to death for insulting the Prophet. A Sudanese woman who grew up Christian but had a Muslim father was charged with apostasy and threatened with execution. An atheist blogger from Morocco had to apply for asylum in Switzerland. Two politicians in post-Gaddafi Libya faced death over a cartoon that some rather oddly thought was blasphemous. Iran executed Mohsen Amir-Aslani, who had held discussion sessions in his house devoted to his idiosyncratic interpretations of the Quran, for heresy. An atheist from Afghanistan, where blasphemy accusations are used against liberal Muslims as well as nonbelievers, was granted asylum in the United Kingdom. Kazakhstan prosecuted an atheist for inciting religious conflict and confined him to a psychiatric ward.[36]

These are not isolated incidents. In Egypt, the criminalization of blasphemy has public support and is entrenched in the state. Blasphemy charges are often used against Coptic Christians; for example, a young villager, Kerolos Shouky Attallah, was recently sentenced to six years in prison for defaming a divinely revealed religion—because he "liked" a Facebook page run by converts to Christianity. The Coptic atheist Karem Saber has been sentenced to five years in prison for insulting religion in his collection of short stories called *Where Is God*. Liberals and doubters from Muslim backgrounds also suffer. Poet and journalist Fatima Naoot was sentenced to three years in prison for contempt of Islam; in a Facebook post, she had criticized the ritual slaughter of animals for a Muslim holiday. TV preacher Islam Behery questioned Quranic literalism and cast doubt on some prophetic traditions, and he was sent to prison for a year for contempt of religion. University students Karim al-Banna and Sherif Gaber have been sentenced to prison terms for expressing atheism on Facebook; the case against Gaber was personally filed by his university's president. Conservative Muslims have accused Hamed Abdel-Samad, a political scientist based in Germany, of apostasy due to his criticism of traditional Islam, and have called for his death. Egyptian nonbelievers are afraid of expressing their views. As one atheist put it, "I'm not afraid of the government, I'm afraid of the people. Society is the problem."[37]

Theocratic regimes drive nonbelief further underground. The Persian Gulf States harbor a small number of atheists and anticlerical dissidents who express themselves clandestinely, often using social media. Publicly, they are despised. Recently, Saudi Arabian regulations and royal decrees have equated atheism and questioning Islam with terrorism. Raef Badawi, a blogger responsible for a liberal Muslim website, has been sentenced to ten years and a thousand lashes for insulting Islam. Courts continue to pass death sentences for blasphemy and apostasy, though the sentences may get reduced due to international pressure. A Palestinian poet living in Saudi Arabia, Ashraf Fayadh, was recently condemned to death for apostasy, but had his sentence downgraded to eight years in prison and eight hundred lashes. Meanwhile, the Saudis have also demanded that Norway should better respect human rights—by preventing criticism of religion and the Prophet.[38]

In Pakistan, charges of blasphemy are notoriously used to ruin lives and foment violence against minorities and nonbelievers. Desecrating the Quran, insulting the Prophet, or disrespecting his Companions—as the Shia might do—demand death or life imprisonment. Pakistan has not yet executed anyone for blasphemy, but many suffer from life sentences or are on death row. Blasphemy accusations require little evidence; indeed, courts often fear to hear evidence, as presenting the blasphemous statements may repeat the offense. However, social norms, rather than the blasphemy law, create the most pressure on religious dissent. Individuals accused of blasphemy and those in their community face vigilante violence. Lawyers defending the accused have been murdered. In recent years, Salman Taseer, a former governor, and Shahbaz Bhatti, a Christian and the Federal Minister for Minorities, have been assassinated for opposing the blasphemy laws. Religious minorities such as Christians and the Ahmadi worry daily about oppression, forced conversions, and uncertain legal status. A few atheists and agnostics have an Internet presence, but they cannot express themselves publicly. That would lead to family dishonor and social ostracism.[39]

Bangladesh, which used to in part define its national identity through its struggle against Pakistani-style Islam, has become more conservatively Muslim in its public culture in recent decades. Bangladesh also recently witnessed political conflict with blasphemy as a pretext. In 2013, liberal political groups protested to demand the death penalty for an Islamist leader accused of favoring Pakistan in the Bangladeshi war of independence in 1971. They were soon upstaged by over a hundred thousand religious conservatives who demonstrated against atheist bloggers among the liberals, demanding more Islamization and harsher blasphemy laws. The bloggers were attacked and one was murdered. The government tightened monitoring of social media against blasphemy. In 2015 another wave of assassinations of atheist bloggers began, where the killers acted with every expectation of impunity. Publishers and sellers of books critical of Islam are regularly arrested and charged with harming Muslim sentiments.[40]

Muslim countries with a more democratic reputation are somewhat more lenient toward blasphemy. Open nonbelief has always been rare in Turkey; as far as I knew, I was the only godless infidel among my schoolmates. But the religious conservatism of the last few decades has produced a cultural polarization, and increasing numbers of secular people have drifted from nonobservant belief into more explicit religious dissent. When I get together with old school friends, many will now declare themselves as deists, agnostics, or even atheists. But they are a very unrepresentative sample. Turkish public culture reviles nonbelief. Laws against defaming religion are enforced: I constantly read about blocked websites, bloggers sentenced to prison for insulting the Prophet, and cartoonists prosecuted for poking fun at religion. The official clergy are always ready to support government acts such as social-media bans, reminding believers that freedom cannot mean license. In 2015 Islamic terrorists killed twelve at the offices of the humor magazine *Charlie Hebdo* in France, due to its practice of publishing irreverent cartoons of Muhammad. In Turkey, a secularist newspaper decided to show solidarity by publishing a translated selection from the next issue of *Charlie Hebdo*, without including any material that might be deemed offensive. Even that brought police harassment, obstructions to the paper's distribution, and angry demonstrations by religious groups. Leading politicians denounced mockery of the sacred as beyond the bounds of freedom, and prosecutors launched investigations against the secularist newspaper and its columnists.[41]

Meanwhile, Malaysia, based on worries about possible conversions away from Islam, banned the commonly used word for God, "Allah," from use by non-Muslims. Indonesia is not always hospitable to minority sects such as the Ahmadis, which have been banned in some localities. Indonesia also has a very small population of atheists, who usually form anonymous online groups. Revealing oneself can be dangerous—civil servant Alexander Aan recently served two and a half years in prison for declaring himself an atheist on Facebook and thereby violating the Indonesian blasphemy law. While the Indonesian law against blasphemy has been in effect since 1965, it has only recently begun to be used widely. Amnesty International reports more than one hundred convictions for blasphemy over the last few years.[42]

Many religious authorities defend harsh penalties against blasphemy and atheism. After all, these are serious crimes that undermine a public order based on religion. Conservative scholars give rulings explaining that

> whoever denies the Creator or refuses to worship Him, or joins others
> in worship with Him [worships anything other than God], deserves the
> most severe punishment, because for a man to deny his Creator, or refuse
> to worship Him, or join others in worship with Him, is the most serious
> of human sins, the most abhorrent of beliefs and the worst deviation. If

a person is like this, there is no value in any good deed that he does. The atheist who does deeds that are good in his own eyes, and does whatever good deeds he can for his society, is like a man who kills his father and mother and takes good care of dogs. Does it not make sense that he should be punished and that his good treatment of dogs should not count for anything? The most important rights are the rights of Allaah, which are that He should be acknowledged and worshipped.[43]

Other interpreters may attempt to soften Islamic law, arguing that blasphemy and apostasy should be punished by death only if explicit treason is involved. Even so, the result is hardly freedom of expression. According to Mohammad Hashim Kamali, a prominent scholar and professor of law, Islamic law "entitles the individual to say what he or she pleases, provided that the words so uttered do not involve blasphemy, backbiting, slander, insult or lies, nor seek to give rise to perversity, corruption, hostility, and sedition."[44] Indeed, the law affirms a freedom to criticize the government. Blasphemy, for Kamali, involves deliberate contempt or hostility, and its punishment must follow modern legal norms that allow protection of communities or offended persons from insults. "Freedom of speech, like other liberties, is subservient to the 'essential interests' . . . and values which are needed to maintain a stable sociopolitical order. Therefore, the exercise of this freedom must not jeopardise the five essential values of life, faith, intellect, lineage and property."[45] Islam balances personal freedom with responsibility and respect for the sacred foundations of social life.

Not every Muslim, however, always respects the religious rules. The Middle East also has a tradition of underground humor that eviscerates clerics and other solemn guardians of propriety. And more liberal Muslims, while accepting that most popular and historical understandings of Islam have been hostile to freedom of conscience and expression, seek newer interpretations. After all, reform demands criticism of tradition. Religious writings have to be interpreted, and the community of believers cannot know what interpretation to accept unless they can freely debate alternative points of view.[46] A few Muslim thinkers even defend freedom of conscience while acknowledging religious nonbelief as a live option rather than a possibility from which to recoil in horror. Faith must be voluntary:

God has created humans such that we have a free choice to acknowledge or resist the truth of Islam.[47]

In a climate of religious nationalism, however, liberalizing social attitudes toward religiously offensive speech is not easy. This is not just a Muslim issue. While collecting Muslim examples of the persecution of nonbelief, I also made note of what other religious conservatives were up to, starting with the Pakistani Christians who accused a controversial pastor of blasphemy and forced him to flee.[48]

India, for example, is not much more welcoming toward free expression than its Muslim neighbors. India also ranks very low in the World Press Freedom Index. Indian law penalizes outrages against religious sentiments, so that for example, books have been prevented from publication due to accusations of sexualizing Hindu deities. Intellectuals who criticize the local religion are in danger in India as well. In 2015, the year atheist bloggers were being murdered in Bangladesh, the famous rationalist M. M. Kalburgi was shot dead in India. The Indian government has been criticized for indifference to similar assassinations of secular activists.[49]

Buddhist nationalists can be as sensitive to insult as Hindu nationalists. Sri Lanka deported a British tourist with a tattoo of the Buddha for hurting religious feelings. Buddhist conservatives in Thailand have demanded a law against blasphemy.[50]

Orthodox Christian countries do not usually tolerate blasphemy. In Greece, blogger Filippos Loizos, who ridiculed a popular religious figure online, received a suspended sentence for malicious blasphemy and insulting religion. The Russian parliament overwhelmingly passed a church-supported bill to criminalize insulting religious believers' feelings. Georgia moved toward further solidifying the privileged position of the Georgian Orthodox Church with a law against blasphemy.[51]

Catholic countries such as Poland also have blasphemy laws; indeed, blasphemy as a legal and social concept has been undergoing a revival in Christian countries. Pakistan and other Muslim states have used the example of Irish laws against blasphemy to present criminalizing defamation of religion as an accepted international standard.[52]

More liberal countries also present odd cases. French law protects individuals, not beliefs, from defamation. But the Alsace region has an exceptional status, including a law against blasphemy, so French Islamists have sued the humor magazine *Charlie Hebdo* under Alsatian law. Curiously, blasphemy against Islam can run afoul of anti-racist laws. Firoozeh Bazrafkan, a Danish-Iranian artist, was convicted of racism and fined due to statements on her blog. She had accused Muslim men of supporting a rape culture and described Islam as "a defective and inhumane religion whose textbook, the Koran, is more immoral, deplorable and crazy than manuals of the two other global religions combined."[53]

WHY FREEDOM OF EXPRESSION?

To me, accounts of people persecuted for blasphemy are horror stories. I am not merely indifferent to religion, for example, in the way that ice hockey does nothing for me. In my considered judgment, beliefs in supernatural agents and revelations are seriously mistaken. My intellectual life is shot through with blasphemy. I can easily imagine being subjected to the penalties for nonbelief.

Moreover, freedom of expression is central for me. Together with most secular liberals, I want to order our collective lives through reasoned negotiation rather than deference to sanctified authority. I hope for an expansive public sphere full of debate and disagreement, where we can weigh different options and construct common political goals. None of this can happen if our ability to criticize stops where the sacred begins. I understand why the Enlightenment tradition has taken freedom of expression to be fundamental, and how a political philosopher such as Stephen Eric Bronner can say that "freedom of speech is the precondition for all other freedoms."[54]

But then, Muslims very often think that disrespect toward the sacred is an abuse of freedom. Devout Muslims and I value different things, and maybe that is all there is to say. Still, I also wonder if there is a case for freedom of expression that does more than restate liberal pieties. We might be able to appeal to common interests. After all, liberals celebrate individuality, novelty, and personal self-expression. People everywhere care for their freedom to choose consumer goods, musical tastes, and elected officials. Nobody likes to be told to shut up.

And yet, one does not have to be a puritan to suspect an element of narcissism in an emphasis on self-expression. Most discussions I encounter online are freewheeling and uncensored, but usually they are also vicious and inconsequential. I am not the only one to complain; few of us care about expression just for its own sake. And once we ask what forms of expression we want to promote, we face endless possibilities tied to diverse social practices. Novelty-seekers like me favor social experiments, but traditionalists may want a more regimented community necessary to express moral values higher than the superficialities of consumer choice.[55]

Liberals also provide utilitarian reasons for freedom of speech, pointing, like philosopher Paul Cliteur, to "the fruitful consequences of the development of science, culture, and also religion."[56] But in that case, it is not clear that the useful forms of speech extend to blasphemy. What use is an insult? Conservative Muslims also desire development, particularly economic development. But the pious modernity that has captured the imaginations of many Muslims suggests that the benefits of speech may be realized without tolerating blasphemy.

Indeed, social conservatives who aim to promote virtue and suppress vice have a stronger sense of what is useful than liberals who are more suspicious of overarching social purposes. Some conservatives want to promote a society shaped by a moral aristocracy of saints and religious experts. We must train our desires, improving ourselves in the light of pious exemplars. Liberal freedoms tend to produce a cacophony of speech, which may have to be dampened to let the examples of higher goods shine through.[57] Anthropologist Talal Asad argues that the enticements to vice in a secular liberal environment are *seductions*, with an implied threat to social order.

> Thus in liberal democracies the individual as consumer and as voter is subjected to a variety of allurements through appeals to greed, vanity, envy, revenge, and so on. What in other circumstances may be identified and condemned as moral failings are here essential to the functioning of a particular kind of economy and polity.

In the context of an Islamic moral order, however, "blasphemy is neither freedom of speech nor the challenge of a new truth but something that seeks to disrupt a living relationship."[58]

So I don't think that the attractions of more liberal ways of life will make free speech prevail. Individual freedom is attractive, but so is moral community. Perhaps no one wants to be told to shut up, but a lot of us want offensive speech to be silenced. There is plenty of popular support for preventing insults to religious or ethnic sensibilities.

There may be more persuasive arguments for free speech in restricted domains, such as the academic settings in which I work. Suppressing criticism is anathema to the classroom and the research seminar. If we seek knowledge, we run the risk of offending religious sentiments and moral convictions. And we also have to acknowledge criticism of our own positions. This is basic to scholarly training, internalized by most academics. I have long been interested in challenges to mainstream science, and therefore the readings I assign my students include both skeptics and proponents of paranormal claims. I have invited both defenders of evolution and advocates of intelligent design creationism to speak on campus. I have never felt that I was doing anything unusual.

Speech in academic environments, however, is also tightly controlled. Not everything goes in my classroom—counterarguments are fine, but online-style vitriol is not. Academic debates have high barriers to entry, such as credentials and peer review. Participants have to demonstrate critical engagement with current ideas and win the respect of a community of experts. Outsiders, such as creationists, often accuse mainstream science of excluding their ideas from free and open debate. But controlled environments *enable* productive discussion. We need standards. Our professional standards keep intelligent design out of the biology classroom, and ruin the reputations of creationists. That is what they are supposed to do.

Moreover, academic institutions also have purposes that conflict with free speech. The need to attract corporate and military sponsorship of applied research can interfere with open publication. Some speech—insults to sexual orientation, religious or racial identities—may make some students so uncomfortable, feel so unwelcome, as to impede their free participation in academic debates. In practice, universities are not free-speech utopias but constant battlegrounds over the limits of legitimate expression.

Our political institutions have a much weaker interest in seeking knowledge, and even in liberal societies, our public debates have many purposes other than individual expression. We might also care for inclusion of various religious and ethnic groups; we certainly want to keep the peace. In that case, speech that will be understood as an insult or blasphemy becomes a problem.

Defenders of free speech often portray sensitivity to insult as a disguise for intolerance.[59] An offense caused by speech is merely a psychological response, not a substantial harm that demands a public remedy. But it is not so easy to separate insults from harm. Muslim academics often portray criticism or mockery of Islam as another Western attack on peoples that remain subordinated even after direct colonial rule has expired.[60] Brushing off insults as harmless privileges liberal individualism, overlooking how insults work among people who deeply care about honor and loyalty. Moreover, even liberal political thinkers today put more emphasis on how group membership shapes our personalities. Religious affiliation can be of immense value to individuals. Unlike opinions about wallpaper, religious beliefs might deserve protection. In particular, multicultural societies require respect to be extended to all. Philosopher Charles Taylor argues that

> our identity is partly shaped by recognition or its absence, often by the *mis*recognition of others, and so a person or group of people can suffer real damage, real distortion, if the people or society around them mirror back a confining or demeaning or contemptible picture of themselves. Nonrecognition or misrecognition can inflict harm, can be a form of oppression, imprisoning someone in a false, distorted, and reduced mode of being.[61]

In complex societies full of groups jockeying for advantage, group members usually develop sensitivity to signs of disrespect. Insults probe status hierarchies; what we can get away with indicates how power is structured. So to keep the peace, we often have informal sanctions against criticizing what is sacred to others. Muslims might think that belief in the Trinity is an absurdity, or even a grave sin, but they will not often voice that conviction in the presence of Christian neighbors. Atheists keep quiet. Moreover, even liberals can let informal disapproval harden into legal prohibitions. Promoting inclusion of vulnerable groups may demand penalties against hate speech, homophobia, or Holocaust denial.

We might, perhaps, still try to structure our regulations of speech in order to maximize our liberty. But it is hard to even make sense of maximizing freedom.[62] Sometimes we can rank different countries according to specific freedoms, as with the World Press Freedom Index. But more often, how we weigh different freedoms and how we resolve conflicts between freedoms are the very substance of fierce political contests. The robust sense of religious freedom favored by many social conservatives conflicts with a more expansive freedom of speech. Criticism of religion, especially when expressed irreverently, is an implicit challenge to religious identities in public. The presence of blasphemy marks public space as hostile to the devout—it interferes with their freedom to participate in public debates without the burden of enduring mockery or insult. Our politics, then, includes debates about how to structure our public spheres. We have to decide what freedoms we value the most, what purposes will be served by our public deliberations. Liberal attempts to claim neutrality with respect to comprehensive social purposes are not helpful in this regard.

So we decide what we care about. Secularists like to privatize intense religiosity, seeing it as improper in public debates. Most Muslims prefer, instead, to privatize blasphemy. This does not, however, mean that devout Muslims must be committed to the kinds of harsh penalties against defaming religion that are so common in Muslim lands. Many Muslims seek a balance between protecting religious sensibilities and allowing criticism. A Muslim political order can institute disincentives to public blasphemy that fall short of criminalizing nonbelief. In these postmodern times, we have increasingly fragmented public spheres, which means that no single rule has to apply everywhere. Religious conservatives cannot impose an empire of virtue on everyone. But they can hope to establish islands of virtue, where blasphemy receives formal and informal discouragement. And people like me, perhaps, will have to be satisfied with islands of academic inquiry.

In that case, Muslims may perhaps come to treat blasphemy and infidelity similar to the way Americans handle nudity. Secular liberals such as philosopher Russell Blackford often distinguish between "psychic distress" caused by insult and "nauseating odors or shocking images in public places."[63] Being disturbed by nudity—a mere psychological response on the part of the offended—may well be a historical and cultural artifact. The more liberal-minded among us may even argue that a nudist lifestyle has numerous benefits, or that nude images can be important elements of political speech. Nonetheless, in our present circumstances, we recognize that nudity is usually disruptive in the common public sphere. It is closer to a shocking image than a mere insult. We might allow some nude beaches or clubs where nudists can quietly act on their proclivities. But we do not open up the common public sphere to nudity, or apologize for imposing penalties on transgressions. Similarly, in a Muslim environment, blasphemers and infidels could come to enjoy their own enclaves, but they would be restricted from disrupting a public order sustained by religious convictions.

For me, an expansive, open public sphere is central to my convictions, so that freedom of speech is more important than freedom of dress. I care for open criticism far more than for religious liberty as understood by religious conservatives. I love cartoons that mock pious solemnity. Nonetheless, my aspirations find only ambiguous support within the liberal tradition. In liberal social circles, I find plenty of stultifying politeness—we avoid criticism of identity markers. I do not want a sanitized, shopping-mall-like public sphere, and I am not bothered by the possibility of giving offense. Achieving aims such as mine, however, depends on persuasion and political organization. Liberal pieties alone are not enough.

FEAR OF ISLAM

Most Muslim countries will continue to penalize speech. The religious convictions that keep blasphemers and infidels out of the public sphere are too deeply woven into the values of the majority. Secular liberals will object, but there is little else we can do. The liberal political tradition is divided about interference with nonliberal but "decent" societies; it is not clear that freedom of conscience should be among a set of core human rights.[64] The influence of Western liberals is further limited by a history of neocolonial meddling that has often reinforced illiberal practices.

It is easier to imagine that Muslim countries could reduce the severity of their persecution of blasphemy. Religious nationalists care about the international reputation of their countries, so regular criticism by human-rights organizations has at least some small effect. More important, the rhetoric of pluralism and electoral choice has become integral to the conservative populism of Muslim democracies such as Turkey and Indonesia. As Muslim democrats become more secure in the religious character of their public environments, interpretations of Islam that allow nonbelievers more breathing space could also gain strength. If secularism is perceived to be thoroughly defeated, religious dissent may come to be seen more as an irrelevance than a threat.

Secular liberals also face questions raised by the increased visibility of conservative Muslim communities within liberal societies. Secular public orders have, with some strain, accommodated Jewish or Christian sectarians. Muslim minorities, however, often seem more foreign. Their customs grate more on Western sensibilities. Loud calls to prayer, mass prostrations that block off streets, or sacrificing animals in public for religious holidays bothers secular Western citizens more than it does when Orthodox Jews mark off neighborhoods for the Sabbath or when evangelical men gather to pray in stadiums.

All of this invites debates about animal welfare versus religious freedom, or religious claims to common public spaces. But it has also ignited controversies over speech. After the attacks of September 11, 2001, a cluster of "New Atheist" writers objected to the way religion enjoys immunity from criticism, and they took Islam to be today's clearest example of violent religious irrationality.[65] Conservative Christians and Jews revitalized age-old themes, portraying Islam as the face of religious evil. Among evangelicals, rhetoric such as Charles Colson and Harold Fickett's "millions of fascist-influenced jihadists, feeding on revivalist teachings as a counter to Western decadence, seek death for infidels and global rule for Islam"[66] became common. Although such polemics against Islam found a popular audience, they also met with liberal resistance. Figures such as Ayaan Hirsi Ali, an apostate and women's rights activist, became controversial. Rejected by liberals, Hirsi Ali and some other uncompromising critics of Islam have found homes in American neoconservative think tanks. Liberal and progressive reactions toward such critics has included protests, withdrawn invitations from campus appearances, and other informal sanctions against defaming Islam. Western conservatives and some critics of Islam, especially those who assert Western cultural superiority, have then charged liberals with failing to defend free speech.[67]

Liberal support for free expression *has* been inconsistent. Supporting vulnerable immigrant populations or responding to attitudes akin to racism is all well and good. Islamophobia is a serious problem, especially among the religious rivals of Islam. All too often, Hindu nationalists treat Islam as a disease that has been imposed on South Asia. Many Christian Zionists portray Islam as a demonic faith and Muslims as an impediment to Israel who should be treated as savages.[68] Right-wing networks in Western countries have cultivated a broader fear of Islam as a civilizational enemy.[69] Muslim minorities endure plenty of unwarranted distrust, which sometimes erupts into violence. But partly as a reaction, postmodern anticolonialists have turned Muslims into symbols of innocence. Even mainstream liberals often interpret opposition to Islam as a threat to a romantic notion of cultural authenticity. Such fear of Islamophobia is of no great consequence—it has produced little more than battles of words or the occasional public school banning a book with negative images of Islam.[70] Nonetheless, shouting down criticism of Islam, even bigoted, misinformed criticism of Islam, does not help us construct a politics that has a larger role for reasoned deliberation.

Negative reactions to Islam are often rooted in substantial conflicts of interest.[71] For many secular people, Europe is a test case for progress toward humane societies in the absence of a strong religiosity. Scandinavian countries, for example, appear to be well-functioning societies where organized religion has faded, education levels are high, and inequality has not exploded as elsewhere. Scandinavians still entertain diffuse supernatural beliefs and disorganized forms of spirituality, but their societies provide some hope that secular forms of social solidarity can be sustained.[72] Muslim immigrant communities in Europe, however, cloud this picture of secularization. In North America, Muslim immigrants are often professionals, so that on average, Muslims are slightly better educated and wealthier than North Americans in general. But in Europe, Islam is usually associated with a poorer stratum of economic refugees and a persistent underclass. Among socially conservative immigrants excluded from mainstream society, varieties of Islam compete to shape a communal identity, an oppositional ideology, and a popular culture. Islam inspires rivals to secular politics, inviting debate.

Now, concerns about Islam and immigration can certainly cross over into Islamophobia. According to a narrative popular among many Western conservatives, Europe is being gradually Islamized due to the high birth rates of Muslims and a multiculturalist betrayal of Christian civilization.[73] The reality is more complicated. For example, many Middle Eastern and North African countries that have been sources of immigration to Europe have undergone a demographic transition to below-replacement rates of fertility. The fertility of Muslim populations within Europe has also declined, starting to approach common European values. The imminent Islamization of Europe is a myth.[74] The failure of Muslims to adapt to Europe is also exaggerated; recent policies have enjoyed some success in integrating Muslims.[75]

The questions raised by Muslim minorities are more subtle. Integrating Muslims has called for a measure of multiculturalism rather than assimilation. This has meant that secular nationalists have had to adapt to a Muslim presence. The solidarity that once supported social democratic states in Europe, however, also relied on a degree of social homogeneity that made it easier for citizens to think of themselves as engaged in a common national enterprise. The presence of large Muslim minorities tends to break down trust and makes citizens less willing to pay taxes for projects that benefit others who appear less invested in common projects.[76]

Muslims, in turn, have often been opportunistic about multicultur-alism. Political theorist Bhikhu Parekh points out that the

> Muslim attitude to multicultural society is one-sided. They welcome it largely because it gives them the freedom to retain their religious iden-tity and to familiarize others with their beliefs, practices, and history. However, they also resent it because it puts them on a par with other reli-gions and cultures, denies their absolute superiority, and exposes them and their children to other religions and secular cultures.[77]

But even if more Muslim and non-Muslim Europeans were to become good multicultural citizens, questions would persist, particularly about free speech. After all, multiculturalism comes with a politics of recognition, of affirming difference, of demonstrating respect rather than offering criti-cism, of preventing harms associated with insults and public contempt.[78] But demanding that we all feel respect is overly intrusive. It overlooks the ways we find to live together with others for whose beliefs we may have very little respect.

Consider outspoken atheists, who encounter plenty of fear and mis-trust. But this is understandable. I cannot require positive affirmation from conservative religious people without asking them to abandon important aspects of their faith. Instead, I rely on tolerance and selective invisibility. If I happen to wear a T-shirt that announces my skepticism, that invites comment, disapproval, even debate. I want a vigorous secular public sphere that, when I enter it, allows full rein to criticism. But it is also impor-tant that I do not always have to declare myself when in public. Unless I choose, I do not have to announce my political and religious views in everyday circumstances. Most of the time, I depend on keeping private, remaining invisible, and being granted a measure of tolerance when my views slip out. I can have all of this without my neighbors giving up their belief that people such as me are bound for hell. Acknowledging real dif-ference—not the fake "diversity" of American life with its remarkable uni-formity in the workplace and in public—also implies recognizing deep, irreconcilable disagreements.

Cold civility, I think, is good enough. I do not need respect or warm recognition. I may bow to necessity, but fundamentally, I do not want criticism to be restricted to academic enclaves. I still aspire to an environment of robust public debate, with institutions and informal rules to help us reason productively. I would hope that in such an environment, inaccuracies in Islamophobic misrepresentations would be easier to expose. And if that is not so easy today, then we might have to reconsider how we structure our political debates. Free speech is not in a healthy state, and I think that multicultural reluctance to give offense is only a minor pathology. In a public sphere that has been overrun by entertainment, advertising, and propaganda, controversies about Islamophobia are too often yet another distraction.

OUR TRUE RELIGION

Many religious conservatives liken secular liberalism to a religion, with its own metaphysical assumptions and sacred values. It may be a false religion—idolatry—but secular liberalism has its equivalents of blasphemy and infidelity.

I do not particularly like the analogy. Taking something to be important is not quite the same as considering it sacred, especially when openness to criticism is an important liberal commitment. Still, religious conservatives have a point. Examining how we restrict freedom of expression—how we act—says a lot about what we collectively care about. One reason I live in the United States rather than Turkey is that I feel freer not to be Muslim. So it might be interesting to ask what the functional equivalent of blasphemy is in the United States.

The 2015 World Press Freedom Index ranked the United States in a disappointing forty-ninth place, which was better than any Muslim country, but close to Niger and Taiwan rather than to the Scandinavians. One reason speech is not so free here must be our heightened concerns for security. American Muslims suffer the most. For example, in 2012, pharmacist Tarek Mehanna was convicted for terrorist activity, even though he committed no violence, due to speech expressing sympathy for radical Islamist causes. The FBI and some big-city police departments conduct massive infiltration and surveillance of mosques and Muslim communities, looking for those who criticize American foreign policy and express radical political opinions. They engage in entrapment and anticipatory prosecution, charging "material support" for terrorism based on political speech alone.[79]

Dissent by non-Muslims is not welcome either, as demonstrated, for example, by the absurd "free speech zones" set aside to isolate and remove protestors from major events. When it comes to whistleblowers and organizations like Wikileaks, which expose American surveillance or war crimes, the United States government appears determined to erase the distinction between journalism and espionage.[80]

Liberals recognize national security as a legitimate reason to restrict freedoms, especially in a time of war. But we are *always* at war, as part of the Cold War, the war on terror, or whatever the overarching framework-of-the-day happens to be. We have an immense national security and intelligence apparatus that works largely outside of democratic accountability. And we have a history of repressing political dissent and organizing: we regularly go on witch hunts for socialists, communists, and now, apparently, Islamists. Most Americans have, by and large, either acquiesced in or supported a permanent security exception to free speech. The parallel with popular Muslim attitudes about blasphemy is hard to overlook.

The United States, however, does not stand for national security alone. We also restrict speech when commercial interests are at stake. For example, we have "ag-gag" laws that criminalize speech implying that certain foods are dangerous, or recording images of animal mistreatment.[81] Academics can find themselves fenced in by intellectual property laws. Scholarly and scientific activity has to be public; it critically depends on an intellectual commons. But research in areas as diverse as biotechnology, computer science, and popular culture face privatization of this commons. Corporate funding biases research in favor of industry-friendly conclusions, and large companies try to achieve monopolies of intellectual property on such a scale that they re-create an internal commons under their control.[82] Freedom of speech associated with applied research has become complicated. Perhaps this should be no surprise. After all, in the United States, even religions try to silence blasphemy by appealing to the rights of property, the way Scientologists have charged their critics with copyright violations.[83]

Corporate control extends to more than privatizing parts of our intellectual public sphere. For most of us, the workplace is an environment that affords few freedoms. Employers usually can hire and fire at will. Therefore, they have power not only over speech at work, but also over what happens after hours. Employees have been fired for political speech and activity outside of work. There is little that defenders of free speech can do except ask that employees should not cease to be citizens of a deliberative democracy in and out of work, ineffectually pleading for ethical behavior on the part of businesses.[84]

Observing all of this, a Muslim observer of the United States might conclude that what we hold sacred—what we are not willing to allow insult to—is property, plus our form of nationalism. There is some truth there. In many Muslim countries religion accompanies unaccountable corporate power, and states tend to become bloated security operations in the service of private power. It would be odd if the United States, the center of the neoliberal global order, did not exhibit some of the same symptoms.

There is another parallel between Muslim attitudes toward blasphemy and American restrictions of speech. Except for a small minority of dissenters, most Americans think that our limits on speech are either glitches in a fundamentally sound system or necessary features of a regime of ordered liberty. Free enterprise; freedom of contract; freedom to choose in the marketplace, among churches, and among candidates for office— this is what it means to be a free country. An employee may find that her speech is penalized, but then, she is perfectly free to stop working for that company. If a religious dissenter feels restricted by his community, then that can easily be fixed if he has a right to exit.

For me, such arguments reinforce my suspicion that it is futile to talk about freedom in the abstract. We do need rules to give structure to debate. It does not make sense to speak of maximizing freedom. In that case, it is all the more important to pay attention to what we want to achieve. And from where I stand, neither the United States nor Muslim countries come close to the kind of public political deliberation I would prefer.

In Turkey, outside secular enclaves, I find the Islamic ambience suffocating. Even as electoral democracy has flourished and public rhetoric has come to celebrate difference, many secular Turks feel less free. They thought that free markets would usher in efficient technocratic administration and meritocracy. But they found that the new rulers fused religious, business, and government power, and merit came to mean loyalty to enterprising religious networks. Emine Ülker Tarhan, a judge who became a politician and a member of parliament, voices the frustration of displaced secular elites:

> We know of the prisons we see, those who die inside, who lose their loved ones outside. Yes, but what about the unseen prisons—what official report mentions them? Who mentions the fear of losing their job, becoming unable to find work, surveillance, being denied education? There is no need to fire anyone, everyone knows that they can be fired, that no one will give them a job again. Everyone now censors themselves, censorship has won a victory against truth and this turns everyone's home into a prison.[85]

At the same time, an alliance of religious and business conservatives invested heavily in media companies, which meant that that the reality presented on screens and through newsprint took on an increasingly Islamic character. The government now shapes media coverage through its ability to deny contracts, and in turn, media oligopolies influence policy to favor the business interests of their owners.[86] In Muslim democratic Turkey, private power has made informed public deliberation as naive an expectation as under westernizing authoritarian rule.

So I live in the United States, working in a university where tenure allows me to frighten the horses. I criticize religiously motivated distortions of modern science in complete security. Meanwhile, corporate interests manage to severely distort the public understanding of the reality and urgency of global warming.[87] This is as catastrophic a failure of informed public deliberation as I can imagine. No one's free speech has to be suppressed; after all, scientists can complain all they want. And yet, private power buys all the ignorance, confusion, and political paralysis it needs.

But then, the secular liberal hopes of scientists have been naive. We have long been behind the times. Our dominant ideology today has little investment in deliberation and informed debate. Commercial markets are not structured to improve knowledge or to negotiate competing political interests. And yet, we are supposed to defer to The Market as the ultimate knowledge machine, submit to the "wisdom of crowds," vote with our dollars, revel in our free self-expression through our choice of products. We celebrate our lack of job security, unleashing our freedom to be entrepreneurs, continually reshaping and marketing ourselves to best contract out our services. We adopt fragmented, servile personalities lacking stable long-term interests and unable to participate in public projects.[88]

Much of our debate over free speech and insults ignores power. We focus on laws and states but set aside private coercion. We ponder respect but overlook how we need material conditions to enable debates that can *matter*.

According to stories that have come down from Muslim empires, such as the caliphal court in Baghdad, or Mughal India, the rulers sometimes staged debates between representatives of rival religions. Christians and Jews joined Muslim scholars, as well as the occasional philosopher or theologian of a now-dead religion. They were civil but vigorous, free to argue that they had better knowledge of the True God and that the others were wrong. All of that must have been stimulating intellectual entertainment for the court. There was never any real doubt that Islam would remain the imperial religion. Ordinary believers, going about their lives in their separate communities, would never be exposed to any unsettling arguments.

Today is not that different. Our lords and masters have always known that they can allow free expression, as long as it is inconsequential.

SACRED VIOLENCE

MYTHS OF INNOCENCE

Afew years ago, one of my students was telling me about his classes. Rather artlessly, he said that his favorite was not physics, but a course on world religions. He was particularly excited to have found out that ordinary Muslims did not go around contemplating acts of terror and mayhem. Islam was not, as he had been led to believe, a religion of violence.

I was annoyed that he had so casually associated Islam with blood-shed. But then again, I should not have been surprised. After all, there is a long tradition of thinking of Islam as a religion of the sword. Islam's rivals have all produced extensive literatures of being menaced by the intrinsi-cally violent, savage force that is Islam. For many centuries, Christians told some of the most lurid stories. And in the United States, our recent experi-ence with wars against Muslim countries and Islamic terrorism have made us especially receptive to myths of injured innocence. After the attacks of September 11, 2001, I ran into all sorts of denunciations of Islamic vio-lence in bookstores. Even Serbian nationalist writers appeared among the alleged experts on Islam, airing grievances nurtured in the Balkans, far from American soil.[1]

Christian fears draw on a history of Muslim empires swallowing Eastern Christianities, and Ottoman Turks threatening Western Chris-tendom. Medieval Christians described their foes as cruel and inhumane, while also recognizing that Muslim lands were often wealthier and better versed in the arts of civilization. Well-founded fears of raids and con-quest mixed with religious propaganda to result in a picture of Islam that was ambivalent, contradictory, but also laced with elements of demonic violence.[2]

This identification of Islam with violence is no mere historical curiosity. Just a few decades ago, apologists for the Serbian ethnic cleansing of Bosnian Muslims presented their cause as a defense of Christian civilization against an incurably aggressive population alien to Europe.[3] On the ground, the conflict was more complicated, and memories of the slaughter of Serbs during the Second World War by some Bosnian Muslims allied to Nazis also played a part. But the demonic image of Islam lent a universal, heroic coloring to what would have otherwise been a local story of massacres and retaliations.

Conflicts bring our myths of innocence to the fore. Israeli nationalists today also present themselves as bulwarks of Western civilization resisting a tide of violent, irrational hatred. Christian nationalists in the United States constantly stoke fears of an Islamic threat. Every local conflict becomes evidence of the intrinsic violence of Islam, every atrocity a sign of demonic forces at work. Fire-breathing Muslim preachers speak of expanding into the West, conquering Europe, and winning the world over to Islam. And in their words, Islamophobes perceive a threat of violence instead of the rhetoric of a missionary religion that, much like evangelical Christianity, aspires to convert the world to the True Faith before the End of Days.[4]

Critics of Islam who are aware of the long history of Christian violence avoid the futile adding up of atrocities on either side. Nonetheless, myths of innocence persist. After all, they say, Jesus was a purely spiritual leader, while Muhammad was a military commander and political ruler. Christianity exalts nonviolence, but Islam endorses holy war. Historically, Christians and Muslims have both been violent. But Christians have betrayed the ideal of their founder, while Muslims have been faithful.[5]

Secular liberals have our own myths of innocence. For some of us, Western democracies represent reason, while Islam, identified with lunatic preachers and suicide bombers, becomes an ideal type of fanaticism.[6] The New Atheist writers, who popularize an unapologetic rejection of religion, often take Islam to be the most dangerous, unreconstructed expression of militant monotheistic faith available today.[7] But atheists—and even, perhaps, all of us who identify with the European Enlightenment—have our own history of political violence to answer for, from the Terror following the French Revolution to mass murders by communist dictatorships. Our current way of claiming that we are innocent is to argue that the Stalins of the world did not kill in the name of atheism, while violence in the name of God regularly accompanies monotheism.[8] And yet, on the face of it, proponents of secular ideologies of salvation have persecuted dissenters with no less gusto than monotheists have, and with considerably more effective technologies.

The connection between Islam and violence, then, is a difficult question. We have too many myths of innocence to tempt us, too many opportunities to pay attention to spectacular instances of bloodshed. Examining conflicts between secular liberalism and common varieties of Islam always means picking and choosing. When the conflicts involve violence, this is especially true. So I have to be careful to acknowledge that the acts of terrorists and holy warriors do not represent all of Islam, and they do not directly proceed out of the pages of sacred texts. John L. Esposito, a leading scholar in Islamic studies, observes that

> If a group of Jews or Christians had been responsible for the bombing of the World Trade Center, few would have attributed it to the beliefs of mainstream Judaism or Christianity. The assassination of Prime Minister Yitzak Rabin by a Jewish fundamentalist was not attributed to something in mainstream Judaism; nor was the clergy sex abuse scandal attributed to the heart of Catholicism. The most heinous crimes committed by Jewish or Christian extremists are not tagged as reflections of militant radical Christianity or Judaism. The individuals who commit such crimes are often dismissed as fanatics, extremists, or madmen rather than labeled Christian or Jewish fundamentalists. By contrast, too often the statements and acts of Muslim extremists and terrorists are portrayed as integral to mainstream Islam.[9]

On the other hand, Esposito overstates his case. Yes, violent fanatics are rarely the best representatives of any religion or political position. But it is also natural to wonder if the distrust of non-Jews reinforced by the

texts Orthodox Jews study has anything to do with the casual dehumaniza-
tion of Arabs so prevalent in Israel today.[10] Perhaps the Christian history
of sexual repression can help us understand sexual abuse by clergy. Secularists such as me should be questioned about our tendency to substitute
secular salvation myths for the old-time religion and go on witch hunts of
our own. And it is legitimate to ask why violent interpretations of Islam
have become so plausible for a significant minority of Muslims today.

THE TEXTS COMMAND

Few present a demonic image of Islam without a list of quotations from
the Quran and the prophetic traditions. After all, the Quran appeared in an
environment of sectarian conflict; though lacking in many details, it refers
to fighting, battles, and raids. The sacred texts encourage distrust of outsiders, promoting loyalty to a community of true believers in the face of
powerful opposition.

References to struggling for the faith are scattered throughout the Quran.
Some passages promise reward for those who do not waver. According to 4
Women 95, "Those who remain at home, except the disabled, are not equal
to those who struggle in the cause of God by means of their property and
their persons. God has favored those who struggle by means of their property
and their persons with a rank above those who sit at home." Faith is not just
inward assent or outward confession: serving God requires active engagement, even personal sacrifice. And struggle extends to fighting for the faith
when necessary. The reward is great: "God has accepted their persons and
their property from the believers in exchange for paradise for them—they
fight in the cause of God, so they kill and are killed—as a promise binding
on God in the Torah, and the Gospel, and the Qur'an" (9 Repentance 111).

As always, however, it is difficult to figure out exactly what such scattered passages add up to. The Quran includes a variety of statements about
fighting for the faith.[11] For example, 16 The Bee 126 calls for patience and
self-restraint, saying that "if you inflict punishment, then inflict punishment equivalent to the vengeance wrought on you." Defensive fighting

is permitted in 22 The Pilgrimage 39–41, which starts with "Victims of aggression are given license because they have been done injustice." Then there is 2 The Cow 217, which allows offensive war with some restrictions: "They ask you about fighting in the sacred month. Say, 'Fighting then is an atrocity; but more atrocious to God is blocking the way to the path of God, denying God, preventing access to the sacred mosque, and driving out its people. And persecution is worse than killing.'" The famous sword verse, 9 Repentance 5, lifts restrictions, commanding believers to "kill idolaters wherever you find them." Accepting war does not mean overlooking prospects for peace: 8 Spoils of War 60 starts with "And prepare what power you can against them, including cavalry to terrify God's enemies and yours," but 61 adds that "now if they incline toward peace, then incline toward it." Similarly, 9 Repentance 29 commands fighting against nonbelievers "among those to whom scripture has been given" but only "until they pay tribute willingly, as subjects." But very little of a coherent Islamic picture of war follows from all of this. Historians and theologians try to fit such verses into an overall narrative, mostly relying on Muslim traditions to provide context. The result, however, is an imposed structure.

Still, even with divergent traditions and historical uncertainties, it is clear that the Quran imagines a regulated form of war. Sacred violence may provide plunder and slaves, but that cannot be its only purpose. It must advance the faith. War must serve a religious conception of justice. Indeed, fighting "in the cause of God, and oppressed men, women, and children" (4 Women 75) is a religious duty. Those killed while fighting for God are rewarded with paradise. As 2 The Cow 190–193 puts it,

> And fight for the sake of God those who fight you; but do not be brutal or commit aggression, for God does not love brutal aggressors. And kill them wherever you catch them, and drive them from where they drove you; for civil war is more violent than execution. But do not fight them in the precincts of the sacred mosque, unless they fight you there. If they fight you, then kill them; such is the reward of the scoffers. But if they stop, God is most forgiving, most merciful. And fight them until there is no more strife, and there is the religion of God. And if they stop, then let there be no hostility, except against wrongdoers.

The prophetic traditions elaborate on the conditions for sacred violence. Volumes of anecdotes provide the raw material for jurists trying to extract the rules that govern legitimate war, the division of spoils, and the disposition of captives. The sense of struggle and small-scale fighting in the Quran becomes filtered through the contexts of an Arab empire rapidly expanding into infidel territories, later Muslim empires as likely to war against one another as non-Muslim states, and then modern states and bureaucratically organized clergy.

Many traditions claim to describe historical events involving warfare and violence. For example, 33 The Confederates 26 mentions some of "the people of scripture," the believers "killed some of them and captured some of them." In the standard sacred history, this gets expanded into a detailed story about a Jewish tribe that was collectively punished for treachery against Muhammad. According to prophetic traditions, all the males, who numbered in the hundreds, were killed. The women and children were enslaved.[12] Naturally, there is an extensive apologetic literature arguing that this treatment was appropriate, while critics of Islam use the story as a prime example of the original violence of the religion.

Whether such events took place as told is very hard to determine. In any case, sacred history provides templates for correct and incorrect action. Jurists, scholars, and holy men take scattered passages of scripture and heaps of anecdotes and construct their meanings: they propose, for the faithful, what is proper during fighting, whose blood can be spilled, and who can legitimately instigate holy war. Among nomadic raiders such as the early Arab Muslims, or the Turks and Mongols who later converted to Islam, religious war shades imperceptibly into a license to plunder the lands of non-Muslims. But elsewhere—in the urban centers of empires, among comfortably established clergy, where Muslims are vulnerable minorities—holy war becomes bound by so many rules and conditions that it becomes barely possible.

Religious scholars try to base their rulings on timeless divine commands. In practice, the meanings of fighting for the faith vary with time and place. The struggles and fighting in the Quran include both sacred violence and a spiritual struggle against selfishness. The prophetic traditions encourage fighting as a means of propagating the True Faith. The classical legal tradition focuses on regulating religious warfare, often turning it into an instrument of empire. Depending on the circumstances, religious leaders have emphasized a struggle to discipline the self or called for violence for the sake of the faith.

Today, Muslims debate the meaning of sacred violence more intensely than ever before. In the twentieth century, some radical factions among Islamists became convinced that Islam faced a dire threat, and that many ostensibly Islamic countries had reverted to a state of nonbelief. In response, true Muslims had to revive their tradition of militant struggle, including the "neglected duty" of religious war.[13] Since fully committed radicals were small in number, their acts of holy war produced terrorism. Naturally, sacred violence became a question for serious public discussion. Traditionalists reiterated the religious rules that declared freelance violence illegitimate. More liberal interpreters portrayed the Muslim concept of holy war as analogous to a Christian "just war," and presented the fighting for the faith demanded in the sacred sources as a form of liberation theology.[14] The ongoing debate over interpretations of sacred violence, and particularly the emphasis on the justice of religious warfare, is a modern phenomenon. Historically, some Muslim philosophers had addressed just wars, but they had very little influence. The classical jurists wrote extensively on the proper conduct of war but rarely concerned themselves about whether a holy war was just.[15] Today, it is a leading topic of debate.

Lists of quotations from the Quran and traditions, then, do not reveal Muslim attitudes toward warfare and violence. The believers are divided about what the texts command. Now, it is true that compared to other world religions, the sacred violence in the texts of Islam attracts more attention. It is, for example, difficult to find Christian equivalents to the Quran's promise that those killed while fighting for God will go to heaven—only, perhaps, distant echoes such as the pope granting plenary indulgences to those going on a crusade, so those killed would be spared the worst of purgatory. Jewish texts can inspire violence against outsiders, but it is hard to see even the most right-wing Jews expanding holy war beyond Israel and any territories Israel may claim.[16] But then, religions are not direct reflections of sacred texts. Buddhists, for example, often emphasize nonviolence, but many varieties of Buddhism are as wrapped up in nationalism and cultural identity as any religion. In the name of defending their faith, some Buddhists have lately been attacking and killing others, including Muslim minorities, in Sri Lanka, Myanmar, and Thailand.[17]

Those of us who are concerned for peace but who have no interest in joining the faithful have plenty to be wary about in traditional Islamic doctrines. Sometimes sacred violence lies too close to the surface. But Muslim tradition is also a resource. After all, Muslims have forthrightly accepted the constant presence of political struggle, including violence, in human affairs. And they have usually sought ways to contain violence and harness it to purposes other than rapacity. That, at least, avoids some forms of hypocrisy fostered by rival traditions that allegedly condemn violence.[18]

DEFENDING THE FAITH

In the early history of Islam, as Arabs took over the territories of the Byzantine and Iranian empires, war was understood to be a prime instrument in establishing the supremacy of the True Faith. God commanded fighting in his cause and confirmed the validity of his religion by granting success on the battlefield.[19]

This aggressive understanding of holy war was common for many centuries, especially at the frontiers of Islam. The slave trade and plunder were important components of the economy for many Muslim empires, not just for the Arabs but also for later empires with Turkish ruling castes, such as the Seljuks and early Ottomans. The legitimacy of a dynasty was often founded on its ability to prosecute war against non-Muslim states.

But usually the role of sacred violence in the advancement of Islam has been more complicated. In Africa south of the Mediterranean coast, and in Asia east of India, Islam has very successfully—and relatively recently— spread through vast areas with little warfare. Missionary religious orders appealed to new populations, but perhaps more important, trade networks also made Islam attractive. Where a Muslim merchant class established itself, it came to determine norms of commercial activity. Islam, in many regions, spread in part because it represented the rule of law, an advanced civilization, and effective trade.

For example, Islam did not arrive in Indonesia and Malaysia by conquest. Merchants brought Islam and its rules. Some among the local aristocracies adopted the new religion. Rulers engaged, as always, in power struggles with neighboring principalities, and they occasionally mobilized Muslim concepts of holy war to expand their control at the expense of rival Hindu and Buddhist princes. The population developed an allegiance to Islam through a complex interaction between Islam's association with state power, the influence of merchants, and the gradual establishment of the scholarly class and Sufi orders as religious authorities. The religious scholars acquired control over education, law, and the legitimation of elites. Over time, urban populations were Islamized, and rural religion also became at least nominally Islamic in most regions. The process of Islamization continues today.[20]

In the heartlands of Islam, where the protected communities of non-Muslims became small, subdued, and subject to tribute taxes, regulations of holy war remained among the religious rules, but in many circumstances were irrelevant to the peaceful conduct of ordinary life far from any frontiers. Sometimes, however, sacred violence could be reactivated—as a tool of revolt.

An interesting example is the Wahhabi movement that began in the Arabian Peninsula in the eighteenth century. Muhammad bin Abd al-Wahhab, a charismatic religious scholar, opposed the settled forms of Islam of his time, demanding a return to the sacred sources.[21] His followers considered Islam to have been purest in the first generations after Muhammad, and they proposed to cleanse the faith of later accretions such as Sufi forms of organization and observance. Directed inward, such an impulse can produce pietistic enclaves. In this case, however, the reformers of faith allied with tribal chiefs, such as Muhammad bin Saud and his descendants, and attempted to use sacred violence to establish a puritan order. The Wahhabis rebelled against the Ottoman Empire, and the empire then suppressed what was considered a band of uncivilized fanatics. Eventually, in the early twentieth century, the Wahhabis succeeded, founding Saudi Arabia.

After the industrialized West came to dominate the lands of Islam, declarations of holy war were often part of anticolonial struggles. After all, the colonial powers were infidels ruling over Muslims, often with the collaboration of westernizing local elites. Even today, the most credible calls for religious warfare involve places such as Kashmir, Chechnya, Palestine, or Iraq under occupation, where Muslims might be described as oppressed by foreign invaders. Bringing up these conflicts, preachers remind Muslims of their collective obligation to defend the faith against its enemies. Saudi history, however, shows that sacred violence can be considerably more complicated. Wahhabi fundamentalism arose as a movement for reform and renewal, one of many examples in Muslim history. It was not a reaction against Western modernity or domination by non-Muslim powers. Indeed, the Wahhabi revolts targeted other, what they considered laxer, forms of Islam. To attain and keep power, Saudis later allied themselves with Western colonial powers; they maintain a very close alliance with the United States today. Both Saudi and Western interests converged to support a puritan form of religion against independent nationalism.

The Saudis continue to finance Wahhabi-like expressions of Islam throughout the world.[22] In their revivalist fervor, puritan movements often take a hard line against insufficiently fundamentalist varieties of Islam. They may also revive sacred violence, so that holy war once more becomes a possibility. Offshoots of Wahhabi-style Islam inspired international volunteers to join the fighting in Afghanistan against the Soviets and in Bosnia against the Serbs. Lately, they have been encouraging violence against the Shia as well.

Today, the landscape of religious warfare is very different from centuries ago. There are no more conquering armies of the faithful, no more raids at the borderlands. The rhetoric of holy war still appears with resistance against foreign occupation. Furthermore, in conservative Muslim areas where states have collapsed, such as Afghanistan, Somalia, Libya, or Iraq and Syria, rigorous fundamentalist movements often make up the core of attempts to re-form a state. They activate notions of sacred violence while trying to establish a local monopoly on violence. Minorities and the insufficiently orthodox suffer. Our most common media image of Islamic violence, however, is associated not with armies or guerrillas, but with tiny bands of terrorists. The targets of their violence are not just soldiers and occupiers, but civilians. The perpetrators are not armies, but loosely connected networks of freelance holy warriors. For many of us who see the world through our screens, fighting for Islam has come to mean suicide bombings and beheadings, not just in war-torn lands but in the midst of cities. This is something new; it has very little historical precedent.

The media image can be misleading, particularly if we imagine that Muslims are especially violent. Muslim societies enjoy unusually low murder rates. And contrary to perceptions that Islam is associated with war, statistically, Muslim populations are not linked to large-scale political violence such as armed conflicts. Muslims, however, are disproportionally involved with terrorism. The most spectacular acts of terror, such as suicide bombings, often target foreign occupiers. But even accounting for such factors, Muslims are overrepresented.[23]

Naturally, Muslims have been subjects of many surveys that probe whether terrorism, as a new variety of sacred violence, enjoys popular support. A Pew Research Center poll finds that

> Muslims in some countries surveyed in South Asia and the Middle East– North Africa region are more likely than Muslims elsewhere to consider suicide bombing justified. Four-in-ten Palestinian Muslims see suicide bombing as often or sometimes justified, while roughly half (49%) take the opposite view. In Egypt, about three-in-ten (29%) consider suicide bombing justified at least sometimes. Elsewhere in the region, fewer Muslims believe such violence is often or sometimes justified, including fewer than one-in-five in Jordan (15%) and about one-in-ten in Tunisia (12%), Morocco (9%) and Iraq (7%).[24]

It is difficult to interpret such numbers. Clearly, a strong majority of Muslims condemn terrorist violence, especially against civilians. On the other hand, the existence of a substantial minority that find terror attacks justified suggests that some varieties of Islam too readily affirm violence.

To further complicate matters, focusing on suicide bombing as an unacceptable tactic overlooks how martyrdom operations are the smart bombs used by people without access to drones and cruise missiles. Many Muslims who feel ambivalent about terror tactics point out, with considerable justification, that Muslim populations have suffered mass slaughter from aerial bombings, drone strikes, or economic sanctions directed by Western powers. Such means of killing civilians are less often condemned by Westerners wrapped up in their myths of innocence. For example, a 2006 poll, at the height of the American occupation of Iraq, found that "only 46 percent of Americans think that 'bombing and other attacks intentionally aimed at civilians' are 'never justified,' while 24 percent believe these attacks are 'often or sometimes justified.'" At the same time, in most Muslim countries, about 80 percent agreed that terrorist attacks are never justified.[25]

Indeed, sociologist Charles Kurzman argues that, given the circumstances, there are surprisingly *few* Muslim terrorists. The globalized terrorist version of sacred violence receives some superficial pop-culture support, particularly online. But the holy warriors have been unable to recruit substantial numbers from among Muslim populations. Their literature is full of complaints about how the vast majority of Muslims are unwilling to fight.[26]

Nevertheless, there are enough acts of terror to influence perceptions of Islam, among Muslims as well as outsiders. The invitation to violence has not convinced many Muslims, but it has once again become an important part of religious discourse. Terrorists use the language of martyrdom, of righteous sacrifice, of religious duty. As with other aspects of Islam, sacred violence has mutated and modernized.

SPREADING TERROR

Sometime during the late 1970s, as we were playing in the backyards between apartment buildings in Istanbul, my friends and I heard gunshots. After a few minutes of quiet, with the foolhardiness of youth, we went to investigate. In the few more minutes before the authorities arrived, we saw what might have been a small bloodstain on the pavement, but little more. Later, we heard a rumor that an army colonel had been shot at, maybe wounded, and returned fire.

In Turkey at that time, it was typical to have ten to twenty people killed every day due to political violence. Few places were safe. Every bank had begun to be guarded by soldiers, as terrorist groups had taken to frequent armed robbery to finance their activities. At night, it was not a good idea to go out. In the mornings, we would often find fresh slogans painted on the neighborhood walls, advertising the presence of one armed faction or another.

Some of the terrorists were radical Islamists trying to establish an Islamic state. But most were sectarian Marxists, similar to the Red Brigades and other groups in Europe that had delusions of ushering in the Revolution. Much of the bloodshed was due to leftist clashes with ultranationalist gangs who saw themselves as defending the state, and for whom Islam was just one part of a right-wing identity.

In 1980, to most peoples' relief, the military staged a coup and clamped down on the street violence. They also suppressed all forms of left-wing politics. In the period of military rule and in the following decades, terrorist attacks on civilians in Turkey mostly came from Kurdish separatists. They included suicide bombings. The separatists were nominally Marxist—a relic of the days when ethnic nationalists thought they needed a modern but anti-imperialist ideology. Meanwhile, many disappointed Marxists turned to Islam. This was not a complete transformation since, at this time, opposition Islamist politics in Turkey still had a radical edge. Occasionally, Islamic terrorists would again make the news, particularly when they assassinated secularist intellectuals. But the most spectacular forms of Islamic violence again had roots in Kurdish rejection of the Turkish state. Toward the end of the 1990s, an exceptionally brutal Kurdish Islamic terrorist group made its mark. The security establishment had at first encouraged it, since the radical Islamists initially targeted the more secular Kurdish nationalists.[27] One gets used to such items in the news. Terrorism became a nasty but manageable part of life in Turkey, comparable to IRA terror in Britain and Northern Ireland or the ETA in Spain. Traffic accidents claim many more lives.

More recently, the violence associated with Kurdish nationalism and Turkish repression has intensified. The conflict has become further complicated by state failure in Iraq and Syria, neighboring countries that also have large Kurdish minorities. Turkey has involved itself in these regional wars.[28] And so in the news, I now encounter suicide bombings by radical Islamists linked to Syria as well as bombings by Kurds, all against a background of security forces engaging in urban warfare in Kurdish-majority towns in eastern Turkey. Knowing about Islamic doctrines concerning holy war is not very useful in understanding all of this violence. Sectarian divisions, ethnic conflicts, and gambles by geopolitically ambitious governments are far more relevant.

So the Islamic terrorism I have been most familiar with does not stand out as very different from other kinds of ideologically colored violence. Recent Turkish history has produced various forms of failed aspirations for radical social change, suppressed social movements, and militants lashing out at an oppressive state and indifferent society. In a conservative religious environment, political violence often invokes Islam. When religion is everywhere, religion will provide the language of rebellion as well as submission.

Much of the street violence I read about in other Muslim countries seems both broadly similar and strangely different. People with beards and headscarves use guns and bombs, citing chapter and verse, hoping that violence will cleanse the world of sin. Underground terror organizations imperceptibly shade into drug smuggling and mafia-like organized crime networks, eventually laundering money through the most mainstream financial institutions.[29] But the local, often ethnic grievances that feed into armed struggles are usually foreign to me. Recently, when suicide bombings began to afflict Pakistan, the concept of "Islamic terrorism" was not very helpful. The holy warriors cite the usual verses, say that they are defending the faith against all who are complicit in oppressing the faithful, and vow to fight for the justice that will be manifested by an Islamic political order. But while the rhetoric is similar, I am bewildered by the Pakistani ethnic and political landscape in which the holy warriors operate. Foreign intervention, such as drone strikes, further exacerbates the violence in Pakistan.[30] If I look for similarities with Turkey, what stands out are ethnic and sectarian tensions, and the effects of a failed state next door. The language of sacred violence appears in both Turkey and Pakistan, but it seems incidental to the conditions that promote violence.

This is not to say that the rhetorical similarities between Muslim terrorist groups are irrelevant. Sacred violence does not emerge unless the conditions are right, but the availability of ideas associated with religious violence is also significant. These ideas often have a common history, most recently in Arab Islamist movements. Egypt, for example, has had considerable experience with radical Islamist violence. In the mid-twentieth century, even the Muslim Brotherhood went through a period where it engaged in armed opposition. Some of its most persecuted leaders, such as Sayyid Qutb, were instrumental in spreading the practice of describing less rigorous Muslims as nonbelievers and elevating sacred violence to the level of a religious obligation. The most enthusiastic holy warriors found inspiration from previously obscure medieval authorities such as Ibn Taymiyya, who had denounced the incompletely Islamized Mongol invaders of his time as apostates who had failed to implement Islamic law. They called on Muslims everywhere to resist the modern forms of infidelity.[31]

With the global Islamic revival that became visible in the 1970s, much Arab Islamist literature, including the works of radicals such as Qutb, was translated and made available throughout the Muslim world. Turkish Muslims, no less than those in Morocco or Indonesia, began debating the heady new ideas percolating in. This was a new ideology, like Marxism, that could make sense of and help voice grievances linked with everything from ethnic exclusion to alienation from economic opportunities. Radical Islamists throughout the Muslim world saw overwhelming corruption in the modernizing, partly secular states they inhabited. They imagined themselves as a community of the truly faithful, surrounded by enemies and scattered across the globe. They dreamt of seizing power for an Islamic state, and some factions convinced themselves that they were part of a renewed holy war to purify and defend the faith.

Today, this globalized, floating concept of holy war has taken on a life of its own, even as hopes for an Islamic state have faded. There are always armed groups who express their local struggles in the universalist language of sacred violence. Most stereotypical terrorist groups primarily oppose corrupt, insufficiently puritan Muslim governments. If they strike Western targets, it is with the hope that casualties might prompt Western powers to withdraw from their region. At the same time, however, there is also an odd collection of highly decentralized, born-again warriors organizing online or through informal networks. They may attach themselves to various local causes or be drawn toward a kind of apocalyptic violence abstracted from the usual list of conflicts. But in any case, they are marginal actors who find themselves continually driven further from mainstream Islamic discourse.[32]

What, then, should a secular liberal make of Islamic terrorism? The language of sacred violence appears to have been revitalized, ready to use in a wide range of conflicts, mixed in with a variety of invented traditions and redeployed religious symbols and identities. Most interesting, perhaps, is how a heady blend of armed resistance, authenticity, and puritanism can be detached from local conflicts and exercise a narrow but global attraction. But then again, although decentralized networks of would-be holy warriors can be dangerous, they rarely produce more than online posturing. Indeed, it is hard to see such activity growing into much more than another modern nuisance, comparable, at its worst, with the organized crime it so often devolves into. In conditions of state collapse, such as the remains of Iraq and Syria, a lust for cleansing the world of sin may feed into puritan state-forming movements. But even then, the need to conquer and hold territory soon entangles sacred violence in messy local politics.

All of this should, perhaps, come as no surprise. Religion bends to political needs. Violent groups will selectively use aspects of their religious tradition to inspire and justify their bloodletting. And yet, I also do not want to suggest that religion is a mere veneer over worldly interests. There is something unmistakably religious in the fervor of holy warriors. The fanatics ripping Iraq and Syria apart are not just trying to form a state; they have some intensely apocalyptic ideas. So I have considerable sympathy for those Muslims who have to worry about how their religion has become entangled with so much recent bloodshed. There is no easy answer, no honest way to say that sacred violence is no part of True Islam. But then, secularists also face questions about our history with political violence. If we continue to value our political tradition, it is not because we are innocent but because we think our tradition captures something important for us—even after we acknowledge the blood spilled in its name, and the never-vanishing possibility that more will come. Muslims can surely do the same.

SEVENTY-TWO VIRGINS?

Conflicts have complex causes. But secular liberals might be especially disturbed by religious violence. Faith makes conflicts scarier: more primal, less subject to negotiation. We do not fully understand the motives of suicide bombers or those who gun down cartoonists. Martyrdom is no part of our aspirations. We think we might be able to reason about worldly grievances, but not about violations of an alien sense of the sacred.

Terrorists usually have long-term political objectives. Abu Musab al-Suri, a leading theorist among recent holy warriors, advocates easy-to-perform acts that will attract media attention, such as assassinating liberal intellectuals. Such violence will induce fear in unbelievers, and then provoke repression of Muslims. This repression should then provoke a backlash, inspiring recruitment to the sacred cause and promoting solidarity among the Muslim masses.[33] All of this, however, is thoroughly mixed with otherworldly motives. Al-Suri lists the reasons that a believer should fight as:

1. So that infidelity does not prevail.
2. That men who are willing to fight are scarce.
3. Fear of damnation.
4. Performing a duty that is an answer to a divine call.
5. Following the teaching of the worthy ancestors.
6. Establishing a firm base for the development of real Islam.
7. Protection of the weak.
8. In hope of martyrdom.

Violence becomes a form of piety, of self-sacrifice for the greater good.[34]

So we have terrorists, such as those responsible for the attacks of September 11 in the United States, who think of themselves as performing a sacred duty. For some, it seems that religious loyalties are intimately linked with spectacular violence. Moreover, the American response to Islamic terrorism has often invoked Christian and biblical themes, claiming an injured innocence which is to be avenged by righteous wrath directed against evildoers.[35] Secular liberals might feel caught in a religious war we want no part of.

Social scientists, however, usually find that religious rewards, such as admission to paradise, are only incidental in motivating religious terrorism, including suicide attacks. Terrorism has strategic calculations behind it and can be attractive to secular as well as religious actors.[36] Very often, the common element is self-sacrifice. Terrorists, especially suicide terrorists, act out of altruism. They love the group they belong to, and they sacrifice themselves in the cause of their nation or their religious community. Therefore suicide bombers need not come from among the disaffected and the socially marginal. They tend to be better educated and economically better off within their societies.

Such altruistic motivations can serve secular nationalist purposes, such as in the suicide bombings performed by the Tamil Tigers in Sri Lanka and Kurdish separatists in Turkey. Nonetheless, religion makes a difference. Religious terrorism—which is almost exclusively associated with Islam today—is more effective, more lethal than secular terrorism such as that of the Marxist factions of the 1970s. Small-scale religious groups, including mystical Sufi orders, are very good at harnessing intense love and self-abnegation. They can more easily channel religious emotions to the service of spectacular violence.[37] Indeed, religious terrorism is often successful because close-knit, intensely religious groups have effective mechanisms to suppress free riding and individual defection from the goals of an organization. Ultraorthodox religious communities separate their members from the wider society and require them to engage in costly demonstrations of loyalty. In return, they provide intimate networks of mutual aid within the group. There may be theological rationales for martyrdom. But it is more important that when terror and suicide operations are effective tactics to attack otherwise-inaccessible targets, religious groups can often count on their members to sacrifice themselves rather than take a bribe to turn the rest of the organization in.[38]

Beyond small, ultraorthodox groups, rivalry between secular and religious concepts of nationalism can also encourage conflict. Secular liberals can claim some success in reducing the level of violence that used to characterize everyday life, in large part because modern states have established a monopoly on legitimate violence within their territories.[39] But religious ideals of social order challenge secular nationalist attempts to monopolize violence. Our religions often use metaphors of warfare, mobilizing believers against cosmic and social disorder. But defense of the sacred order inspires total commitment from religious overachievers. As sociologist Mark Juergensmeyer points out, "religious violence is especially savage and relentless since its perpetrators see it not merely as part of a worldly political battle but as part of a scenario of divine conflict."[40] One does not compromise with the enemies of God. Political scientist Pauletta Otis observes that religion is a significant component of many conflicts today, and she argues that "religious conflicts tend to have higher levels of intensity, severity, brutality, and lethality than other forms of war."[41]

The possibility that whole communities may be engulfed in bitter conflict is one of the most worrisome aspects of sacred violence, more than the spectacular but limited actions of a handful of terrorists. For example, in the mid-1960s, Indonesian mobs massacred hundreds of thousands of communists, non-Muslims, and nominally Muslim peasants affiliated with left-wing organizations. These mobs were typically made up of observant Muslims who were mobilized to exterminate alleged atheists. Their leaders and participants included large numbers of religious students and scholars, including many from more traditionalist, Sufi-influenced organizations that had a reputation for moderation and flexibility in their interpretations of religion. The sacred violence against atheism was not confined to Islam, since the richer classes took the opportunity to have leftist activists slaughtered in Hindu Bali as well.[42] To further complicate matters, the Indonesian massacres were steeped in Cold War politics and American complicity.

If secular liberals find faith-based violence scary, however, it is not primarily because of what the texts of any supernatural religion command, or even those episodes where secular people have been targets. It is because of the potential for violence inherent in all creeds of salvation. Again, it does not hurt to remember our own history of utopian violence, whether it is to make Indian or Irish peasants starve in the name of free markets[43] or to ignore collateral damage on the path to a Workers' Paradise. When we add intense loyalties that call for self-sacrifice, which religions often do better than secular ideologies do, we have even more cause to be wary. Secular liberals tend to be cool toward tight-knit communities and unquestioned loyalties. One reason is our suspicion that such loyalties can be dangerous.

Many, perhaps most, Muslims might agree—not only the more liberal-minded Muslims whom I know best, but also traditionalists who think of Islam as the religion of moderation, of the middle path. They want to cultivate loyalty, disciplining and subordinating themselves to a larger divine purpose. They may even acknowledge that fighting has its place, in the service of an Islamic sense of justice. They think, however, that they can do all of this without descending into fanaticism.

How Muslims will deal with fanatics will largely be up to them. After all, so far terrorists have mainly hurt their fellow Muslims. Meanwhile, secular liberals also have a balancing act. After the demise of communism, we appear to have few radicals among us today. If we have learned to accept imperfection, if we have abandoned hopes of salvation, perhaps this is a sign of maturity. And since we hold heaven and hell at arm's length, disillusionment might come more naturally to us than to conservative monotheists. But in that case, I worry that losing sight of the radical aspects of our own political tradition will mean that we imagine politics to be limited to a complacent management of worldly ambitions. Fanaticism is a danger for everyone, but so is growing cynical and abandoning all dreams of remaking the world. Our balancing act is not so different from, or easier than, that faced by devout Muslims.

CONTAINING FANATICISM

Most of the violence related to religious fanaticism can be contained through ordinary, boring policies. For example, not too long ago, Indonesia inspired much concerned commentary on the increasing influence of violent Islamist movements. But the more radical Islamists failed. Noorhaidi Hasan, who specializes in Islam and politics, explains that

> attempts made by radical Islamists to impose a totalitarian world order by disseminating religious doctrines and activism that espoused norms, symbols, and rhetoric imbued with animosity ended in failure, and this ultimately serves to highlight the marginal position of radical Muslims and their unsuccessful efforts to popularize their discourse glorifying militancy and violence. In the face of this failure radical Islamists have shifted toward a strategy of implementing the shari'a from below (or adopting it at the personal level), promoting da'wa (Islamic proselytizing) and nonviolent endeavors with the aim of making Indonesian Muslims aware of their duty to uphold the supremacy of Islam. . . . The circle of militancy and violence is believed to only jeopardize the struggle for the victory of Islam.[44]

In Indonesia, effective security measures combined with democratization to provide more space for moderate, market-friendly varieties of Islamist politics. Activist demands for an Islamic public order were channeled into work for Islamization from below. Instead of aiming to violently take control of the state, Islamists came to have more confidence in opportunities to create an Islamic public ambiance through personal piety, or even through pop culture and the marketplace. Radical Islamist hopes for social salvation were assimilated into mainstream religious nationalism.

Limiting the influence of fanatics often depends upon undermining their religious appeal. And traditionalist, conservative religious authorities actively try to do so. Opponents of Islam often allege that Muslim leaders do not denounce terror with sufficient rigor. But Muslim condemnations of the September 11 attacks on the United States, for example, were global and widespread, and included a broad range of political Islamists. After all, traditional Islamic law does not allow freelance, anarchic violence. Religious warfare must be declared and conducted by a properly constituted authority, usually understood to be a legitimate Islamic state.[45] Mainstream religious figures also regularly issue general condemnations of freelance terror. Turkish religious leader Fethullah Gülen, for example, states that terrorist killers are not true Muslims; indeed, they are as bad as atheists:

> The Qur'an says that killing one person is the same as killing all people. Ibn Abbas said that a murderer will stay in Hell for eternity. This is the same punishment that is assigned to unbelievers. . . . In short, in Islam, in terms of the punishment to be dealt on the Day of Judgment, a murderer will be considered to be as low as someone who has rejected God and the Prophet (an atheist in other words).[46]

Religious scholars are more divided about suicide attacks against occupying powers, such as in Israel and Palestine. Some condemn such bombings as sinful suicides and as gross crimes, but others affirm them as legitimate attacks against oppressors.[47] But freelance holy warriors draw the ire of almost every scholar, including established puritans. Saudi rulings, for example, often compare terrorists to Kharijites, a seventh-century sect that separated themselves from other Muslims, declared the majority to be apostates, and made war against the community. Highlighting the near-universal religious opinions against freelance holy war can effectively isolate fanatics inclined toward terrorism.[48]

Efforts to bring sacred violence back under control can join with reinterpretations of religious warfare. Historically, Muslims have been proud of the conquests achieved by their ancestors. But more recently, as Muslim populations came under Western domination, Muslim apologists have been compelled to answer charges that Islam has depended on violent expansion. Moreover, it became uncomfortable to oppose colonial rule while celebrating past Muslim imperialism. Therefore, especially in writings produced for foreign consumption, Muslim apologists began to describe holy war as a nonaggressive, strictly defensive enterprise.[49]

This impulse is still alive today. One of my favorite examples comes from sociologist Hammudah 'Abd al-'Ati, according to whom the notion that the first generations of Muslims engaged in armed conquest is just a misunderstanding:

Now they had, by the Order of God, to make Islam known to the outside world, but there was no telecommunication system or press or any other mass medium of communication. There was only one course to take, namely, personal and direct contacts, which meant that they had to cross the borders. But they could not do that in small or unarmed groups. So they had to move in large protected groups which must have appeared like an army, but was not an army in the real sense.[50]

Among ordinary believers, the imperialist aspect of Muslim history draws ambivalent responses. The Pakistani diplomat Iqbal Akhund observes that "the Pakistani Muslim thinks of himself as the heir to the Muslim empire, descended from a race of conquerors and rulers. There is therefore a streak of militarism in Pakistan's ethos, even at the popular level."[51] As I was growing up in Istanbul, almost all Turks affirmed the Muslim conquest of what was once Constantinople as a forthright military triumph by their forebears. Over the years, religious nationalists have put ever more emphasis on celebrating the conquest. And yet, I also read conservative Muslim intellectuals describing the conquest as an act of liberation, indeed, part of a struggle for human rights. Journalist Abdurrahman Dilipak, for example, says that the conquest of Istanbul "can also be considered the overthrow of an oppressive regime with the help of the people."[52]

Muslim apologetics can reach a surreal state where Muhammad's fighting as described in the sacred history was always purely defensive in nature, or that acts of terror are always committed by false Muslims under the influence of alien ways of thinking. Fethullah Gülen says that "religion, religious values, spiritual things, and morals based on religion are being seriously undermined; this constitutes the most important causal factor of terrorism, and of many other important social problems that threaten humanity today."[53] The Turkish creationists who write under the name Harun Yahya blame terrorism on Darwinian evolution in education, which apparently promotes a godless philosophy of a struggle for existence that inevitably leads to violence.[54]

I do not want to suggest that any of this is intellectually serious, still less that it represents True Islam as a religion of peace and that the holy warriors of today are complete deviants. But it is important to recognize that most Muslims have no interest in what have been traditional forms of sacred violence. Renunciations of violence are not confined to liberal intellectuals or meant just for foreign consumption. They are rooted in the incoherent, superstitious mess of popular religion as well as in scholarly resources that help interpreters to read black to mean white. The texts of Islam can be exceptionally unstable in meaning. Orthodoxy is fractured. And religious intellectuals are followers as well as leaders, translating tacit, unreflective convictions about the sacred into doctrines and rules. Where Muslims have been able to lead reasonably prosperous, ordinary lives, they have not been attracted to interpretations that proclaim that the situation is so dire that a sacred order must be restored through violence.

In that case, secular liberals also have to consider how militaristic policies by Western countries encourage interpretations of Islam that present sacred violence as legitimate armed resistance. After all, we too often seek the causes of "Muslim rage" in shared traits of psychology or culture. Historian Bernard Lewis, for example, famously argued that Muslim hostility to Western powers was due not to the violence of Western imperialism but to Muslims displaying a sense of cultural woundedness, a perception that the wrong people are on top.[55] There are some signs of this. But Muslim literature that denounces Western policies, including writings by radical Islamists, emphasizes corruption and bloodshed. It incessantly points out the injustices visited upon innocent Muslims.

Polls support this view: anti-American sentiment is linked to foreign policy rather than a blanket opposition to Western countries. Muslims often condemn the United Kingdom, which typically participates in American military actions, but they are warmer toward Germany, France, or Canada.[56] Invasion and occupation of Muslim lands creates an environment where deploying sacred violence against imperial powers becomes much more attractive. And even then, very few Muslims are seduced by freelance terrorism.

This is no less clear to many members of the American security establishment. Graham Fuller, who spent a long career in the State Department, the CIA, and defense-related think tanks, observes that a major problem is the violent and sweeping nature of the American "global war on terror," with its high dependency upon military action, accompanied by an avowedly hegemonistic American geopolitical strategy. . . . Indeed, the forces of terrorism in the Muslim world must be brought to heel. But that will not happen unless we see a change in hegemonistic U.S. policies, America's explicit embrace of Israeli right-wing policies in the occupied West Bank, and its linkage with fundamentalist Christian attitudes.[57]

Furthermore, the manner in which the United States has conducted its war on terror reinforces radical Islamist narratives of injured innocence. Pakistani political analyst Abid Ullah Jan argues that "the way in which the victims of the present American concentration camps have been treated, their public humiliation in so widespread a fashion, and the lack of any convictions indicate that the U.S. extremists wish to send a message to the Muslims: Do not expect mercy if you dare to oppose American designs. The gratuitous employment of unrestrained torture further demonstrates and emphasizes this point."[58] The American use of torture is particularly disturbing because of the public support it has received. After the publication of the Senate Intelligence Committee Report on CIA Torture in 2014, a poll found that 51 percent of Americans thought that the torture was justified, and only 29 percent thought that it was not.[59] Traditionalist Muslim scholars may emphasize the religious rules against harming noncombatants, but in the ideology of freelance holy war, civilians who approve of and enable the savagery of imperial war against Muslims become legitimate targets.

While American policy creates the impression of a war against Islam, however, the United States more often intervenes through complex and shifting alliances. Many conservative Muslims support American policy; the Saudi dynasty is a prominent and constant example. Fethullah Gülen's movement admires the United States as a conservative world power; Gülenists have reliably supported Israel and even the American invasion of Iraq. In most cases, however, alliances between the United States and local Muslim factions are opportunistic. The ruling moderate Islamists in Gülen's Turkey, for example, have often served American interests but have not been completely reliable. They did not fully support the war on Iraq, and they have been too closely entangled with radical Islamist groups involved in the Syrian civil war.[60] Pakistan's alliance with the United States has been similarly complicated. Historically, ruling conservatives in Pakistan have found common ground with the United States in anticommunism, encouraging Islamist politics at home and in Afghanistan. However, Pakistani intelligence services have also supported the Afghan Taliban even as the Taliban confronted the United States. American involvement in Afghanistan has also channeled some Islamist factions in Pakistan in a more violent direction.[61]

And so the United States both fights terror and creates the unstable conditions that promote violence. Our media often assumes that Western powers act in favor of democracy, human rights, and liberal values in Muslim lands. I don't know how seriously I should take such a notion. The United States allies with conservative, even puritan Muslims such as the Saudis, as long as they do not tolerate forms of either religious or secular nationalism that might pursue independent interests. In turn, conservative Muslim elites use Western support as a way to keep on top of rival factions.

Outsiders tend to attribute sacred violence among Muslims either to internal religious reasons, or to the impulse to resist imperial domination. But such causes have become so entangled with each other that they are inseparable. Muslim violence is not a simple, straightforward reaction to Western policies. But Western foreign policy—a consistently militaristic, violent policy—is not helping the prospects for peace.

RULE BY FEAR

The scholars of Sunni Islam have often advised believers to submit to unjust leaders. The rulers may steal, overtax, and indulge in immoralities in their palaces. But as long as they are at least nominally committed to Islam, revolt is not an option. Tyranny is better than anarchy. A fear of social disorder, reinforced by historical experience, runs through traditional Sunni political thought.

Secular liberalism is also stamped by a fear of disorder, especially the violence we think will be unleashed when rival absolutist faiths contend for power. As represented by Thomas Hobbes, our tradition of political philosophy also includes counsel to submit to a ruler. The Hobbesian sovereign can even determine our religion, in an effort to end the war of all against all. Secular liberals acknowledge Hobbes's concern with security, but we think his solution goes too far. Instead, we have preferred to make religion private and to prevent the state from endorsing any comprehensive idea about the social good. We are preoccupied with security, but we also want to avoid coercion.

Therefore liberals often face the accusation of being relativists who abandon any strong sense of an overarching moral purpose binding on all. This does not bother me. Our moral perceptions are inseparable from our interests and our agreements; they are rooted in who we are. In complex societies with multiple successfully reproducing ways of life, value pluralism, even relativism, seems to be merely accurate. Conservatives, however, have more practical worries than questions about the nature of morality. We still need a basis for social coherence. Without any common purpose acknowledged, we have little more to rely on than a concern for security, plus ephemeral alliances for mutual material advantage.

In that case, stabilizing a liberal order might require illiberal guidance, perhaps by elites educated to apprehend a transcendent good beyond our worldly interests and negotiations.[62] Even better, an external threat can produce the required social cohesion. After all, liberals still fear violence.

Liberal democracies have often appeared to function this way. In the United States, there is a longstanding tendency for ruling elites to bypass the ignorant masses, particularly in foreign policy. From the Cold War to today's confrontations with Muslim countries, illiberal practices such as extreme secrecy and constant deception have been held necessary, ultimately for the good of the people. Especially in times when foreign policy appears to be run mainly by neoconservative or so-called realist factions, it becomes easy to suspect that our policies are shaped by anti-liberal political philosophies such as that of Leo Strauss.[63]

Perhaps. But attributing our violence to illiberal tendencies overlooks how secular liberalism can also feed into a militaristic foreign policy. Historically, liberalism has been closely associated with nationalism, which has not had a peaceful record. But even when we think we are at our most internationalist and humanitarian, we remain susceptible to messianic violence. For

example, since the end of the Cold War, many liberal human-rights organizations have been enamored of the notions of smart power and humanitarian
intervention. The United States has prominently used such justifications for
invasions in the remnants of Yugoslavia, Iraq, and Afghanistan. The results
have hardly been humanitarian.[64] Even the much-maligned neoconservative
approach to the Middle East has a lot in common with a conventional liberal
developmentalist view that seeks to establish market economies and electoral democracy and to reduce the role of religion.[65]

War, I suspect, reveals one of the fundamental weaknesses in liberalism. The grade-school versions of the stories we tell about liberal democracy overlook how financial power and political power are interlinked, and
then we profess disappointment about how our elected representatives primarily serve corporations and the rich. Similarly, we ignore how modern
states use security concerns to bolster their legitimacy, and how they have
enormous incentives to create and inflate threats.

Across the world, an exaggerated fear of terrorism has provided pretexts to restrict civil liberties. After the attacks of September 11, the United
States inflicted significant damage on itself due to irrational fear and the
absurd costs of dubious security measures.[66] We resign ourselves to regular
mass shootings as a price of the freedom to own guns, but we panic when
faced with the far less frequent events of Islamic terrorism at home. Meanwhile, our militaristic tendencies have been unrestrained: immune to
austerity, untethered from meaningful oversight, free to engage in preemp-
tive strikes. In our permanent war on terror, liberal politicians and liberal
interventionists also call for national unity, rarely questioning the security
rationales undergirding the use of force. The Muslim democracies are not
far behind. In Turkey today, accusations of involvement with terrorism
are used to narrow civil rights, repress opposition figures, and restrict the
capabilities of the defense in legal proceedings.[67] At the same time, the
Turkish government has encouraged radical Islamist factions in the Syrian
civil war and let Turkey become an easy transit point for holy warriors
crossing into Iraq and Syria.

It is easy to provoke fear of terrorism, of various enemies. And an environment of fear provides a reliable stream of pretexts to tighten control over

citizens. Liberal political thought gives us few reasons to resist coercion in the name of security. In liberal democracies, forcing people to conform to religious or moral dictates is difficult, but coercion to provide security is much less controversial.[68] And the more that politics takes place in a climate of fear, the more difficult it becomes to sustain reasoned public deliberation.

The founding myths of secular liberalism emphasize ending religious violence. But where it has made headway, secular liberalism has been established through nation-forging violence. We might want to put all that behind us; indeed, many secular liberals today are cosmopolitan internationalists, suspicious of deep ethnic as well as religious loyalties. And yet, I also wonder if we have done a better job of ignoring how coercion appears in liberal politics than we have of reasoning about it.

Consider, for example, right-wing libertarianism. Today, libertarianism appears as a variety of conservatism reduced to market worship, stripped of concerns for community and religion. But as a political philosophy, libertarianism has liberal roots, attempting to base a political order on a common liberal aversion to use force against others unless it is necessary to defend individual rights.[69] In the libertarian utopia, however, the lion does not lie down with the lamb. There is plenty of force needed to create and maintain a political order centered on property, and plenty of coercion concealed in the freedom of contract. Contract enforcement depends on pervasive bureaucratic regulation of society, and armies of corporate lawyers to keep commercial relationships in line with the law. Control over the disposition of property requires ubiquitous implicit threats of violence, in the form of police and military action.[70] Libertarians ignore all the low levels of coercion that goes into maintaining a social order, concentrate almost exclusively on the force exerted at the point of a sword, and justify liberal use of the sword in protecting established power and property.

The invisibility of force except overt violence is not just a right-wing libertarian peculiarity. It is also relevant in understanding how secular liberalism has so easily capitulated to today's neoliberal political order. Privatization of public spheres, deification of markets, encouraging religious identity politics, and magnifying the security role of the state have all come about with large doses of liberal rhetoric. No less than conservative Muslims, we secular liberals are very good at empty denunciations of violence, pious disavowals of coercion, and dishonest apologetics in the face of the considerable violence embedded in our politics. In the Western democracies, however, we also display our cultural heritage by drawing on Christian hypocrisy about violence.

Muslims are not, and historically have not been, exceptionally violent—certainly not compared to the Western destruction of the New World, scramble for Africa, or colonization of India. Even Islamic terrorism, so far, has been manageable. In the end, what most often bothers me is not the bomb-throwing or holy war, as bad as they are. It is the everyday coercion that happens, for example, when conservative Muslim university students threaten their more secular classmates, quoting violent verses of the Quran to let everyone know that they will defend an Islamic public ambience, that nonbelievers are not welcome.[71] What such conservative students do is an extension of community-based, organic policing of the boundaries of morality. Most often a threat is enough. It might progress to a beating—only rarely to bloodshed. I object to this thuggery not because of a blanket aversion to the use of force but because I favor a different sort of public order, with a different regime of coercion. Our disagreements cannot be resolved just by adding up and comparing the amounts of blood spilled.

This is not to say that I do not care about levels of violence. One of the most important accomplishments of secular modernity is how we have been able to increase the material security of large numbers of people in advanced industrialized countries. Indeed, much of the world's population now enjoys a more middle-income status, far from the abject poverty of just a century ago. Reducing the risk of dying in wars and street violence is part of this story. Because of that, I do not like what the Western democracies have been doing in our war on terror. Our ruling elites have been behaving like they want to extend insecurity at home as an instrument of social control and produce chaos and civil war among Muslims abroad. And too many of us as citizens have far too easily succumbed to a climate of fear, waving our flags and worrying about a Muslim threat.

Some of the worst offenders have been those who have spoken the loudest in the name of secular liberalism. For example, the New Atheists, who were spurred to condemn religion in the aftermath of September 11, have persistently portrayed Islam as an especially violent faith today. According to one such atheist, Sam Harris:

> To see the role that faith plays in propagating Muslim violence, we need only ask why so many Muslims are eager to turn themselves into bombs these days. The answer: because the Koran makes this activity seem like a career opportunity. Nothing in the history of Western colonialism explains this behavior (though we can certainly concede that this history offers us much to atone for). Subtract the Muslim belief in martyrdom and jihad, and the actions of suicide bombers become completely unintelligible, as does the spectacle of public jubilation that invariably follows their deaths; insert these particular beliefs, and one can only marvel that suicide bombing is not more widespread. . . .
>
> The bottom line is that devout Muslims can have no doubt about the reality of paradise or about the efficacy of martyrdom as a means of getting there. Nor can they question the wisdom and reasonableness of killing people for what amount to theological grievances. In Islam, it is the "moderate" who is left to split hairs, because the basic thrust of the doctrine is undeniable: convert, subjugate, or kill unbelievers; kill apostates; and conquer the world.[72]

And so we go off to war against the irrationally violent Muslims, to defend the secular liberal West. My reaction after September 11 has been different. I am more used to seeing conservative Muslims as political adversaries, not uncivilized fanatics. And the years immediately after the war on terror began, with a chest-thumping nationalism and intolerance of dissent pervading the United States, reminded me too much of Turkey during the period of military dictatorship.

All too many secular liberals joined in, in the usual conservative-lite fashion. We worried about a few civil liberties, and harrumphed at the worst Islamophobic excesses, but by jingo, we were in. In our fear, we have demonstrated that we are capable of fanaticism. And we have been far more deadly than the holy warriors.

THE FUTURE, IF IT HAPPENS, WILL BE CONFUSING

THERE MUST BE PROGRESS

A few years ago, an Egyptian religious scholar declared on television that the Prophet Muhammad's urine was not unclean like that of other people, and therefore it would be permissible for Muslims to drink it. Muhammad must, after all, have been superior to any ordinary human, and evidently this scholar thought it was necessary to emphasize the supernatural aura surrounding the bearer of revelation. There are prophetic traditions classified as authentic that speak of the purity of Muhammad's urine. Some viewers, however, were not impressed. Such rulings were outrageous: they associated the sacred with superstition, turning the divine religion into an embarrassment. So critics expressed indignation, and the Egyptian media launched yet another heated debate over a religious question.[1] Controversy attracts viewers.

Secular liberals are also party to these debates, even those of us with no use for the sacred. I read about such episodes with some amusement, but I can't be completely detached—I also feel obligated to worry about rampant magical thinking. Even though I should know better, my first urge is to mutter something about the absurdity of how, *in this day and age*, people can still care about Muhammad's urine. In a time when we casually use smartphones and continually learn more about planets around faraway stars, we should have progressed beyond such absurdities.

And so, secular liberals immersed in conflicts with strong religion inevitably start wondering about the future. Our political tradition has been forged in criticism of old-fashioned faith, nurtured on promises of progress. Detailed predictions about social changes may be foolhardy, but we still hope to glimpse the overall shape of things to come. In a world of technological advances, where information is so easily available to so many people, we think that at least the crazier aspects of our religions should fade away. We want those who make weird pronouncements about Muhammad to be rarely heard beyond the enclaves of religious overachievers. We certainly hope that they will stop influencing elections and public policies.

Those of us who live in rich Western countries often encounter Islam through immigrants with unfamiliar customs. So we want to know if Muslims will assimilate. Since even our varieties of conservatism are laced with liberal convictions, we often express our worries in a liberal political language. *We* represent progress, and we want to know if Muslim citizens will catch up. Will they make their religion a more private affair? Will they stop being so communal? Will they stop beating their wives? We hope, eventually, to weave Islam into our social fabric of fake diversity, along with ethnic restaurants and new choices in carpet patterns.

Some social scientists reassure us about the future. We have, after all, seen similar developments before, when industrializing Protestant countries absorbed waves of Catholic and Jewish immigrants who attracted suspicion for being uncivilized, acting overly religious, and breeding like rabbits. Today's Muslim immigrant populations are adapting as well. Their fertility is becoming comparable to European norms. Pop culture and the consumer society, much more than the dictates of divines, are shaping the lives of younger Muslims. Even fundamentalist Muslim assertiveness in Europe, some experts argue, is part of a process of transition, as the distinctiveness of immigrant populations inevitably dissolves in secular, consumer-oriented societies.[2] Muslims, like everyone else, are caught up in the tide of social change.

But then, the future might not be as clear as that. While religious populations show a trend toward declining fertility, they still reproduce at a rate slightly higher than secular populations. More people are losing interest in organized religion in rich countries, but the world as a whole is getting more intensely religious.[3] The Muslim share of the world's population is rising the fastest, while the proportion of the most secular people is expected to decline.[4] Past Catholic and Jewish immigrants to technologically advanced countries joined rapidly expanding industrial economies. Muslim immigrants today find themselves in deindustrializing, increasingly unequal societies with declining prospects for social mobility. Lately, Europe has been more hospitable to secular liberal aspirations than the persistently conservative United States has been.[5] But a Europe of austerity and a "democracy deficit" can just as easily lead to a future where European nationalist and Muslim identity politics reinforce one another, not only blocking Muslim adaptation but also making Europe less liberal. Even in a Europe that appears irreversibly secularized, our social scientists may turn out to have underestimated the adaptability of modern religious conservatism.

In that case, perhaps Muslim countries themselves can fulfill secular liberal hopes for progress. After all, they have younger, more dynamic populations that are embracing modern communication technologies and chafing under stuffy religious restrictions. And liberal observers have recently found hope in mass protests in the Middle East.

In 2009, the Green Movement in Iran attempted to revive a reforming impulse that had peaked in the early 2000s, before theocratic conservatives reasserted their control of the state. The Greens inspired street protests, which the government repressed. The protestors, drawn largely from middle- and upper-class youth, supported a relatively liberal presidential candidate and even challenged some aspects of clerical rule. But opposition to theocracy and corruption is not the same as rejecting a religiously legitimated public order, or a desire to change the thoroughly religious nature of most of Iranian society. The protestors most often chanted "God is Great," drawing on religious tradition to oppose the clerical leadership.[6] As international-relations professor Mahmood Monshipouri remarks, many observers thought that the Green Movement "embraced a post-Islamist democracy struggle to reclaim citizenship within a religio-political order. It typified the long-standing aspirations for a dignified life free from fear, moral surveillance, corruption, and arbitrary rule."[7] But a combination of repression by the government and limited appeal beyond privileged classes meant that the Green Movement had little chance to attain political power. To the extent that it took on secular associations or attracted Western support, its influence faded.

And then came the Arab Spring. Those of us used to authoritarian rule in Arab states watched our screens in amazement as youthful crowds occupied main squares, defied security forces, and drove dictators from power. Surely, pundits began to say, liberal democratic reforms would follow. But the Persian Gulf States, the closest allies of the United States, crushed the protests in their own neighborhoods. The Egyptian protests succeeded at first. But afterward, Egypt first elected a president from the Muslim Brotherhood and then lapsed back into military dictatorship. Syria and Libya were pushed into chaos and civil war. Tunisia, where the Arab Spring began, just about stumbled along, but continued corruption and economic stagnation led to sporadic unrest and demonstrations by the unemployed.[8]

Western liberals celebrated the uprisings, and the Western media was fascinated by the young urban protestors who organized through social media and smartphones. We did not, however, pay as much attention to how the protest movements in Tunisia and Egypt also attracted support from the working classes. Economic and food insecurity due to long-standing neoliberal policies contributed motivations for a broad-based revolt. And yet, even as the uprisings deposed an older set of dictators, the neoliberal, Western-dominated order remained in place. Some Arab commentators observed how the United States had long been training Arab cyberactivists and darkly wondered how much of the Arab Spring was due to Western manipulation.[9]

In any case, the protests of the Arab Spring did not voice many overtly secularist demands. The youthful rebellion expressed by Arab hip-hop artists, for example, deployed an Islamic rhetoric of divine justice.[10] Like the Iranians, the Arabs cried that there was no power greater than God in order to object to the earthly powers oppressing them. And after the uprisings, the more religiously defined and monarchical Arab regimes remained in place, while those still incorporating a hint of secular nationalism fell apart.

In 2013, Turkey witnessed nationwide, month-long mass demonstrations against the long-ruling moderate Islamist government. As in Iran and the Arab countries, youths with smartphones and social-media experience took the lead. Young women were prominent in the crowds and among the organizers. But in Turkey, the protests developed a secularist edge. The westernized segment of the middle class reacted against the government's authoritarian tendencies and intrusions into secular lifestyles. Very few of the protesting women wore headscarves. Again, however, the protests did not accomplish much. The working class did not show up in force. Among perennially oppressed identity groups, the heterodox Alevi religious minority took to the streets, but the Kurds mostly did not support the protests.

The religious conservatives in power interpreted the demonstrations as an attempt to overthrow a democratically elected government, and resorted to further repression. At the same time, they fell out with their longtime allies, the Gülen movement. The Gülenists, who had come to dominate the police and judiciary with the collusion of the ruling party, released tapes exposing extensive corruption at the highest levels of government. The government responded with fury, starting a purge of Gülenists from the state.[11] And throughout all of this, the ruling party enjoyed crushing victories in repeated elections, retaining their parliamentary majority and their complete grip on Turkish institutions. Most Turks apparently acquiesce in the Islamization of public life and accept corruption as long as some of the money trickles down to their circles. The secular members of the middle class who have joined in protests and led opposition movements are thoroughly alienated from the conservative majority.

In the longer term, the ruling Islamists will perhaps not be as successful, as their reliability as neoliberal economic managers has begun to come into doubt. Their ill-conceived meddling in Syria and their kleptocratic tendencies threaten stability, and hence undermine investor confidence. Nonetheless, they have permanently transformed Turkish politics. Today's viable opposition parties do not contest the religious legitimation of social order or neoliberal policies—they offer kinder, gentler versions. Pious modernity is now the established way of things, regardless of which personal clique or political party administers the state.

Many of my secular liberal Turkish friends, some who were closely involved in the 2013 protests and the 2015 parliamentary elections, now express despair. And they may be right. It is bad enough to continually lose politically, to have nothing come of mass protests that seemed to promise so much. But the problems run deeper. Increasingly, secular liberal aspirations have come to seem futile, an object of nostalgia rather than the cutting edge of progress. We can defend secularity only as a lifestyle, not as a way to advance common human interests or as the best way to deal with technological modernity. We have no hope of winning elections. We can ask only that we be granted our own enclaves, free from religious interference.

Where secularity is stronger, as in Europe, secular liberals might just about entertain hopes that strong religion will find it more difficult to reproduce itself, that Muslims will follow the religious groups that came before and become more liberal as they adjust to local conditions. But in majority-Muslim countries, secularity remains superficial. There, secular liberalism does not represent progress or the future. Among Muslims, secularism will find it hard to become more than the identity politics of a small minority. Preachers on television will continue to make weird pronouncements about Muhammad for a long time yet.

IMAGINARY RESISTANCE

Secular liberals have a history of using Islam to more sharply define our political views. We have thought of ourselves as standing for freedom, democracy, and rationality. We have figured out how the world works and shaped it according to our needs; we have tamed our religions, made them modern. Our picture of Islam, in contrast, has been one of despotism, blind faith, and fatalism. We have not been entirely accurate. Worse, the liberal image of Islam has been inseparable from Western imperial domination of Muslim lands.[12] Nonetheless, we liberals still have a habit of imagining Islam in a way that makes it represent what we want to avoid. Islam becomes the perfect bad example, standing for all that is illiberal, theocratic, and violently anti-modern. We often try to identify a timeless essence of Islam, mirroring the futile quest for a True Islam engaged in by true believers.[13]

I don't want to chase after essences. Still, my own interest in Islam has been similar: I have most often noticed varieties of Islam when they intruded into my life. My curiosity is piqued most when, in the name of religion, Muslims oppose science, become moral scolds, or support conservative political movements. I am intrigued by Muslim objections to secular modernity, and thinking about Islamic critiques of my secular liberal ways helps me to define where I stand. My focus on conflicts means that I am selective: what grabs my attention is not representative of everyday piety or the wide variety of ways to be a Muslim.

What strikes me as most interesting, however, is not those varieties of Islam that make secular people recoil with fear and loathing. Fanatics who display automatic weapons and dream of reestablishing the caliphate are easy to oppose. Religious overachievers who try to resurrect an imaginary seventh century within their enclaves are easy to ignore. Instead, when conservative Muslims assimilate aspects of secular modernity, when they do not appear to be a perfect bad example, I think they present a more important challenge to people like me. Piously modern Muslims today emphasize religious liberty, civil society, and free enterprise. They favor cultural authenticity and denounce the cultural imperialism that expects everyone to become secular, but they also often admire and are inspired by the United States. Their intellectuals are not marginal but part of the mainstream, deploying familiar postmodern and libertarian arguments in their cause. These arguments have liberal as well as conservative resonances. I do not think secular liberals have responded adequately. At the very least, we have to recognize that standard defenses of our position, such as invoking fears of theocracy, are no longer to the point.

Piously modern interpretations of Islam are not just culturally and politically vigorous. Regardless of intellectual pretenses, they deeply penetrate into the lives of believers. For example, televangelists such as Amr Khalid of Egypt and Abdullah Gymnastiar of Indonesia are wildly popular. They promote an ethos of individual empowerment, self-help, and positioning for market success that fit very well with a neoliberal environment. Their emotional presentations normalize the piety of the more privileged classes and appeal to the aspiring young. As sociologist Asef Bayat observes, Khalid's "message operated within the consumer culture of Egypt's nouveaux riches, where piety and privilege cohabit as enduring partners. Analogous to the Methodist Church of the well-to-do in the American Bible Belt, where faith and fortune are happily conjoined, Khalid's style made rich Egyptians feel good about themselves."[14]

Islam today is very often associated with a modern consumer culture, with Islamic popular music, movies, and television shows. Political scientists Amel Boubekeur and Olivier Roy point out that "the old idea of the Islamist protest of cultural consumption has been replaced by pious artists who promote religious diversity as well as a commitment to the free market, consumerism and individualism in order to get empowered."[15] The details are different, but expressions of Islam in our globalized consumer culture are looking increasingly like religion in the Bible Belt of the United States, with its Christian popular music, movies, and television shows. Amel Boubekeur elaborates:

> In the new forms of political Islam, the values of market and competition are replacing those of self-denial and amateurish charity for the former activist. Henceforth the production of a CD of spiritual songs, the commercialization of an Islamic soda, or the latest publication on the situation of Muslims must meet the standards of the global market. This desire among committed Muslims to be competitive actors is visible in the construction of an Islamic ethic of "work well done," of the image of the Prophet as a great merchant, or of wealth valued by God. . . . A sign of the times is the tendency of young Muslims to pursue studies in finance, rather than the natural or human sciences that were favored by their re-Islamized elders. To ensure the defense of Islam, money now seems more efficient than philosophical debates on what an Islamic society looks like.[16]

There is some variety of Islam for everyone to consume. In the Istanbul bookstores I regularly visit, I invariably run into bestselling volumes of inspirational literature that adapt traditional Muslim spiritual writings to provide personal therapy for urban professionals.[17] The religious rules fade away into suggestions, and mystical expressions come to the fore. All of this is, again, very similar to Protestant-inflected management literature and self-help ideology in the United States. It is ostensibly nonpolitical, often becoming a neo-Sufi variety of New Age spirituality, presenting religion as an individual coping mechanism. But it also breathes new life into the sacred, and it reinforces the historical Muslim tendency to seek practical solutions in ancient texts—with attendant political consequences.

Modern technology and industrial economies promote individualism. And in today's cities, where millions from different backgrounds pile on top of each other, some degree of social and political pluralism has become inescapable. But all of this does *not* necessarily lead in a secular direction, especially in conditions of faltering economic growth or entrenched insecurity. These, today, are our normal conditions.[18]

Technological progress has enabled secular liberal projects, including our peculiar insistence on personal autonomy and independence from sacred tradition. Nonetheless, pious modernity has been resilient and adaptable. The staying power of examples such as conservative Christianity in the United States and Hindu nationalism in India suggests that people can get by, and even flourish, without embracing a secular liberal political framework.[19] I expect the Muslim version of pious modernity to thrive as well. Whether in the form of political movements demanding a more Islamic public ambiance, or fundamentalist currents seeking more purity in personal life, updated but conservative forms of Islam look like formidable alternatives to secular ways of being modern.

Piously modern varieties of Islam worry me, partly because they reinforce what I see as negative aspects of secular modernity today: its sanctification of plunder, its entertainment-pacified consumer society, its undermining of prospects for a robust public sphere. To some extent, I am resigned to this. The past half century has not been kind to my political aspirations; with a few exceptions, I have grown accustomed to defeat.

And yet, I still harbor a desire for resistance. And in that case, perhaps religion can help. After all, many devout Muslim intellectuals also resist what they see as the corruptions that accompany modern life. Some even think that piously modern Islam is an attempt to mask a love of money and worldly ambitions with a superficial faith that is not true to the deeper spirituality found in Islamic tradition. Writers calling for a return to Islam used to argue that consumer society led to a flattening out of life, that it obscured a higher, divine purpose to our existence. Even today, there are many who think that secular modernity was a disastrous turn away from God in pursuit of an ultimately dehumanizing conception of freedom. Islamist intellectual Ali Bulaç, for example, finds fault with even the seemingly most obvious successes of secular ways of thinking. He denounces the reductionist, materialist tendencies within science-based medicine, endorsing traditional Islamic forms of alternative medicine as part of a more holistic, God-honoring approach.[20]

Islamic resistance also appeals to disillusioned leftists. British diplomat Alastair Crooke praises "the Islamist effort to haul human society away from a flawed western utopia with no purpose higher than achieving mere affluence, towards another 'old truth,' which is that human happiness and harmoniousness depend more on struggling and sacrificing for ideals, rather than in accumulating material possessions."[21] He presents Shia Islamism as similar to Catholic social theology: a principled, deep-rooted rejection of secular hedonism and individualist moral nihilism. Moreover, Crooke's Islamists represent resistance to colonial depredations and the mass terror by which free markets have been imposed on modernizing populations. More academic writers also pick up the torch, celebrating Muslims who stand up against Western hegemony. I often read ritual denunciations of capitalism as an engine of empire that denatures local cultures, alienating colonized populations from their authentic heritage.[22]

Much of this seems out of date, an echo of a few decades ago when political Islam had not yet made peace with business conservatism. In any case, even if all of this were to represent a genuine form of resistance, it has little to do with my stubbornly secular liberal hopes.

Yes, our industrial civilization has given free rein to human rapacity for far too long, and catastrophic problems like global warming and ocean acidification have become far too urgent. In the face of a relentless capitalist imperative to grow, to extract resources, and to convert all values into prices, it is recklessly optimistic to trust that a technological fix or a free-market solution will always become available. But in order to deal with such problems, we need our best available understanding of the world. It may be tempting to discard modern knowledge, or to attempt to redeem it by injecting more supernatural purpose into our picture of nature. Invariably, the result is an intellectual disaster such as intelligent design creationism or alternative medicine. Neither the California New Ager who claims a higher environmental consciousness nor the Muslim who claims that our problems are due to a Western, materialist conception of nature is at all helpful. It is important to get our science right.

We *are* too caught up in our possessions. We need to ask how much is enough for a good life,[23] and most of us who live comfortably today almost certainly do not need more. And yet, I am an unrepentant secular hedonist. I am wary of romanticism about a simpler life that overlooks the drudgery required to live off the land. I want my modern comforts and my occasional escapist entertainments—in their right places. When I get sick, I want proper healthcare, not superstition wrapped in spiritual drivel. Many of us lack balance in our individual lives, and we certainly lack power in our increasingly plutocratic political systems. But I don't see any way out of our predicament in finger-wagging moralizing, religious or otherwise.

I cannot deny that becoming modern has, for many, meant uprootedness, inauthenticity, and colonial oppression. But I have very little sympathy for postmodern conservatives and their outrage about colonized people being alienated from their own heritage. Cultures change; traditions come and go. We acquire culture as a result of historical accidents, and we may or may not affirm our inheritance upon later reflection. Our local cultures are invariably shot through with deep falsehoods; even their supposedly time-honored practices are often recent inventions. Very often they endorse oppressions of their own. I find the constant defense of islands of cultural authenticity wearying. In my experience, postmodern academic posturing is more a problem than a solution. It tends to be anti-science, moralizing, and trivial. It contributes to fragmenting our public sphere, instead of helping us to collectively address our difficulties. The resistance that postmodern conservatives offer to a neoliberal order is as imaginary as that of organic food fads and televangelism.

I can have very little to object to if a Muslim draws on the rich history of ethical and political reflection in the Islamic tradition. I have friends and relatives who consider themselves perfectly good Muslims and who are secular liberals as much as I am. Religion is open to interpretation, and I run into an occasional book that argues that True Islam endorses a liberal outlook. It may even gesture toward substantial resistance, adopting a form of liberation theology.[24] Still, it is hard not to observe that today, the center of gravity of Muslim political views is very conservative.

I am not sure why monotheistic religiosity is so often associated with right-wing politics. What, after all, does belief in gods and prophets have to do with conservative personality traits? Still, world religions have been remarkably successful in joining our human tendency to perceive supernatural agency with our moral psychology. Religions cement powerful social bonds.[25] And in doing so, common forms of religion far more often infuse existing power structures with a feeling of righteousness than inspire resistance due to a transcendent sense of justice. In the end, however unhappy I may be about how some secular liberal enterprises have worked out, I cannot support any politics that places revelation at its center. It will be far too conservative for my taste.

WHAT, THEN, DO WE DO?

I have long been interested in ideas on the fringes of science that are rejected by mainstream science. I am fascinated by creationism, psychic powers, and alternative medicine. The best evidence shows that such ideas are mistaken, but they enjoy popular support nonetheless. Scientists are annoyed: we often think that with better science education and communication we should be able to banish such pseudoscientific nonsense to the outer darkness.

This never happens. Scientists usually assume that science represents impartial expertise, that religious doctrines should be set aside in deciding questions of empirical fact, that the public interest is best served by attending to what *we* consider to be the merits of each case. Therefore, when we enter less stereotypically secular liberal environments than that of the scientific community, we implicitly challenge convictions that are more deeply rooted than beliefs about a particular fossil or the honesty of any individual miracle worker. We are politically naive. Moreover, we uncritically absorb a notion of science as a nonpolitical, religiously neutral enterprise. But our very ability to produce genuine knowledge depends on political preconditions. We may prefer to be absorbed in our equations or our lab equipment, but politically independent institutions still need funding. And as climate scientists have learned, when our results challenge the powerful, we can be vulnerable. When scientists pay no attention to the political environment in which we work, we risk becoming agents for whomever can hire our services—little more than tools for purposes we ignore.

Science is just the example that is closest to my experience. I think that whatever the context in which we operate, secular liberals have to become more politically astute. We no longer represent the default way of being modern. Our ideals about organizing our collective enterprises are not shared by all. We like to think that the basic political frameworks we favor—secularism, human rights, liberal democracy—are universally applicable, but that is an aspiration, not a reality. It is certainly not true that our political convictions are supported by universally convincing reasons. Many varieties of Islam shape believers' deepest interests and purposes, and are very successful at reproducing themselves as stable, satisfying ways of life. Few of these varieties are liberal. Indeed, secular liberalism is often an obstacle for conservative religious interests. Those Muslims who reject our pieties are not irrational.

Debates involving religion contest fact claims as well as moral ideals. But getting the facts right does not mean much. Evolution is real, the Quran is not an obvious miracle, and we can never strip away human interpretation to be left with pure divine commands. Talk about Muhammad's urine is untethered from reality. Nonetheless, facts are not automatically socially potent. There are many ways to deflect or deny facts, including corporate campaigns of obfuscation, fundamentalist assertions of faith, and postmodern paranoia about the materialist, even colonialist, metaphysical assumptions that surely must underlie our claims of fact. Even without such defensive maneuvers, getting the facts right is costly. In the context of a conservatively religious way of life, the costs may be too high.

If all of this bothers those of us who are secular liberals, we have no alternative to political action. We need to seek allies, appeal to a broader constituency, and gain and exercise power in order to influence our common social environment. We cannot afford to harden the liberal separation between public and private domains and seek to escape into the private. For too long, too many of us have emphasized our freedom to be left alone, acting like a scientist who might retreat to her lab and treat politics as a dirty business to be avoided. Freedom within a private realm is fine. But we need to balance it with another conception of freedom, manifested in our ability to participate in decisions about our collective affairs.[26] Secular liberals have been inspired by Enlightenment ideals: to shake off arbitrary authority, to take responsibility, to stand with others as equals in shaping our public sphere. To do otherwise is to resign ourselves to acting as tools.

Appealing to the Enlightenment feels odd, in a time when the Enlightenment tradition is in decline. It raises suspicions of arrogance and ethnocentricity, not to mention the ghosts of rationalist utopias from past centuries. I should not forget that if the shine has come off the Enlightenment, this is in large part of our own doing. We have been at our worst at our most utopian: when we have sought worldly salvation in the coming Revolution or in the frictionless paradise of the Free Market.

And yet, Enlightenment ideals—indeed, Enlightenment ideals at their most radical[27]—define where I take my stand. I cannot believe in any sort of salvation. I am not sure I can even imagine what a perfectly secular liberal world could look like. But I can still dream of finite improvements in our condition. After all, medicine is not futile because death remains inevitable. I can hope for partial secularities, expanding bubbles of rationality, liberal social spaces where we experiment to find a balance that avoids both suffocating conformity and private isolation. And as I do so, Islam will always be present: a source of both inspiration and obstacles, a bad example *and* a resource for experiments in civilization.

Coming from Turkey, and being interested in the fringes of science, I naturally developed a fascination with Islamic creationism. Adnan Oktar, the figurehead of the Harun Yahya enterprise that promotes one of the splashiest brands of creationism, has lately taken to televangelism. He regularly hosts a show that seems to consist of religious chat interwoven with semi-flirtatious banter between him and a handful of young women. Curiously, the women usually appear with no headscarves on, and they make few concessions to conservative Muslim norms of modesty. Indeed, they are most notable for their absurdly thick layers of makeup. Since I am known as an observer of Islamic creationism, I occasionally get questions about Oktar's televangelism: What is going on? Is Oktar appealing to wealthier Muslims who want to cast off the headscarf? Is this a sign of some kind of backhanded secularization in progress? And I have to admit that I really don't know.

The future, if it happens, will be confusing.

ACKNOWLEDGMENTS

W riting a book like this has been a solitary experience, but it has depended on the work of many others. I should first of all express my gratitude to the many public institutions this book has relied upon, in particular, the libraries of Truman State University and Iowa State University, and MOBIUS, the excellent interlibrary-loan system of Missouri. I also want to thank Truman State University for taking the liberal arts and sciences seriously and allowing me to pursue intellectual interests that might seem out of place in a physics department.

I am especially grateful for the time and efforts of those who read my early drafts and found at least some of the places where I was not making sense. This book owes a lot to Osman Ataker, Stefano Bigliardi, Amy Bix, Maarten Boudry, Joanna Marshall, Tom Marshall, and Richard Woo. Thanks are also due Steven L. Mitchell and Jade Zora Scibilia of Prometheus Books, whose editorial work significantly improved the book.

NOTES

CHAPTER 1: VARIETIES OF ISLAMIC EXPERIENCE

1. Shabbir Akhtar, *The Quran and the Secular Mind: A Philosophy of Islam* (New York: Routledge, 2008), p. 7.

2. Omid Safi, ed., *Progressive Muslims: On Justice, Gender, and Pluralism* (Oxford, UK: Oneworld, 2004).

3. Ronald A. Lindsay, *The Necessity of Secularism: Why God Can't Tell Us What to Do* (Charlottesville, VA: Pitchstone , 2014).

4. David Shankland, *The Alevis in Turkey: The Emergence of a Secular Islamic Tradition* (London: RoutledgeCurzon, 2003).

5. All translations from Turkish are mine, unless otherwise noted.

6. Necdet Subaşı, *Alevi Modernleşmesi: Sırrı Faş Eylemek* (İstanbul: Timaş Yayınları, 2010).

7. Rıza Yürükoğlu, *Okunacak En Büyük Kitap İnsandır: Tarihte Ve Günümüzde Alevilik* (İstanbul: Alev Yayınevi, 1995).

8. Kayhan Karaca, "AİHM: Nüfus cüzdanında din ibaresi olmamalı," *NTV*, February 1, 2010, http://www.ntvmsnbc.com/id/25051819/ (accessed September 25, 2015).

9. James Helicke, "Turks in Germany: Muslim Identity 'between' States," in *Muslim Minorities in the West: Visible and Invisible*, ed. Yvonne Yazbeck Haddad and Jane I. Smith (Walnut Creek, CA: Altamira, 2002), p. 185.

10. Simon Ross Valentine, *Islam and the Ahmadiyya Jama'at: History, Belief, Practice* (New York: Columbia University Press, 2008).

11. Ali Usman Qasmi, *The Ahmadis and the Politics of Religious Exclusion in Pakistan* (London and New York: Anthem, 2015).

12. Nevval Sevindi, *Contemporary Islamic Conversations: M. Fethullah Gülen on Turkey, Islam, and the West* (Albany: State University of New York Press, 2008).

13. Leila Ahmed, *A Border Passage: From Cairo to America—A Woman's Journey* (New York: Penguin Books, 2000), pp. 125–27.

14. Taner Edis, "A False Quest for a True Islam," *Free Inquiry* 27, no. 5

(2007): 48–50. Jan Hjärpe, "What Will Be Chosen from the Islamic Basket?" *European Review* 5, no. 3 (1997): 267–74.

15. OECD, "Alcohol Consumption," in *OECD Factbook 2011–2012: Economic, Environmental and Social Statistics* (OECD), http://dx.doi.org/ 10.1787/factbook-2011-108-en (accessed September 25, 2015). World Health Organization, *Global Status Report on Alcohol and Health 2014*, http://www.who .int/substance_abuse/publications/global_alcohol_report/en/ (accessed September 25, 2015).

16. M. Steven Fish, *Are Muslims Distinctive? A Look at the Evidence* (New York: Oxford University Press, 2011).

17. Sachiko Murata and William C. Chittick, *The Vision of Islam* (St. Paul, MN: Paragon House, 1994).

18. Asef Bayat, *Making Islam Democratic: Social Movements and the Post-Islamist Turn* (Stanford, CA: Stanford University Press, 2007), p. 187.

19. Jacques Berlinerblau, *The Secular Bible: Why Nonbelievers Must Take Religion Seriously* (New York: Cambridge University Press, 2005).

20. Olivier Roy, *Globalized Islam: The Search for a New Ummah* (New York: Cambridge University Press, 2004).

CHAPTER 2: THE SACRED SOURCES

1. Ernest Gellner, "Foreword," in *Islam, Globalization and Post-Modernity*, ed. Akbar Ahmed and Hastings Donnan (London: Routledge, 1994), p. x.

2. Farid Esack, *The Qur'an: A Short Introduction* (Oxford, UK: Oneworld, 2002), chap. 1.

3. I most often use Thomas Cleary, *The Qur'an: A New Translation* (Chicago: Starlatch, 2004), and I consult other translations as well. Usually I find Cleary's translation to be most poetic while still remaining close to the text.

4. F. E. Peters, *A Reader on Classical Islam* (Princeton, NJ: Princeton University Press, 1994), pp. 243–46.

5. Mustafa Akyol, "What Does Islam Say about Being Gay?" *International New York Times*, July 29, 2015, http://nyti.ms/1HYvcFx (accessed February 26, 2016). Ziauddin Sardar, *Reading the Qur'an: The Contemporary Relevance of the Sacred Text of Islam* (New York: Oxford University Press, 2011), pp. 323–28.

6. Shabbir Akhtar, *The Quran and the Secular Mind: A Philosophy of Islam* (New York: Routledge, 2008).

7. G. R. Hawting argues that the Quranic polemic may be directed toward fellow monotheists seeking angelic intercession. G. R. Hawting, *The Idea of Idolatry and the Emergence of Islam: From Polemic to History* (Cambridge: Cambridge University Press, 1999).

8. Ron Cameron, ed., *The Other Gospels: Non-Canonical Gospel Texts* (Philadelphia: Westminster, 1982), pp. 85–86.

9. Here I prefer Ahmed Ali, *Al-Qur'an: A Contemporary Translation* (Princeton, NJ: Princeton University Press, 1984); it is clearer about the reference to witchcraft.

10. J. Edward Wright, *The Early History of Heaven* (New York: Oxford University Press, 2000); Taner Edis, *An Illusion of Harmony: Science and Religion in Islam* (Amherst, NY: Prometheus Books, 2007), pp. 97–100.

11. For example, Mondher Sfar, *In Search of the Original Koran: The True History of the Revealed Text*, trans. Emilia Lanier (Amherst, NY: Prometheus Books, 2008), pp. 57–61.

12. Uri Rubin, "Muhammad's Message in Mecca: Warnings, Signs, and Miracles," in *The Cambridge Companion to Muhammad*, ed. Jonathan E. Brockopp (New York: Cambridge University Press, 2010).

13. *Sahih al-Bukhari*, vol. 4, book 54, no. 429 (http://www.sahih-bukhari .com); *Sahih Muslim*, book 1 (*The Book of Faith*), no. 309 (http://www .sahihmuslim.com).

14. Michael Cook, *The Koran: A Very Short Introduction* (Oxford: Oxford University Press, 2000), pp. 100–103.

15. Esack, *Qur'an*, p. 127.

16. *Sahih al-Bukhari*, vol. 4, book 54, no. 421 (http://www.sahih-bukhari .com). I have corrected some typographical errors in the quoted text.

17. M. Fethullah Gülen, *Muhammad, the Messenger of God: An Analysis of the Prophet's Life* (Somerset, NJ: Tughra Books, 2009), p. 340.

18. Ibid., p. 345.

19. Ibid., p. 346.

20. Fred M. Donner, "The Historical Context," in *The Cambridge Companion to the Qur'ān*, ed. Jane Dammen McAuliffe (New York: Cambridge University Press, 2006).

21. Andrew Rippin, *Muslims: Their Religious Beliefs and Practices*, 3rd ed. (New York: Routledge, 2005), pp. 48–49.

22. For example, F. E. Peters, *Muhammad and the Origins of Islam* (Albany: State University of New York Press, 1994).

23. Patricia Crone, *Slaves on Horses: The Evolution of the Islamic Polity* (Cambridge: Cambridge University Press, 1980), pp. 6–7.

24. Rippin, *Muslims*, p. 34.

25. Montgomery Watt and Richard Bell, *Introduction to the Qur'an* (Edinburgh: Edinburgh University Press, 1970), chap. 6; Sfar, *In Search of the Original Koran*, pp. 40–48.

26. Rippin, *Muslims*, pp. 35–36.

27. Peters, *Reader on Classical Islam*, pp. 178–79.

28. Keith E. Small, *Textual Criticism and Qur'ān Manuscripts* (Lanham, MD: Lexington Books, 2011), p. 180.

29. Yehuda D. Nevo and Judith Koren, *Crossroads to Islam: The Origins of the Arab Religion and the Arab State* (Amherst, NY: Prometheus Books, 2003).

30. John Wansbrough, *The Sectarian Milieu: Content and Composition of Islamic Salvation History*, expanded by G. R. Hawting (Amherst, NY: Prometheus Books, 2006). I am in no position to evaluate this much-criticized work, so for an overview of the radical revisionist position of Wansbrough and his students I have also relied on Tom Holland, *In the Shadow of the Sword: The Birth of Islam and the Rise of the Global Arab Empire* (New York: Doubleday, 2012).

31. Angelica Neuwirth, "Structural, Linguistic, and Literary Features," in McAuliffe, *Cambridge Companion to the Qur'ān*.

32. Fred M. Donner, "Muhammad and the Debates on Islam's Origins in the Digital Age," in *Muhammad in the Digital Age*, ed. Ruqayya Khan (Austin: University of Texas Press, 2015), p. 25. Fred M. Donner, *Muhammad and the Believers: At the Origins of Islam* (Cambridge, MA: Belknap Press of Harvard University Press, 2010).

33. Taner Edis, *The Ghost in the Universe: God in Light of Modern Science* (Amherst, NY: Prometheus Books, 2002), chap. 5.

34. Bart D. Ehrman, *Did Jesus Exist? The Historical Argument for Jesus of Nazareth* (New York: HarperOne, 2012).

35. Andrew Rippin, "Western Scholarship and the Qur'ān," in McAuliffe, *Cambridge Companion to the Qur'ān*. Ibn al-Rawandi, "On Pre-Islamic Christian Strophic Poetical Texts in the Koran: A Critical Look at the Work of Günter Lüling," in *What The Koran Really Says: Language, Text, and Commentary*, ed. Ibn Warraq (Amherst, NY: Prometheus Books, 2002).

36. Esack, *Qur'an*, p. 9.

37. Seyyed Hossein Nasr, *The Need for a Sacred Science* (Albany: State University of New York Press, 1993), p. 161.

38. Mohammed Arkoun, *Islam: To Reform or to Subvert?* (London: Saqi Books, 2006), pp. 280–83.

39. For example, Anouar Majid, *Unveiling Traditions: Postcolonial Islam in a Polycentric World* (Durham: Duke University Press, 2000).

40. "Intercourse" in the Ahmed Ali translation. For a survey of popular possibilities, see Neil MacFarquhar, "Verse in Koran on Beating Wife Gets a New Translation," *New York Times*, March 25, 2007, http://nyti.ms/1mCqqXV (accessed February 26, 2016).

41. Fazlur Rahman, *Major Themes of the Qurʾān* (Minneapolis: Bibliotheca Islamica, 1994).

42. Asma Barlas, *"Believing Women" in Islam: Unreading Patriarchal Interpretations of the Qurʾān* (Austin: University of Texas Press, 2002), p. 14.

43. This is exactly how classical scholarship treated these verses. Cook, *Koran*, pp. 37–41.

44. Ignoring historical context is a potent source of misreadings. Hasan Aydın, *Felsefi Antropolojinin Işığında Hz. Muhammed ve Kuran* (İstanbul: Bilim ve Gelecek Kitaplığı, 2014).

45. L. Carl Brown, *Religion and State: The Muslim Approach to Politics* (New York: Columbia University Press, 2000), p. 137. Dale Eickelman, "Inside the Islamic Reformation," *Wilson Quarterly* 22, no. 1 (1998): 80–89.

46. Saba Mahmood, "Feminist Theory, Embodiment, and the Docile Agent: Some Reflections on the Egyptian Islamic Revival," *Cultural Anthropology* 16, no. 2 (2001): 202–36.

47. Mehran Kamrava, "Introduction: Reformist Islam in Comparative Perspective," in *The New Voices of Islam: Rethinking Politics and Modernity*, ed. Mehran Kamrava (Berkeley: University of California Press, 2006).

48. Cihan Tuğal, *Passive Revolution: Absorbing the Islamic Challenge to Capitalism* (Stanford, CA: Stanford University Press, 2009), pp. 148–49.

49. Ibrahim M. Abu-Rabiʻ, ed., *Islam at the Crossroads: On the Life and Thought of Bediuzzaman Said Nursi* (Albany: State University of New York Press, 2003).

50. Olivier Roy, "Islam in Europe: Clash of Religions or Convergence of Religiosities?" in *Religion in the New Europe*, ed. Krzysztof Michalski (Budapest: Central European University Press, 2006), p. 131. Olivier Roy, *Globalized Islam: The Search for a New Ummah* (New York: Cambridge University Press, 2004), pp. 30–33.

51. Jean-Pierre Filiu, *Apocalypse in Islam*, trans. M. B. DeBevoise (Berkeley: University of California Press, 2011).

52. Ali Bulaç, "Tutarlılık Sorunu," *Zaman*, July 28, 2012, http://www.zaman.com.tr/yazar.do?yazino=1324299 (accessed February 12, 2016).

53. Aisha Y. Musa, *Ḥadīth as Scripture: Discussions on the Authority of Prophetic Traditions in Islam* (New York: Palgrave Macmillan, 2008), chaps. 4–5.

54. Faik Bulut, *Şeriat ve Siyaset: Küresel Çağda İslam 3* (İstanbul: Cumhuriyet Kitapları, 2008), pp. 67–69.

55. Gülen, *Muhammad, the Messenger of God*, pp. 47–59.

56. Edis, *An Illusion of Harmony*, chap. 3. Stefano Bigliardi, "What We Talk about When We Talk about Iʿjāz," *Social Epistemology Review and Reply Collective* 4, no. 1 (2014): 38–45.

57. Norman L. Geisler and Abdul Saleeb, *Answering Islam: The Crescent in Light of the Cross* (Grand Rapids, MI: Baker Books, 2002). An unrelated prominent website is Answering Islam: A Christian-Muslim Dialog, http://www.answering-islam.org.

58. Quoted in Ibn Warraq, ed., *Leaving Islam: Apostates Speak Out* (Amherst, NY: Prometheus Books, 2003), p. 65.

59. From Turkey: Turan Dursun, *Tabu Can Çekişiyor: Din Bu* (İstanbul: Kaynak Yayınları, 1991), İlhan Arsel, *Şeriat'tan Kıssa'lar* (İstanbul: Kaynak Yayınları, 1996). From Pakistan and Britain: Anwar Shaikh, *Islam: The Arab Imperialism* (Cardiff, Wales: Principality, 1998). From prerevolutionary Iran: Ali Dashti, *Twenty-Three Years: A Study of the Prophetic Career of Mohammad*, trans. F. R. C. Bagley (London: Allen & Unwin 1985).

60. Ali Sina (http://alisina.org), Faith Freedom International (http://www.faithfreedom.org), Mukta-Mona (Bengali; http://www.mukto-mona.com/).

61. Taner Edis, "An Ambivalent Nonbelief," in *50 Voices of Disbelief: Why We Are Atheists*, ed. Russell Blackford and Udo Schüklenk (Malden, MA: Wiley-Blackford, 2009).

CHAPTER 3: A MUSLIM MODERNITY

1. Timur Kuran, *Islam and Mammon: The Economic Predicaments of Islamism* (Princeton, NJ: Princeton University Press, 2004), p. 123. Timur Kuran, *The Long Divergence: How Islamic Law Held Back the Middle East* (Princeton, NJ: Princeton University Press, 2011), chap. 1.

2. Prime Minister's High Level Committee (Government of India), "Social, Economic and Educational Status of the Muslim Community of India: A Report,"

(2006); this document is known as the Sachar Committee report. See also Akbar Ahmed, *Journey into Islam: The Crisis of Globalization* (Washington, DC: Brookings Institution, 2007), pp. 76–78.

3. Anatol Lieven, *Pakistan: A Hard Country* (London: Allen Lane, 2011).

4. Michael L. Ross, *The Oil Curse: How Petroleum Wealth Shapes the Development of Nations* (Princeton, NJ: Princeton University Press, 2012).

5. Conservatives today still resent this minor materialist influence. Hasan Gümüşoğlu, *Modernizm'in İnanç Hayatına Etkileri ve Jön Türklük* (İstanbul: Kayıhan Yayınları, 2012).

6. Taha Parla and Andrew Davison, *Corporatist Ideology in Kemalist Turkey* (New York: Syracuse University Press, 2004).

7. Daniel Lerner, *The Passing of Traditional Society: Modernizing the Middle East* (New York: Free Press, 1958).

8. *Sahih al-Bukhari*, 7:71:641, 642, 4:52:253, 7:71:635, 636 (http://www.sahih-bukhari.com).

9. Talip Küçükcan and Ali Köse, *Doğal Afetler ve Din: Marmara Depremi Üzerine Psiko-Sosyolojik Bir İnceleme* (İstanbul: Türkiye Diyanet Vakfı, 2000).

10. M. Steven Fish, *Are Muslims Distinctive? A Look at the Evidence* (New York: Oxford University Press, 2011), chap. 2.

11. Catharina Raudvere and Leif Stenberg, eds., *Sufism Today: Heritage and Tradition in the Global Community* (London: I. B. Tauris, 2009). New Age Sufism attracts some Western seekers as well; Ron Geaves, Markus Dressler, and Gritt Klinkhammer, eds., *Sufis in Western Society: Global Networking and Locality* (London and New York: Routledge, 2009).

12. Robert Pringle, *Understanding Islam in Indonesia: Politics and Diversity* (Honolulu: University of Hawai'i Press, 2010), chap. 4. Robert W. Hefner, *Civil Islam: Muslims and Democratization in Indonesia* (Princeton, NJ: Princeton University Press, 2000).

13. For similarities and differences in the trajectories of Indonesia and Malaysia, see Gordon P. Means, *Political Islam in Southeast Asia* (Boulder, CO: Lynne Rienner Publishers, 2009).

14. M. Hakan Yavuz, *Islamic Political Identity in Turkey* (New York: Oxford University Press, 2003).

15. Haluk Nurbaki, *Kur'an-ı Kerim'den Ayetler ve İlmi Gerçekler*, 7th ed. (Ankara: Türkiye Diyanet Vakfı, 1998), pp. 146–47. A more recent example: "Dark Matter," *Miracles of Quran*, http://www.speed-light.info/miracles_of_quran/seven_heavens.htm (accessed October 16, 2015).

16. Taner Edis, "Islamic Creationism in Turkey," *Creation/Evolution* 34 (1994): 1–12. Taner Edis, *An Illusion of Harmony: Science and Religion in Islam* (Amherst, NY: Prometheus Books, 2007), chap. 4.

17. Edis, *Illusion of Harmony*, pp. 130–31.

18. James Bell et al., *The World's Muslims: Religion, Politics and Society* (Washington, DC: Pew Research Center, 2013), pp. 132–33.

19. Taner Edis and Saouma BouJaoude, "Rejecting Materialism: Responses to Modern Science in the Muslim Middle East," in *International Handbook of Research in History, Philosophy and Science Teaching*, vol. 3, ed. Michael R. Matthews (Dordrecht: Springer, 2014).

20. Edis, *Illusion of Harmony*, chap. 4. Raymond A. Eve and Francis B. Harrold, *The Creationist Movement in Modern America* (Boston: Twayne, 1991).

21. Taner Edis and Amy Sue Bix, "Biology and 'Created Nature': Gender and the Body in Popular Islamic Literature from Modern Turkey and the West," *Arab Studies Journal* 12, no. 2 and 13, no. 1 (2005): 140–58.

22. Meera Nanda, *Prophets Facing Backward: Postmodern Critiques of Science and Hindu Nationalism in India* (New Brunswick, NJ: Rutgers University Press, 2003). Meera Nanda, *Science in Saffron: Skeptical Essays on History of Science* (Gurgaon: Three Essays Collective, 2016).

23. Pervez Hoodbhoy, "Science and the Islamic World—The Quest for Rapprochement," *Physics Today* 60, no. 8 (2007): 49–55. Edis, *Illusion of Harmony.*

24. David Masci, "Scientists and Belief," *Pew Research Religion & Public Life Project*, November 5, 2009, http://pewrsr.ch/13sqTMm (accessed February 26, 2016).

25. For the last three decades, about 40–45 percent of Americans have expressed at least a loose sympathy with young-earth creationism in Gallup polls; Frank Newport, "In U.S., 42% Believe Creationist View of Human Origins," *Gallup*, June 2, 2014, http://www.gallup.com/poll/170822/believe-creationist -view-human-origins.aspx (accessed February 14, 2016). With more specific questions about the age of the earth, agreement with a young-earth position can drop to 18% or lower; George F. Bishop, Randall K. Thomas, Jason A. Wood, and Misook Gwon, "Americans' Scientific Knowledge and Beliefs about Human Evolution in the Year of Darwin," *Reports of the National Center for Science Education* 30, no. 3 (2010): 16–18.

26. Ümit Sayın and Aykut Kence, "Islamic Scientific Creationism," *Reports of the National Center for Science Education* 19, no. 6 (1999): 18–20, 25–29.

27. Hasan Aydın, *Postmodern Çağda İslam ve Bilim* (İstanbul: Bilim ve Gelecek Kitaplığı, 2008). Edis, *Illusion of Harmony*, chap. 5.

28. Pervez Hoodbhoy, *Islam and Science: Religious Orthodoxy and the Battle for Rationality* (London: Zed Books, 1991). Stefano Bigliardi, *Islam and the Quest for Modern Science* (Istanbul: Swedish Research Institute, 2014). Magdi Abdelhadi, "Muslim Call to Adopt Mecca Time," *BBC News*, April 21, 2008, http://news.bbc .co.uk/2/hi/middle_east/7359258.stm (accessed September 25, 2015).

29. Aydın, *Postmodern Çağda İslam ve Bilim*, p. 174.

30. Osman Bakar, *The History and Philosophy of Islamic Science* (Cambridge: Islamic Texts Society, 1999), p. 31.

31. Ibid. Seyyed Hossein Nasr, *Knowledge and the Sacred* (Albany: State University of New York Press, 1989). Tariq Ramadan, "The Way (*Al-Sharia*) of Islam," in *The New Voices of Islam: Rethinking Politics and Modernity*, ed. Mehran Kamrava (Berkeley and Los Angeles: University of California Press, 2006), pp. 91–97.

32. Edis, *Illusion of Harmony*, chap. 3.

33. Salim T. S. Al-Hassani, ed., *1001 Inventions: The Enduring Legacy of Muslim Civilization* (Washington, DC: National Geographic, 2012), p. 64.

34. Taner Edis and Sonja Brentjes, "A Golden Age of Harmony? Misrepresenting Science and History in the *1001 Inventions* Exhibit," *Skeptical Inquirer* 36, no. 6 (2012): 49–53. Taner Edis and Amy Sue Bix, "Flights of Fancy: The *1001 Inventions* Exhibition and Popular Misrepresentations of Medieval Muslim Science and Technology," in *1001 Mistakes*, ed. Sonja Brentjes, Taner Edis, and Lutz Richter-Bernburg (Würzburg: Ergon Verlag, forthcoming).

35. George Saliba, *Islamic Science and the Making of the European Renaissance* (Cambridge: MIT Press, 2007).

36. Toby E. Huff, *The Rise of Early Modern Science: Islam, China, and the West*, 2nd ed. (New York: Cambridge University Press, 2003).

37. Edis, *Illusion of Harmony*, chap. 3.

38. Bakar, *History and Philosophy of Islamic Science*, p. 66; Edis, *Illusion of Harmony*, chap. 2.

39. Nidhal Guessoum, *Islam's Quantum Question: Reconciling Muslim Tradition and Modern Science* (London: I. B. Tauris, 2011), pp. 174–75. Guessoum proposes a non-supernatural interpretation of scriptural miracles; he even rather oddly claims that the miracle of the Quran is its constant relevance throughout history as well as its openness to new interpretations. Bigliardi, *Islam and the Quest for Modern Science*, chap. 6.

40. Guessoum, *Islam's Quantum Question*, p. 218.

41. Taner Edis, *Science and Nonbelief* (Westport, CT: Greenwood, 2006), chap. 7.

42. Doron Aurbach, "Intelligent Design vs. Evolution Theory," in *Divine Action and Natural Selection: Science, Faith and Evolution*, ed. J. Seckbach and R. Gordon (New Jersey: World Scientific, 2009), pp. 687–705.

43. Robert J. Russell, "Divine Action and Quantum Mechanics: A Fresh Assessment," in *Philosophy, Science and Divine Action*, ed. F. LeRon Shults, Nancey C. Murphy and Robert J. Russell (Boston: Brill, 2009), pp. 351–403. For critiques see Jeffrey Koperski, "Divine Action and the Quantum Amplification Problem," *Theology and Science* 13, no. 4 (2015): 379–394; Taner Edis, *The Ghost in the Universe: God in Light of Modern Science* (Amherst: Prometheus Books, 2002).

44. David Shearman and Joseph Wayne Smith, *The Climate Change Challenge and the Failure of Democracy* (Westport, CT: Praeger, 2007).

45. Morris H. Shamos, *The Myth of Scientific Literacy* (New Brunswick, NJ: Rutgers University Press, 1995).

46. The trend is most obvious for the humanities, but the sciences face similar pressures. Christopher Newfield, *Unmaking the Public University: The Forty-Year Assault on the Middle Class* (Cambridge, MA: Harvard University Press, 2008). Martha C. Nussbaum, *Not for Profit: Why Democracy Needs the Humanities* (Princeton, NJ: Princeton University Press, 2010).

47. David Edgerton, *The Shock of the Old: Technology and Global History Since 1900* (New York: Oxford University Press, 2007).

48. Diego Gambetta and Steffen Hertog. "Why Are There So Many Engineers among Islamic Radicals?" *European Journal of Sociology* 50, no. 2 (2009): 201–30. Diego Gambetta and Steffen Hertog, "Engineers of Jihad," *Oxford Department of Sociology Working Papers*, 2007, http://www.sociology .ox.ac.uk/materials/papers/2007-10.pdf (accessed September 25, 2015).

49. Taner Edis, "Is There a Political Argument for Teaching Evolution?" paper presented at the Religions, Science and Technology in Cultural Contexts: Dynamics of Change conference in Trondheim, Norway, March 2, 2012.

50. Michael Oakeshott, *Experience and Its Modes* (Cambridge, UK: University Press, 1966). Michael Oakeshott, *Rationalism in Politics* (London: Methuen, 1962), pp. 7–12.

51. Yıldız Atasoy, *Islam's Marriage with Neoliberalism: State Transformation in Turkey* (New York: Palgrave McMillan, 2009), pp. 130–31.

52. Joshua D. Hendrick, "Küreselleşme, İslami Aktivizm, ve Türkiye'de Pasif Devrim: Fethullah Gülen Örneği," in *Neoliberalizm, İslamcı Sermayenin Yükselişi ve AKP*, ed. Neşecan Balkan, Erol Balkan, and Ahmet Öncü (İstanbul: Yordam Kitap, 2013).

53. Stephen C. Stearns and Jacob C. Koella, eds., *Evolution in Health and Disease*, 2nd ed. (New York: Oxford University Press, 2008). Peter D. Gluckman, Alan Beedle, and Mark Hanson, *Principles of Evolutionary Medicine* (New York: Oxford University Press, 2009).

54. Ernest Gellner, "Trust, Cohesion, and the Social Order," in *Trust: Making and Breaking Cooperative Relations*, ed. Diego Gambetta (Cambridge, MA: B. Blackwell, 1990), p. 154. Kuran, *Islam and Mammon*, p. 142.

55. Lawrence Rosen, *The Culture of Islam: Changing Aspects of Contemporary Muslim Life* (Chicago: University of Chicago Press, 2002), p. 43.

56. Kuran, *Long Divergence*, p. 5.

57. Ibid., chap. 5.

58. Ibid., chap. 6.

59. Bernard Lewis, *Islam in History: Ideas, People, and Events in the Middle East* (Chicago and La Salle: Open Court, 1993), p. 267.

60. Kuran, *Long Divergence*, p. 141.

61. Ibid., chap. 8.

62. Ibid., p. 142.

63. For criticism of Islamist economics, see Kuran, *Islam and Mammon*.

64. Saadia Toor, *The State of Islam: Culture and Cold War Politics in Pakistan* (London: Pluto, 2011).

65. Ebru Deniz Ozan, *Gülme Sırası Bizde: 12 Eylül'e Giderken Sermaye Sınıfı Kriz ve Devlet* (İstanbul: Metis Yayınları, 2012).

66. Cihan Tuğal, *Passive Revolution: Absorbing the Islamic Challenge to Capitalism* (Stanford, CA: Stanford University Press, 2009). Nilüfer Göle, *İslam ve Modernlik Üzerine Melez Desenler* (İstanbul: Metis Yayınları, 2000).

67. Atasoy, *Islam's Marriage with Neoliberalism*, p. 125.

68. Dilek Yankaya, *Yeni İslâmî Burjuvazi: Türk Modeli* (İstanbul: İletişim Yayınları, 2014). Evren Hoşgör, "İslami Sermaye," in Balkan, Balkan, and Öncü, *Neoliberalizm, İslamcı Sermayenin Yükselişi ve AKP*.

69. Tuğal, *Passive Revolution*, pp. 248–56. Yasin Durak, *Emeğin Tevekkülü: Konya'da İşçi-İşveren İlişkileri ve Dindarlık* (İstanbul: İletişim Yayınları, 2011). Evidently this does contribute to suppressing unions; Aziz Çelik, "AKP Döneminde Sendikal Haklar: Sendikasız-Grevsiz Kaynaşmış Bir Kitleyiz!" in

Himmet, Fıtrat, Piyasa: AKP Döneminde Sosyal Politika, ed. Meryem Koray and Aziz Çelik (İstanbul: İletişim Yayınları, 2015).

70. Dani Rodrik, "The Turkish Economy after the Global Financial Crisis," *Ekonomi-tek* 1, no. 1 (2012): 41–61.

71. Dani Rodrick, "How Well Did the Turkish Economy Do over the Last Decade?" *Dani Rodrik's Weblog: Unconventional Thoughts on Economic Development and Globalization*, June 20, 2013, http://rodrik.typepad.com/dani_rodriks_weblog/2013/06/how-well-did-the-turkish-economy-do-over-the-last-decade.html (accessed October 16, 2015).

72. "Turkey Ranks Last in OECD's 'Better Life' List," *Today's Zaman*, May 28, 2013, http://www.todayszaman.com/news-316732-turkey-ranks-last-in-oecds-better-life-list.html (accessed October 16, 2015).

73. Atasoy, *Islam's Marriage with Neoliberalism*, pp. 131–32. Kuvvet Lordoğlu and M. Hakan Koçak, "AKP Döneminde İstihdam, İşgücü ve İşsizlik," in Koray and Çelik, *Himmet, Fıtrat, Piyasa*.

74. Roland Bénabou, Davide Ticchi, and Andrea Vindigni, "Forbidden Fruits: The Political Economy of Science, Religion, and Growth," National Bureau of Economic Research Working Paper No. 21105 (2015), http://www.nber.org/papers/w21105 (accessed November 5, 2015).

75. Tuğal, *Passive Revolution*, pp. 284–91. Mohamed Mosaad Abdel Aziz, "The New Trend of the Muslim Brotherhood in Egypt," in *Whatever Happened to the Islamists? Salafis, Heavy Metal Muslims and the Lure of Consumerist Islam*, ed. Amel Boubekeur and Olivier Roy (New York: Columbia University Press, 2012).

76. Steve Keen, *Debunking Economics—Revised and Expanded Edition: The Naked Emperor Dethroned?* (London: Zed Books, 2011).

77. Ian Buruma and Avishai Margolit, *Occidentalism: The West in the Eyes of Its Enemies* (New York: Penguin , 2004), pp. 38–39.

78. Nanda, *Prophets Facing Backward*. A similar term is *half-modernity*, Bassam Tibi, *Islam between Culture and Politics* (Basingstoke: Palgrave, 2001), p. 6. Ibrahim Kaya, *Yeni Türkiye: Modernliği Olmayan Kapitalizm* (Ankara: İmge Kitabevi, 2014) takes secularity and autonomy to be essential to modernity, and so describes the Turkish experience as de-modernization while adopting capitalism; I prefer to refer to "pious modernity."

79. Vivek Chibber, *Postcolonial Theory and the Specter of Capital* (London: Verso, 2013).

80. Nanda, *Prophets Facing Backward*. Nanda, *Science in Saffron*.

81. Gordon Gauchat, "Politicization of Science in the Public Sphere: A Study

of Public Trust in the United States, 1974 to 2010," *American Sociological Review* 77, no. 2 (2012): 167–87.

82. Barbara Forrest, "Rejecting the Founders' Legacy: Democracy as a Weapon against Science," *Logos* 12, no. 2 (2013), http://logosjournal.com/2013/forrest/ (accessed September 25, 2015).

83. James B. Stewart, "New Metric for Colleges: Graduates' Salaries," *New York Times*, September 14, 2013, http://nyti.ms/1ACzwVe (accessed February 26, 2016).

84. Nuray Mert, *İslâm ve Demokrasi: Bir Kurt Masalı* (İstanbul: İz Yayıncılık, 1998).

85. Nader Hashemi, *Islam, Secularism, and Liberal Democracy: Toward a Democratic Theory for Muslim Societies* (New York: Oxford University Press, 2009), pp. 58–61.

86. Armando Salvatore, "Modernity," in *Islamic Political Thought: An Introduction*, ed. Gerhard Bowering (Princeton and Oxford: Princeton University Press, 2015). In scholarly circles, the term *post-Islamist* is sometimes used for moderate political movements with Islamist roots that express such an alternative, pious modernity. Asef Bayat, ed., *Post-Islamism: The Changing Faces of Political Islam* (New York: Oxford University Press, 2013).

CHAPTER 4: DIVINE LAW

1. Muhammad Saalih al-Munajjid, ed., "Is Artificial Insemination Regarded as Taking Back a Wife Who Is Revocably Divorced?" *Islam Question and Answer*, n.d., http://islamqa.info/en/178477 (accessed October 16, 2015). Muhammad Saalih al-Munajjid, ed., "Ruling on Doing the Marriage Contract over the Phone or Internet," *Islam Question and Answer*, n.d., http://islamqa.info/en/105531 (accessed October 16, 2015).

2. Muhammad Saalih al-Munajjid, ed., "Responding to Greeting of Parrot," *Islam Question and Answer*, n.d., http://islamqa.info/en/140497 (accessed October 16, 2015).

3. Lawrence Rosen, "Islamic Law as a Common Law System," in *The Justice of Islam: Comparative Perspectives on Islamic Law and Society*, by Lawrence Rosen (Oxford, UK: Oxford University Press, 2000).

4. G. P. Makris, *Islam in the Middle East: A Living Tradition* (Malden, MA: Blackwell, 2007), chap. 5.

5. F. E. Peters, *A Reader on Classical Islam* (Princeton, NJ: Princeton University Press, 1994), pp. 231–36.

6. Christopher Melchert, *The Formation of the Sunni Schools of Law: 9th–10th Centuries C.E.* (Leiden: Brill, 1997).

7. Richard W. Bulliet, *Islam: The View from the Edge* (New York: Columbia University Press, 1994).

8. Andrew G. Bostom, *Sharia versus Freedom: The Legacy of Islamic Totalitarianism* (Amherst, NY: Prometheus Books, 2012).

9. Dale F. Eickelman and James Piscatori, *Muslim Politics* (Princeton, NJ: Princeton University Press, 1996), chap. 3.

10. L. Carl Brown, *Religion and State: The Muslim Approach to Politics* (New York: Columbia University Press, 2000), p. 34.

11. This rough general description, naturally, overlooks many complexities. Anver M. Emon, *Religious Pluralism and Islamic Law:* Dhimmīs *and Others in the Empire of Law* (Oxford, UK: Oxford University Press, 2012).

12. Timur Kuran, *The Long Divergence: How Islamic Law Held Back the Middle East* (Princeton, NJ: Princeton University Press, 2011), chap. 9.

13. Antony Black, *The History of Islamic Political Thought: From the Prophet to the Present* (New York: Routledge, 2001), p. 212.

14. Richard W. Bulliet, *The Case for Islamo-Christian Civilization* (New York: Columbia University Press, 2004), chap. 2. Noah Feldman, *The Fall and Rise of the Islamic State* (Princeton, NJ: Princeton University Press, 2008).

15. Bernard Lewis, *Islam in History: Ideas, People, and Events in the Middle East* (Chicago and La Salle: Open Court, 1993), chap. 6.

16. Black, *History of Islamic Political Thought*, p. 214.

17. Sayyid Mujtaba Musavi Lari, *The Seal of the Prophets and His Message: Lessons on Islamic Doctrine*, book 2, trans. Hamid Algar (Potomac, MD: Islamic Education Center, n.d.), p. 20.

18. Sayyid Abul A'la Maududi, *Towards Understanding Islam*, trans. and ed. Khurshid Ahmad (Indianapolis: Islamic Teaching Center, 1977).

19. Raşit el Gannuşi, *Laiklik ve Sivil Toplum Üzerine Değerlendirmeler* (İstanbul: İlimyurdu, 2010).

20. John L. Esposito and Dalia Mogahed, *Who Speaks for Islam? What a Billion Muslims Really Think* (New York: Gallup, 2007), p. 48.

21. James Bell et al., *The World's Muslims: Religion, Politics and Society* (Washington, DC: Pew Research Center, 2013), p. 9.

22. Esposito and Mogahed, *Who Speaks for Islam?* p. 6.

23. Damon Linker, *The Theocons: Secular America under Siege* (New York: Doubleday, 2006), pp. 96–99.

24. National Legal Foundation, "NLF Mission Statement," *National Legal Foundation*, 2006, http://www.nlf.net/About/mission.html (accessed October 16, 2015).

25. Pew Research Center, "Iranians' Views Mixed on Political Role for Religious Figures," *Pew Research Center Religion and Public Life*, June 11, 2013, http://pewrsr.ch/14geFg4 (accessed February 26, 2016).

26. Anatol Lieven, *Pakistan: A Hard Country* (London: Allen Lane, 2011).

27. Bell, *World's Muslims*, p. 16.

28. *Sahih al-Bukhari*, vol. 9, book 84, no. 57 (http://www.sahih-bukhari .com).

29. Arshiya Khullar, "Brunei Adopts Sharia Law amid International Outcry," *CNN*, May 1, 2014, http://www.cnn.com/2014/05/01/world/asia/brunei -sharia-law/ (accessed February 17, 2016).

30. United Nations, "The Universal Declaration of Human Rights," n.d., http://www.un.org/en/documents/udhr/index.shtml (accessed October 16, 2015).

31. Hanibal Goitom, "Laws Criminalizing Apostasy in Selected Jurisdictions," *Law Library of Congress, Global Legal Research Center*, 2014, http://www.loc .gov/law/help/apostasy/apostasy.pdf (accessed August 5, 2015). David Batty and Mona Mahmood, "Palestinian Poet Ashraf Fayadh's Death Sentence Quashed by Saudi Court," *Guardian*, February 2, 1016, http://gu.com/p/4fqjv/sbl (accessed February 16, 2016).

32. Bekir Topaloğlu, *İslâm'da Kadın* (İstanbul: Rağbet Yayınları, 2001).

33. M. Steven Fish, *Are Muslims Distinctive? A Look at the Evidence* (New York: Oxford University Press, 2011), chap. 4.

34. Bernard Lewis, *What Went Wrong? Western Impact and Middle Eastern Response* (New York: Oxford University Press, 2002), pp. 92–93.

35. Black, *History of Islamic Political Thought*, pp. 250–53.

36. Muhammad Saalih al-Munajjid, ed., "Islam and Slavery," *Islam Question and Answer*, n.d., http://www.islam-qa.com/en/94840 (accessed October 16, 2015). Some implausibly argue that there was a security rationale for slavery; Ali Bulaç, *İnsanın Özgürlük Arayışı* (İstanbul: İnkılap Kitabevi, 2015), pp. 18–19.

37. Mawil Izzi Dien, *Islamic Law: From Historical Foundations to Contemporary Practice* (Notre Dame, IN: University of Notre Dame Press, 2004), chap. 6.

38. Khaled Abou El Fadl, *The Great Theft: Wrestling Islam from the Extremists* (New York: Harper San Franscisco, 2005), p. 131.

39. For example, Chandra Muzaffar, "Islam, Justice, and Politics," in *The New Voices of Islam: Rethinking Politics and Modernity*, ed. Mehran Kamrava (Berkeley: University of California Press, 2006).

40. Dien, *Islamic Law*, pp. 132–33.

41. Mohammad Ali Syed, *The Position of Women in Islam: A Progressive View* (Albany: State University of New York Press, 2004), p. 102.

42. Human Rights Education Associates, "The Moroccan Family Code (Mou-dawana) of February 5, 2004," *HREA*, 2005, http://www.hrea.org/programs/gender -equality-and-womens-empowerment/moudawana/ (accessed October 16, 2015).

43. Mohamed Talbi, "Religious Liberty: A Muslim Perspective," in Kamrava, *New Voices of Islam*, pp. 113–15.

44. Faraz Sanei, *Codifying Repression: An Assessment of Iran's New Penal Code* (Human Rights Watch report, 2012), https://www.hrw.org/report/2012/08/28/codifying-repression/assessment-irans-new-penal-code (accessed September 27, 2015).

45. 'Abdullahi Ahmed An-Na'im, "*Shari'a* and Basic Human Rights Concerns," in *Liberal Islam: A Sourcebook*, ed. Charles Kurzman (New York: Oxford University Press, 1998), p. 234. Abdullahi Ahmed An-Na'im, *Islam and the Secular State: Negotiating the Future of Shar'ia* (Cambridge, MA: Harvard University Press, 2008).

46. Tariq Ramadan, "The Way (*Al-Saharia*) of Islam," in Kamrava, *New Voices of Islam*. Ramadan has been accused of saying different things to Western and Muslim audiences; Caroline Fourest, *Brother Tariq: The Doublespeak of Tariq Ramadan* (New York: Encounter Books, 2008). This seems overblown.

47. Anthony Chase and Kyle M. Ballard, "Status of Human Rights Treaty Ratifications, with Notable Reservations, Understandings, and Declarations," in *Human Rights in the Arab World: Independent Voices*, ed. Anthony Chase and Amr Hamzawy (Philadelphia: University of Philadelphia Press, 2006). Robert F. Drinan, *Can God and Caesar Coexist? Balancing Religious Freedom and International Law* (New Haven: Yale University Press, 2004), pp. 32–38.

48. Ophelia Benson and Jeremy Stangroom, *Does God Hate Women?* (London: Continuum, 2009), pp. 113–27.

49. Kerem Altıparmak and Onur Karahanoğulları, "European Court of Human Rights," *European Constitutional Law Review* 2 (2006): 268–92.

50. Quoted in Yıldız Atasoy, *Islam's Marriage with Neoliberalism: State Transformation in Turkey* (New York: Palgrave Macmillan, 2009), p. 191. (Mazlum-Der is misspelled as "Maslum-Der" in the text.)

51. Abdulaziz Sachedina, *Islam and the Challenge of Human Rights* (New York: Oxford University Press, 2009). Bulaç, *İnsanın Özgürlük Arayışı*, pp. 64–70.

52. Atasoy, *Islam's Marriage with Neoliberalism*, pp. 194–200.

53. Mohammed el-Nawawy and Sahar Khamis, *Islam Dot Com: Contemporary Islamic Discourses in Cyberspace* (New York: Palgrave Macmillan, 2009), chap. 4.

54. Mark Juergensmeyer, *Global Rebellion: Religious Challenges to the Secular State, from Christian Militias to al Qaeda* (Berkeley, CA: University of California Press, 2008), p. 240.

55. Russell Blackford, *Freedom of Religion and the Secular State* (Malden, MA: Wiley-Blackwell, 2012).

56. Stephen Eric Bronner, *Reclaiming the Enlightenment: Toward a Politics of Radical Engagement* (New York: Columbia University Press, 2004), p. 145.

57. Anthony Chase, "The Tail and the Dog: Constructing Islam and Human Rights in Political Context," in Chase and Hamzawy, *Human Rights in the Arab World*.

58. Abdulwahab al Masseri, "The Imperialist Epistemological Vision," *American Journal of Islamic Social Scientists* 11, no. 3 (1994): 413.

59. Nicholas Mercuro and Steven G. Medema, *Economics and the Law: From Posner to Postmodernism and Beyond* (Princeton, NJ: Princeton University Press, 2006).

60. Wilfried Hinsch and Markus Stepanians, "Human Rights as Moral Claim Rights," in *Rawls's Law of Peoples: A Realistic Utopia?* ed. Rex Martin and David A. Reidy (Oxford, UK: Blackwell, 2006).

61. Meredith Tax, *Double Bind: The Muslim Right, the Anglo-American Left, and Universal Human Rights* (New York: Centre for Secular Space, 2012).

62. Examples include the International Covenant on Economic, Social and Cultural Rights, the Convention on the Rights of the Child, the Convention on the Rights of Persons with Disabilities, and others. On the reasons for American conservative resistance to human rights, see Michael Ignatieff, ed., *American Exceptionalism and Human Rights* (Princeton: Princeton University Press, 2005).

63. For a liberal invocation of human dignity, see Martha C. Nussbaum, *Creating Capabilities: The Human Development Approach* (Cambridge, MA: Belknap Press of Harvard University Press, 2011), pp. 29–36. For a conservative example, where dignity is better integrated into an overall theological view, see Robert P. George, *Conscience and Its Enemies: Confronting the Dogmas of Liberal Secularism* (Wilmington, DE: ISI Books, 2013), chap. 1.

64. Shibley Telhami, *The World through Arab Eyes: Arab Public Opinion and the Reshaping of the Middle East* (New York: Basic Books, 2013), p. 159.

65. Dien, *Islamic Law*, pp. 126–29.

66. Laura Levitt, "Other Moderns, Other Jews: Revisiting Jewish Secularism in America," in *Secularisms*, ed. Janet R. Jakobsen and Ann Pellegrini (Durham: Duke University Press, 2008).

67. Ali Bulaç, "Medina Document," in Kurzman, *Liberal Islam*.

68. Tariq Ramadan, *To Be a European Muslim: A Study of Islamic Sources in the European Context* (Leister, UK: Islamic Foundation, 1999).

69. Machteld Zee, *Choosing Sharia?: Multiculturalism, Islamic Fundamentalism and Sharia Councils* (The Hague: Eleven International Publishing, 2016). Other scholars find sharia councils to be harmless; for example, John R. Bowen, *Blaming Islam* (Cambridge, MA: MIT Press, 2012), chap. 3. There are also arguments that British law effectively has become, and indeed should be, more pluralistic. Prakash Shah, *Legal Pluralism in Conflict: Coping with Cultural Diversity in Law* (London: Glasshouse, 2005).

70. Jocelyne Cesari, *Why the West Fears Islam: An Exploration of Muslims in Liberal Democracies* (New York: Palgrave Macmillan, 2013), pp. 116–20.

71. Glenn Greenwald, *With Liberty and Justice for Some: How the Law Is Used to Destroy Equality and Protect the Powerful* (New York: Picador, 2012).

72. Jessica Silver-Greenberg and Michael Corkery, "In Arbitration, a 'Privatization of the Justice System,'" *New York Times*, November 1, 2015, http://nyti.ms/1N4UNfI (accessed February 17, 2016). Michael Corkery and Jessica Silver-Greenberg, "In Religious Arbitration, Scripture Is the Rule of Law," *New York Times*, November 2, 2015, http://nyti.ms/1izsuOf (accessed February 17, 2016).

CHAPTER 5: WOMEN AND MEN

1. Yasmin Alibhai-Brown, "The Talibanisation of British Childhood by Hardline Parents," *Daily Mail*, August 5, 2010, http://www.dailymail.co.uk/debate/article-1300449/The-Talibanisation-British-childhood-hardline-parents.html (accessed February 18, 2016).

2. Valentine M. Moghadam, "Women, Citizenship, and Civil Society in the Arab World," in *Human Rights in the Arab World: Independent Voices*, ed. Anthony Chase and Amr Hamzawy (Philadelphia: University of Pennsylvania Press, 2006).

3. *Sahih al-Bukhari*, vol. 1, book 6, no. 301 (http://www.sahih-bukhari .com).

4. Hayat Alvi, "Women's Rights Movements in the 'Arab Spring': Major Victories or Failures for Human Rights?" *Journal of International Women's Studies* 16, no. 3 (2015): 294–318. Amel Grami and Karima Bennoune, "Tunisia's Fight against Fundamentalism: An Interview with Amel Grami," *50.50 Inclusive Democracy*, July 8, 2013, https://www.opendemocracy.net/5050/amel-grami -karima-bennoune/tunisias-fight-against-fundamentalism-interview-with-amel -grami (accessed October 17, 2015).

5. Elias Biryabarema, "Uganda Passes Law Meaning Life in Prison for Some Homosexual Acts," *Reuters*, December 20, 2013, http://reut.rs/19h9oHq (accessed February 18, 2016).

6. Leila Ahmed, *Women and Gender in Islam* (New Haven, CT: Yale University Press, 1992), p. 45.

7. Elvan Ezber, "10 günlük evli çifte kanlı infaz," *Hürriyet*, December 12, 2010, http://www.hurriyet.com.tr/gundem/16513216.asp?gid=373 (accessed February 18, 2016).

8. Bernard Lewis, *What Went Wrong? Western Impact and Middle Eastern Response* (New York: Oxford University Press, 2002), p. 66.

9. Joseph Henrich, Robert Boyd, and Peter J. Richerson, "The Puzzle of Monogamous Marriage," *Philosophical Transactions of the Royal Society B* 367 (2012): 657–69.

10. Alison Wolf, *The XX Factor: How the Rise of Working Women Has Created a Far Less Equal World* (New York: Crown, 2013).

11. Khadijeh Aryan, "The Boom in Women's Education," in *Women, Power and Politics in 21st Century Iran*, ed. Tara Povey and Elaheh Rostami-Povey (Burlington, VT: Ashgate Publishing, 2012). Education does not always translate into employment for women.

12. Hans Groth and Alfonso Sousa-Poza, eds., *Population Dynamics in Muslim Countries: Assembling the Jigsaw* (Heidelberg: Springer-Verlag, 2012).

13. Bernd Hayo and Tobias Caris, "Female Labour Force Participation in the MENA Region: The Role of Identity," *Review of Middle East Economics and Finance* 9, no. 3 (2013): 271–92. Elhum Haghighat, "A Comparative Analysis of Neopatriarchy and Female Labor Force Participation in Islamic Countries," *Electronic Journal of Sociology* (2005), http://www.sociology.org/content/2005/ tier1/__islamLaborforce.pdf (accessed October 17, 2015).

14. M. Steven Fish, *Are Muslims Distinctive? A Look at the Evidence* (New York: Oxford University Press, 2011), p. 201.

15. Ibid., p. 203.

16. Cihan Tuğal, *Passive Revolution: Absorbing the Islamic Challenge to Capitalism* (Stanford, CA: Stanford University Press, 2009), pp. 211–14.

17. 'Abd al-'Azeez ibn Baaz, "Meaning of the Lack in Reason and Religious Commitment in Women," *Islam Question and Answer*, n.d., http://islamqa.info/en/111867 (accessed October 17, 2015). Süleyman Ateş, *Gerçek Din Bu*, vol. 1 (İstanbul: Yeni Ufuklar Neşriyat, 1991), pp. 36–37.

18. Şanar Yurdatapan and Abdurrahman Dilipak, *Opposites: Side by Side*, trans. İsfendiyar Eralp (New York: George Brazillier, 2003), pp. 123–24.

19. Raşit el Gannuşi, *Laiklik ve Sivil Toplum Üzerine Değerlendirmeler* (İstanbul: İlimyurdu, 2010), pp. 86–89.

20. Taner Edis and Amy Sue Bix, "Biology and 'Created Nature': Gender and the Body in Popular Islamic Literature from Modern Turkey and the West," *Arab Studies Journal* 12, no. 2 and 13, no. 1 (2005): 140–58.

21. Bekir Topaloğlu, *İslâm'da Kadın* (İstanbul: Rağbet Yayınları, 2001).

22. Suzanne Haneef, *What Everyone Should Know about Islam and Muslims*, 14th ed. (Chicago: Library of Islam, 1996), pp. 113–14.

23. Ibid., p. 172.

24. Ibid., p. 173.

25. Tuğal, *Passive Revolution*, pp. 80–82. Jenny B. White, *Islamist Mobilization in Turkey: A Study in Vernacular Politics* (Seattle and London: University of Washington Press, 2002).

26. "Gericilik hız kesmiyor: Tüm çalışanları kadın olan hastane geliyor!" *soL Haber Portalı*, May 11, 2013, http://haber.sol.org.tr/devlet-ve-siyaset/gericilik-hiz-kesmiyor-tum-calisanlari-kadin-olan-hastane-geliyor-haberi-72805 (accessed October 17, 2015). "Kadınlar plajına çam ağacı kamuflajı," *soL Haber Portalı*, August 11, 2014, http://haber.sol.org.tr/devlet-ve-siyaset/kadinlar-plajina-cam-agaci-kamuflaji-haberi-95706 (accessed September 27, 2015). Reza Arjmand, "Women-Only Parks," *Center for Middle Eastern Studies*, November 8, 2013, http://www.cmes.lu.se/research/research-areas/iran-working-group/ (accessed August 21, 2015).

27. Ali Bulaç, "Başörtülü aday yoksa oy da yok!" *Zaman*, January 14, 2013, http://www.zaman.com.tr/ali-bulac/basortulu-aday-yoksa-oy-da-yok_2040305.html (accessed February 18, 2016).

28. Selin Ongun, *Başörtülü Kadınlar Anlattı: Türbanlı Erkekler* (İstanbul: Destek Yayınevi, 2010).

29. Leila Ahmed, *A Border Passage: From Cairo to America—A Woman's Journey* (New York: Penguin Books, 2000), pp. 125–29.

30. Haideh Moghissi, *Feminism and Islamic Fundamentalism: The Limits of Postmodern Analysis* (London and New York: Zed Books, 1999).

31. Janet Afary, *Sexual Politics in Modern Iran* (New York: Cambridge University Press, 2009).

32. Margot Badran, *Feminism in Islam: Secular and Religious Convergences* (Oxford, UK: Oneworld, 2009).

33. Asma Afsaruddin, "Accommodating 'Moderation': A Return to Authenticity or Recourse to Heresy?" in *Debating Moderate Islam: The Geopolitics of Islam and the West*, ed. M. A. Muqtedar Khan (Salt Lake City: University of Utah Press, 2007), p. 149.

34. Ahmed, *Women and Gender in Islam*, chap. 4.

35. Amina Wadud-Muhsin, *Qur'an and Woman* (Shah Alam: Penerbit Fajar Bakti Sd. Bhd., 1992), p. 68. Wadud-Muhsin has become better known as Amina Wadud.

36. Asma Barlas, *"Believing Women" in Islam: Unreading Patriarchal Interpretations of the Qur'ān* (Austin: University of Texas Press, 2002), p. 189.

37. Ahmed, *Women and Gender in Islam*, pp. 64–67.

38. Barlas, *"Believing Women" in Islam*, pp. 133–39; Wadud-Muhsin, *Qur'an and Woman*, pp. 17–23.

39. Wadud-Muhsin, *Qur'an and Woman*, pp. 70–71.

40. Ibid., p. 73.

41. Ahmed, *Women and Gender in Islam*, chap. 9.

42. Pieternella Van Doorn-Harder, *Women Shaping Islam: Indonesian Women Reading the Qur'an* (Urbana: University of Illinois Press, 2006), p. 2.

43. Robert Pringle, *Understanding Islam in Indonesia: Politics and Diversity* (Honolulu: University of Hawai'i Press, 2010), p. 141. Azyumardi Azra, Dina Afrianty, and Robert W. Hefner, "Pesantren and Madrasa: Muslim Schools and National Ideals in Indonesia," in *Schooling Islam: The Culture and Politics of Modern Muslim Education*, ed. Robert W. Hefner and Muhammad Qasim Zaman (Princeton, NJ: Princeton University Press, 2007).

44. Yoginder Sikand, "Why Can't Muslim Women Also Lead the Whole Community? Interview with Zakia Nizami Soman, Bharatiya Muslim Mahila Andolan," *MR Zine*, May 11, 2009, http://mrzine.monthlyreview.org/2009/sikand051109.html (accessed February 18, 2016).

45. Pragna Patel, in "We Should Not Abandon Secularism: Interview with Pragna Patel and Gita Sahgal," by Maryam Namazie, *Fitnah: Time for Change*, n.d., http://fitnah.org/fitnah_articles_english/interview_with_patel_and_sahgal.html (accessed October 17, 2015).

46. Robert N. McCauley, *Why Religion Is Natural and Science Is Not* (New York: Oxford University Press, 2011), p. 266. See also Melanie Elyse Brewster, "Atheism, Gender, and Sexuality," in *The Oxford Handbook of Atheism*, ed. Stephen Bullivant and Michael Ruse (Oxford, UK: Oxford University Press, 2013).

47. Fish, *Are Muslims Distinctive?* chaps. 2, 6.

48. Pippa Norris and Ronald Inglehart, *Sacred and Secular: Religion and Politics Worldwide* (Cambridge: Cambridge University Press, 2004). There are disputes over drivers of secularity; for example, education might be more important than security: Claude M. J. Braun, "Explaining Global Secularity: Existential Security or Education?" *Secularism and Nonreligion* 1 (2012): 68–93.

49. David Sehat, *The Myth of American Religious Freedom* (New York: Oxford University Press, 2011), pp. 149–50.

50. Lila Abu-Lughod, "Do Muslim Women Really Need Saving? Anthropological Reflections on Cultural Relativism and Its Others," *American Anthropologist* 104, no. 3 (2002): 788.

51. Susan Moller Okin, *Justice, Gender, and the Family* (New York: Basic Books, 1989).

52. Neil Levy, *Moral Relativism: A Short Introduction* (Oxford, UK: Oneworld, 2002), pp. 174–92.

53. Saba Mahmood, "Feminist Theory, Embodiment, and the Docile Agent: Some Reflections on the Egyptian Islamic Revival," *Cultural Anthropology* 16, no. 2 (2001): 202–36. Quotations from p. 205.

54. Ibid.

55. Sylva Frisk, *Submitting to God: Women and Islam in Urban Malaysia* (Copenhagen: NIAS, 2009), pp. 96–97.

56. Olivier Roy, *Globalized Islam*. Nilüfer Göle, "Islam, European Public Space and Civility," in *Religion in the New Europe*, ed. Krzysztof Michalski (Budapest: Central European University Press, 2006).

57. Joan Wallach Scott, *The Politics of the Veil* (Princeton, NJ: Princeton University Press, 2007), p. 128.

58. David Novak, "Human Dignity and the Social Contract," in *Recognizing Religion in a Secular Society: Essays in Pluralism, Religion, and Public Policy*, ed. Douglas Farrow (Montreal & Kingston: McGill-Queen's University Press, 2004), p. 60.

59. My description of secular and religious selves owes something to Charles Taylor, *A Secular Age* (Cambridge, MA: Belknap Press of Harvard University Press, 2007).

60. A secular analogue might be feminist suspicion of analytical reason in favor of an ethic of self-giving love. Within the secular liberal tradition, however, it is easy to find fault with such an approach: see Martha Nussbaum, *Sex and Social Justice* (Oxford, UK: Oxford University Press, 1999), pp. 74–80.

61. Ilkka Pyysiäinen, *Magic, Miracles, and Religion: A Scientist's Perspective* (Walnut Creek, CA: AltaMira, 2004).

62. Religion is often used to illustrate conflicts between "factual realism" and "practical realism." For example, David Sloan Wilson, "The Truth Is Sacred," in *The Joy of Secularism: 11 Essays for How We Live Now*, ed. George Levine (Princeton, NJ: Princeton University Press, 2011).

63. Ruth Abbey, *Charles Taylor* (Tweddington, UK: Acumen, 2000), chap. 3.

64. John R. Bowen, *Why The French Don't Like Headscarves: Islam, the State, and Public Space* (Princeton, NJ: Princeton University Press, 2007), p. 232.

65. Karima Bennoune, "The Law of the Republic versus the 'Law of the Brothers': A Story of France's Law Banning Religious Symbols in Public Schools," in *Human Rights Advocacy Stories*, ed. Deena R. Hurwitz et al. (New York: Foundation, 2009).

66. Yıldız Atasoy, *Islam's Marriage with Neoliberalism: State Transformation in Turkey* (New York: Palgrave McMillan, 2009), chap. 6.

67. Özlem Çelik, "Türkiye sahtekârlıklar ülkesi . . ." *soL Haber Portalı*, October 30, 2010, http://haber.sol.org.tr/kadinin-gunlugu/turkiye-sahtekarliklar -ulkesi-haberi-35172 (accessed September 27, 2015).

68. Fish, *Are Muslims Distinctive?* pp. 89–98.

69. Topaloğlu, *İslam'da Kadın*, pp. 249–50.

70. For example, Marnia Larzeg, *Questioning the Veil: Open Letters to Muslim Women* (Princeton, NJ: Princeton University Press, 2009).

CHAPTER 6: ISLAM VERSUS SECULARISM

1. Abdullahi Ahmed An-Na'im, *Islam and the Secular State: Negotiating the Future of Shari'a* (Cambridge: Harvard University Press, 2008), p. 85.

2. Martha C. Nussbaum, *Creating Capabilities: The Human Development Approach* (Cambridge: Belknap Press of Harvard University Press, 2011), p. 90.

3. David Sehat, *The Myth of American Religious Freedom* (New York: Oxford University Press, 2011).

4. Ryan T. Cragun, Stephanie Yeager, and Desmond Vega, "Research

Report: How Secular Humanists (and Everyone Else) Subsidize Religion in the United States," *Free Inquiry* 32, no. 4 (2012): 39–46.

5. John J. DiIulio, Jr., *Godly Republic: A Centrist Blueprint for America's Faith-Based Future* (Berkeley: University of California Press, 2007).

6. Barbara Forrest, "Rejecting the Founders' Legacy: Democracy as a Weapon against Science," *Logos* 12, no. 3 (2013), http://logosjournal.com/2013/forrest/ (accessed September 28, 2015).

7. Jacques Berlinerblau, *How to Be Secular: A Call to Arms for Religious Freedom* (Boston: Houghton Mifflin Harcourt, 2012), pp. 123–36.

8. Gary David and Kenneth K. Ayouby, "Being Arab and Becoming Americanized: Forms of Mediated Assimilation in Metropolitan Detroit," in *Muslim Minorities in the West: Visible and Invisible*, ed. Yvonne Yazbeck Haddad and Jane I. Smith (Walnut Creek, CA: Altamira, 2002), pp. 133–35.

9. Berlinerblau, *How to Be Secular*, pp. 46–47.

10. John R. Bowen, *Why The French Don't Like Headscarves: Islam, the State, and Public Space* (Princeton, NJ: Princeton University Press, 2007), p. 158.

11. Ibid., pp. 12–13, 186.

12. AFP, "Scientology's Fraud Conviction Upheld in France," *Telegraph*, October 17, 2013, http://www.telegraph.co.uk/news/worldnews/europe/france/10384877/Scientologys-fraud-conviction-upheld-in-France.html (accessed February 20, 2016).

13. Bowen, *Why the French Don't Like Headscarves*, chap. 3.

14. William Galston, "Religion and the Limits of Liberal Democracy," in *Recognizing Religion in a Secular Society: Essays in Pluralism, Religion, and Public Policy*, ed. Douglas Farrow (Montreal & Kingston: McGill-Queen's University Press, 2004), pp. 42–43.

15. Jocelyne Cesari, *When Islam and Democracy Meet: Muslims in Europe and in the United States* (New York: Palgrave MacMillan, 2004), p. 78.

16. Stefan Korioth and Ino Augsberg, "Religion and the Secular State in Germany," in *German National Reports to the 18th International Congress of Comparative Law: Washington, 2010*, ed. Jürgen Basedow, Uwe Kischel and Ulrich Sieber (Tübingen: Mohr Siebeck, 2010), pp. 1–18.

17. Mani Shankar Aiyar, *Confessions of a Secular Fundamentalist* (New Delhi: Penguin Books, 2006), pp. 90–91.

18. Neera Chandhoke, *Beyond Secularism: The Rights of Religious Minorities* (New Delhi: Oxford University Press, 1999).

19. Meera Nanda, *The God Market: How Globalization Is Making India More Hindu* (Noida: Random House India, 2009), p. 108.

20. Graeme Smith, *A Short History of Secularism* (London: I. B. Tauris, 2008).

21. Bernard Lewis, *Islam in History: Ideas, People, and Events in the Middle East* (Chicago and La Salle: Open Court, 1993), chap. 21.

22. Mark Lilla, *The Stillborn God: Religion, Politics and the Modern West* (New York: Knopf, 2007).

23. William T. Cavanaugh, *The Myth of Religious Violence: Secular Ideology and the Roots of Modern Conflict* (New York: Oxford University Press, 2009).

24. David Biale, *Not in the Heavens: The Tradition of Jewish Secular Thought* (Princeton, NJ: Princeton University Press, 2011).

25. Antony Black, *The History of Islamic Political Thought: From the Prophet to the Present* (New York: Routledge, 2001).

26. Hasan Gümüşoğlu, *Modernizm'in İnanç Hayatına Etkileri ve Jön Türklük* (İstanbul: Kayıhan Yayınları, 2012), p. 248.

27. A similar pattern of entanglement between nationalism and religion appears with Greek Orthodoxy. Ioannis N. Grigoriadis, *Instilling Religion in Greek and Turkish Nationalism: A "Sacred Synthesis"* (New York: Palgrave Macmillan, 2013).

28. Adeed Dawisha, *Arab Nationalism in the Twentieth Century: From Triumph to Despair* (Princeton, NJ: Princeton University Press, 2016). Aziz Al-Azmeh, *Islams and Modernities* (London: Verso, 1996).

29. L. Carl Brown, *Religion and State: The Muslim Approach to Politics* (New York: Columbia University Press, 2000). Islamization has often proceeded both from above, through state policies, and below, through popular culture and democratic demands. Nureddin Nebati, *Milli Görüşten Muhafazakâr Demokrasiye* (İstanbul: Alfa Basım Yayım, 2014).

30. Joseph Chinyong Liow, *Piety and Politics: Islamism in Contemporary Malaysia* (New York: Oxford University Press, 2009).

31. Geneive Abdo and Jonathan Lyons, *Answering Only to God: Faith and Freedom in Twenty-First-Century Iran* (New York: Henry Holt, 2003), pp. 113–15.

32. Christopher Houston, *Islam, Kurds and the Turkish Nation State* (New York: Berg, 2001). Cengiz Güneş, *The Kurdish National Movement in Turkey: From Protest to Resistance* (New York: Routledge, 2012).

33. Mainstream liberal authors are some of the worst offenders in this regard. Examples such as John Feffer, *Crusade 2.0: The West's Resurgent War against Islam* (San Francisco: City Lights Books, 2012), are full of delusionary assessments of countries such as Turkey.

34. Humeira Iqtidar, *Secularizing Islamists? Jama'at-E-Islami and Jama'at-Ud-Da'wa in Urban Pakistan* (Chicago: University of Chicago Press, 2011). Nuray Mert, *İslâm ve Demokrasi: Bir Kurt Masalı* (İstanbul: İz Yayıncılık, 1998). Nader Hashemi, *Islam, Secularism, and Liberal Democracy: Toward a Democratic Theory for Muslim Societies* (New York: Oxford University Press, 2009).

35. Ali A. Allawi, *The Crisis of Islamic Civilization* (New Haven and London: Yale University Press, 2009), p. 185.

36. M. Steven Fish, *Are Muslims Distinctive? A Look at the Evidence* (New York: Oxford University Press, 2011), p. 245.

37. Ibid., p. 63.

38. Ergün Yıldırım, *Yeni Türkiye'nin Yeni Aktörleri: AK Parti ve Cemaat* (İstanbul: Hayat Yayın Grubu, 2010).

39. Carrie Rosefsky Wickham, *The Muslim Brotherhood: Evolution of an Islamist Movement* (Princeton, NJ: Princeton University Press, 2013).

40. James Chin, "Malaysia: Pseudo-Democracy and the Making of a Malay-Islamic State," in *Routledge Handbook of Southeast Asian Democratization*, ed. William Case (London: Routledge, 2015). Simon Tisdall, "Democracy Falters in South-East Asia as Malaysia's PM Cleared of Corruption," *Guardian*, January 26, 2016, http://gu.com/p/4g667/sbl (accessed February 20, 2016).

41. Gareth H. Jenkins, *Between Fact and Fantasy: Turkey's Ergenekon Investigation* (Washington DC: Central Asia–Caucasus Institute and the Silk Road Studies Program, 2009). Some of these decisions were reversed following the later split between Gülenists and the ruling Islamists, but the damage had already been done.

42. Mark Lowen, "The Problem with Insulting Turkey's President Erdogan," *BBC News*, April 16, 2015, http://www.bbc.com/news/world-europe-32302697 (accessed February 20, 2016). "Turkey's AK Party: Another Victory for Illiberalism," *Economist*, November 7, 2015, http://www.economist.com/news/europe/21677997-turkeys-government-escalated-its-conflict-kurds-then-ran-promises-security-it-won (accessed February 20, 2016).

43. Asef Bayat, *Making Islam Democratic: Social Movements and the Post-Islamist Turn* (Stanford: Stanford University Press, 2007).

44. Turkish secularists tend to repeat outdated arguments that do not engage with contemporary conservatism. For example, Server Tanilli, *Din ve Politika: "Laik Barış"ın Dostları ve Düşmanları* (İstanbul: Cumhuriyet Kitapları, 2008).

45. Yalçın Akdoğan, *AK Parti ve Muhafazakar Demokrasi* (İstanbul: Alfa Yayınları, 2004). Bekir Berat Özipek, *Muhafazakarlık: Akıl, Toplum, Siyaset* (İstanbul: Timaş Yayınları, 2011).

46. For example, Mustafa Akyol, *Islam without Extremes: A Muslim Case for Liberty* (New York: W. W. Norton, 2011).

47. Christos Teazis, *İkincilerin Cumhuriyeti: Adalet ve Kalkınma Partisi* (İstanbul: Mızrak Yayınları, 2010), p. 188. For similar observations, see Cihan Tuğal, "Islam and the Retrenchment of Turkish Conservatism," in *Post-Islamism: The Changing Faces of Political Islam*, ed. Asef Bayat (New York: Oxford University Press, 2013), pp. 119–20.

48. Dinesh D'Souza, *The Enemy at Home: The Cultural Left and Its Responsibility for 9/11* (New York: Broadway Books, 2007).

49. Feisal Abdul Rauf, *What Is Right with Islam: A New Vision for Muslims and the West* (San Francisco: HarperOne, 2005). Akyol, *Islam without Extremes*.

50. Raşit el Gannuşi, *Laiklik ve Sivil Toplum Üzerine Değerlendirmeler* (İstanbul: İlimyurdu, 2010), pp. 20, 31.

51. Jean Bethke Elshtain, "A Catholic Understanding of Human Rights," in *Recognizing Religion in a Secular Society: Essays in Pluralism, Religion, and Public Policy*, ed. Douglas Farrow (Montreal & Kingston: McGill-Queen's University Press, 2004). Samuel Scheffler, "Responsibility, Reactive Attitudes, and Liberalism in Philosophy and Politics," *Philosophy and Public Affairs* 21, no. 4 (1992): 299–323.

52. Russell Blackford, *Freedom of Religion and the Secular State* (Chichester, UK: John Wiley & Sons, 2012), p. 82.

53. Judgments of harm depend on differing conceptions of the good. John Gray, *Two Faces of Liberalism* (New York: New Press, 2000), pp. 85–89.

54. Peter Berkowitz, "The Liberal Spirit in America and Its Paradoxes," in *Liberalism for a New Century*, ed. Neil Jumonville and Kevin Mattson (Berkeley: University of California Press, 2007), p. 23.

55. Tariq Modood, *Multiculturalism: A Civic Idea* (Cambridge, UK: Polity, 2007), p. 25.

56. El Gannuşi, *Laiklik ve Sivil Toplum Üzerine Değerlendirmeler*, pp. 17–31.

57. Anouar Majid, *Unveiling Traditions: Postcolonial Islam in a Polycentric World* (Durham, NC: Duke University Press, 2000), p. 65.

58. Charles Colson et al., "In Defense of Religious Freedom: A Statement by Evangelicals and Catholics Together," *First Things*, March 2012, http://www.firstthings.com/article/2012/03/in-defense-of-religious-freedom (accessed October 17, 2015).

59. Şanar Yurdatapan and Abdurrahman Dilipak, *Opposites: Side by Side*, trans. İsfendiyar Eralp (New York: George Brazillier, 2003), pp. 150–51.

60. "4+4+4'ün diğer hatırlattıkları: Gericiliğin kutsal ittifakı," *soL Haber Portalı*, March 31, 2012, http://haber.sol.org.tr/devlet-ve-siyaset/444un-diger -hatirlattiklari-gericiligin-kutsal-ittifaki-haberi-53279 (accessed October 17, 2015). On conservative social welfare policy in Turkey and its peculiar neoliberal use of welfare state rhetoric, see Meryem Koray, "AKP Dönemi: Neo-Liberalizm, Neo-Muhafazakarlık, Neo-Popülizm Beşiğinde Sallanan Sosyal Devlet ve Sosyal Politika," in *Himmet, Fıtrat, Piyasa: AKP Döneminde Sosyal Politika*, ed. Meryem Koray and Aziz Çelik (İstanbul: İletişim Yayıncılık, 2015).

61. Berlinerblau, *How to Be Secular*, p. 16.

62. Alan Brinkley, "Liberalism and Belief," in Jumonville and Watson, *Liberalism for a New Century*. Thomas A. Spragens Jr., *Getting the Left Right: The Transformation, Decline, and Reformation of American Liberalism* (Lawrence: University Press of Kansas, 2009), pp. 85–91.

63. H. Tristram Englehardt Jr., "Taking Moral Difference Seriously: Morality after the Death of God," in Farrow, *Recognizing Religion in a Secular Society*.

64. George Crowder, *Liberalism and Value Pluralism* (London: Continuum, 2002).

65. Anouar Majid, *We Are All Moors: Ending Centuries of Crusades against Muslims and Other Minorities* (Minneapolis: University of Minnesota Press, 2009), p. 47.

66. William E. Connolly, *Why I Am Not a Secularist* (Minneapolis: University of Minnesota Press, 1999). Banu Gökarıksel and Katharyne Mitchell, "Veiling, Secularism, and the Neoliberal Subject: National Narratives and Supranational Desires in Turkey and France," *Global Networks* 5, no. 2 (2005): 147–65.

67. Saba Mahmood, "Secularism, Hermeneutics, and Empire: The Politics of Islamic Reformation," *Public Culture* 18, no. 2 (2006): 323–47.

68. See contributions to Farrow, *Recognizing Religion in a Secular Society*.

69. For a critical discussion, see Kwame Anthony Appiah, *The Ethics of Identity* (Princeton: Princeton University Press, 2005), chap. 2.

70. Bhikhu C. Parekh, *Rethinking Multiculturalism: Cultural Diversity and Political Theory*, 2nd ed. (New York: Palgrave Macmillan, 2006).

71. Tariq Modood, *Multiculturalism*, p. 61.

72. Robert F. Drinan, *Can God and Caesar Coexist? Balancing Religious Freedom and International Law* (New Haven, CT: Yale University Press, 2004), pp. 126–29.

73. Paul M. Sniderman and Louk Hagendoorn, *When Ways of Life Collide: Multiculturalism and Its Discontents in the Netherlands* (Princeton, NJ: Princeton University Press, 2007), p. 18.

74. Tariq Modood, "Muslims and European Multiculturalism," in *Religion in the New Europe*, ed. Krzysztof Michalski (Budapest: Central European University Press, 2006); Modood, *Multiculturalism*, pp. 78–84.

75. El Gannuşi, *Laiklik ve Sivil Toplum Üzerine Değerlendirmeler*, pp. 187–88. See also contributions in *Cultural Diversity and Islam*, ed. Abdul Aziz Said and Meena Sharify-Funk (Lanham, MD: University Press of America, 2003).

76. Noam Chomsky and Gilbert Achcar, *Perilous Power: The Middle East & U.S. Foreign Policy: Dialogues on Terror, Democracy, War and Justice* (Boulder, CO: Paradigm, 2007), p. 128.

77. Efraim Karsh, *Islamic Imperialism: A History* (New Haven, CT: Yale University Press, 2006), chap. 6.

78. Sniderman and Hagendoorn, *When Ways of Life Collide*, pp. 135–38.

79. Gilles Kepel, *Beyond Terror and Martyrdom: The Future of the Middle East* (Cambridge, MA: Harvard University Press, 2008), pp. 243–56.

80. Taner Edis and Maarten Boudry, "Beyond Physics? On the Prospects of Finding a Meaningful Oracle," *Foundations of Science* 19, no. 4 (2014): 403–22.

81. Taner Edis, *The Ghost in the Universe: God in Light of Modern Science* (Amherst, NY: Prometheus Books, 2002), chap. 9.

82. I appear to fit a stereotypically liberal profile, as described in Jonathan Haidt, *The Righteous Mind: Why Good People Are Divided by Politics and Religion* (New York: Pantheon Books, 2012).

83. My conception of discourse in a secular public sphere has a family resemblance to those elaborated by Jürgen Habermas, *The Structural Transformation of the Public Sphere: An Inquiry into a Category of Bourgeois Society* (Cambridge, MA: MIT Press, 1989) and Lincoln Dahlberg, "The Internet and Democratic Discourse: Exploring the Prospects of Online Deliberative Forums Extending the Public Sphere," *Information, Communication & Society* 4, no. 4 (2001): 615–33.

84. Kent Greenawalt, "Five Questions about Religion Judges Are Afraid to Ask," in *Obligations of Citizenship and Demands of Faith*, ed. Nancy L. Rosenblum (Princeton, NJ: Princeton University Press, 2000).

85. Taner Edis, "Is There a Political Argument for Teaching Evolution?" Paper presented at the Religions, Science and Technology in Cultural Contexts: Dynamics of Change conference in Trondheim, Norway, March 2, 2012.

86. Alberto Alesina and Edward L. Glaeser, *Fighting Poverty in the U.S. and Europe: A World of Difference* (Oxford, UK: Oxford University Press, 2004). While there appears to be such a trend, the overall empirical picture is more

complicated; Holger Stichnoth and Karine Van der Straeten, "Ethnic Diversity, Public Spending, and Individual Support for the Welfare State: A Review of the Empirical Literature," *Journal of Economic Surveys* 27, no. 2 (2013): 364–89.

87. Stephen Macedo, *Diversity and Distrust: Civic Education in a Multicultural Democracy* (Cambridge, MA: Harvard University Press, 2000).

88. David Voas, "The Rise and Fall of Fuzzy Fidelity in Europe," *European Sociological Review* 25, no. 2 (2009): 155–68.

89. Valentina Frate, "Veiled Artists in Egypt," in *What Happened to the Islamists? Salafis Heavy Metal Muslims and the Lure of Consumerist Islam*, ed. Amel Boubekeur and Olivier Roy (New York: Columbia University Press, 2012).

90. Sheldon S. Wolin, *Democracy Incorporated: Managed Democracy and the Specter of Inverted Totalitarianism* (Princeton, NJ: Princeton University Press, 2010).

91. For example, legislative outcomes follow the preferences of the wealthy and ignore middle-class preferences. Martin Gilens, "Inequality and Democratic Responsiveness," *Public Opinion Quarterly* 69, no. 5 (2005): 788–96. Martin Gilens and Benjamin I. Page, "Testing Theories of American Politics: Elites, Interest Groups, and Average Citizens," *Perspectives on Politics* 12, no. 3 (2014): 564–81.

92. Philip Mirowski, *Never Let a Serious Crisis Go to Waste: How Neoliberalism Survived the Financial Meltdown* (London: Verso, 2014).

93. Ibid., pp. 53–67.

94. Tarek Masoud, "Arabs Want Redistribution, So Why Don't They Vote Left? Theory and Evidence from Egypt," Harvard Kennedy School Faculty Research Working Paper Series, RWP13-007 (2013).

95. Flynt Leverett and Hillary Mann Leverett, *Going to Tehran: Why the United States Must Come to Terms with the Islamic Republic of Iran* (New York: Metropolitan Books, 2013). Cihan Tuğal, *Passive Revolution: Absorbing the Islamic Challenge to Capitalism* (Stanford, CA: Stanford University Press, 2009), pp. 255–62.

CHAPTER 7: BLASPHEMERS AND INFIDELS

1. Hind Al-Abadleh, "Edis Paints Poor Picture of Islam," *Cord Weekly,* October 3, 2007, p. 21.

2. Rory Fenton, "Atheist Students Must Fight Back," *Huffpost*

Students, June 4, 2014, http://www.huffingtonpost.co.uk/rory-fenton/atheism -students_b_5434739.html (accessed February 21, 2016).

3. Mesut Hasan Benli, "Yargıtay: Say'ın paylaşımları düşünce ve ifade özgürlüğü," *Hürriyet*, October 26, 2015, http://www.hurriyet.com.tr/yargitay -sayin-paylasimlari-dusunce-ve-ifade-ozgurlugudur-40005948. "Ayhan Sefer Üstün'den skandal Fazıl Say açıklaması!" *soL Haber Portalı*, April 27, 2013, http:// haber.sol.org.tr/devlet-ve-siyaset/ayhan-sefer-ustunden-skandal-fazil-say-aciklamasi -haberi-72106. "RTÜK'ten Pınar Kür'ün 'türban' açıklamalarına ceza!" *soL Haber Portalı*, May 4, 2014, http://haber.sol.org.tr/medya/rtukten-pinar-kurun -turban-aciklamalarina-ceza-haberi-91908. (All accessed October 26, 2015).

4. Farid Esack, *The Qur'an: A Short Introduction* (Oxford, UK: Oneworld, 2002), pp. 146–47.

5. For example, stories about Ka'b ibn al-Ashraf: *Sahih al-Bukhari*, vol. 3, book 45, no. 687; vol. 5, book 59, no. 369 (http://www.sahih-bukhari.com).

6. *Sahih Muslim*, book 26, no. 5389 (http://www.sahihmuslim.com/).

7. Yohanan Friedmann, *Tolerance and Coercion in Islam: Interfaith Relations in the Muslim Tradition* (New York: Cambridge University Press, 2003), pp. 35–36.

8. Reza Aslan, *No God but God: The Origins, Evolution, and Future of Islam* (New York: Random House, 2005), p. 262.

9. David Nirenberg, *Communities of Violence: Persecution of Minorities in the Middle Ages* (Princeton, NJ: Princeton University Press, 1996). Bat Ye'or's work arguing that Muslims almost uniformly oppressed the protected peoples has become popular in Islamophobic circles; for criticism see Anver M. Emon, *Religious Pluralism and Islamic Law:* Dhimmīs *and Others in the Empire of Law* (Oxford, UK: Oxford University Press, 2012), pp. 39–42; Michael A. Sells, "Christ Killer, Kremlin, Contagion," in *The New Crusades: Constructing the Muslim Enemy*, ed. Emran Qureshi and Michael A. Sells (New York: Columbia University Press, 2003), pp. 362–63.

10. Philip Jenkins, *The Lost History of Christianity: The Thousand-Year Golden Age of the Church in the Middle East, Africa, and Asia—And How It Died* (New York: HarperOne, 2008).

11. Hasan Gümüşoğlu, *Modernizm'in İnanç Hayatına Etkileri ve Jön Türklük* (İstanbul: Kayıhan Yayınları, 2012), pp. 44–46. Bernard Lewis, *What Went Wrong? Western Impact and Middle Eastern Response* (New York: Oxford University Press, 2002), chap. 4.

12. Ilgaz Zorlu, *Evet, Ben Selanikliyim: Türkiye Sabetaycılığı* (İstanbul: Zvi-Geyik Yayınları, 2000).

13. Rıfat N. Bali, *Musa'nın Evlatları, Cumhuriyet'in Yurttaşları* (İstanbul: İletişim Yayıncılık, 2001).

14. Sahih Muslim, Book 41 (*The Book of Tribulations and the Signs of the Last Hour*), no. 6985 (http://www.sahihmuslim.com).

15. Jean-Pierre Filiu, *Apocalypse in Islam*, trans. M. B. DeBevoise (Berkeley: University of California Press, 2011). David Cook, *Contemporary Muslim Apocalyptic Literature* (Syracuse, NY: Syracuse University Press, 2005).

16. Patrick Sookhdeo, *Freedom to Believe: Challenging Islam's Apostasy Law* (McLean, VA: Isaac Publishing, 2009), pp. 63–64.

17. Abu Amina Elias, "Hadith of the Gharqad Tree: Is It a Good Deed to Kill Jews in Islam?" *Faith in Allah*, February 27, 2013, http://abuaminaelias.com/hadith-of-the-gharqad-tree-is-it-a-good-deed-to-kill-jews-in-islam/ (accessed February 22, 2016).

18. Ruşen Çakır and Semih Sakallı, *100 Soruda Erdoğan × Gülen Savaşı* (İstanbul: Metis Yayınları, 2014), pp. 33–37.

19. Mun'im Sirry, *Scriptural Polemics: The Qur'ān and Other Religions* (New York: Oxford University Press, 2014).

20. Feisal Abdul Rauf, *Moving the Mountain: Beyond Ground Zero to a New Vision of Islam in America* (New York: Free Press, 2012), pp. 43, 97–99.

21. James Bell et al., *The World's Muslims: Religion, Politics and Society* (Washington, DC: Pew Research Center, 2013), chap. 6.

22. M. Steven Fish, *Are Muslims Distinctive? A Look at the Evidence* (New York: Oxford University Press, 2011), pp. 22, 60.

23. Samuli Schielke, "The Islamic World," in *The Oxford Handbook of Atheism*, ed. Stephen Bullivant and Michael Ruse (Oxford, UK: Oxford University Press, 2013), pp. 647–48.

24. Sookhdeo, *Freedom to Believe*.

25. Max Blumenthal, *Goliath: Life and Loathing in Greater Israel* (New York: Nation Books, 2013), pp. 304, 309–10.

26. Bernard Lewis, *Islam in History: Ideas, People, and Events in the Middle East* (Chicago: Open Court, 1993), p. 290.

27. Anouar Majid, *A Call for Heresy: Why Dissent Is Vital to Islam and America* (Minneapolis: University of Minnesota Press, 2007), pp. 206–208.

28. Shabbir Akhtar, *The Quran and the Secular Mind: A Philosophy of Islam* (New York: Routledge, 2008), p. 82. Perceptions of divine unfairness are often important for individual Muslim atheists, but this is not a matter for public debate. Brian Whitaker, *Arabs without God: Atheism and Freedom of Belief in the Middle East* (CreateSpace Independent Publishing Platform, 2014).

29. For example, Harputizâde Hacı Mustafa Efendi, *Red ve Isbât: Alman Feylesoflarından Louis Büchner'in Ahmed Nebil, Baha Tevfik Efendiler Tarafından Tercüme Olunan* Madde ve Kuvvet *Nâm Eserine Reddiyedir*, ed. Ibrahim Hakkı Kaynak and Ali Utku (İstanbul: Çizgi Kitabevi, 2014).

30. For example, Fazlur Rahman, *Major Themes of the Qur'ān* (Minneapolis: Bibliotheca Islamica, 1994), p. 11. Muslims also rarely engage in philosophical apologetics for theistic belief; examples such as Zain Ali, *Faith, Philosophy and the Reflective Muslim* (New York: Palgrave Macmillan, 2013) are few and far in between when compared to Christian efforts.

31. Mark Juergensmeyer, *Global Rebellion: Religious Challenges to the Secular State, from Christian Militias to al Qaeda* (Berkeley: University of California Press, 2008), p. 237.

32. Whitaker, *Arabs without God*, chap. 1.

33. Bahey El-Din Hassan, "A Question of Human Rights Ethics: Defending the Islamists," in *Human Rights in the Arab World: Independent Voices*, ed. Anthony Chase and Amr Hamzawy (Philadelphia: University of Pennsylvania Press, 2006), p. 48.

34. Reporters without Borders, "World Press Freedom Index 2015," https://index.rsf.org/ (accessed October 29, 2015). Benoît Hervieu, *Blasphemy: Information Sacrificed on Altar of Religion* (Reporters without Borders, December 2013).

35. International Humanist and Ethical Union, *Freedom of Thought 2015: A Global Report on Discrimination against Humanists, Atheists, and the Non-religious; Their Human Rights and Legal Status*, http://freethoughtreport.com (accessed February 22, 2016).

36. AFP, "Mauritania Issues First Apostasy Death Sentence," *Daily Mail*, December 25, 2014, http://www.dailymail.co.uk/wires/afp/article-2886801/Mauritania-issues-apostasy-death-sentence.html. Associated Press, "Nigerian Atheist Faces Death Threats after Release from Psychiatric Ward," *Guardian*, July 3, 2014, http://gu.com/p/3qkam/sbl. "Nigeria Court in Kano Sentences Nine People to Death for Blasphemy," *BBC News Africa*, June 26, 2015, http://www.bbc.com/news/world-africa-33283261. "Sudan Woman Faces Death for Apostasy," *BBC News Africa*, May 15, 2014, http://www.bbc.com/news/world-africa-27424064. James Kirchick, "Exiled after Threats: Blogger Wants More Freedoms in Morocco," *Der Spiegel*, March 29, 2013, http://www.spiegel.de/international/world/moroccan-blogger-champions-freedom-in-swiss-exile-a-891561.html. "Libya: Politicians Face Death Penalty over Blasphemous Cartoon," *Amnesty International*, February 27, 2014, https://www.amnesty.org/

en/latest/news/2014/02/libya-politicians-face-death-penalty-over-blasphemous
-cartoon/. Saeed Kamali Dehghan, "Iran Executes Man for Heresy," *Guardian*,
September 29, 2014, http://gu.com/p/4222y/sbl. "Atheist Afghan Granted
Religious Asylum in UK," *BBC News UK*, January 14, 2014, http://www.bbc
.com/news/uk-25715736. Joanna Lillis, "Kazakhstan: Atheist Faces Seven Years
for Stoking Religious Tension," *Eurasianet.org*, May 15, 2014, http://www
.eurasianet.org/node/68375. (All accessed February 21, 2016).

37. Morning Star News, "Christians Convicted of 'Blasphemy' in Egypt
for 'Liking' Facebook Page," *Christian Post*, June 25, 2014, http://www
.christianpost.com/news/christians-convicted-of-blasphemy-in-egypt-for-liking
-facebook-page-122210/. "Egyptian Author Sentenced to Five Years for Insulting Religion," *Aswat Masriya*, June 13, 2013, http://en.aswatmasriya.com/
news/view.aspx?id=dafd1593-29e5-4fe6-ae42-e38cb7cb7647. "Poet Fatima
Naoot Sentenced to 3 Years in Prison for Contempt of Religion," *Mada Masr*,
January 26, 2016, http://www.madamasr.com/news/culture/poet-fatima-naoot
-sentenced-3-years-prison-contempt-religion. "Behery to Remain in Jail after
Legal Challenge Denied in Blasphemy Case," *Ahram Online*, February 2, 2016,
http://english.ahram.org.eg/News/186557.aspx. Emir Nader, "Student in Hiding
after Prison Sentence for Atheism," *Daily News Egypt*, March 14, 2015, http://
www.dailynewsegypt.com/2015/03/14/student-in-hiding-after-prison-sentence
-for-atheism-confirmed/. Emir Nader, "Egyptian Student Given Prison Sentence
for Atheist Facebook Posts," *Daily News Egypt*, February 17, 2015, http://www
.dailynewsegypt.com/2015/02/17/egyptian-student-given-prison-sentence-for
-atheist-facebook-posts/. Sherif Tarek, "Egyptian Author Appeals for Protection
following Islamist Threats," *Al-Ahram Online*, June 10, 2013, http://english
.ahram.org.eg/NewsContent/1/64/73680/Egypt/Politics-/Egyptian-author-appeals
-for-protection-following-I.aspx. Patrick Keddie, "Egypt's Embattled Atheists," *Al
Jazeera*, November 18, 2013, http://www.aljazeera.com/indepth/features/2013/11/
egypt-embattled-atheists-20131114184645790660.html. (All accessed February
22, 2016).

38. Sultan Sooud Al Qassemi, "Gulf Atheism in the Age of Social Media,"
Al Monitor, March 3, 2014, http://www.al-monitor.com/pulse/originals/2014/03/
gulf-atheism-uae-islam-religion.html. "Saudi Arabia: New Terrorism Regulations
Assault Rights," *Human Rights Watch*, March 20, 2014, http://www.hrw.org/
news/2014/03/20/saudi-arabia-new-terrorism-regulations-assault-rights. AFP, "Saudi
Court Upholds 10-Year Term for Rights Activist," *Gulf News Saudi Arabia*,
September 2, 2014, http://gulfnews.com/news/gulf/saudi-arabia/saudi-court

-upholds-10-year-term-for-rights-activist-1.1379805. Lizzie Dearden, "Man to Be Beheaded in Saudi Arabia after Ripping Up a Koran and Hitting It with His Shoe," *Independent*, February 24, 2015, http://www.independent.co.uk/news/world/middle-east/man-to-be-beheaded-in-saudi-arabia-after-ripping-up-a-koran-and-hitting-it-with-his-shoe-10067392.html. David Batty and Mona Mahmood, "Palestinian Poet Ashraf Fayadh's Death Sentence Quashed by Saudi Court," *Guardian*, February 2, 2016, http://gu.com/p/4fqjv/sbl. Felicity Morse, "Saudi Arabia Criticises Norway over Human Rights Record," *Independent*, April 29, 2014, http://www.independent.co.uk/news/saudi-arabia-criticises-norway-over-human-rights-record-9301796.html. (All accessed February 22, 2016).

39. Human Rights Commission of Pakistan, *State of Human Rights in 2013* (Lahore: Human Rights Commission of Pakistan, 2014), pp. 83–126. Ali Sethi, "Pakistan's Tyranny of Blasphemy," *New York Times*, May 20, 2014, http://nyti.ms/1giqkkd. Mina Sohail, "Young Pakistanis Are Asking: If There Can Be Secular Jews, Why Not Atheist Muslims?" *Tablet*, March 10, 2014, http://www.tabletmag.com/jewish-news-and-politics/165226/pakistans-secular-muslims. (All accessed February 21, 2016.)

40. John Chalmers, "Islamist Agitation Fuels Unrest in Bangladesh," *Reuters*, April 15, 2013, http://reut.rs/XCXsHQ. "Bangladesh Blogger Niloy Neel Hacked to Death in Dhaka," *BBC News*, August 7, 2015, http://www.bbc.com/news/world-asia-33819032. Associated Press, "Bangladesh Arrests Publisher for Books Said to Hurt Muslims," *New York Times*, February 16, 2016, http://nyti.ms/1QbdvYN. (All accessed February 22, 2016).

41. Nick Ashdown, "Atheists, the 'Ultimate Other' in Turkey," *Inter Press Service*, June 24, 2014, http://www.ipsnews.net/2014/06/atheists-the-ultimate-other-in-turkey/. "Turkish-Armenian Scribe Sentenced to 13 Months for Blasphemy in Blog Post," *Hürriyet Daily News*, May 22, 2013, http://www.hurriyetdailynews.com/turkish-armenian-scribe-sentenced-to-13-months-for-blasphemy-in-blog-post-.aspx?pageID=238&nID=47371&NewsCatID=341. Serdar Kulaksız, "Karikatürist Baruter hakkında 1 yıl hapis istendi!" *Habertürk*, September 28, 2011, http://www.haberturk.com/yasam/haber/673827-karikaturist-baruter-hakkinda-1-yil-hapis-istendi. "Diyanet'ten internet yasaklarına destek: Hürriyet başıboşluk değildir!" *soL Haber Portalı*, March 28, 2014, http://haber.sol.org.tr/devlet-ve-siyaset/diyanetten-internet-yasaklarina-destek-hurriyet-basibosluk-degildir-haberi-90158. DHA, "Cumhuriyet yazarları ifadeye çağrıldı," *soL Haber Portalı*, January 16, 2015, http://haber.sol.org.tr/turkiye/cumhuriyet-yazarlari-ifadeye-cagrildi-105480. (All accessed February 21, 2016).

42. Eileen Ng, "Malaysia's Top Court Upholds Ban on Non-Muslims Using 'Allah' to Refer to God," *Globe and Mail*, June 23, 2014, http://www.theglobeandmail.com/news/world/malaysias-top-court-upholds-ban-on-non-muslims-using-allah-to-refer-to-god/article19286167/. "Indonesia Province Bans Ahmadiyah from Spreading Minority Islamic Sect," *Reuters*, January 26, 2016, http://reut.rs/1OM8jZa. Marcel Thee, "The Rise of Indonesian Atheism," *Jakarta Globe*, December 7, 2010, http://www.thejakartaglobe.com/archive/the-rise-of-indonesian-atheism/. "Atheist Alexander Aan Gets out of Prison," *Jakarta Post*, January 31, 2014, http://www.thejakartapost.com/news/2014/01/31/atheist-alexander-aan-gets-prison.html. Gabriel Domínguez, "Amnesty Slams Indonesia's 'Oppressive' Blasphemy Laws," *Deutsche Welle*, November 21, 2014, http://dw.de/p/1DqG6. (All accessed February 22, 2016.)

43. 'Abd al-Rahmaan al-Barraak, "The Atheist Who Does Good Deeds Is Worse Than the One Who Kills His Mother and Takes Care of Dogs," *Islam Question and Answer*, n.d., http://islamqa.info/en/10300 (accessed October 17, 2015).

44. Mohammad Hashim Kamali, *Freedom of Expression in Islam* (Cambridge, UK: Islamic Texts Society, 1997), p. 12.

45. Ibid., p. 166.

46. Abdullahi Ahmed An-Na'im, *Islam and the Secular State: Negotiating the Future of Shar'ia* (Cambridge, MA: Harvard University Press, 2008), pp. 30–31. Wahid al-Din Khan also took advantage of the comparative freedom in India to advance an internal critique of the Islamic legal tradition. Muhammad Qasim Zaman, "Tradition and Authority in Deobandi Madrasas of South Asia," in *Schooling Islam: The Culture and Politics of Modern Muslim Education*, ed. Robert W. Hefner and Muhammad Qasim Zaman (Princeton, NJ: Princeton University Press, 2007), p. 69.

47. Mohamed Talbi, "Religious Liberty: A Muslim Perspective," in *The New Voices of Islam: Rethinking Politics and Modernity*, ed. Mehran Kamrava (Berkeley and Los Angeles: University of California Press, 2006).

48. Rana Tanveer, "Blasphemy Bandwagon: Parishioners Force Pastor to Flee Church, Home," *Express Tribune*, February 25, 2013, http://tribune.com.pk/story/512022/blasphemy-bandwagon-parishioners-force-pastor-to-flee-church-and-home/ (accessed October 17, 2015).

49. Hemchhaya De, "Books in a Bind," *Telegraph*, February 26, 2014, http://www.telegraphindia.com/1140226/jsp/opinion/story_18022320.jsp. "Outspoken Indian Scholar Killed by Gunmen," *Al Jazeera*, August 30, 2015, http://www

.aljazeera.com/news/2015/08/outspoken-indian-scholar-rationalist-killed -150830093019963.html. (All accessed February 22, 2016.)

50. "Sri Lanka to Deport Buddha Tattoo British Woman," *BBC News Asia*, April 22, 2014, http://www.bbc.com/news/world-asia-27107857. Anuradha Sharma and Vishal Arora, "Nirvanaless: Asian Buddhism's Growing Fundamentalist Streak," *Religion News Service*, May 1, 2014, http://www.religionnews.com/ 2014/05/01/nirvanaless-asian-buddhisms-growing-fundamentalist-streak/. (All accessed February 22, 2016.)

51. "Man Sentenced to Jail in Greece for Mocking Monk," *Reuters*, January 17, 2014, http://reut.rs/1dAX2cC. "Russian Lawmakers Back Jail Terms for Insulting Religion," *Sputnik*, June 11, 2013, http://sptnkne.ws/UZD. Giorgi Lomsadze, "Georgia Divided over 'Blasphemy Bill,'" *Eurasianet*, February 4, 2016, http://eurasianet.org/node/77156. (All accessed February 22, 2016.)

52. David Nash, *Blasphemy in the Christian World: A History* (New York: Oxford University Press, 2007). "Atheist Ireland Asks Constitutional Convention to Remove Blasphemy Offence," *Atheist Ireland*, July 19, 2013, http://www .atheist.ie/2013/07/atheist-ireland-asks-constitutional-convention-to-remove -blasphemy-offence/ (accessed October 17, 2015.)

53. "French Islamists Seek to Use Blasphemy Law to Silence Critics," *National Secular Society*, February 18, 2014, http://www.secularism.org.uk/ news/2014/02/french-islamists-seek-to-use-blasphemy-law-to-silence-critics. Peter Stanners, "Danish-Iranian Artist Convicted of Racism," *Copenhagen Post*, September 18, 2014, http://cphpost.dk/news/danish-iranian-artist-convicted-of -racism.6906.html. (All accessed October 17, 2015.)

54. Stephen Eric Bronner, *Reclaiming the Enlightenment: Toward a Politics of Radical Engagement* (New York: Columbia University Press, 2004), p. 68.

55. Jeffrey Stout, *Democracy & Tradition* (Princeton, NJ: Princeton University Press, 2004), p. 83.

56. Paul Cliteur, *The Secular Outlook: In Defense of Moral and Political Secularism* (Malden, MA: Wiley-Blackwell, 2010), p. 140.

57. Stout, *Democracy & Tradition*, pp. 166–68.

58. Talal Asad, "Free Speech, Blasphemy, and Secular Criticism," in *Is Critique Secular? Blasphemy, Injury and Free Speech*, by Talal Asad, Wendy Brown, Judith Butler, and Saba Mahmood (Berkeley: University of California Press, 2009), pp. 31, 46.

59. Cliteur, *Secular Outlook*, p. 154.

60. Majid, *Unveiling Traditions*, chap. 1.

61. Charles Taylor, "The Politics of Recognition," in *Multiculturalism: Examining the Politics of Recognition*, ed. Amy Gutmann (Princeton, NJ: Princeton University Press, 1994), p. 25.

62. John Gray, *Two Faces of Liberalism* (New York: New Press, 2000), chap. 3.

63. Russell Blackford, *Freedom of Religion and the Secular State* (Chichester, UK: John Wiley & Sons, 2012), p. 77.

64. Rex Martin and David A. Reidy, eds., *Rawls's Law of Peoples: A Realistic Utopia?* (Malden, MA: Blackwell, 2006).

65. Taner Edis, "Finding an Enemy: Islam and the New Atheism," in *Muhammad in the Digital Age*, ed. Ruqayya Khan (Austin: University of Texas Press, 2015), pp. 172–90.

66. Charles Colson and Harold Fickett, *The Faith: What Christians Believe, Why They Believe It, and Why It Matters* (Grand Rapids, MI: Zondervan, 2008), p. 27.

67. Ibn Warraq, *Why the West Is Best: A Muslim Apostate's Defense of Liberal Democracy* (New York and London: Encounter Books, 2011), chap. 6.

68. John L. Esposito, *The Future of Islam* (New York: Oxford University Press, 2010), pp. 21–23.

69. Nathan Lean, *The Islamophobia Industry: How the Right Manufactures Fear of Muslims* (London: Pluto, 2012).

70. Tiffany Gabbay, "Chicago Public School Bans 'Islamophobic' Novel—and Now Parents & Teachers Are Protesting," *Blaze*, March 15, 2013, http://www.theblaze.com/stories/2013/03/15/chicago-public-school-bans-islamophobic-novel-and-now-parents-teachers-are-protesting/ (accessed September 28, 2015).

71. Edis, "Finding an Enemy."

72. Phil Zuckerman, *Society without God: What the Least Religious Nations Can Tell Us about Contentment* (New York: New York University Press, 2008). Ingvild Sælid Gilhus, "Angels in Norway: Religious Border-Crossers and Border Markers," in *Vernacular Religion in Everyday Life: Expressions of Belief*, ed. Marion Bowman and Ülo Valk (New York: Routledge, 2014). The Nordic welfare state is under more stress than often acknowledged; Asbjørn Wahl, *The Rise and Fall of the Welfare State* (London: Pluto, 2011).

73. Christopher Caldwell, *Reflections on the Revolution in Europe: Immigration, Islam, and the West* (New York: Doubleday, 2009).

74. Raphaël Liogier, *İslamlaşma Efsanesi: Kolektif bir Anksiyite Hakkında Deneme* [*Le Mythe de l'Islamisation—Essai sur une Obsession Collective*] (Ankara: Epos Yayınları, 2012).

75. Jonathan Laurence, *The Emancipation of Europe's Muslims: The State's Role in Minority Integration* (Princeton, NJ: Princeton University Press, 2012).

76. Paul M. Sniderman and Louk Hagendoorn, *When Ways of Life Collide: Multiculturalism and Its Discontents in the Netherlands* (Princeton, NJ: Princeton University Press, 2007).

77. Bhikhu Parekh, "Is Islam a Threat to Europe's Multicultural Democracies?" in Michalski, *Religion in the New Europe*, p. 120.

78. Tariq Modood, *Multiculturalism: A Civic Idea* (Cambridge, UK: Polity, 2007).

79. Glen Greenwald, "The Real Criminals in the Tarek Mehanna Case," *Salon*, April 13, 2012, http://www.salon.com/2012/04/13/the_real_criminals_in_the_tarek_mehanna_case/. AP, "Highlights of AP's Pulitzer Prize–Winning Probe into NYPD Intelligence Operations," *Associated Press*, 2015, http://www.ap.org/media-center/nypd/investigation. Glenn Greenwald, "The FBI's Anticipatory Prosecution of Muslims to Criminalize Speech," *Guardian*, March 19, 2013, http://gu.com/p/3eh2q/sbl. (All accessed February 26, 2016). Arun Kundnani, *The Muslims Are Coming! Islamophobia, Extremism, and the Domestic War on Terror* (New York: Verso, 2014).

80. Chris Hedges, "The Death of Truth," *TruthDig*, May 6, 2013, http://www.truthdig.com/dig/item/the_death_of_truth_20130505. Peter Van Buren, "*1984* Was an Instruction Manual," *TomDispatch*, December 3, 2013, http://www.tomdispatch.com/blog/175779/tomgram%3A_peter_van_buren,_1984_was_an_instruction_manual_. (All accessed September 28, 2015.)

81. Richard A. Oppel Jr., "Taping of Farm Cruelty Is Becoming the Crime," *New York Times*, April 6, 2013, http://nyti.ms/17VD50p (accessed February 21, 2016).

82. Kembrew McLeod, *Freedom of Expression®: Resistance and Repression in the Age of Intellectual Property* (Minneapolis: University of Minnesota Press, 2007). Justin Bekelman, Yan Li, and Cary Gross, "Scope and Impacts of Financial Conflicts of Interests in Biomedical Research," *Journal of the American Medical Association* 284 (2003): 454–65. Philip Mirowski, *ScienceMart: Privatizing American Science* (Cambridge, MA: Harvard University Press, 2011).

83. McLeod, *Freedom of Expression®*, pp. 215–16.

84. Bruce Barry, *Speechless: The Erosion of Free Expression in the American Workplace* (San Francisco, CA: Berrett-Koehler, 2007).

85. Emine Ülker Tarhan, *Beni Susturabilecek Tek Şey . . .* (İstanbul: Ka Kitap, 2014), p. 107.

86. Anita Oğurlu and Ahmet Öncü, "Türkiye Egemen Sınıfında Laik/İslami Hizipleşme ve Medya," in *Neoliberalizm, İslamcı Sermayenin Yükselişi ve AKP*, ed. Neşecan Balkan, Erol Balkan, Ahmet Öncü (İstanbul: Yordam Kitap, 2013). Mehmet Altan, *Alo Fatih! Medyanın RTE ile İmtihanı* (İstanbul: Klas Kitaplar, 2014).

87. Naomi Oreskes and Erik Conway, *Merchants of Doubt: How a Handful of Scientists Obscured the Truth on Issues from Tobacco Smoke to Global Warming* (New York: Bloomsbury, 2011).

88. Philip Mirowski, *Never Let a Serious Crisis Go to Waste: How Neoliberalism Survived the Financial Meltdown* (London: Verso, 2013).

CHAPTER 8: SACRED VIOLENCE

1. Serge Trifkovic, *The Sword of the Prophet: Islam—History, Theology, Impact on the World* (Boston: Regina Orthodox Press, 2002).

2. Franco Cardini, *Europe and Islam*, trans. Caroline Beamish (Malden, MA: Blackwell, 2001). Özlem Kumrular, *Türk Korkusu: Avrupa'da Türk Düşmanlığının Kökeni* (İstanbul: Doğan Kitap, 2008).

3. Mujeeb R. Khan, "The Islamic and Western Worlds: 'End of History' or the 'Clash of Civilizations'?" in *The New Crusades: Constructing the Muslim Enemy*, ed. Emran Qureshi and Michael A. Sells (New York: Columbia University Press, 2003).

4. For example, the movie *Obsession*, which was distributed as an insert to tens of millions of newspaper readers in 2008; http://www.obsessionthemovie .com (accessed October 5, 2015).

5. Robert Spencer, *The Truth about Muhammad: Founder of the World's Most Intolerant Religion* (Washington, DC: Regnery Publishing, 2006), pp. 10–11. Bernie Power, *Understanding Jesus and Muhammad: What the Ancient Texts Say about Them* (Moreland, Australia: Acorn, 2016), chaps. 12–14.

6. Lee Harris, *The Suicide of Reason: Radical Islam's Threat to the Enlightenment* (New York: Basic Books, 2007).

7. Sam Harris, *The End of Faith: Religion, Terror, and the Future of Reason* (New York: W. W. Norton, 2004).

8. Victor J. Stenger, *The New Atheism: Taking a Stand for Science and Reason* (Amherst, NY: Prometheus Books, 2009), pp. 113–16.

9. John L. Esposito, *The Future of Islam* (New York: Oxford University Press, 2010), p. 6.

10. Israel Shahak, *Jewish History, Jewish Religion: The Weight of Three Thousand Years* (London: Pluto, 2008). Or Kashti, "Israeli Teenagers: Racist and Proud of It," *Haaretz*, August 23, 2014, http://www.haaretz.com/news/features/1.611822 (accessed February 23, 2016).

11. Michael Bonner, *Jihad in Islamic History: Doctrines and Practice* (Princeton, NJ: Princeton University Press, 2006), pp. 25–27.

12. F. E. Peters, *Muhammad and the Origins of Islam* (Albany: State University of New York Press, 1994), pp. 222–24.

13. David Cook, *Understanding Jihad* (Berkeley: University of California Press, 2005), p. 107.

14. Reza Aslan, *No God But God: The Origins, Evolution, and Future of Islam* (New York: Random House, 2005), pp. 84–88.

15. Bonner, *Jihad in Islamic History*, pp. 5–6.

16. Max Blumenthal, *Goliath: Life and Loathing in Greater Israel* (New York: Nation Books, 2013), chap. 47.

17. Anuradha Sharma and Vishal Arora, "Nirvanaless: Asian Buddhism's Growing Fundamentalist Streak," *Religion News Service*, May 1, 2014, http://www.religionnews.com/2014/05/01/nirvanaless-asian-buddhisms-growing-fundamentalist-streak/ (accessed October 17, 2015).

18. Shabbir Akhtar, *Islam as a Political Religion: The Future of an Imperial Faith* (New York: Routledge, 2011).

19. Reuven Firestone, *Jihad: The Origin of Holy War in Islam* (New York: Oxford University Press, 1999).

20. Robert Pringle, *Understanding Islam in Indonesia: Politics and Diversity* (Honolulu: University of Hawai'i Press, 2010), chap. 1.

21. Abd Al-Wahhab's own writings evidence a more nuanced, less rigid style of fundamentalism than displayed by some Wahhabis today. Natana J. Delong-Bas, *Wahhabi Islam: From Revival and Reform to Global Jihad* (New York: Oxford University Press, 2004).

22. Beverley Milton-Edwards, *Islamic Fundamentalism since 1945*, 2nd ed. (New York: Routledge, 2014). Gilles Kepel, *The War for Muslim Minds: Islam and the West* (Cambridge, MA: Belknap Press of Harvard University Press, 2004), chap. 5.

23. M. Steven Fish, *Are Muslims Distinctive? A Look at the Evidence* (New York: Oxford University Press, 2011), pp. 126–30, chap. 5.

24. James Bell et al., *The World's Muslims: Religion, Politics and Society* (Washington, DC: Pew Research Center, 2013), p. 70.

25. Kenneth Ballen, "The Myth of Muslim Support for Terror," *Christian Science Monitor*, February 23, 2007, http://www.csmonitor.com/2007/0223/p09s01-coop.html (accessed October 5, 2015).

26. Charles Kurzman, *The Missing Martyrs: Why There Are So Few Muslim Terrorists* (New York: Oxford University Press, 2011).

27. Ruşen Çakır, *Derin Hizbullah: İslamcı Şiddetin Geleceği* (İstanbul: Metis Yayınları, 2001).

28. Fehim Taştekin, *Suriye: Yıkıl Git, Diren Kal* (İstanbul: İletişim Yayınları, 2015).

29. Richard Labévière, *Dollars for Terror: The United States and Islam* (New York: Algora, 2000).

30. Eamon Murphy, *The Making of Terrorism in Pakistan: Historical and Social Roots of Extremism* (New York: Routledge, 2013), chap. 8.

31. Devin R. Springer, James L. Regens, and David N. Edger, *Islamic Radicalism and Global Jihad* (Washington, DC: Georgetown University Press, 2009), pp. 28–29.

32. Ibid., pp. 41–51, chap. 3.

33. Gilles Kepel, *Beyond Terror and Martyrdom: The Future of the Middle East* (Cambridge, MA: Belknap Press of Harvard University Press, 2008), pp. 160–71.

34. Springer, Regens, and Edger, *Islamic Radicalism and Global Jihad*, p. 143.

35. Bruce Lincoln, *Holy Terrors: Thinking about Religion after September 11* (Chicago: University of Chicago Press, 2006).

36. Robert Pape, *Dying to Win: The Strategic Logic of Suicide Terrorism* (New York: Random House, 2005).

37. Ariel Glucklich, *Dying for Heaven: Holy Pleasure and Suicide Bombers—Why the Best Qualities of Religion Are Also Its Most Dangerous* (New York: HarperOne, 2009).

38. Eli Berman, *Radical, Religious, and Violent: The New Economics of Terrorism* (Cambridge, MA: MIT Press, 2009).

39. Steven Pinker, *The Better Angels of Our Nature: Why Violence Has Declined* (New York: Viking, 2011).

40. Mark Juergensmeyer, *Global Rebellion: Religious Challenges to the Secular State, from Christian Militias to Al Qaeda* (Berkeley: University of California Press, 2008), pp. 254–55.

41. Pauletta Otis, "Religious Warfare on the Global Battlefield," in *The*

Just War and Jihad: Violence in Judaism, Christianity, and Islam, ed. R. Joseph Hoffmann (Amherst, NY: Prometheus Books, 2006), p. 173.

42. Pringle, *Understanding Islam in Indonesia*, pp. 80–84.

43. Mike Davis, *Late Victorian Holocausts: El Niño Famines and the Making of the Third World* (New York: Verso, 2001).

44. Noorhaidi Hasan, "Post-Islamist Politics in Indonesia," in *Post-Islamism: The Changing Faces of Political Islam*, ed. Asef Bayat (New York: Oxford University Press, 2013), p. 176.

45. Esposito, *Future of Islam*, pp. 29–33, 99–102.

46. M. Fethullah Gülen, "In True Islam, Terror Does Not Exist," in Ergün Çapan, *Terror and Suicide Attacks: An Islamic Perspective* (Somerset, NJ: Light, 2006), p. 8. Also see other contributions in the book.

47. Esposito, *Future of Islam*, pp. 102–105.

48. Springer, Regens, and Edger, *Islamic Radicalism and Global Jihad*, p. 231.

49. Cook, *Understanding Jihad*, pp. 35–44.

50. Hammudah 'Abd al-'Ati, *Islam in Focus* (Cairo, Egypt: Al-Falah Foundation, 2003), p. 291.

51. Quoted in Anatol Lieven, *Pakistan: A Hard Country* (London: Allen Lane, 2011), p. 42.

52. Abdurrahman Dilipak, in *Opposites: Side by Side*, by Şanar Yurdatapan and Abdurrahman Dilipak, trans. İsfendiyar Eralp (New York: George Brazillier, 2003), p. 195.

53. Nevval Sevindi, *Contemporary Islamic Conversations: M. Fethullah Gülen on Turkey, Islam, and the West* (Albany: State University of New York Press, 2008), pp. 58–59.

54. Harun Yahya, *Islam Denounces Terrorism*, 3rd ed. (Bristol, UK: Amal, 2002).

55. Bernard Lewis, "The Roots of Muslim Rage," and "Targeted by a History of Hatred," in *From Babel to Dragomans: Interpreting the Middle East* (New York: Oxford University Press, 2004).

56. Esposito, *Future of Islam*, pp. 143–44.

57. Graham E. Fuller, "Freedom and Security: Necessary Conditions for Moderation," in *Debating Moderate Islam: The Geopolitics of Islam and the West*, ed. M. A. Muqtedar Khan (Salt Lake City: University of Utah Press, 2007), p. 38.

58. Abid Ullah Jan, "Moderate Islam: A Product of American Extremism," in Khan, *Debating Moderate Islam*, p. 47.

59. "About Half See CIA Interrogation Methods as Justified," *Pew Research*

Center, December 15, 2014, http://pewrsr.ch/13r482z (accessed February 24, 2016). On US torture, see Jennifer K. Harbury, *Truth, Torture, and the American Way: The History and Consequences of U.S. Involvement in Torture* (Boston: Beacon, 2005); Amrit Singh, *Globalizing Torture: CIA Secret Detention and Extraordinary Rendition* (New York: Open Society Foundation, 2013).

60. Sungur Savran, "İslamcılık, AKP, Burjuvazinin İç Savaşı," in *Neoliberalizm, İslamcı Sermayenin Yükselişi ve AKP*, ed. Neşecan Balkan, Erol Balkan, Ahmet Öncü (İstanbul: Yordam Kitap, 2014). Taştekin, *Suriye*.

61. Saadia Toor, *The State of Islam: Culture and Cold War Politics in Pakistan* (London: Pluto, 2011).

62. Khan, "Islamic and Western Worlds: 'End of History' or the 'Clash of Civilizations'?" in Qureshi and Sells, *New Crusades*.

63. John Trumpbour, "The Clash of Civilizations: Samuel P. Huntington, Bernard Lewis, and the Remaking of Post-Cold War World Order," in Qureshi and Sells, *New Crusades*.

64. Jean Bricmont, *Humanitarian Imperialism: Using Human Rights to Sell War*, trans. Diana Johnstone (New York: Monthly Review, 2006). George Szamuely, *Bombs for Peace: NATO's Humanitarian War on Yugoslavia* (Amsterdam: Amsterdam University Press, 2013).

65. Olivier Roy, *The Politics of Chaos in the Middle East*, trans. Ros Schwartz (New York: Columbia University Press, 2008), pp. 33–39.

66. Clark R. Chapman and Alan W. Harris, "9/11: Perspectives from a Decade Later," *Skeptical Inquirer* 35, no. 5 (2011): 14–15.

67. Orhan Gazi Ertekin and Faruk Özsu, *Türkleşmek, İslamlaşmak, Memurlaşmak: Ak Parti, Cemaat ve Yargının Hikayesi* (Ankara: Nika Yayınevi, 2013), p. 50.

68. Corey Robin, "The Language of Fear: Security and Modern Politics," in *Fear: Across the Disciplines*, ed. Jan Plamper and Benjamin Lazier (Pittsburgh, PA: University of Pittsburgh Press, 2012).

69. Robert Nozick, *Anarchy, State, and Utopia* (New York: Basic Books, 1974).

70. David Graeber, *The Utopia of Rules: On Technology, Stupidity, and the Secret Joys of Bureaucracy* (Brooklyn, NY: Melville House, 2015).

71. "Ankara'da gericilerden saldırı tehdidi: Yarın Hrant ve Charlie Hebdo eylemi var," *soL Haber Portalı*, January 18, 2015, http://haber.sol.org.tr/turkiye/ankarada-gericilerden-saldiri-tehdidi-yarin-hrant-ve-charlie-hebdo-eylemi-var -105603 (accessed October 17, 2015).

72. Harris, *End of Faith*, pp. 32–33, 113.

CHAPTER 9: THE FUTURE, IF IT HAPPENS,
WILL BE CONFUSING

1. Faik Bulut, *Şeriat ve Siyaset: Küresel Çağda İslam 3* (İstanbul: Cumhuriyet Kitapları, 2008), pp. 200–204. On the traditions, see *WikiIslam*, s.v. "Qur'an, Hadith and Scholars: Urine," August 3, 2013, http://wikiislam.net/wiki/ Qur'an,_Hadith_and_Scholars:Urine (accessed February 24, 2016).

2. Doug Saunders, *The Myth of the Muslim Tide: Do Immigrants Threaten the West?* (New York: Vintage Books, 2012), pp. 150–57.

3. Pippa Norris and Ronald Inglehart, *Sacred and Secular: Religion and Politics Worldwide* (Cambridge: Cambridge University Press, 2004). Eric Kaufmann, *Shall the Religious Inherit the Earth? Demography and Politics in the Twenty-First Century* (London: Profile Books, 2010).

4. Pew Research Center, "The Future of World Religions: Population Growth Projections, 2010–2050," April 2, 2015, http://pewrsr.ch/1MFjWTx (accessed February 24, 2016).

5. Steven Hill, *Europe's Promise: Why the European Way Is the Best Hope in an Insecure Age* (Berkeley and Los Angeles: University of California Press, 2010).

6. The graphic novel by Amir and Khalil, *Zahra's Paradise* (New York: First Second, 2011), captures the Green Movement, including its piety, from a protester's point of view.

7. Mahmood Monshipouri, *Democratic Uprisings in the New Middle East* (Boulder, CO: Paradigm, 2014), p. 73. Asef Bayat, "The Making of Post-Islamist Iran," in *Post-Islamism: The Changing Faces of Political Islam*, ed. Asef Bayat (New York: Oxford University Press, 2013).

8. Chris Stephen, "Tunisia Imposes Curfew as Unrest Grows over Lack of Jobs," *Guardian*, January 22, 2016, http://gu.com/p/4g3j9/sbl (accessed February 23, 2016).

9. Tariq Ramadan, *Islam and the Arab Awakening* (New York: Oxford University Press, 2012), pp. 29–32, has an analysis that does not resort to such conspiracy theories.

10. Monshipouri, *Democratic Uprisings in the New Middle East*, pp. 92–95.

11. Ruşen Çakır and Semih Sakallı, *100 Soruda Erdoğan × Gülen Savaşı* (İstanbul: Metis Yayınları, 2014).

12. Joseph A. Massad, *Islam in Liberalism* (Chicago and London: University of Chicago Press, 2015).

13. Taner Edis, "Finding an Enemy: Islam and the New Atheism," in *Muhammad in the Digital Age*, ed. Ruqayya Khan (Austin: University of Texas Press, 2015). Taner Edis, "A False Quest for a True Islam," *Free Inquiry* 27, no. 5 (2007): 48–50.

14. Asef Bayat, "Egypt and Its Unsettled Islamism," in Bayat, *Post-Islamism*, p. 200. John L. Esposito, *The Future of Islam* (New York: Oxford University Press, 2010), pp. 132–39.

15. Amel Boubekeur and Olivier Roy, "What Happened to the Islamists or . . . Political Islam Itself?" in *What Happened to the Islamists? Salafis, Heavy Metal Muslims and the Lure of Consumerist Islam*, ed. Amel Boubekeur and Olivier Roy (New York: Columbia University Press, 2012), p. 9.

16. Amel Boubekeur, "Reinventing Political Islam: The Disengagement of European Islamists," in Boubekeur and Roy, *What Happened to the Islamists?* pp. 123–24.

17. For example, Uğur Koşar, *Allah De Ötesini Bırak* (İstanbul: Destek Yayınları, 2013).

18. James K. Galbraith, *The End of Normal: The Great Crisis and the Future of Growth* (New York: Simon & Schuster, 2014).

19. John Gray, *Two Faces of Liberalism* (New York: New Press, 2000), pp. 96–97.

20. Ali Bulaç, *İnsanın Özgürlük Arayışı* (İstanbul: İnkılap Kitabevi, 2015), pp. 115–48. Islamic-flavored alternative medicine is attractive because of its aura of cultural authenticity; it generates some amusingly bad pseudoscientific publications. For example, Asif Ahmed, "Innovative Energy Standard of Curative Cupping/Hijama," *Journal of Basic & Applied Sciences* 11 (2015): 445–53.

21. Alastair Crooke, *Resistance: The Essence of the Islamist Revolution* (London: Pluto, 2009), pp. 119–20.

22. For example, Anouar Majid, *Unveiling Traditions: Postcolonial Islam in a Polycentric World* (Durham, NC: Duke University Press, 2000).

23. Robert Skidelsky and Edward Skidelsky, *How Much Is Enough? Money and the Good Life* (New York: Other Press, 2013) ask many of the right questions, though I am not entirely convinced by the answers they offer.

24. Books for a wider audience can be more promising in this regard; for example, Eren Erdem, *Devrim Ayetleri: Egemenlerin İslam'ı değil Ezilenlerin İslam'ı* (İstanbul: Kırmızı Kedi Yayınevi, 2013.) Academic efforts are often barely coherent, such as Hamid Dabashi, *Islamic Liberation Theology: Resisting the Empire* (New York: Routledge, 2008).

25. Scott Atran and Joseph Henrich, "The Evolution of Religion: How Cognitive By-Products, Adaptive Learning Heuristics, Ritual Displays, and Group Competition Generate Deep Commitments to Prosocial Religions," *Biological Theory* 5, no. 1 (2010): 18–30.

26. Matthew Flinders, *Defending Politics: Why Democracy Matters in the Twenty-First Century* (New York: Oxford University Press, 2012).

27. Jonathan I. Israel, *Radical Enlightenment: Philosophy and the Making of Modernity 1650–1750* (New York: Oxford University Press, 2002).

INDEX